Landscape and Material Life
in Franklin County, Massachusetts,
1770–1860

Landscape and Material Life

in Franklin County,

Massachusetts,

1770–1860

J. Ritchie Garrison

The University of Tennessee Press

KNOXVILLE

Publication of this book has been aided by grants from the
Universtiy of Delaware and The National Endowment
for the Humanities.

The paper in this book meets the minimum requirements
of the American National Standard for Permanence of Paper
for Printed Library Materials.

The binding materials have been chosen for strength
and durability.

Library of Congress Cataloging in Publication Data

Garrison, J. Ritchie, 1951–
  Landscape and material life in Franklin County, Massachusetts
  1770–1860 / J. Ritchie Garrison.—1st ed.
      p.   cm.
  Includes bibliographical references and index.
  ISBN 0-87049-680-8 (cloth: alk. paper)
    1. Landscape—Massachusetts—Franklin County—History.
  2. Material culture—Massachusetts—Franklin County.
  3. Anthropology—geography—Massachusetts—Franklin County.
  4. Franklin County (Mass.)—Industries.
  5. Franklin County (Mass.)—Social life and customs.   I. Title.
  F72.F8G37   1991
  974.4'2203—dc20   90-48067   CIP

iv

To My Family

The land, manipulated nature,
is the people's great work.
HENRY GLASSIE

Contents

Illustrations

Tables

Preface

This book is about material life and the transformation of a New England landscape. The study focuses on one place and one time—Franklin County, Massachusetts, between the years 1770 and 1860—in order to examine intensively the choices open to people of that era living in an agrarian culture and how they adjusted to the coming of an industrial and commercial order. There are several reasons why Franklin County is an appropriate and useful region for studying rural life in New England. One reason is that I lived there for nine years while I worked at Historic Deerfield, Inc., and I came to know its history in great detail. Another reason is that the landscape shares many of the topographical and climatic characteristics of greater New England and, to a lesser extent, of the rural North. Located in the upper Connecticut Valley of Massachusetts, the land ranges from broad fertile meadows to rugged hills, from some of the region's richest soil to the rock-infested till covering much of the glacially scoured uplands.

While the landscape is representative of the larger New England region, the county's settlement patterns were unusual because they took so long to complete. Parts of the lowlands were occupied in the seventeenth century, only a generation or two after settlers participated in the Great Migration. After a hesitant beginning in the late 1660s, settlers slowly moved up the valleys of the area's rivers and streams into the uplands. The entire process lasted nearly a hundred and seventy years. New settlements around factory sites coexisted with nucleated agricultural villages surrounded by open fields. Isolated farmsteads stood just down the road from a field system little changed from feudal traditions. If these tangled webs of families and communities represented unique juxtapositions, they also reflected cultural systems in place elsewhere and they responded to forces that were much broader than those confined to town or county boundaries. Individual characteristics of each town were peculiar, but the combination of separate experiences mirrored those shared by other New Englanders and Americans.

As scholars, we attempt to perceive an order to this historical process, but the job is hard because the range of behavior was so great. Folk traditions continued in the midst of changes wrought by people debating the creation and nature of the Republic, moral values and discipline, self-interest and public interest, and control of information, land, and the next generation. The people of Franklin County sculpted elements of this discourse into their landscape. Much of it has survived. The county is old enough to retain a record of America's early history and remote enough to have escaped some of the consequences of post–World War II suburban expansion. Still visible in the folds of the region's hills are the tool marks of the people who imposed a European mentalité on native and natural order, chipping steadily at a process that remains uncompleted. Viewed at the level of what Fernand Braudel has called the "elementary forms of everyday life," then, the landscape of Franklin County and of its material life forms an important text on how and why people changed their world.[1]

There are inevitably limits to this kind of study. Some result from lack of evidence; others are imposed by the constraints of time and space. This book confines itself to the years 1770 to 1860 largely as a matter of convenience since the history of the county's landscape is much longer. The story begins in the 1770s, a date chosen because, in 1771, the Commonwealth of Massachusetts made a provincial tax valuation that provides us with a comprehensive look at the region's landscape prior to the Revolution. The story ends ninety years later because the 1860 agricultural census provides an equally appropriate ending point.

This study began as a dissertation but evolved into something much different. I have benefited from the encouragement, comments, and observations of many gifted scholars, several with deep knowledge of the valley's history. Anthony Garvan, Henry Glassie, Donald Friary, and Karin Calvert all made helpful contributions as the dissertation evolved. Former students Max van Balgooy, Gregory Gross, Prudence Proctor Haines, Philip Hayden, Leslie Keno, James Male, Laurie Mitchel, Peter Templeton, and especially Mark Mastromarino contributed to this study with portions of their own research. Alan Swedlund and Robert Paynter of the University of Massachusetts added immeasurably to my understanding of the county's demography and archaeology. Rick Melvoin and I had several memorable exchanges about the early history of the area, particularly on the details of the Deerfield massacre and the town's landscape at that time. Amelia Miller kept feeding me important items about the local landscape based upon her lifetime of research. Susan McGowan and especially Suzanne Flynt helped me find some of the Memorial Hall Museum's rich resources. Bill Flynt passed along pertinent information on the rich architectural landscape of the Connecticut Valley. Winifred Rothenberg shared her perspective on the Massachusetts economy, as did Robert Gross, Greg Nobles, and Christopher Clark. Kevin Sweeney,

Richard Candee, and Bernard Herman read the entire manuscript carefully and made numerous suggestions and criticisms, most of which I followed and a few of which I obstinately resisted.

The National Endowment for the Humanities and the L. J. and Mary C. Skaggs Foundation made it possible for a fascinating team of historians and archaeologists to look at the landscape of Deerfield for a year and a half. I would like to think that portions of this book are a credit to that support. Historic Deerfield, Inc., quite literally gave me the opportunity to pursue this work during the years I served as director of education there. The Pocumtuck Valley Memorial Association's extraordinary collections and library were essential to this venture, and its librarians, David Proper, Louise Perrin, and Sharmen Prouty, were congenial colleagues and unfailingly indulged my requests for manuscripts and assistance.

The University of Delaware provided generous research assistance that enabled me to spend two summers in Northfield, Massachusetts, studying the architecture and account books of Calvin and George Stearns. The university also provided important support for the publication of this book. While I was in Northfield, Rosa Johnston and a number of residents generously allowed me to do field work in their houses and barns. Most of the information on the Stearnses awaits another book, but what I learned in Northfield helped make sense of patterns of barn construction and domestic architecture in the entire county. I also am indebted to Myron Stachiw, Nora Pat Small, and Jack Larkin of the research department at Old Sturbridge Village for sharing research on the New England square plan form of house, and especially to John Worrell, whose study of Stratton Tavern provided essential archaeological information on earthmoving and hydrological systems in early Northfield. Carol Wallace Orr and her staff at the University of Tennessee Press were both helpful and patient as we pushed this project forward. Butch Hewlett did a superb job of printing my photographs, working with great skill to get the best possible print. Mary Tabinowski entered the original dissertation into the computer and helped with various requests connected with this book. Bryant Tolles, Jr., was always supportive and made certain that I had time to work on this project.

My parents have sustained me and the book in more ways than I can adequately acknowledge; my children, Eric, Nathan, and Rebecca, have never known a time when I was not working on some aspect of this study, and on a few occasions even helped measure buildings (sometimes willingly); my wife Carla has made it all possible, has helped me keep it in perspective, and has tried to keep the kids from playing with my drafting equipment. She especially is glad that it is coming to an end. It is to my family, then, that this book is dedicated.

Chapter 1

Introduction

In 1841, the Reverend Henry Colman published a study of agriculture in two of Massachusetts's counties—Franklin and Middlesex. Sanctioned by the state and published under its auspices, his report attempted to evaluate the commonwealth's agriculture in a time of great political and social change. Despite advances in manufacturing and growth in competition from western farmers, he noted that "the condition of the agricultural population of Franklin County is that of general comfort and prosperity." Describing, praising, and criticizing the region as an example for others, he reviewed agricultural conditions in Massachusetts's most sparsely settled county (Fig. 1:1). Dominated by the Connecticut River Valley and hemmed in by hills— the upland plateau of Worcester County to the east and the Berkshires to the west—it was an area of contrasts: of some of the best land in New England and some of the worst, of towns settled in the seventeenth century and others newly made on dam and mill sites, of farmers who were prosperous and many more who struggled ceaselessly to make ends meet, of families whose children stayed on to farm while others moved elsewhere to seek their fortune, and of things that hardly changed yet in the end changed more than most people understood.[1]

Colman's choice of Franklin County was not accidental. A former minister who gave up his pastorate in Salem for reasons of ill health, he bought Cephas Hoyt's farm in Deerfield, in August 1831, and headed inland to recuperate. The Hoyt farm was one of the best in the county, and he farmed, raising corn and hogs, and continued to write letters to his friends back in Essex County. By temperament he seemed poorly suited to serious farming, and his restless intellect soon gained him contacts with some of the most talented men in the region. Describing the region's agricultural practices and recommending improvements in his thorough report, he approached his subject with the zeal of a minister exhorting his flock, praising the worthy, chastising the unconverted, and calling for reformation.[2]

Like other agricultural reformers, Colman felt changes came too slowly.

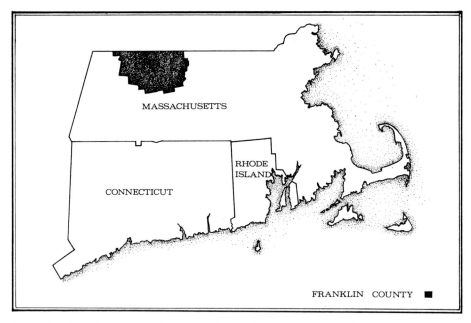

Figure 1:1. Location of Franklin County, Massachusetts. (Drawn by the author.)

But if some farmers plowed in the same direction, planted the same crops, used the same tools, and processed their harvest in the same ways as genera-tions of forebears, he also would have acknowledged that their lives were different from their fathers' and mothers'. Some contemporaries lauded the changes as evidence of progress, of enlightened minds using science and reason to elevate mankind to new heights of civilization. Others, Colman among them, were not so sure. They warned of the consequences for human values if the winds of change blew too strongly or in the wrong directions. No material gain, they reasoned, justified the loss of moral virtue. Addressing the new materialistic, technological, and economic pressures that people faced, he and they cautioned their listeners to look past visible things and search for what was truly meaningful.

The transformation of the Franklin County landscape between 1770 and 1860 was multi-layered. A decade of studying archaeological, architectural, and documentary records has made it clear that this transformation was a process rather than a dramatic shift in world view. What is also clear is that the transformation was not caused by the coming of industrial order; it was preceded by important changes in the pre- and post-Revolutionary country-side which in turn were built on foundations set down in the seventeenth and early eighteenth centuries. Moreover, the signs of these changes were visible in other parts of the country as Americans continued the task of disciplining their landscape to European standards of order, enclosing fields, supplanting traditions of customary rights with systems of law, intensifying efforts to increase the yields of their fields, and expanding production for the market rather than household or local needs. In these respects the landscape of Franklin County shared characteristics of this great transformation with other sections of the country and wider world, but because the landscape was made by individuals and families there were idiosyncrasies as well as patterns. Our distance in time allows us to distinguish between individual actions and general practices, to see patterns and consistencies that contemporaries were often only dimly aware of or worried about. But the task is difficult. To recover the early landscape demands the consideration of a great many actions and objects; to understand the relationship of actions and objects requires that we elevate the stories of individual actors as well as the stages on which everyday dramas took place.[3]

Although the landscape was a stage for ordinary events, it was not remade freely. In a variety of ways the choices made by generations of forebears constrained how descendants could alter their world. These choices created a form of durable history. Informing the placement of lot lines, the direction of roads, the form of dwellings, and the location of fences were a range of assumptions and action statements about how the world worked, who controlled it, and what future generations might do. Thus the surveyors who laid out the county's towns in the seventeenth and eighteenth centuries established conditions that affected how people have lived in these communities ever since (Fig. 1:2). Such conditions were inherently conservative, favoring evolutionary rather than revolutionary change. To remake the material world on a grand scale was nearly impossible without great social trauma, and such traumas directly threatened the security of family and cultural life.[4]

Arrayed against these constraints were formidable forces for change. Population growth prompted the creation of new farms; new cultural expectations led people to modify, tear down, or replace old houses with new dwellings; and changing social and economic imperatives impelled farmers to redesign barns and barnyards to accommodate new standards of material abundance and personal convenience. Confronting these pressures and attractions, men and women throughout Franklin County and the rural North worked hard to reshape their landscape, aware that their vision of progress sometimes required them to sacrifice things earlier generations valued.[5]

Transforming the landscape was the physical manifestation of the growth of capitalism, a subject that has sometimes fostered acrimonious debate among historians who have analyzed the nature and timing of capitalism's influence on rural life. In the 1970s historians such as Michael Merrill and James Henretta proposed a profound dichotomy between the values of pre-industrial rural families and those who participated in and shared a capitalistic world view. Much of their interpretation focused on the issue of production. They argued that pre-industrial farm families were not motivated principally by a drive for profits but by the need to provide for family security and to affirm communally held values. In a later study of the Connecticut Valley, Christopher Clark proposed an explanation of how this pre-industrial economy changed. He argued that family needs prompted people to enter the marketplace, that involvement with the market served to change economic priorities, and that commercial growth increased class consciousness, broadening the distance between rich and poor and promoting competition.[6]

Other historians have seen commercial motives in the pre-industrial world. Robert St. George's study of the material life of seventeenth-century New Englanders explored some of the changes that occurred as yeomen created specialized and disciplined spaces in their homes and yards. Similarly, Stephen Innes's book on seventeenth-century Springfield, Massachusetts, posited the existence of different types of New England communities, some of which were market oriented from their beginnings. For a later period, Kevin Sweeney has looked at the social, economic, and material history of the Connecticut Valley gentry, documenting their extensive ties to centers of power, their use of material symbols to affirm their social position, and their importance as economic patrons. Winifred Rothenberg has examined thousands of account book entries to document the existence of markets in Massachusetts's economy before and after the Revolution. She demonstrated how commodity prices in hinterland and metropolitan regions fluctuated in the same cycles, a classic test of market penetration. She has also shown how wage prices converged over time as labor costs became one more commodity by which people adjusted their economic affairs. While variations in the price of farm labor according to task continued, traditional market regulations on wages and commodities eventually failed or were abandoned. Over time and space, wages for the same task evened out. The integration of wages with commodity and capital markets challenged and replaced what some social historians, such as E. P. Thompson, have termed the "moral economy," the face-to-face network of exchanges they associate with life in traditional communities.[7]

The entries Rothenberg painstakingly analyzed indicated that a market existed, grew in importance, and altered society prior to industrialization. Decades before factories were built in Lowell, or the agricultural press began calling for improved agricultural techniques, ordinary farm laborers began working more efficiently. Productivity increased during the 1780s and accelerated thereafter as farm families improved their fields and stock, learned more efficient management practices, and worked harder. Market integration and higher rates of productivity contributed to capital accumulation in the countryside and provided the foundation for industrialization. Jeremy Atack

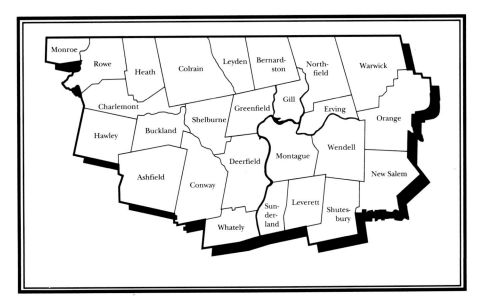

Figure 1:2. Map of Franklin County Towns. (Drawn by the author.)

and Fred Bateman's extensive study of northern agriculture in the antebellum period supports several of Rothenberg's arguments. They found that by the 1850s, New England farms were more highly capitalized than farms in the Midwest, population fertility was lower, and the mix of agricultural production had shifted to dairying, pasture, and truck crops. In general they found New England farms profitable and increasingly specialized rather than backward or stagnant.[8]

Reconciling these views remains difficult, in part because historians posit such divergent views of what early America was like, and in part because they differ on the amount and meaning of conflict in American history. Can we better comprehend the pre-industrial world by looking at material life for the values encoded in houses and barns, fences, fields patterns, and work? Do these things record the persistence of traditional social forms and household modes of production as a critique of capitalistic values, or did the landscape mirror attempts to adapt to a competitive market-oriented culture? To what degree were the reform-minded texts of men like Henry Colman a reflection of the direction progressive farmers were going in or a codification of existing behavior?

At one level, then, the history of Franklin County's landscape helps to illuminate the interpretive issues social historians struggle with; at a different level the story contributes to an appreciation of how folk traditions and popular culture interacted in creating a vernacular landscape. Although the region's landscape retained many traditional forms, some of which evoked a distinct regional flavor, these traditions were never static because people continually recombined traditional culture with new ideas and fashions. Thus, the world men and women built between 1770 and 1860 in Franklin County was a continuous discourse on the directions their culture would take. At times these discursive forms are quite eloquent but there are pitfalls to interpreting them too freely. To casual viewers, the perception of antiquity in the region's old houses evokes a sense of quaint charm and of timelessness. That perception is not supported by careful study of the evidence. The landscape that seems so old to the tourists who come to view the colorful hues of October foliage was constantly being remade and reused, sometimes in ways close to those envisioned by the original owner, sometimes not. The surviving landscape is an archaeological artifact of immense, sometimes chaotic complexity. It abounds with layers, accidental survivals, individual whimsy, and pattern.

This landscape is complex because families and groups painstakingly constructed its elements over time. Usually, they developed their landscape in patterned ways to limit confusion about their intentions toward their neighbors. Some patterns were apparent to contemporaries; others were clear only to later generations. Sometimes, however, individuals and families expressed themselves in novel fashions their neighbors did not choose to emulate. Recovering these patterns, filtering out the idiosyncracies, is hard because people unsystematically destroyed or altered their landscape in response to broad social and economic forces. We can reconstruct landscape patterns and locate individual whimsy only by combining a wide range of evidence from documentary and artifactual texts. Nevertheless, the search for a more precise picture of what the past was like is not enough. We must ask why the landscape looked as it did and why it changed.[9]

The answers to these questions may surprise those who expected the landscape to reflect a rather static past. Much of the county's present landscape looks very old, but most of what is visible reflects the great reformation of America's rural landscape between the late eighteenth and the mid-nineteenth centuries. As they did in the wheat fields of central Delaware studied by Bernard Herman, or the dairies of Chester County, Pennsylvania, that Joan Jensen documented, or the connecting barns of southeastern Maine that Thomas Hubka compellingly analyzed, Franklin County farm families progressively intensified their use of the landscape. They accomplished this in several ways: by clearing and enclosing more land, by eliminating many "customary" landscape uses such as common field fences, by restricting the freedom of wandering livestock, by building district schools, by improving roads and building bridges, by expanding production of marketable surpluses, by moving astonishing amounts of dirt with relatively simple tools, and by building more efficient dwellings and outbuildings. With the intensification of land use came an increased segmentation of work and living spaces into separately defined units—well before the agricultural press, thoroughly studied by Sally McMurray, began publishing plans for improved farmhouses. This realignment was accomplished by assigning specialized functions to rooms, yards, and outbuildings.[10]

The long-term implications of these changes were profound. Gender roles were more often relegated to separate spheres, domestic space was arranged into hierarchies of formality and work, and community boundaries were atomized and redefined as neighborhoods or interest groups. Space was further divided by class and sometimes by race, resulting in the creation of poor farms, the emergence of neighborhoods for mill workers and laborers, and the construction of partitions to keep apart family and hired help. Public and central spaces also changed. Where once towns had used a centrally placed meetinghouse as a compelling symbol of community unity, villages began to grow wherever commercial opportunities were greatest—sometimes far from geographical town centers. In other towns energetic citizens rebuilt the village centers and public buildings to reflect the new realities of sectarianism and secularism years before the state formally got around to disestablishing religious life. In ways that were often quite direct, then, Franklin County's landscape echoed the effects of broader cultural trends.[11]

Responding to and driving this transformation were changes in production strategies. Household production of a wide range of goods from foodstuffs to cloth declined as men and women increasingly turned to the marketplace to meet even basic needs. This shift took decades to accomplish. Population growth on fixed natural resources and greater participation in regional and international markets sharpened competition and encouraged progressive farmers to invest in technological change. Simultaneously, the consequences of competition seem to have prompted a measured withdrawal from face-to-face relationships with the entire community. House form and family life adapted, if only modestly, to these changes. More intensive use of resources, greater productivity, smaller family size, increased education, and the accumulation of capital from previous generations contributed substantially to a rise in material abundance for many people, providing the rationale for supporting and participating in new forms of production. Prodded by the zeal of reformers who advocated the ethos of cultural improvement and human perfectibility and confronted by choices of how to live, families in Franklin County and elsewhere struggled to make and find a life that was more productive and convenient. Henry Colman could cite numerous successes and deficiencies in his report on the county's agricultural population, but the story behind the rhetoric is more interesting and thought-provoking than he realized.[12]

Chapter 2

The Past

Eunice Allen died on July 18, 1818. The *Franklin Herald*, Greenfield's newspaper, devoted an unusually long obituary to her, for, in her native town of Deerfield where she was born and where she died, she had been a living reminder of the struggle to settle the region. During King George's War, in 1746, when she was thirteen years old, she and several others were ambushed in the Deerfield meadows by a band of French Mohawks who had participated in the recent capture of Fort Massachusetts. As her father fought a hopeless delaying action, Eunice and her younger brother ran for home pursued by Indians, one of whom fired a musket at her. The ball passed harmlessly through her clothing but in her terror she fell down thinking that she had been hit. Catching up to her, the Indian split open her skull with a blow of his tomahawk, then fled as reinforcements approached to find out what all the shooting was about. Because of her flight she had fallen some distance from the other victims, and it was some time before her uncle and others found her and relized she was still alive. Although they expected her to die from her wounds, they carried her home and sent for Dr. Thomas Williams. He removed bits of bone and brain tissue, cleaned out the wound as best he could, and applied a dressing. When she died at the age of eighty-five, she was a legend in her own time, a subject of some curiosity and awe, and a reminder of the price some paid as the frontier was settled.[1]

Eunice Allen was not the only one injured by war. The Connecticut Valley had a long history of violence and suffering, and the past was a strong influence for the people who settled the region. Allen's story was only one small episode in a much larger drama. By the time of her death, she was a link with a distant time, one that for most people in Franklin County was the substance of stories and legends about the remote past. For those who were unusually reflective or observant, however, remnants of the past were all about. The old houses, the layout of farmland, the day-to-day patterns of community life—all were reminders of the choices made by forebears. Their beliefs, traditions, and values, established at the first period of settlement, would linger to affect the opportunities and decisions of succeeding generations. Farm families were sensitive to this cultural baggage because they often had literally inherited land, equipment, and buildings. While this inheritance provided families with a means of support, it also bound families to assumptions and decisions about the world made several generations earlier — assumptions that constrained the choices later generations might make.

In 1841, when Henry Colman published his survey, a considerable portion of Franklin County could be seen by standing on the tops of ridges and looking out over the landscape. To the south lay the great valley of the Connecticut River where it widened to a flat plain, dotted at intervals by the towns of Amherst, Hadley, Hatfield, and Northampton. In the distance, to the east, north, and west were the uplands, broken here and there by valleys or swift-flowing rivers, dominated by the hills that in summer light extended blue-grey until the eye lost them on the horizon. It was a landscape of nature and civilization, incomplete and always changing as human needs came and went. Only by including and understanding that world, do we begin the process of recapturing the dimensions of human lives and historical process.[2]

The principal topographic reality of Franklin County was its hills. Every town in the county had them, but some had them in greater abundance than others. The Great River, as the Connecticut River was called by the area's early settlers, roughly bisected the county on its southerly course to Long Island Sound. Here and there, it turned to go around rock impasses, or, in gentler land, as in the broad meadowlands that spread from Mt. Sugarloaf in South Deerfield to the Holyoke Range, it meandered. Like the ridges that flanked it to the east and west, the Connecticut River headed south, and that fact had profound consequences for those who settled the area and for their descendants. No matter what cultural changes would come, the orientation of people in the valley was bifurcated and pulled in two directions — to the east where the seat of Massachusetts's government was firmly entrenched and to the south along a natural transportation route (Fig. 2:1).[3]

Not all of the county's topography was oriented north and south. Two important rivers interrupted the long rows of ridges that ran on the northerly axis. The largest of the two was the Deerfield River. Its headwaters rose in the hills of south-central Vermont. From there the river flowed south, then turned to the east. It meandered somewhat gently through the length of Charlemont, but at Shelburne Falls it dropped more quickly until it reached the Deerfield meadows. At that point the river snaked north for about three miles past the village of Deerfield before turning east again, passed through a gap in the Pocumtuck range, and emptied into the Connecticut. Thousands of years before Europeans entered the valley, native tribes had used the Deer-

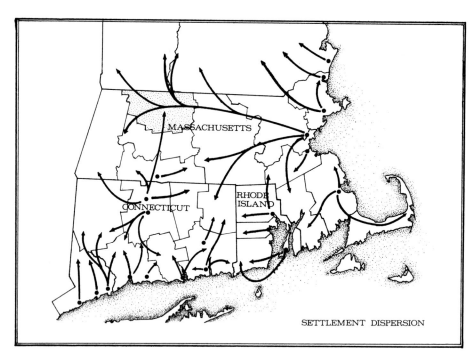

Figure 2:1. Settlement Dispersion in the eighteenth century. (Drawn by the author after the map of linguistic patterns, Hans Kurath, *Handbook of the Linguistic Geography of New England,* [Providence, 1939], 241–2.)

field River and its tributaries as a highway. During the eighteenth century, white settlers also used the river to move westward beyond the Connecticut Valley lowlands.[4]

While the Deerfield River linked towns in the western uplands, the Miller's River performed a similar function to the east. Although it was smaller than the Deerfield River, the Miller's River had its headwaters in the upland areas of northwestern Worcester County and southwestern New Hampshire. The river flowed west, dropping fairly swiftly through the towns of Orange and Erving until it reached Miller's Falls, where it too joined the Connecticut, several miles upstream from the Deerfield River. Taken together, the three rivers formed a rough cross with the Connecticut River as the main axis, the Deerfield River as the western and the Miller's River as the eastern axes (Fig. 2:2).

Rivers were only one of the forces that shaped the topography of the valley and the county. Four major periods of glaciation had ground down the mountains, widened the valleys, and churned up the region's soils. Remnants of the last glacial period survived until nearly ten thousand years ago, and the present topography of the area is rather new judged against the scale of geologic time. Moreover, the glacial epochs left several legacies that had conse-

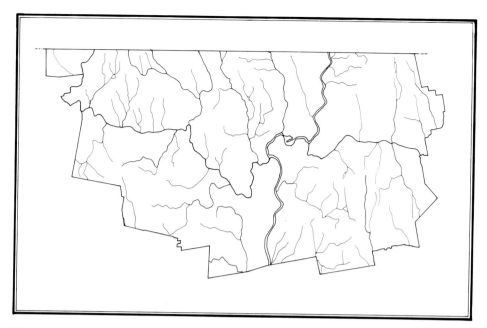

Figure 2:2. Major Streams and Rivers, Franklin County, Massachusetts. (Drawn by the author.)

quences for the development of agriculture. Much of the Connecticut Valley was covered by Lake Hitchcock, a glacial lake that at its furthest extent stretched about 160 miles from Rocky Hill, Connecticut, to Lyme, New Hampshire. The lake is believed to have existed for about 2400 years, during which many layers of silt and gravel were built up on the lake's bottom. These layers eventually became the fertile bottomlands of the Connecticut Valley lowlands.[5]

Evidence of the glacial period still abounds. On the edges of the lake are the remains of alluvial fans left from rivers and streams that flowed into it. In some areas, such as Montague, there are ancient sand dunes, signs of an old shore line, overgrown now with oaks, birches, and sumac. Above the high water mark rise the hills. The glaciers rounded off the peaks, scooped out valleys, and scoured rocky outcrops. Giant blocks of bedrock were ripped off in the process and pushed south. Some rocks were ground into fine dust. As the glaciers melted, glacial till was left on the slopes of the area's tilted, bedrock hills—a mixture of dust, sand, gravel, and boulders. This glacial waste would form the basis of the soils in much of the New England uplands, and Franklin County was no exception. Many farmers would curse the stones that seemed to sprout from their fields each spring. Miles of stone walls, deeply shrouded now in woodland, testify mutely to the tenacity with which farmers struggled to improve their lands.[6]

The bedrock in the valley and in Franklin County varies considerably and the quality of county soils differs accordingly. The valley lowland forms a rough wedge shape that points north. About 200 million years ago the sedimentary rock at the eastern side of the present lowland cracked into several faults. As this bedrock rose it formed the ridges of the eastern uplands. The sedimentary layers to the west also tilted upward. The tilted bedrock is the reason the western uplands rise gradually to a ridge, drop off more steeply, then rise gently once again. The slope of the bedrock also accounts for the tendency of the hills and ridges in the area to run north and south.[7]

Beginning at Mount Sugarloaf in South Deerfield and extending north through Greenfield is a ridge of harder rock that divides the lowland into two sections. The Connecticut River flows through the eastern half of the division and the Green and Deerfield rivers occupy the western half. This ridge is composed of harder layers of rock rising gently from east to west, then dropping off abruptly. Occasionally, harder dikes of igneous rock rise steeply on both sides, especially in Greenfield where the ridge separates the town from the Connecticut River. This ridge also forms a rough dividing line as to the quality of the soil between the eastern and western parts of the county. In general, lands west of the Connecticut River and this ridge are more fertile than the lands to the east.[8]

The bedrock of the lowland areas is Triassic sandstone with a rather distinctive reddish hue. Rock in the uplands is principally composed of schists and gneisses, metamorphic rock found across much of New England. Occasionally, there are intrusions of harder granitic rock, but there are few deposits of lime in the area. The soils tend to reflect the bedrock in the area. The softer bedrock of the lowlands has weathered and broken into fine particles that have washed down from the hills to the east and west to form the fertile lowland soils. In many areas these soils are free of gravel and rocks and make excellent farmland. The gneisses and schists of the uplands have resisted weathering better. Soils in the uplands therefore tend to be thinner and to reflect glacial action in the mixing of gravel, boulders, and finer soils. Many parts of the uplands were and still are suitable for farming depending on the gradient, but the steepest slopes were always poorly suited to agriculture. Soils in most cases are fairly fertile. Abandoned fields grow forest cover in a matter of a decade or two, and there are many areas in the uplands where stone walls in deeply wooded areas mark the boundaries of fields abandoned years ago. Steep grades, stones, thinner soils with bedrock outcrops, and a colder climate all made farming more difficult in the uplands. Colman noted that the uplands were well suited for grazing as they were fertile and produced grasses well. Advertisements in the local newspapers also claimed that upland farms were "well watered and suitable for farming." Soil types varied considerably in most of the region's towns, however, and farmers who lived next to each other could have different topography and dirt to work with.[9]

Modern soil surveys by the Department of Agriculture have broken down the soils in the county to twelve basic types with a number of subdivisions. As in most of New England, the soils are acidic. The best soils lie in the low-lands, especially along the interval lands of the Connecticut and Deerfield rivers. The towns of Whately, Sunderland, Deerfield, Montague, Greenfield, and Northfield contain the largest areas of fine well-drained, fertile soils with gentle gradients. (See Fig. 2:3, nos. 7 and 8.) Gill, Bernardston, Charlemont, and Buckland also contain smaller areas of alluvial soils. (See Fig. 2:3, nos. 3 and 4.) The eastern uplands are crowded with steeply sloped hills, but there are some areas with arable land along river valleys and on gentler slopes. New Salem contained sizable areas of rolling farmland. (See Fig. 2:3, nos. 11 and 12.) To a lesser extent, so did Warwick, Orange, Wendell, Shutesbury, and Leverett. Erving had little arable land and was not incorporated as a town until the 1830s. The rugged topography and the small quantity of good tillage land were among the reasons the population in the eastern towns grew slowly. Until manufacturing started along the area's developable mill sites, only New Salem could boast a substantial population.[10]

The western uplands generally contained good lands suited for farming. By the early nineteenth century, Conway, Ashfield, Shelburne, Leyden, and Colrain were active farming towns with substantial populations of modest farmers. But the further west people settled in Franklin County, the further they moved from transportation routes and into rugged terrain. On the tops of high ridges, farming was a struggle. Heath and Rowe contain some good farm land, but the bulk of western land consisted of areas of thin soils and rock. Hawley, Monroe, and the western sections of Rowe are rugged and rock strewn. The Hoosac range rises abruptly to the west of the Deerfield River. Gradients there are often steeper than 30 degrees. Tiny Monroe's farmland is situated chiefly in the mountains that divide the Deerfield and Hoosac river valleys. To the southeast is Hawley, a town splintered into several smaller com-munities by the steeply sloped mountains that fracture its surface.[11]

Given the topographic differences between county towns, it is hardly sur-prising that farming and community life varied across the region. Many of the differences were tied to geographic elevation. Upland towns are normally several degrees cooler than towns in valley lowlands. Towns where the mean elevation is more than five hundred feet above sea level generally are less suit-able for agriculture. The present growing season in the lowland towns along the Connecticut River averages about 142 days of frost-free temperatures. By contrast, the eastern and western uplands average about 110 to 120 days, and in the higher portions of the county the growing season may be only about

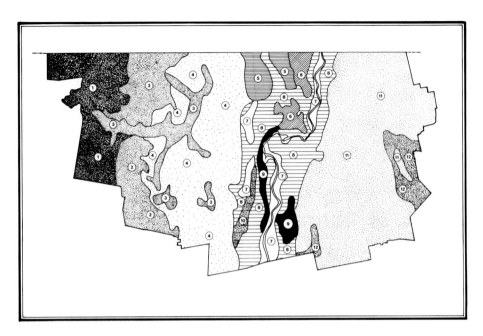

Key to Soils in Franklin County

1. Lyman-Berkshire-Peru association: Shallow and deep, well-drained and moderately well-drained soils that have a reddish subsoil and are in the Berkshire hills
2. Westminster-Marlow, dark subsoil-Peru association: Shallow and deep, well-drained and moderately well-drained soils that have an olive subsoil and are in the Berkshire Hills
3. Merrimac-Ondawa association: Well-drained and somewhat excessively drained sandy and gravelly soils in the Berkshire Hills and foothills
4. Westminster-Colrain-Buckland association: Shallow and deep, well-drained and moderately well-drained soils that have a dull-brown or olive subsoil and are in the foothills west of the Connecticut Valley
5. Nassau-Bernardston-Dutchess association: Shallow and deep, well-drained silty soils that have an olive-gray subsoil and are in the north-central part of the county
6. Hollis-Charlton association: Shallow and deep, well-drained soils that have a yellowish-brown subsoil and are in the north-central part of the county
7. Hadley-Winooski-Limerick association: Well-drained to poorly-drained silty soils on flood plains in the Connecticut Valley
8. Hinckley-Windsor-Merrimac association: Droughty and somewhat sandy and gravelly soils in the Connecticut Valley
9. Holyoke-Sunderland-Cheshire association: Shallow and deep, well-drained soils that have a red subsoil and are on bedrock ridges in the Connecticut Valley
10. Hartland-Ninigret, silty substratum-Belgrade association: Well-drained and moderately well-drained silty and sandy soils in the Connecticut Valley
11. Shapleigh-Essex-Gloucester association: Shallow and deep, well-drained soils in dandy glacial till in the uplands east of the Connecticut Valley
12. Hinckley-Merrimac association: Droughty to somewhat droughty sandy and gravelly soils that are nearly level to gently sloping and are in the eastern part of the county

Figure 2:3. Soil Map, Franklin County, Massachusetts. (Drawn by the author, after General Soil Map, Franklin County Massachusetts, U.S. Department of Agriculture Soil Conservation Service.)

100 days.[12] These numbers are only averages, however, and the actual climate conditions could differ considerably from year to year. Yearly fluctuations were significant forces for the area's farmers, and farm journals frequently reported the arrival of apple blossoms, one of the period's signals for the start of planting. These observations could vary by several weeks depending on location and the year. Always there were risks of an untimely frost. In 1816, farmers in the county lost crops or did very poorly when frosts were recorded in many areas every month of the year.[13] Small wonder, then, that the weather was a subject of discussion, speculation, and watchful concern. It spelled the difference between good or indifferent years and, unlike many other elements in the farmer's economic equation, was not susceptible to human control.

Temperatures also fluctuated greatly. Winters, according to Rodolphus Dickinson in 1811, generally averaged between 33 degrees and 10 degrees with temperatures often descending to 1 to 5 degrees. Occasionally, he noted, the temperature descended as low as −20 degrees, but this was uncommon. Summers were warm and humid with high temperatures generally registering in the 80s and often in the 90s. While readings of 100 degrees or greater were rare, in some years there were a few days in July when the thermometer registered readings at that level. Such temperatures were suitable for a wide variety of crops, providing that the cycle of growth fitted into the length of the growing season. Farmers who lived in the uplands, or whose lands were shaded by hills from the spring and fall sun, or who guessed wrong about planting or harvesting, faced greater risks than did those in more favored locations. For them, family security meant carefully treading the narrow path between ruin and prosperity.[14]

Although temperatures varied greatly according to location and elevation, precipitation was probably distributed fairly evenly throughout the year. Presently, in the lowlands, approximately 44 inches of rain falls each year. In the western uplands the average is a bit higher with 50 inches a common figure. While there are dry spells, they seldom last long enough to damage crops severely. Snowfall varies greatly. Modern data indicate that for roughly six out of thirty-one years the upland community of Shelburne Falls did not have continuous snow cover. A rough average of precipitation for the county between 1790 and 1860 was about 50 inches a year, but this varied considerably from place to place and year to year. Snow cover was important to logging and teaming operations in the early nineteenth century but often was inconsistent. Too much snow clogged roads; too little made sled runners unusable.[15]

For all farmers, the climate dictated seasonal rhythms. Historians have long noted that seasonality set farmers apart from industrial culture, but they have been slower to recognize that nature was often a taskmaster almost as tyrannical as factory life. If the day-to-day tasks varied, over time farming itself followed a repetitive and never-ending course. Nature dictated when to plant, when to harvest, when to slaughter, and when to get in the wood for winter's cold. Farm labor was less regimented than industrial work but only in a relative sense. Nature's parameters were often unyielding and farmers chose tasks within rather strict confines. What did perhaps distinguish farm work from the industrial world was that tasks were adapted to fit natural cycles and that farmwork frequently gave the worker the opportunity to participate in productive processes from start to finish. Those features of farm life were conditioned by the reciprocal relationship of the individual, nature, and community—still the dominant forces in farming.[16]

The natural landscape was altered rapidly by human hands, despite the difficulties imposed by soil and climates. The activities of native tribes in the lowlands were certainly extensive enough that the first white settlers did not confront a land that was entirely natural. Even before the English arrived, Native Americans had cleared tracts of land on river plains. The region's seventeenth-century communities were placed on lands that the Indians had already cleared. Native fires had burned out the underbrush to improve hunting, and these left a rather open understory that made travel through the forest fairly easy by foot or on horse. Indian activities on the land were restrained in comparison with the European settlers' systematic alteration of the landscape to fit English cognitive perceptions. The pace of those alterations accelerated steadily through the eighteenth and during the first half of the nineteenth centuries. Farmers cut back forest cover, filled in low spots, drained marshes and swamps, cut away hillocks, and leveled the ground. Clearing reached its widest extent in the 1880s, when it was estimated that only about 20 percent of the county's land was still forested.[17]

Most of the county was covered with trees when the first settlers arrived in the area. The trees were part of a general mixed hardwood forest that covered most of southern and a considerable part of northern New England. Birch, beech, and maples dominated this type of forest, but hickory, ash, red and white oak, chestnut, and walnut trees were common. Softwoods were also prevalent. Spruce, hemlock, and white pine predominated, but red and yellow pines and firs also grew. The pre-European forest contained mature trees of a very large size and great age. Some of these trees, such as the white pines, may have reached heights of 150 feet with trunks that exceeded 4 feet at the base. Even hardwoods may have exceeded 120 feet in height. The size of these trees may be judged in part by the width of boards found in some of the area's eighteenth-century houses. Some of these boards exceed twenty-two inches in width and are nearly free of knots. This type of lumber comes from very large trees—trees that were rare by 1800.[18]

The burning that Native Americans had undertaken did not clear away all of the shrubbery growing on the forest floor. Wherever light reached and conditions were right, shrubbery and young trees flourished. Mountain laurel grew on the rocky ridges on the acidic and stoney uplands to the east of the Connecticut Valley, particularly in association with stands of oaks. There are also areas of mountain laurel in the western uplands. Wild grapes apparently attracted the attention of English troops just before they were ambushed at Bloody Brook in 1675 during King Philip's War. Barberry and other plants also competed for space. More detailed information about the types of shrubbery in the region at the time of settlement is not presently available, but Stephen West Williams's carefully gathered herbarium provides information on the types of plants found in the area around Deerfield. Williams, a physician, gathered some of these plants for their medicinal value, but most of them were collected because he was a dedicated and talented amateur naturalist. His 1819 herbarium listed the plants common to the region. Some of these plants were probably introduced as European settlement progressed, but others undoubtedly were indigenous.[19] (See Appendix 1.)

As the axe, plow, harrow, and stoneboat erased the ancient forests, the region assumed a very different look. The vision of a cultivated garden about which Henry Colman rhapsodized was achieved slowly through the determination and hard work of several generations of farm families. These people developed their lands without a sophisticated knowledge of faults or upthrusts, soil surveys and chemical analysis by the agricultural extension services, or advice from foresters. Their approach to farming was predicated upon experience and common sense. Most of the time they knew good land when they saw it, and whenever possible they sought it out.[20]

Although white settlement in the Massachusetts part of the Connecticut River valley occurred as early as 1636 when William Pynchon and his associates settled Springfield, towns further north were not established for several decades more. English settlers first moved into the northern part of the valley in the late 1660s and early 1670s when Deerfield was founded. During the next three decades settlement slowly expanded. Deerfield was abandoned in 1675 during King Philip's War but was permanently established in 1682. The town was heavily damaged in a French and Indian attack in 1704, but by the 1710s other areas in the lowlands were being settled. Northfield was finally incorporated in 1713 after a series of abortive attempts to settle the rich lands on the former Pocumtuck site known as Squakeag. Sunderland was incorporated a year later but continued military threats retarded settlement of the uplands for more than fifty years.[21]

Until the conclusion of the French and Indian Wars in 1763, upland settlements grew slowly. Eunice Allen's experience was enough to sober the most enthusiastic pioneer. There were a few lone settlers or small communities established in the uplands in the 1740s and 1750s, but the area's marginality was reflected in the fact that most of the people living in the uplands in that period were located in the forts that the Massachusetts government had set up to act as a buffer for the towns further south. The town histories for the area always stress the early pioneers and the difficulties they encountered. A quick look at the dates of incorporation, however, reveals how slowly and cautiously settlement proceeded beyond the lowlands. Of the twenty-six towns that made up Franklin County in 1860, only one was established before 1700. Two more were added by 1730 and another three by 1760. All of these towns except New Salem were located in the lowlands along the Connecticut, Deerfield, and Green rivers.[22]

The capture of Quebec and Montreal by British regulars dramatically changed the history of the valley. Before 1760, a total of six towns in the region were founded. Between 1760 and 1790, fourteen more towns were incorporated. Ten of these towns were established between 1760 and 1775. The wave of town-founding had a variety of consequences for people in the region that are worth examining in somewhat greater detail, for the patterns of settlement in the old and new towns differed considerably and these differences reflected a rather significant shift in values and assumptions about the landscape. In a number of obvious and quite crucial ways the towns of the 1760s and 1770s did not look like the old nucleated villages of Deerfield, Northfield, and Sunderland—the oldest towns in the region. Moreover, the differentiation of space in the region continued. The towns that were set up between 1790 and 1820 were scattered in various parts of the county. These newer towns either were started rather late because of their remoteness or were hived off from older communities. The last town to be incorporated in the county was Erving, a section of land in the eastern part of the county where the Miller's River flowed. It was established when various manufacturers set up small mills on the river to use the water power. Erving was not a farming community. The forces that led to its creation were echoed in factory villages elsewhere in New England.[23]

All three of the earliest towns in the region had similar plans. Each town was laid out in a nucleated village form centered on a long street. Tillage fields, mowing land, and wood lots either surrounded the village or were located nearby. Nucleated villages surrounded by common fields were known in England and the continent and were the predominant mode of settlement in the Connecticut Valley in the seventeenth and early eighteenth centuries. Springfield, Hadley, Hatfield, Deerfield, Sunderland, and Northfield all followed this type of plan, which was well adapted for the flat lands of the fertile valley. Home lots were laid out along the village street, and tillage lands were parceled out in various divisions by the towns' proprietors. A fragment of the Deerfield proprietor's map illustrates how the village was laid out (Fig. 2:4). Made about 1671, the map shows the north end of the Deerfield street, and the lot lines in the north meadows. Home lots were generous in size, ranging between 1.7 and nearly 8 acres. Land in the meadows was given in several divisions as needs arose and as lots were developed.[24] The tillage fields ran towards the northwest in long narrow strips; these parcels were a convenient size for a day's plowing and the long run enabled farmers to plow for a considerable distance before the team had to be turned. All settlers also received areas of meadow and wood lot, essential components for establishing a farm with mixed resources. In the early years when so much land was available, it was easy to provide all families with a variety of land. As the population expanded and, more importantly, as land was handed out, new settlers would find it harder to acquire the same variety of property as the early settlers.[25]

Deerfield and the other lowland towns in the region were set up by second and third generations of Puritans. Individuals lived and worked in a complex web of relationships within the family and community. Consensual politics was a cultural value inculcated through the family, church, and town meeting. These values were reinforced by the landscape which reflected the town's emphasis on group habits and goals. The lots in the meadows were owned by individuals, but the fields themselves were managed to a certain degree as a unit. The most visible manifestation of this cooperative management was the common field fence that bordered the village's fields. In a marginal community like early Deerfield, a common fence made a great deal of sense. It was more efficient to fence animals out of one giant field and let them forage on open range land than to fence individual lots. For settlers struggling to create farms where there had been only wilderness, the efficient use of resources and time was an important consideration. At the same time, cultural values that emphasized shared responsibilities and order, both human and divine, encouraged the creation of communities predicated on cooperative systems.[26]

The emphasis placed on cooperation and sharing fit in easily with the realities of life in a new community. What is important to remember is that the tangible manifestations of these values — the town plan, its early field systems, and its land divisions — fixed some elements of the early community in place for later generations. The proprietors of the common fields in Deerfield continued to meet until the 1850s to decide when to close the field to livestock in the spring and when to open it in the fall so that animals could browse on the stubble left over from the harvest. These decisions were made by the group because the actions of one affected everyone who owned land

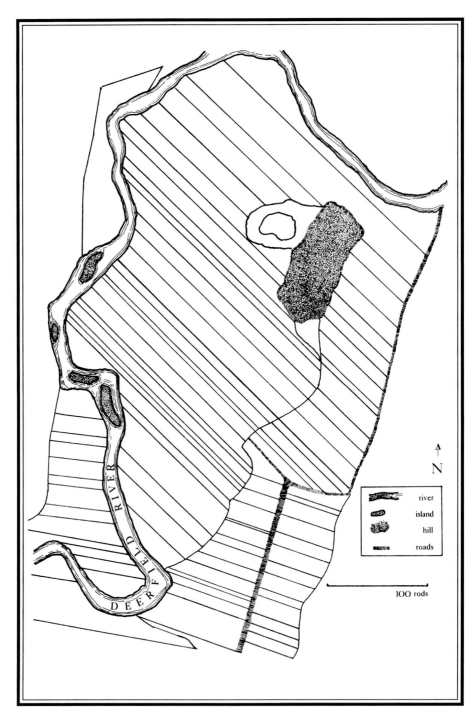

Figure 2:4. Fragment of Proprietor's Map, Deerfield, Massachusetts, 1671.
(Drawn by the author after the original owned by the Pocumtuck Valley
Memorial Association.)

in the meadows. Hence, farmers in the nineteenth century who found the common field system a nuisance put up with it anyway because it was traditional, and because changing it would cause more inconvenience than leaving things the way they were.[27]

While the evidence is clearest for Deerfield, other lowland towns followed the same general organizational scheme. Northfield's Bennett Meadows were laid out in a similar fashion to the Deerfield meadows (Fig. 2:5). Like Deerfield, Northfield made use of a common field fence to bar animals from the meadow areas. Sunderland seems to have followed a similar system. The county's three early towns reflected seventeenth-century values in other ways as well. The relatively uniform size of the three early towns suggests there was a consensus on what the proper size of a community was. It was possible to expand these towns, either by extending the town street or by laying out side streets. But in fact these options were seldom used. Until the end of the eighteenth century, relatively few settlers seemed to have considered dividing up the original home lots to increase population density. While some subdivision occurred in all the villages, expansion of the early towns was normally accomplished by splitting off lands to form sub-communities. Some of these sub-communities were like Wapping, a small neighborhood south of the Deerfield street that was established in the late seventeenth century when the original home lots in the village were all given out. Others, like the Green River area of Deerfield, would eventually become separate towns. In both of these cases, however, these new areas were formed because the process of settlement had crossed an unsurveyed cultural boundary in which continued growth on the original plat was unacceptable.

Expansion of these early lowland settlements proceeded very slowly, largely because the continuing threat of attack discouraged settlers from moving to the area. The apprehension of Indian attack was justified. English settlers in Northfield suffered from several raids and abandoned the town twice before they finally established a lasting community. As danger lessened, new settlements were set up. Bernardston was begun in the 1730s, and after towns on the fringes of existing communities developed, they served as a kind of buffer to the older areas. During the 1740s, the first tentative settlements were established in the uplands. These efforts remained small in scale until the late 1750s and early 1760s when the threat of Indian attack was effectively ended by the British capture of Canada.[28]

When these new settlements were established, they looked different from the nucleated village communities such as Deerfield or Sunderland. As Joseph Wood has shown convincingly, nucleated village patterns were not the only model followed by seventeenth-century New Englanders, although they were the dominant mode in the Connecticut Valley lowlands. The difference in

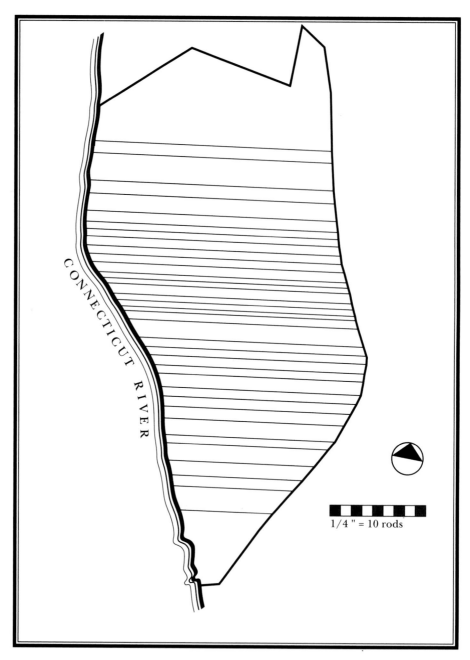

CONNECTICUT RIVER

1/4 " = 10 rods

Figure 2:5. Bennet Meadows, Northfield, Massachusetts, ca. 1730.
(Drawn by the author after the original owned by the Town of Northfield.)

Landscape and Material Life in Franklin County, Massachusetts

appearance of the newer towns reflected both a shift in values and in the way towns were created. Land in lowland towns had been gradually apportioned in divisions as needed or demanded. Starting in the 1730s, however, the surveyors who laid out new towns divided up all the land on paper. The practical effect of this system was to scatter settlers over the entire geographical area of the town from its beginning. The town center was established as a site for the meetinghouse, perhaps a tavern, and maybe some stores or craftsmen's houses, but few people lived in the center of town and traveled out to the fields.[29]

Conway, the town west of Deerfield, is a good example of how the newer process worked. The land from which Conway was created had been a part of the original eight-thousand-acre Deerfield tract granted by the Massachusetts General Court in 1661. When the Deerfield proprietors divided the land in Conway, they simply gridded off the land on paper, drew lots, and chose parcels (Fig. 2:6). In the early 1760s people began moving to the new town, settling on lands they had either chosen or purchased from the original proprietors. The area was incorporated in 1767 as a district and was named after General Henry Conway, a member of the British ministry. Almost two decades later, in 1786, the community was incorporated as a town. There are several points to keep in mind regarding the formation of Conway. The town was laid out in a dispersed farmstead plan even though many of its original proprietors were familiar with or were a part of the nucleated village community of Deerfield. If there were strong advantages in the nucleated plan as an emblem of corporate community, they were not important enough to prompt the proprietors to organize a similar scheme for Conway. Instead, these men chose a different plan that followed an alternative rationale.[30]

The isolated farmsteads that punctuated the Conway landscape illustrated by John Warner Barber in 1839, were a reminder of how much had changed since the old interval lands were laid out (Fig. 2:7). Like Conway, the uplands were organized around more rationalized economic principles, but the change in town planning also symbolized a shift in values toward a more individualistic type of community in which family needs and goals were elevated over the importance of the group. The shift was a subtle one. By isolating farmsteads on sizable blocks of land, Conway families need not depend on others in the community to decide when and how their land could be used. But at the same time they would have to find new ways to weave a fabric of community support since the land no longer bound them in a common cause.

In the older lowland towns the same trend occurred. When Deerfield families moved beyond the early settled areas in the 1750s, they set up farms in the new mode. The South Deerfield section of the town was five miles south

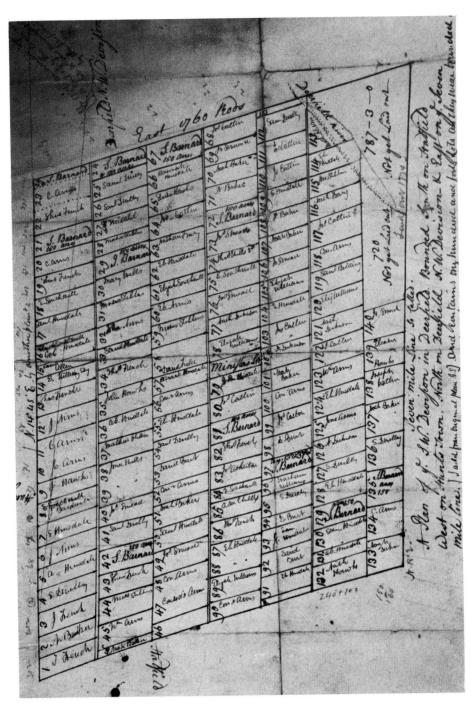

Figure 2:6. Proprietor's Map, Conway, Massachusetts, ca. 1762.
(Courtesy, Pocumtuck Valley Memorial Association.)

Figure 2:7. View of Conway, Massachusetts. From John Warner Barber, *Historical Collections*, 1839. (Courtesy, Pocumtuck Valley Memorial Association.)

of the original village street, but it was organized on new lines of thought rather than old ones. The settlers who moved to this section of town, people like Nathan Frary or Elijah Arms, built up extensive farms on large blocks of contiguous land. Instead of common fields with long strips of tillage fields, to which farmers came from a closely knit village, the fields were near the house and barn. The dispersed homes in the area focused on the crossroads tavern that Nathan Frary built in 1752. Eventually, Frary became one of the town's largest landowners, but in the 1750s, the stout log walls of his modest one-story house served as a reassuring haven for his family and others in a region still wary of Indian raids.[31]

Although settlement of the area was a dynamic process, once instituted, the plans of lowland and upland towns established cultural rules that were difficult to alter. Lots were subdivided, consolidated, and modified in various ways, but most things changed in a series of small accretions over time. It was not possible to easily turn nucleated villages into dispersed farmsteads even if the values that once encouraged communal forms of social and economic life later evolved into something rather different. Change occurred constantly in the minute scale of everyday living, but a radical restructuring of the three-dimensional world, if it occurred at all, took time to achieve — years in most cases, but sometimes decades. It was often easier to change ideas and values than the forms that reflected those values. As an 1837 map of the north meadows in Deerfield demonstrates, the values of people living in the old nucleated villages may have paralleled those of people who settled the uplands, but the forms set down decades earlier had a life of their own. Although 166 years had elapsed from the time the 1671 proprietor's map was made, the lay of the land, the direction of tillage lots were much the same (Figs. 2:4 and 2:8).[32]

Viewed on the level of the family where so much seemed to be the same, the pace of change appears slow, but the forces of many families combined altered the landscape in most of the region from wilderness to farms in two generations. Proud of the civilizing efforts waged by the original settlers to the Connecticut Valley, Timothy Dwight observed, "the hardships encountered by the first planters are not easily conceivable. The labor of converting an American forest into a habitable country is immense."[33] We have begun to grasp the magnitude of the task and the complexity of reading human discourse in the guise of landscape. We now proceed to weigh the implications of how towns at very different stages of development interacted.

Because contiguous towns evolved at different rates, economic strategies depended upon the stage of a farmstead's and of a community's development. Timothy Dwight waxed enthusiastic about the process of ordering the wilderness, writing, "In Maine, in New Hampshire, in Vermont, in Massachusetts, and in New York, I have passed the dwellings of several hundred thousands of these people, erected on grounds which in 1760 were an absolute wilderness. A large part of these tracts they have already converted into fruitful fields, covered it with productive farms, surrounded it with enclosures, planted on it orchards, and beautified it with comfortable and in many places with handsome houses. Considerable tracts I have traced through their whole progress from a desert to a garden, and have literally beheld the wilderness blossom as a rose." Despite the romanticism, Dwight made several telling observations about what he regarded as a proper landscape. The New England world Dwight idealized was largely a human creation, with a balance of different types of lands and proper buildings to meet agricultural needs and to support civil and ecclesiastic order. Starting a farm or a community involved the construction of houses, barns, outbuildings, and "fruitful fields" hacked out of forest.[34]

The Massachusetts Provincial Tax Valuation List of 1771 provides a quantifiable context for the appearance of the area's landscape about the time Dwight would have considered much of it a desert. One striking conclusion is how much time had to elapse before human activity converted it to the rose he lauded. Not all of the towns that were eventually located in the county existed in 1771 and some of the ones listed were quite new. There are a number of ways to compare and analyze the data in the list, but one of the most

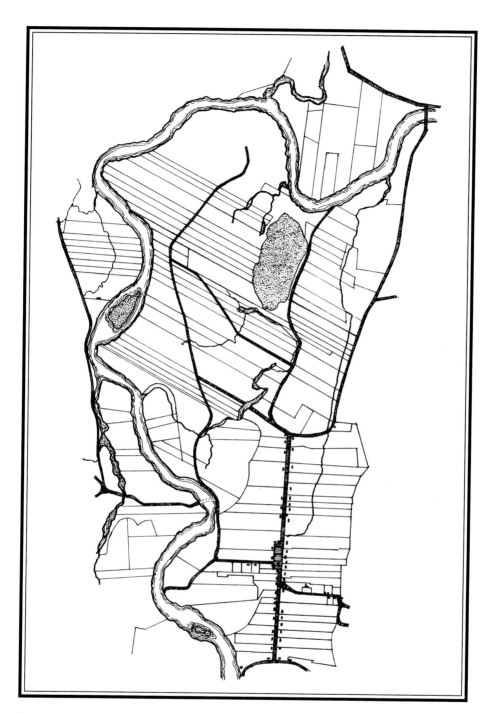

Figure 2:8. Survey of Deerfield's North Meadows, by Boutelle, 1837.
(Drawn by the author, after original owned by Pocumtuck Valley
Memorial Association.)

Table 2:1
Real and Personal Estate, Selected Towns, Hampshire (later Franklin) County, 1771

	Date of Incorporation	Heads of Household	No. of Houses	No. of Tan Houses	No. of Mills
Deerfield	1682	128	95	2	1
Northfield	1713	92	66	4	4
Sunderland	1714	56	77	2	3
Greenfield	1753	84	59	6	6
Montague	1753	87	74	11	5
New Salem	1753	130	76	2	4
Shutesbury	1761	95	66	2	3
Charlemont	1765	56	39	2	5
Ashfield	1765	84	62		3
Conway	1767	124	42	1	3
Shelburne	1768	30			1
Whately	1771	85	40	1	3

revealing is to list the information chronologically from the first date of settlement to the last (Table 2:1; Fig. 2:9). The first three towns—Deerfield, Northfield, and Sunderland—settled between 1670 and 1720 rank as the wealthiest and most highly developed towns in nearly every category. Although there is no way to adjust the category of the mean annual worth of the whole real estate to insure that all the towns were valued at the same rate, the ratio between these three towns and the others shows that they were valued two to four times higher than the other communities. If we include Greenfield and Montague, settled between 1720 and 1750 (ignoring the dates of incorporation for the moment), with these first three, and look at the figures for livestock and crops, it is equally clear that there were substantial differences between lowland and upland communities (Table 2:2). The lowland towns all have substantially more acres of tillage, grain production, and mowing land. The figures are also striking for another barometer of landscape development, the mean number of barrels of cider. These figures are obviously dependent upon the maturity of fruit trees and reflect directly the degree to which farm families in the lowlands were intensifying the use of the landscape.[35]

Several upland communities established before 1760 had progressed far enough by 1771 to equal the lowland towns in categories such as livestock. Although the realities of topography and climate precluded parity in some areas of crop production, upland towns such as New Salem, Ashfield, Charlemont, and, to a lesser extent, Shutesbury established a strategy of general mixed agriculture adapted to their local conditions. Using Bettye Hobbs Pru-

	No. of Iron Works	Mean Worth (£) of the Whole Real Estate	Slaves	Value of Merchandise (£)	Money at Interest (£)
Deerfield		1297	3	800	290
Northfield		1375		85	990
Sunderland		621	1	70	
Greenfield	59	194		37	
Montague		417		100	
New Salem		313		100	347
Shutesbury	36	288			98
Charlemont		217			
Ashfield		198			
Conway		226			60
Shelburne		116			
Whately		334			

itt's figures for subsistence, it appears that several of these towns showed small surpluses of grains and livestock which farm families may have marketed.[36]

The most recently established communities—Whately, Conway and Shelburne—appear poorer by comparison with these other towns. In these three towns fewer than half the heads of household owned houses, and no one produced any cider. While these last towns were not truly impoverished, they were underdeveloped relative to their neighbors, particularly in certain categories. Whately had the highest mean number of acres of pasture of all the towns in the table and its crop production figures were relatively impressive. Perhaps there were few dwellings because Whately was formed by taking land from Hatfield, one of the valley's oldest and wealthiest towns. Presumably portions of Whately were already in use by residents of Hatfield before it was incorporated as a separate community. Shelburne's valuation figures appear to be incomplete but the livestock numbers compare favorably with New Salem's and Charlemont's. Despite having to import food, even lowly Conway had enough potential to attract a large number of settlers; only Deerfield and New Salem had a greater number of heads of household. These last three towns shared some characteristics—most notably a small stock of buildings—yet differed in their individual trajectories of development. Over time, as families created a common farm landscape, these differences would diminish and the three communities would resemble towns with similar geographical conditions.

There were reasons why towns in Franklin County shared many char-

Table 2:2

Livestock and Produce, Selected Towns, Hampshire (later Franklin) County, 1771

	Date of Incorporation	Horses	Oxen	Cattle	Goats and Sheep	Swine	Acres of Pasture
Deerfield	1682	165	167	310	735	130	836
Northfield	1713	106	129	210	420	158	601
Sunderland	1714	104	116	191	384	108	275
Greenfield	1753	107	144	176	683	116	594
Montague	1753	70	92	150	407	110	199
New Salem	1753	61	153	250	668	134	294
Shutesbury	1761	47	70	128	393	95	206
Charlemont	1765	37	60	91	211	78	202
Ashfield	1765	37	69	102	291	67	209
Conway	1767	50	86	146	258	83	445
Shelburne	1768	14	32	33	123	28	212
Whately	1771	45	60	99	375	56	858

acteristics. An ideal farm contained at least four types of land: tillage, mowing, pasture, and wood lot. Real estate advertisements in the Greenfield newspapers made it clear that farmers sought such a mixture. Even so, there was considerable variation. The real estate advertisements seem to have fairly represented the general types of farms in the region, large as well as small. Henry Gould advertised his Colrain farm on January 1, 1795. His notice indicated that the farm consisted of a hundred acres, a house, a forty-foot barn, a wood lot, and a blacksmith shop located near the center of Colrain. Simeon Nash's land was located in Greenfield, a half mile west of the meetinghouse. His three-and-a-half-acre home lot contained a house, barn, blacksmith shop, and orchard. He owned another fifty acres of land a short distance away. Ephraim Leach's Bernardston farm was even smaller. He advertised a forty-two acre farm with a house, barn, outbuildings, and twenty acres of improved land. For farmers who could not afford existing farms there was still unimproved land available in some sections of the uplands in the 1790s. Land speculators like John Lowell, Jr., of Boston, advertised five thousand acres of land in Rowe and Heath for sale in lots of five hundred to one thousand acres, but most common farmers could not finance the purchase of such large acreage. Regional entrepreneur/farmers like Col. Hugh Maxwell of Heath bought some of these large tracts and turned their purchase to profit by subdividing them for ordinary folk. After the Revolution, the price of good land in the fertile bottoms of river valleys quickly escalated in price. By the 1830s, the

Acres of Tillage	Bu. of Grain/ Year	Barrels of Cider	Acres of English Mowing	Tons of Hay	Acres of Fresh Meadow	Tons of Fresh Meadow Hay
1611	11684	517	831	825.5	330.3	276.5
1226	7576	161	299.6	341.3	339.6	303.4
1007	6561	316	648.9	289.5	326.6	224
1065	9972	199	672.5	556	121	106
1010	7440	284	191.2	182.1	253.7	192
328	4856	175	367	282	400	269
237	1994	132	433.5	246	67	42
332	3064	14	452	267		
388	4031	38	348	335		
348	2901		365.8	296.3		
144			171			
490	3465		321.5	205.5	3	4

Table 2:3
Size of Farms Advertised in the Greenfield Newspaper, 1792-1820

No. of Farms	Amount of Land
23	Under 30 acres
51	31-60 acres
33	61-90 acres
52	91-120 acres
22	121-150 acres
22	Larger than 151 acres

best alluvial land in Deerfield's famed north meadows cost two hundred dollars per acre. At that price even the town's wealthiest residents could not afford to consolidate much property. For those seeking cheap undeveloped land, only towns on the peripheries, the areas with the shortest growing seasons, steepest slopes, and thinnest topsoil, had much to offer.[37]

Most farms in Franklin County were fairly small. Some were too small to have provided the mixture of land generally claimed as the minimum for adequately sustaining a family. A careful reading of the Greenfield newspaper between 1792 and 1820 turned up 203 real estate advertisements for properties identifiable as farms. (See Table 2:3.) Very few farms, however, were listed as having more than 250 acres. By far the greatest concentration

Figure 2:9. Periods of Incorporation, Franklin County Massachusetts.
(Drawn by the author.)

of the farms advertised for sale ranged between 45 and 100 acres. The land
on these farms varied in quality. Hence, the majority of farmers could not
actually use all of the land they owned. At least some land of marginal quality,
particularly in the uplands, was recorded as unimprovable and other areas
were not suitable for certain agricultural purposes. Land that was satisfactory
for pasture seldom made very good tillage fields. The reality for most farmers
was that they rarely owned the ideal mixture of land in the correct proportions. Most families had to make do with what they had or devise strategies
of exchanging goods and services to compensate.[38]

Wealthy lowland farmers who tilled the region's rich interval lands also
suffered sometimes from less than ideal circumstances. These farmers might
have sizable acres of good tillage fields, but according to Rodolphus Dickinson some families in lowland towns like Deerfield faced a shortage of pasture
land in 1815. He reported that "the want of convenient pasture has long been
a serious inconvenience to the inhabitants of the village, but this is gradually
becoming less, by the opening of the woodlands on the eastern hills."[39] Prominent lowland farm families who could afford to do so held onto their undeveloped lands, banking them for future generations. Consequently, older valley
towns like Deerfield and Northfield grew far more slowly than most upland
towns between 1790 and 1830 because newcomers seldom found land to buy

there at a reasonable price. Farmers who moved to Deerfield in the 1820s and 1830s were either wealthy, married into the town's prosperous farm families, inherited land from relatives, or bought less desirable property.

Wealthier farmers generally had the recommended types of land or could purchase what they needed, but poorer farmers did not and could not. Although the effects of unequal resources were evened out considerably by reciprocal economic ties within kinship networks and the community in general, some farmers necessarily looked to other communities to fulfill their needs for pasture, woodland, or tillage. Moreover, the opportunities to acquire a competence through inheritance became increasingly limited. It was not possible to divide up some of the small farms in the county in the early 1800s without wrecking their economic potential entirely.[40]

We can test for evidence of specialization and dependency only by reconstructing the biographies of individual families. Tax valuation lists are suggestive but they are not sufficiently detailed to quantify neatly the dynamic qualities of household patterns. Nor are they always accurate reflections of social status because communities judged individuals on a variety of criteria, not just those deemed taxable. Two case studies illustrate this point. By any measure, Joseph Barnard was one of Deerfield's most prominent residents in 1771. Although he was a merchant, Barnard owned several substantial farms. His valuation listed 11 horses, 5 oxen, 14 cattle, 40 sheep, 2 hogs, 35 acres of pasture, 47 acres of tillage, 30 barrels of cider, 56 acres of mowing, and 10 acres of fresh meadow. This property yeilded 470 bushels of grain and 66 tons of hay. Using Pruitt's estimate that 30 bushels of grain would feed an average family for a year, it appears that Barnard's farm yielded a substantial surplus of grain. Down the street from Barnard's elegant mansion house stood Thomas Williams's smaller but still pretentious home. In 1771, Williams, a physician, owned 1 horse, 4 cows, 4 acres of pasture, 6 acres of tillage, 10 barrels of cider, and 13.5 acres of mowing.[41]

Ranked with other farmers, the figures for Williams are modest. Evaluating the figures by linking them with other documents, we see that in terms of his professional reputation, education, kinship ties, public offices, mansion house, and furnishings, Williams was a member of the town's elite. Both men, then, were members of the region's gentry. Barnard's farms contained the complete variety of the types of land farmers were supposed to have and he raised substantial surpluses. Williams's farm seems to have met only a portion of the family's food requirements with the balance made up from payments for his medical services. His son, William Stoddard Williams, would inherit only a part of his father's estate because he was one of eleven children who reached adulthood. A physician like his father, he struggled for years to acquire farmland in a town where the real estate values were high. After his

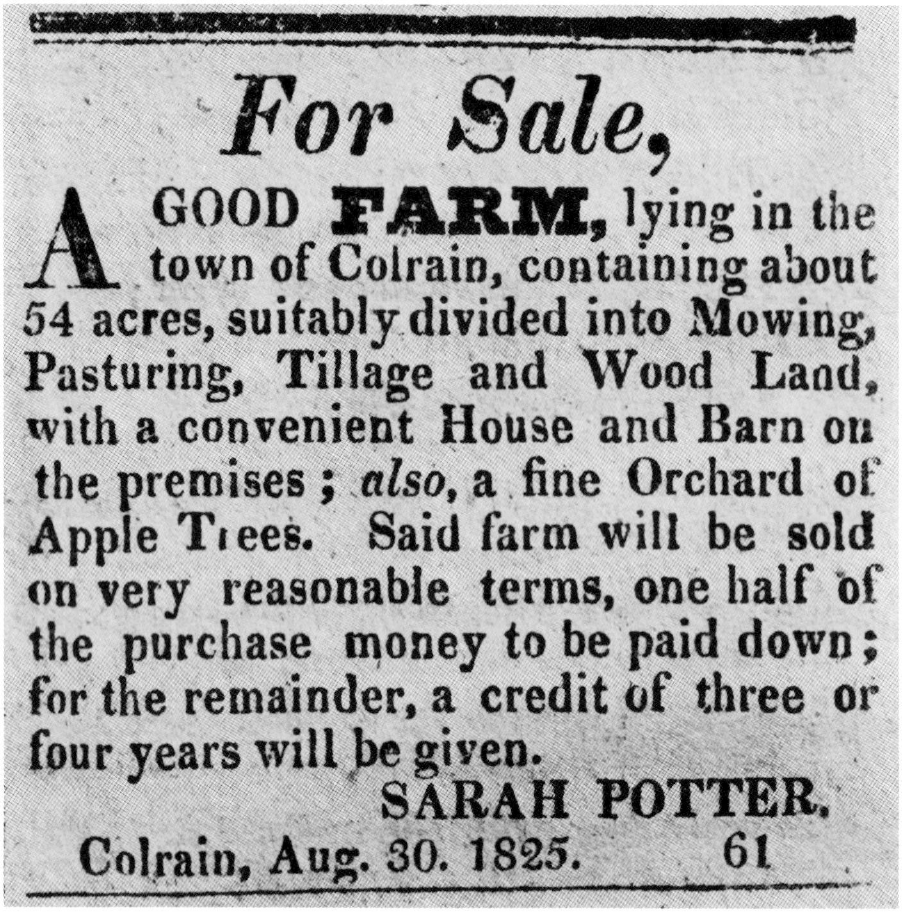

For Sale,

A GOOD **FARM,** lying in the town of Colrain, containing about 54 acres, suitably divided into Mowing, Pasturing, Tillage and Wood Land, with a convenient House and Barn on the premises; *also*, a fine Orchard of Apple Trees. Said farm will be sold on very reasonable terms, one half of the purchase money to be paid down; for the remainder, a credit of three or four years will be given.

SARAH POTTER.

Colrain, Aug. 30. 1825. 61

Figure 2:10. Real Estate Advertisement, *Greenfield Gazette and Franklin Herald*, August 30, 1825. (Courtesy, Pocumtuck Valley Memorial Association.)

death, his son, Stephen West Williams, wrote to Elihu Hoyt on 1 February 1829: "Why should my father's estate be very large? He has [brought] up an expensive family, & for many of us has expended a great deal of money. If his landed estate is worth something it is because in the purchase of a good deal of it he has taken advantage of the market and bought cheap, & that land has increased in value since he purchased." However, the increase in the value of land William Stoddard Williams benefited from closed off opportunity for many who came after him. For the Williamses and other families a trade or profession could coexist with farming because more and more they had little choice. By necessity these households reached out to the rest of the community, wider networks of kin, and to strangers seeking their services in order to insure family security.[42]

Because towns in Franklin County were settled and developed at different times, they evolved at different rates. As Conway farmers were converting their forests to a habitable country in the 1760s and 1770s, Deerfield families were entering a period of rebuilding that transformed the town's early architecture and landscape. A similar process of rebuilding occurred later in newly settled towns. Just as towns adjacent to one another could exist at very different stages of development, so could individual farms. The inequalities in development forced families and newer communities to trade locally and interregionally to meet basic needs. In newly established communities or households people purchased tools, building materials, foodstuffs, seed, livestock, textiles, furniture, tableware, and a host of other items from outside sources — from merchants like Elisha Alvord of Northampton, who had many accounts with people from newly settled towns in the 1760s and 1770s. Eventually, families and communities could become more self-sufficient through home production or local exchange, but because of inequalities in the distribution of property and the character of the landscape, local and interregional forms of trade and cooperation continued long after the first generation of settlers were in their graves. We can decode patterns in the region's history by examining the landscape's development in 1771 when Massachusetts ordered a valuation list made, but the patterns are accurate only in a relative sense. Behind them were the actions of individuals and families who collectively were making a new world.[43]

Chapter 3

Change

It was on November 27, 1812, that citizens of Deerfield escorted John Wilson on horseback from his farm to the old town street of Deerfield. He was "saluted on his arrival by a discharge of cannon—and most cordially received and congratulated by a large number of his fellow townsmen." The occasion for all this pomp and circumstance was Wilson's redemption from Canada where, in the sensitive months after war was declared, he had been arrested and charged with spying. Although it caused his family and friends great anxiety at the time, in retrospect the entire event had comical overtones. While on a business trip to Canada, Wilson, who was interested in military science, strayed too close to a British garrison near St. Johns and was detained as he reviewed the maneuvers of English troops. Fascinated with the professionalism of British regulars, he was probably not very discreet or was prepared to ignore that a state of war was in existence. His subsequent imprisonment lasted only a short time before he was released and sent safely back home to Deerfield, but it was sufficient. He returned as a hero, a rather ordinary man suddenly plucked from obscurity by happenstance and ill-timed curiosity.[1]

It was precisely curiosity and a willingness to experiment and take risks that was characteristic of John Wilson and many other progressive farmers in the early nineteenth century. When Alexis de Tocqueville wrote about the restless American and called him a "new man," he might have been referring to someone like Wilson. When relatives wrote about John Wilson, they called him "enterprising." If one word could describe him, that was as good as any. And in the enterprises of Wilsons's life one could almost trace the shifting patterns of farming and business in antebellum Franklin County. While Henry David Thoreau withdrew to the solitude of Walden Pond to listen to the rhythms of his different drum, Wilson was intently engaged in the very pursuit of recognition and fortune that Thoreau viewed with such suspicion. He and other progressive farmers led the movement to reform the landscape, reshaping material life with new technology, speculative ventures, and aggressive acquisitiveness.[2]

John was born in 1782, in Montague, Massachusetts, a town across the river from Deerfield. While he was still a child, his father swapped farms with someone in the Great River section of Deerfield, near the juncture of the Connecticut and Deerfield rivers. The land in the Great River area was indifferent, but the Wilsons' move opened new opportunities. When he grew up, John became active in the local militia which was as much a men's club as it was an arm of state authority. Soon, he became associated with the Deerfield social library. This widened his chances to meet with some of the local social and intellectual elite and he made the most of it. Two years after joining the social library, Wilson married Betsey Hoyt, sealing his connection to one of the town's most respected and politically active families. An ambitious man without title to his own farm, he apparently undertook a variety of business activities, some of which included trips to Canada. It was during one of these trips that he was captured and detained.[3]

Despite his Canadian adventure and a brief stint with his militia regiment in Boston during the War of 1812, Wilson was somewhat unclear about the direction of his life until his father's death in 1815. He inherited the farm equally with his two brothers but bought sole title to the property from them. He soon turned in another direction, however, joining with his brothers-in-law, John Churchill Hoyt and Rodolphus Dickinson, to start up a book-printing venture. Dickinson provided the press and the copy to be published; Hoyt offered land near his house on which to build a printing office; and Wilson managed the business. While Dickinson remained in Greenfield to continue his law practice, Hoyt and Wilson traded houses so that Wilson could be near the printing venture. The business initially employed two printers, two bookbinders, and probably several apprentices. Their first publication was an inexpensive reprint of biblical excerpts edited by Dickinson. This book sold moderately well and the partners soon embarked on a more ambitious and expensive undertaking—a digest of the laws of Massachusetts, written once again by Dickinson. Unlike the biblical compendium, the new work was an expensive product with quality paper and simply tooled binding, but a digest of Massachusetts laws had limited popular appeal and the business soon became dangerously overextended.[4]

His partners were little help. Dickinson, whose personal characteristics might kindly be called erratic, soon quit writing, gave up his law practice, and set off to pursue a new career as an Episcopal minister in North Carolina. John Churchill Hoyt soon followed, sent by the family to help keep the Dickinson's affairs in a semblance of order. These moves left Wilson with the press, type, and a hopelessly large debt just when some of the new books' bigger bills were coming due. In desperation, Wilson turned to contract printing to stay afloat for a few more months, but the financial panic of 1819 proved to be too much and the venture failed. Wilson sold what he could, paid off the workers with the press and type, and returned to his farm in 1821 still under the cloud of a sizable debt.[5]

His reverses did not diminish his reputation or his energy. He served as a selectman in 1820 and took over responsibility for the town's poor. When his term of office ended, he contracted with the town to continue caring for the poor over a period of ten years at $450 a person. Although it must have seemed attractive at the time, perhaps because of the large debt he still carried, it is not entirely clear what he hoped to achieve from this arrangement. He may have believed that the contract would yield him a steadier income than agriculture or printing, for he was free to employ town paupers ". . . in farming or the mechanic arts, according to their several abilities." Using the guaranteed income as collateral, he built a new house, paying for the construction by mortgaging his farm. Despite the potential financial rewards, the mortgage added to his debts by two thousand dollars, and the prospects of getting work from the town's poor soon dimmed. Wilson fulfilled the terms of his contract, but when it ended in 1832, neither he nor the town elected to repeat the experiment.[6]

Farming rather than care of the poor was Wilson's principal occupation and he would return to his farm after failed business ventures. Always a risk taker and experimenter, he tried new seed types and crops, participated in the local agricultural society, and sought friendships with men like Henry Colman. He recorded a variety of agricultural experiments in his personal memorandum book, subscribed to the *New England Farmer*, and, like other progressive agriculturalists, tinkered with inventing. Sometime in the 1820s or 1830s he became involved with designing a cast iron plow—an implement that many others were also striving to improve (Fig. 3:1). Like the printing venture, plow manufacturing also depended on kinship ties. His brother William ran Greenfield's most enduring foundry and had married one of the Pierces of Greenfield, a family of experienced metalworkers. These ties were not enough for success, however. Although he received a patent for his design and Henry Colman reviewed it favorably, few people bought it.[7]

By 1832, these schemes—the pauper contract and the plow venture—combined with financial improvidence had brought Wilson to the brink of financial ruin. Some in the area estimated his debt to be six thousand dollars, and he was forced to assign his affairs to his brother William and a local insurance agent, Horatio Newcomb. Much of his personal estate was auctioned, but he managed to hold on to the farm and directed his energies to planting cash crops that would help retire his debts. True to his interests in advanced

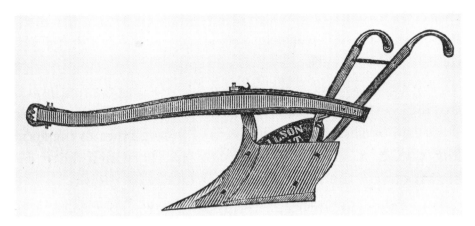

Figure 3:1. John Wilson's Plow. (Courtesy, Pocumtuck Valley Memorial Association.)

agriculture and anxious to pay his creditors by exploiting the market, he experimented during the 1830s with several cash crops. He planted teasels (for the textile industry), grew broom corn, and tried to raise silkworms. In the end, however, it was his business contacts and friends that enabled him to regain a measure of financial security.[8]

These personal contacts ultimately led to his participation in the development of East Boston between 1834 and 1836. That an obscure farmer from east Deerfield could become involved with the development of East Boston offers some insight into the complexity of social and economic systems in the early nineteenth century and is worth studying in some detail. The East Boston Company was founded in 1833 to improve and develop Noddles Island. The company's president was William H. Sumner. It is unclear how Sumner and Wilson became associated, but it was probably through Wilson's brothers-in-law, Elihu and Epaphras Hoyt. Like Sumner, Epaphras Hoyt was a general in the Massachusetts militia. He may have introduced Wilson to Sumner in the fall of 1826 when Sumner passed through Deerfield while on tour of western Massachusetts with the governor. By that time, Wilson was a colonel in the state militia and may have had a chance to meet with Sumner. Wilson may also have met Sumner through Elihu Hoyt who was a senator in the Massachusetts legislature until his death in 1833. Elihu Hoyt's political connections had helped others. Perhaps Wilson used the same avenues to seek patronage.[9]

Whatever the means by which he met Sumner, Wilson's many years of service to Deerfield as a surveyor and road commissioner, and his political credentials were apparently sufficient qualifications. At various times during 1834, he supervised road construction in East Boston. During the opening ceremonies in May 1835, he was asked to say a few words about his work.

With appropriate modesty, he explained that he believed his work was "accomplished with credit to the company and to his own credit." He then asked to be excused from saying anything further as he was unaccustomed to speaking publicly. "General Sumner begged him to keep on," according to one account, "as he said his speech was like his road, very well constructed, but only wanted a smoother surface." The flattering remarks must have been deeply satisfying, but Wilson's success with the East Boston venture underscored the fact that opportunities for financial reward and personal recognition were limited in rural towns like Deerfield. Wilson's association with the East Boston Company was made possible by family contacts, but relatively few rural people had similar kinds of connections.[10]

With the successful completion of the East Boston project behind him, Wilson entered into a different business arrangement with Sumner. This time the project was far removed from Boston. Sumner had become involved as a trustee and attorney with the Galveston Bay and Texas Land Companies, a land-speculation scheme organized by eastern capitalists to sell land to settlers who were willing to move to Texas. Wilson became the agent for Franklin County and began to recruit settlers for Texas. In return for his work as an agent he was promised sizable tracts of land. He lost little time in taking out a large advertisement in the *Greenfield Gazette* and *Franklin Herald*, pledging to go to Texas himself to aid the settlers in setting up, "for a reasonable compensation." Within a month twenty-five families from the county were signed up to go, but the entire enterprise was starting to unravel.[11]

Although the Mexican government had initially encouraged settlers to move into the sparsely settled region, the subsequent flood of Americans searching for cheap Texas land threatened to overwhelm the influence of Mexican officials. Just as Wilson finished signing up settlers to move from Franklin County to Texas, word arrived from Sumner that the company's Texas agent had reported that conditions there were very bad. The recruitment of settlers was halted. Once again Wilson's highest expectations failed to materialize. Sumner offered Wilson a small commission of the land sales that were still open, but the company soon dissolved. There would be no move to Texas for the Wilsons nor any fortune from land speculation. Instead, Wilson was stuck with more debts incurred by his promotional activities for the Texas scheme. To keep afloat financially, he turned to his surveying skills again, traveling to Southport, Pennsylvania, to work on another development project. Once again personal and business contacts staved off ruin.[12]

In 1836, he became steward of Deerfield Academy, a position he would hold for seven years. During these years, he continued to work on his plow design and maintained an active interest in agriculture. In the 1820s he had tried raising merino sheep; in the 1830s he raised broom corn; by the early

1850s he was experimenting with tobacco. Throughout his life he manipulated opportunities as they became available, demonstrating flexibility when faced with obstacles. John Wilson died on April 29, 1869, with a comfortable estate of a little less than ten thousand dollars. Like many others of his era he had worked hard and succeeded—moderately.[13]

Several patterns characterized Wilson's approach to life. For most of his adult years he aspired to the "main chance," the opportunity to become someone special in the world. He sought this goal by participating in activities that would admit him to the circles of the local social, intellectual, and political elite, and he took risks to attain his ends. He was prepared to move to Texas, he contracted out his surveying expertise far from home and community, and he experimented with farming and other ventures in hopes of gaining financial and social position. Although his social status remained relatively secure, his economic status fluctuated wildly. He was probably saved from insolvency and disgrace because he had a network of kin and friends who helped him, and because over the long run the economy remained vigorous enough for him to recoup his losses. His debts were as much a product of his ambition and his improvidence as of a competitive capitalistic system, and he did not reject that system even when he nearly foundered in it.

Wilson's story also underscores several other concepts central to understanding the development of the region's landscape. The first is that change is finally a consequence of individual actions on the part of many people. Seen at a personal level these actions are not very significant, yet individuals mattered; they modified culture through their families and communities. Secondly, the landscape reflected cultural change, often quite directly. Men and women reshaped patterns of production, the layout of farmsteads, and the architecture of farmhouses and barns not only because they responded to broad intellectual, social, and economic currents but because they were constantly altering portions of their world. Finally, the dynamic qualities of everyday life did not drown out older traditions entirely. Old networks of patronage, the habits of face-to-face relationships, and a sense of community responsibility were transmuted but not dissolved by new commercial strategies. Wilson depended upon the connections and support implicit in these older traditions, yet he consciously embraced the possibilities of capitalistic production and progressive agriculture.

Was Wilson's interest in progressive farming widely shared? How many other families in the region took similar financial risks? What persuaded the region's farmers to adopt new agricultural techniques, improve crops and livestock, and expand productivity? Tax valuations and census reports convey information on the social and economic structure of the area, but we must also study tools to determine how much technological change influenced rural life. Assaying the impact of reformers, the agricultural press, libraries, and agricultural fairs is harder because cause and effect are far less clear. Most men and women in the area were literate and had access to a broad spectrum of didactic discourse. The most persuasive agents of change were probably local families who tried out new, sometimes expensive, ideas and contraptions. When these innovations proved their merits, the neighbors adopted them.

While the leaders of progressive agriculture were at or near the top deciles of wealth in most towns, those who followed came from the region's sizable middle class. Northfield's 1815 tax valuation list provides an overview of its taxable wealth. The town's progressive farmers came from the top 30 percent of the tax rolls. These were the men who built the community's biggest houses and barns, owned the most outbuildings, land, livestock and tools, and who consistently raised market surpluses for commercial purposes. It is unclear whether their status as economic leaders enabled them to be progressive or whether their progressive attitudes contributed to their prosperity. It is clear that names like Stratton, Mattoon, Field, and Wright were among the wealthiest members of the town when the 1771 tax valuation was made and that these leading families remained prominent. Most of the men at the top of the list were middle-aged or older in 1815, and Northfield's list paralleled the stratification of wealth by age that prevailed in other towns in New England.[14]

The middle 40 percent were by no means impoverished. The majority owned land and houses, and some had sizable personal estates associated with their trade, profession, or family farm. In general these people were younger than those further up the list. Some would move up after they inherited their parents' estate; a few were widows. The size of this middle group contributed in important ways to the reform of the county's landscape. While the middling farm families lacked the capital to reshape their world on the same scale as their wealthy neighbors, they were able to accommodate some of the innovations that the elite pioneered. By the 1810s and 1820s many of them were adding ells and sheds to their houses; some built new outbuildings to improve the storage of feed and to shelter livestock. Most of them improved yields by using better seed types, by planting timothy and clover, and by more careful fertilizing. Equally important, the relative prosperity of the middle group prevented wealthier residents from appropriating control of the landscape or local politics.

The bottom 30 percent of Northfield's tax rolls was composed principally of younger men. Some of them were sons of prominent local families and would eventually improve their status as they aged. In other cases their opportunities were clearly limited and they would move on. Augustus Richardson, for example, was a journeyman carpenter working for his brother-in-law, Calvin Stearns. He would subsequently move to Boston. William Norton who also worked for Stearns was barely old enough to pay a poll tax and would move on after his employment ended. This pattern does not mean that residents of the town did not suffer from poverty or inequalities, but the people listed in the lower deciles of the town's valuations did not represent a permanently disenfranchised underclass with little hope of improvement. The gap between rich and poor was real in Northfield, as it was in all towns in the county, but it was not enormous. Three men (.9 percent) on the 1815 tax rolls owned more than five hundred acres of land, and only about fifteen (5 percent) owned more than two hundred acres. While the town's highest taxpayer, Rufus Stratton, paid $720 annually, he did not own enough land or control enough of the economy to compel complete deference from his more modestly situated neighbors.

The relatively small size of holdings does not seem to have encouraged extensive farm tenancy. Many families rented pasture or bought cutting rights in local woodlots, but they do not seem to have leased entire farms very often. Frequently tax valuations did not indicate leaseholds or specify tenants because property owners stipulated that their leaseholders assume payment for all taxes. Local account books seldom mentioned tenancy of farms, but they did occasionally refer to renting of houses or sections of farm land. The 1798 Federal Direct Tax Census is not complete for the region or for the valley, but where the schedules do survive, it appears that between two and six families per town leased farms, a small number compared with the figures Lucy Simler reported in her study of tenancy in Chester County, Pennsylvania.[15]

The large middle-class and small holdings prevented most farm families in Franklin County from participating fully in the economies of scale that benefited midwestern farmers by the 1850s. For that reason the county's farmers shared production dilemmas with other old farm regions in the East. The Delaware farmers Jack Michel studied faced similar pressures from western competition and responded by intensifying production. Franklin County families did too and, like the husbandmen in New Castle County, Delaware, found that increased productivity led to surpluses that drove down prices. Only those farmers who could continue to turn profits as they increased capital and labor inputs would prosper under these conditions—a situation that favored families in Franklin County who owned larger farms on good land and who prevented population growth from segmenting their holdings into smaller units. Increasingly siblings or fathers and sons ran the family farm as a single entity, although they might live separately as nuclear families. The 1815 Northfield tax list illustrates this development. Of the 311 names on the list, 38 (12 percent) owned shares in a farm. Several of these owners were widows, but in the majority of cases the farm was operated jointly by father and son or by brothers.[16]

These partnerships skew the ranking of the Northfield valuation because they make individuals look poorer than they actually were. If holdings are combined and repositioned in the ranking, most partnerships look competitive with farms in the top three or four deciles. This pattern of shared responsibility became characteristic of many mature farms. The pressures of population growth, the impact of competition from northern farms, and the fixed resources of farms tended to concentrate innovation in the hands of families who were committed to farming as a way of life, who were willing and able to participate in economies of scale, and who could cooperate with other family members if it was necessary to preserve the productivity of the farm unit. These forces and conditions also affected habits of work.

Managing labor was crucial to the economic security of local families if farmers were to mitigate the effects of seasonal production. In an agrarian system, labor, commodity prices, and profit were inseparably linked with seasonal shifts. For most farmers, income was available when there was a surplus to exchange or sell, usually in the months following harvest. Because nearly everyone brought in their crops at about the same time, there were cyclical fluctuations in the demand for farm labor and in the prices of commodities. As a result, labor was hired by season or task and frequently was handled in a quasi-cooperative fashion with neighbors by "changing work." Such labor was seldom given gratis. The work was often credited on farm account books and given a monetary value. The presumption was that the debt would be paid for later, perhaps with cash, but more likely with an equivalent amount of labor or value of goods. As communities developed and population increased, more farmers hired wage laborers rather than changing work with their neighbors. Nevertheless eighteenth-century habits changed slowly. Traditional practices like changing work persisted among neighbors through the entire period of this study but gave ground to cash wages. During busy seasons, farmers paid hired help for plowing, haying, hoeing, and harvesting; sometimes they contracted for longer periods in return for board and room. Later, in the 1850s, wealthy farmers in the lowlands began to hire Irish laborers as long-term farm hands.[17]

Agricultural work might mean intensive efforts for several weeks followed by periods of relatively light demands. When Cephas Hoyt had to get his corn harrowed, his father wrote in his diary, "We are harrowing corn with 5 or 6 hands. I harrowed today and am very tired. I am to old to work so hard but Cephas took the Physic and the work must be done." As one of the most prosperous farmers in Deerfield, Cephas Hoyt could afford to hire labor, but even his seventy-two-year-old father expected to help during busy times. This traditional reliance on family, however, does not alter the fact that most of Hoyt's crop was brought in by hired help. By 1800 the wage rates farm laborers received and the contractual arrangements they negotiated were beginning to follow modern patterns: wage rates fluctuated according to supply and demand, and payment for the same task became congruent throughout the region.[18]

The cyclical system of agricultural production was reflected in most farm account books in two ways: The first was to live within the family's needs by conserving resources. Such an approach placed a premium on "making do" and on learning a broad variety of skills in order to be as self-sufficient as possible—attributes that are still characteristic of the region's farm families. The second was to augment the family income by increasing sales of marketable produce. The first approach was in keeping with the traditional value assigned to frugality and communal reciprocity; the second met the desire of many families to improve tools, crops, and capital stock, learn better farming techniques, and seek out strategies to overcome the constraints of seasonality.[19]

Working a farm in the rural North required tools. Despite the technological innovations that aided grain farmers in the Midwest before the Civil War, farmers in Franklin County did not benefit much from mechanization. Both probate inventories and collections of tools with provenance reflect relatively low amounts of capital invested in technological innovations. Most farmers seem to have invested their capital in land and buildings rather than in consumer durables like farm tools. Basic equipment included: hoes (Fig. 3:2) for weeding corn fields; axes for managing wood lots; dungforks and a two-wheeled cart for cleaning out stalls and fertilizing fields; beetles and wedges for splitting fence posts and rails; corn knives, sickles, scythes, snaiths, handles, pitchforks, and rakes for haying or harvesting grains; spades for digging post holes; tackling for horses and chains and yokes for oxen; flails, winnowing baskets, sieves and grain shovels for threshing (Figs. 3:3 and 3:4); and a variety of wood-working tools such as planes and augers. Some of these goods were made on the farm or in the community; others were imported or bought from manufacturers. Locally, the Lamson family of Shelburne Falls manufactured axes and in the 1830s developed a technique for mass-producing curved, steam-bent scythe snaiths, a clear improvement over the earlier straight-handled models. Thus the common tools in local farmers' sheds and barns included a mixture of forms and finishes that paralleled the condition of the larger material landscape in which old and new buildings coexisted.[20]

There were some significant improvements. By the 1800s plows were common to middling and wealthy farmers, and both "Dutch" and common plows

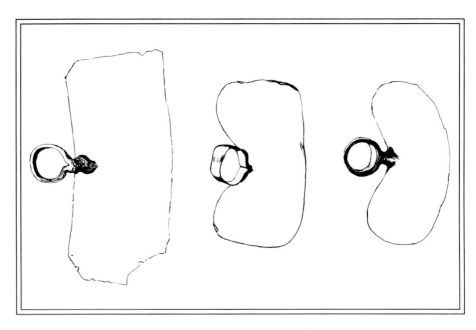

Figure 3:2. Hoe heads, Franklin County, Massachusetts, 1780–1860. (Measured and drawn by the author from the Collections of the Memorial Hall Museum.)

were owned and used in the region (Fig. 3:5). Plows were made locally or were brought up river from Enfield, Connecticut, where there was a well-known plow manufacturer. Cast-iron plows were in use by the 1820s when men like John Wilson experimented with the shape of mouldboards, coulters, and shares, but they do not show up in probate inventories until the late 1830s and early 1840s. The evidence from farm tools indicates that few farmers relied on much of the evolving agricultural equipment to increase yields. Only two labor-saving devices were rapidly accepted in the 1810s and 1820s — corn shellers and fanning mills (Fig. 3:6).[21]

While corn shellers were relatively inexpensive, a fanning mill was not. During a slack period in November and December of 1817, Northfield carpenter Calvin Stearns made seven fanning mills, charging each of his customers the going rate of twelve dollars per mill. Five more orders followed in January 1818. Skilled carpenters like Stearns could fabricate a fanning mill without too much difficulty during winter months when they were not busy with building tasks, buying the metal parts they needed from local merchants or iron founders. An ingenious device, the fanning mill was originally called a "Dutch fan." A few wealthy farmers in the area owned them during the last quarter of the eighteenth century, but it was another generation before they were very common. Threshed grains were poured into the hopper at the top of the machine while an assistant turned the crank on the side to power the

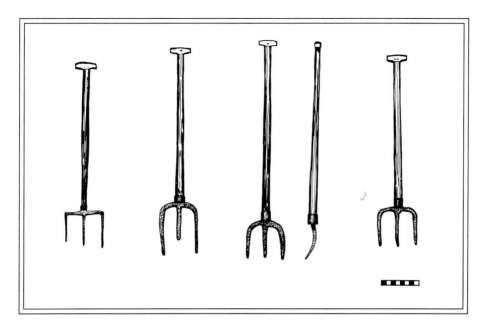

Figure 3:3. Dung Forks, Franklin County, Massachusetts, 1780–1860.
(Drawing by the author from the Collections of the Memorial Hall Museum.)

mill's fan and sieves. The grain descended through a series of wire screens which were automatically shaken from side to side as a forced draft of air blew chaff out the end of the machine. The cleaned grain then slid out a small chute at the bottom of the apparatus into a basket set on the ground.[22]

Corn shellers were generally much simpler; some were little more than two pieces of wood faced with iron spikes that swiveled against each other. The operator applied sufficient friction to a dried ear of corn passed between them to rub off the kernels. Corn-shellers were available from local merchants or carpenters, but after 1830 more farmers ordered them from merchants who specialized in agricultural equipment, occasionally from distant centers like New York. In July 1833, Elisha Wells was in New York selling brooms. In a letter to Elihu Hoyt, Wells mentioned that he had talked to the head man at a store selling corn-shellers and would bring one back upon his return for wealthy Deerfield farmer Asa Stebbins. We do not know if these distant purchases from urban centers were common, but they did occur. Progressive farmers clearly were aware of innovations and prices in urban areas whether they traveled there themselves or heard from neighbors.[23]

While these improvements were effective time-saving devices, most of the region's farmers grew commodities for which the age's famous innovations, such as the reaper, were of little use. Only in the late 1850s did a few progressive farmers begin to acquire mowing machinery, but the expense of the

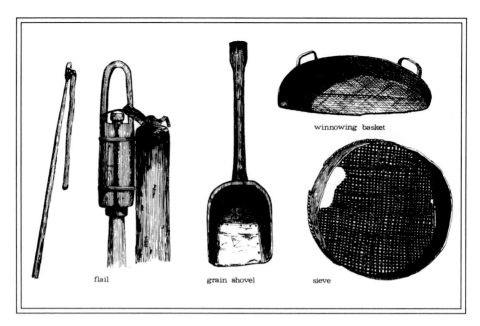

Figure 3:4. Flail, Grain Shovel, Winnowing Basket, Sieve, Franklin County, Massachusetts, 1780–1860. (Drawing by the author from the Collections of the Memorial Hall Museum.)

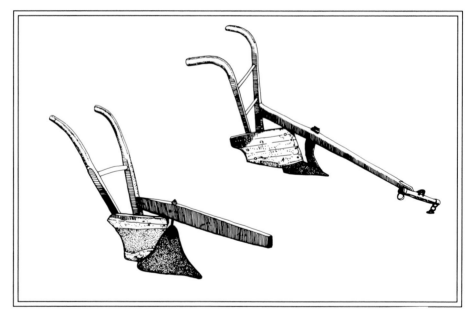

Figure 3:5. *Left:* Dutch Plow, Franklin County, Massachusetts, 1780–1815. *Right:* English or Common Plow, Franklin County, Massachusetts, 1790–1820. (Drawn by the author from the Collections of the Memorial Hall Museum.)

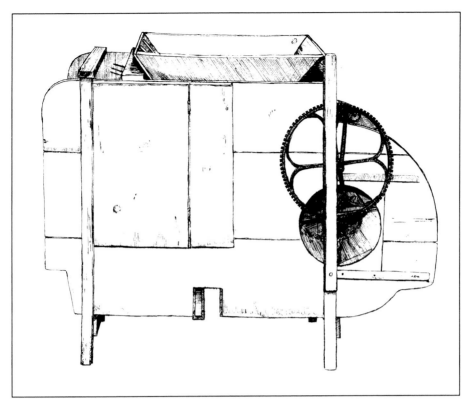

Figure 3:6. Fanning Mill, Franklin County, Massachusetts, 1810–40.
(Drawn by the author from the Collections of the Memorial Hall Museum.)

equipment and the small size of many of the region's mowing fields seem to have retarded early acceptance of power machinery. Although equipment patterns suggest the region's farmers took a conservative approach to farm mechanization, their conservatism was not necessarily an indifference to efficiency. As we will show later, instead of buying expensive equipment, many farmers reorganized their landscape to achieve greater productivity. By the early nineteenth century, most farmers owned a wide variety of tools, but most of them were traditional. When the basic tools younger and poorer farmers owned proved insufficient, they either borrowed or rented what they needed from better-equipped neighbors. Thus, a limited range of tools was usually enough in the old farm areas in the East before the Civil War; what really mattered was that more people had tools than before.

Given the conservative technology of the region's farms, it is tempting to assume that there was little change in the region's production strategies. If the farmers lived with a pre-industrial mentalité that concentrated on meeting basic human needs and on providing for household and community secu-

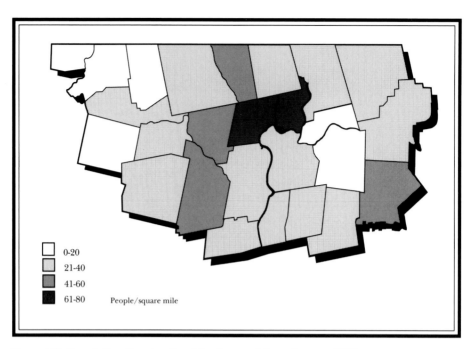

Figure 3:7. Population Density, Franklin County, Massachusetts, 1790.
(Drawn by the author.)

rity, then it seems logical to assume that there would be a fairly uniform system of production from community to community. Since the basic needs of such communities would be similar across space and time, farming strategies would be oriented to providing for these needs, and most towns would use the landscape in roughly the same ways to make the same kinds of things. There would naturally be some exceptions since the land itself would vary from town to town, population figures would differ, and individual families would engage in a variety of productive strategies, but, if we adjust for per capita output, the general economic profile of the county's towns should be relatively similar. Conversely, if communities demonstrated little congruity in production strategies, it seems reasonable to assume that families produced according to their own interests, that individuals produced at least some goods for market, that each community's needs were different, that they were not as constrained by communal goals as some historians have thought, or that they may have been the grasping, acquisitive individualists others have described. If we find that neither of these models is clearly visible, that there is congruity in some farming activities but not in others, the model may be a mixed one requiring closer examination and interpretation to learn why people sometimes acted similarly and at other times divergently.

In fact there were many similarities among community production strategies in the region. Some of these similarities were clearer after 1800 when the towns in the region developed mature landscapes. Depending on environmental factors, most towns seemed to achieve a rough stasis when population density reached twenty-five to thirty-five people per square mile. Many parts of the region attained this density by 1790, particularly in the western part of the county (Fig. 3:7). Thereafter, population in these towns either stabilized or declined. Patterns varied according to a number of factors. The more remote uplands never attained the densities of the more pleasantly situated communities. Elsewhere, the oldest town in the county, Deerfield, grew more slowly in the 1780s and 1790s than towns to its west. While it had the largest number of heads of household on the 1771 tax valuation list, its wealthy residents apparently continued to control enough of the landscape to retard new settlement and to keep population growth lower than other towns nearby. To the east, where the soil map showed poorer soils, population also grew more slowly. Based on the evidence of population density alone it is clear that the county's environmental diversity deeply affected the growth and development of the region.[24] (Compare Figs. 2:3 and 3:7.)

Using the Massachusetts Census of Manufacturers for 1845 and 1855, we can plot the distribution of certain kinds of farm activity with some precision by converting the data to per capita figures to control for population differences in the county's twenty-six towns. The records are incomplete or missing for some towns in some categories, but overall the data is suggestive of the kinds of patterns that existed. When the county is viewed on maps, in order to read spatial patterns more clearly, there appears to be mixed support for the concept of consistency among individual towns. In the areas of food and transportation, people in the county seem to have followed similar productive strategies over time. Horses were widely distributed throughout the region with minimal per capita differences between towns in either 1845 or 1855 (Fig. 3:8). Many people also appear to have owned hogs, but few families seemed to have owned more than an average of one or two in any of the county towns reporting data. While the pattern for hogs may indicate a case of under-reporting, the congruency between towns sustains the interpretation that food-production patterns looked much the same across the county in the two censuses (Fig. 3:9).

In the case of horses and hogs the pattern of even distribution is congruent with the evidence of the 1771 tax valuation list. There is additional evidence that the county towns consistently produced foodstuffs. The figures for grain production show that all county towns produced grains, although the lowland towns with more favorable soil and climate conditions held an advantage in production and raised more than upland communities (Figs. 3:10 and 3:11). The pattern of widespread grain production *and* higher yields in

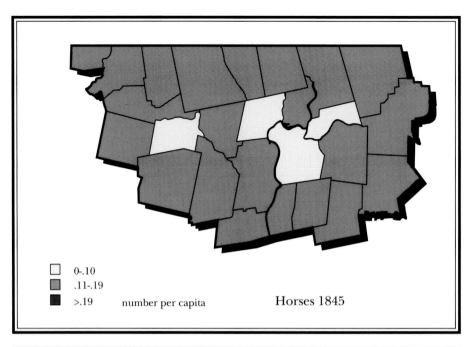

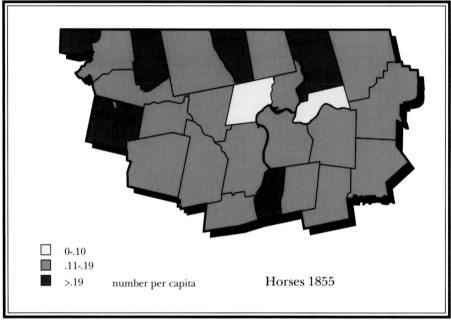

Figure 3:8. Horses per capita, Franklin County, Massachusetts, 1845 and 1855.
(Drawn by the author.)

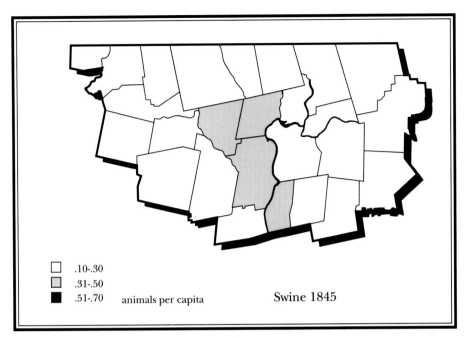

.10-.30
.31-.50
.51-.70   animals per capita   Swine 1845

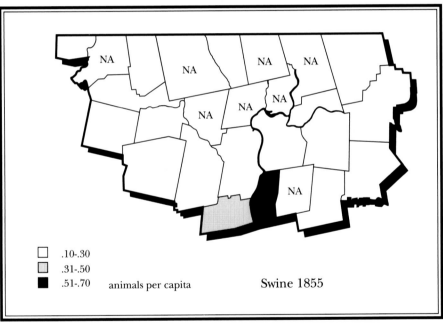

.10-.30
.31-.50
.51-.70   animals per capita   Swine 1855

Figure 3:9. Swine per capita, Franklin County, Massachusetts, 1845 and 1855.
(Drawn by the author.)

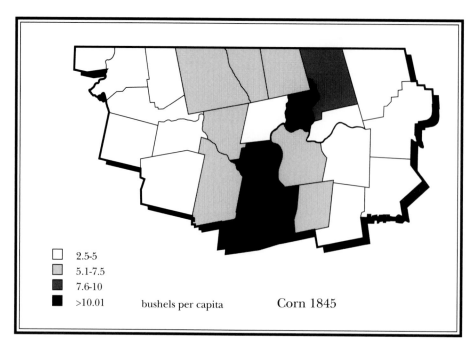

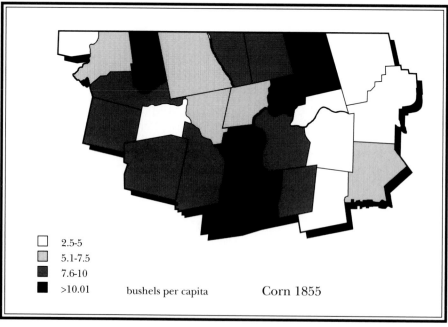

Figure 3:10. Bushels of Corn per capita, Franklin County, Massachusetts, 1845 and 1855. (Drawn by the author.)

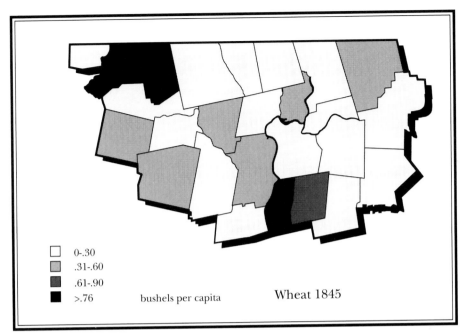

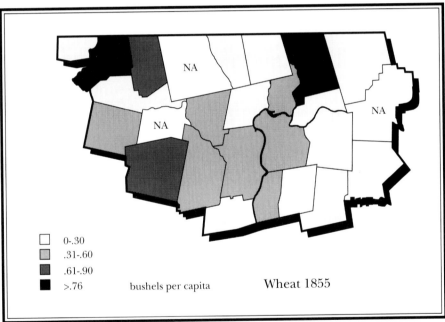

Figure 3:11. Bushels of Wheat per capita, Franklin County, Massachusetts, 1845 and 1855. (Drawn by the author.)

the lowlands is particularly striking for corn, but holds to a lesser degree for wheat, a tillage crop grown only in small quantities—evidently for local use. Among the county's twenty-six towns, only farmers in the rugged hill towns in the eastern portion of the county grew significantly smaller amounts of grain, yet even these towns raised substantial quantities. While the figures for grains are less congruent than those for hogs and horses, they fit the concept that the area's farmers consistently produced foodstuffs for community subsistence needs and in some towns raised surpluses.[25]

Other patterns were more irregular. They imply strongly that there were profit motives that shaped the choices families made. Many farmers raised cattle throughout the county, but the greatest concentration of stockmen was in the western uplands where there were sometimes more cattle than people and where pasture was plentiful. While the total number of cattle in the county declined between 1845 and 1855, the distribution remained much the same (Fig. 3:12). The figures for butter and cheese reinforce the argument that the market and local environmental conditions caused variations in the area's production strategies. The figures for dairying reflect the contributions of women to the local economy since they were the principal agents of milk processing. In 1845 butter production was widely distributed throughout the region with few dramatic differences between towns. Production increased in many towns during the next decade, despite a reduction in the number of cattle, but it remained widely distributed (Fig. 3:13). These patterns imply either a large household consumption of butter or a consistent attempt to produce for modest commercial gain since stores in the region took butter in trade. By contrast, cheese production in 1845 was widely distributed through the region *and* heavily concentrated in the western uplands. This distribution suggests that most towns processed raw milk into cheese but that some towns specialized in levels of production that exceeded household needs; presumably this production was intended for market.

Lowland farmers were less likely to engage in large-scale cheese making than uplanders. They apparently were content to make only enough cheese for local demand. Cheese production declined in the late 1840s and early 1850s in most towns. Towns in the eastern and western fringes of the county produced the most cheese, but even there the number of pounds decreased considerably. It appears that the decline in cattle is related to the decline in cheese. That is, the production of butter held relatively stable while cheese fell. Evidently the decreased supply of raw milk was directed to butter rather than cheese (Fig. 3:14). The size of this shift implies market forces were at work since there is no evidence that people suddenly eliminated cheese from their diets.[26]

Several features stand in relief as we contrast the geographic distribution

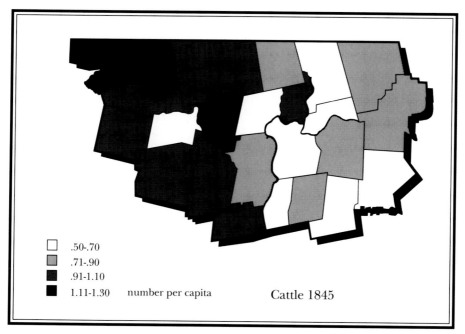

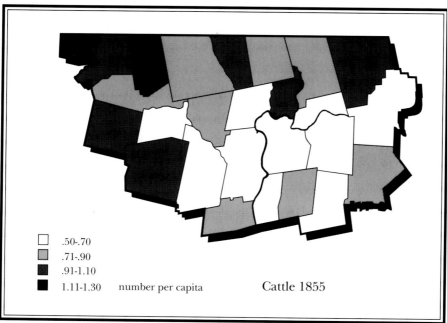

Figure 3:12. Cattle per capita, Franklin County, Massachusetts, 1845 and 1855. (Drawn by the author.)

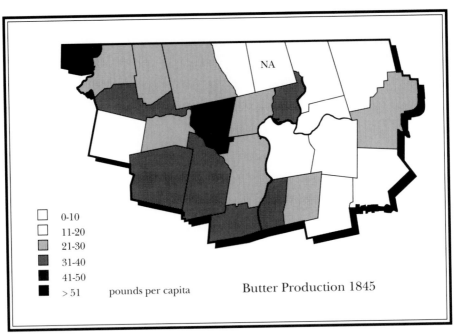

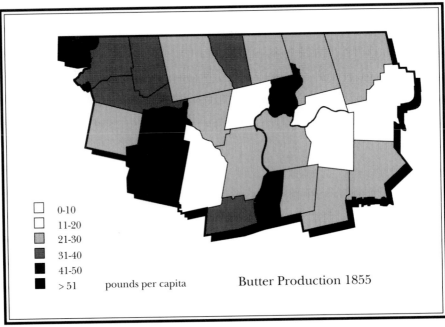

Figure 3:13. Butter, Pounds per capita, Franklin County, Massachusetts, 1845 and 1855. (Drawn by the author.)

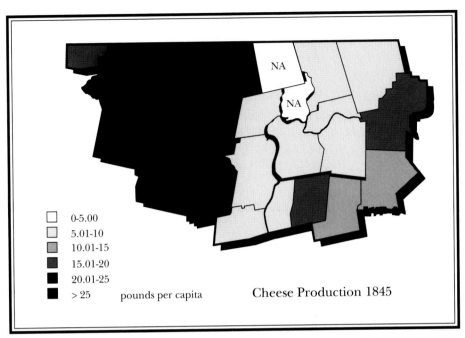

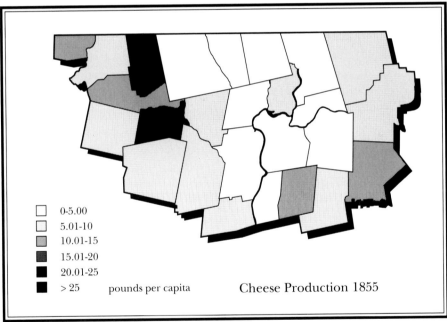

Figure 3:14. Cheese, Pounds per capita, Franklin County, Massachusetts, 1845 and 1855. (Drawn by the author.)

of production. Production of foodstuffs and the demand for transportation throughout the county remained rather stable over time; these patterns imply that farm families in the region regularly produced for household and local needs, that the priority of insuring family security did not wane in the face of a market economy or the number of barrels of flour that local merchants imported. It also appears that many familes in the region produced surpluses of basic foodstuffs that had some commercial potential.

Taken in isolation the surpluses of different towns may or may not support the interpretation that people consistently planned for a marketable surplus because it is hard to know what motivated a family to produce more than it needed. Nevertheless there were consistent patterns of specialized production. The western portion of the county contained substantially more cattle per capita, and produced more, in several instances much more, butter and cheese than towns to the east. It is difficult to sustain the belief that the region's families were unaware of market possibilities when in 1845 seven contiguous towns in the western uplands produced more than twenty-five pounds of cheese per capita, twice as much as towns in the eastern portion of the county were making. It is also difficult to argue that the shifts in the mixture of production were unrelated to market forces and commodity prices or that production in the same community could change so rapidly in the course of one decade. Despite the strong reservoir of generalized agriculture in which farmers raised goods, especially foodstuffs, for home or community purposes, this excess production was driven by market concerns regardless of whether the market was regional, national, or international. To argue that the economy was bifurcated into commercial or household strategies seems pointless. Farmers in Franklin County responded to both imperatives, adopting new strategies and hanging onto old ones when it made sense to do so. Like John Wilson they made rational choices and reshaped their world in a cumulative discourse of many separate voices.

On September 28, 1850, the Franklin County Agricultural Society held its first fair on Main Street in Greenfield. It was a simple event, similar to the earlier Tri-County Fairs that were sponsored annually in Northampton by the Hampshire, Franklin, and Hampden County Agricultural Society from 1818 onward. Franklin County men and women had attended and earned premiums in these fairs over the years, but the trip to Northampton was long and inconvenient and few went. By 1850 when a separate Franklin County Agricultural Society was finally chartered, interest in an annual county fair was strong. Ninety of the Society's original 222 members came from Greenfield, but representatives from other towns were also included. For a donation of ten dollars (later reduced to five) members received lifetime honorary membership entitling them to normal society privileges and two free tickets to the "Agricultural Dinner" at the annual fair. A year later the normal privileges were further defined as free admission to the annual fair, free registration of exhibit animals, agricultural products, or domestic manufactures, free passage over local toll bridges on cattle show days, reserved seats in the church for annual addresses, and rights to purchase extra tickets to the "Agricultural Dinner."

On the appointed day, exhibits of swine and working cattle were set up on Main Street. Displays of fruit, vegetables, and domestic goods were shown in the town hall to all who would pay an admission of six cents. An estimated crowd of eighteen hundred showed up at Clay Hill to watch the oxen pull and the plowing match on Alfred Wells's land. Later, at one o'clock, the Green field Brass Band escorted a parade of the society's members to the Second Congregational Church. Following a suitable blessing, the Hon. Joseph T. Buckingham, former editor of the *Boston Courier*, delivered an address, various committees made their reports and awarded premiums, and the group recessed via another parade to the American House for the "Agricultural Dinner." The evening concluded with several rounds of toasts, singing, and general conviviality.[27]

The first agricultural fair was held in Pittsfield, Massachusetts, in 1811, the product of Elkanah Watson's fertile imagination and his desire to promote improved breeds of Merino sheep. From that small beginning it would grow as an important community ritual during the antebellum period, serving as an educational forum for progressive husbandry, a showcase for local businesses, and entertainment for thousands of rural people. When Julius Robbins of Deerfield attended the first Franklin County fair he simply noted in his diary: "Clear. To Greenfield to the Cattle Show for the first time. Cattle aplenty and other things in proportion." Two years later he joined the society and received admission to the annual lecture as a privileged member. Robbins and others in the region enjoyed the chance to frolic, to watch the contests of oxen struggling up Clay Hill dragging heavy stone boats, and to marvel at town teams of up to fifty-one yoke of oxen decorated with flags, produce, and schoolchildren as they lumbered down Main Street. He also enjoyed the chance to socialize with other farmers and with the movers and shakers of small-town rural society.[28]

For most people, the fair was a chance to break away from the routine of everyday life, have some fun with family and friends, examine new types of agricultural equipment and local handicrafts, do some shopping in Greenfield, and celebrate another season's harvest. While Watson had envisioned a respectable and dignified gathering to uplift public virtue and to proselytize ordinary farmers about the promise of scientific agriculture, the fair evolved by the 1850s into something rather different. Entertainment rather than pure education became central to planning the fair and keeping it financially sound. The Franklin society's members learned this lesson the hard way. During the annual address in 1855, the Welch and Lent Circus, "the two largest and most popular Equestrian Establishments in the world," clopped up Clay Hill with horses, wagons, tents, plows, monkeys, and music "to the great gratification of the boys, and the great annoyance of the assembly in the church." The assembly was the local agricultural society members. Offended though they may have been, society officers could not ignore the fact that the morning train had brought "fifteen cars from the east well-filled with passengers . . . and a good turnout from the south." Life memberships of five dollars paid by local farmers would not meet expenses; crowds of visitors who paid an admission fee would. More and more, the fair's organizers would promote crowd-pleasing activities such as horse racing rather than the traditional exhibition of prize stock, produce, or homemade linens.

Merchants of course quickly understood the fair's effects on their trade. Several local entrepreneurs exhibited their wares at the first fair, including "a case of most beautiful and natural looking teeth manufactured by Doct. J. Beals of Greenfield, surpassing in appearance and excellence . . . anything we have ever seen. To any person in whom the 'sound of the grinders is low,' we would recommend Doct. Beals." Exhibits of similar "Miscellaneous Articles" were a convenient means of alerting the public to the skills or wares that local people offered. By 1853 a wide range of factory goods appeared alongside those of household manufacture, and most of this material was for sale. Many visitors in town for the fair also took advantage of the chance to do some shopping in the stores that lined Main Street. The *Greenfield Gazette and Courier* carried an advertisement on October 3 advising that "Strangers visiting Greenfield at the Cattle Show are invited to call at the Cheap Cash Bookstore." In its own way, then, the Franklin County fair reflected the society and culture the region had become. Its roots were nourished by agriculture, but on its various branches flourished merchants and manufacturers, men and women, yeomen and wage earners, residents and visitors, and a variety of interests and amusements.[29]

The direction Franklin County life was to take was anticipated to some degree by the activities featured at the agricultural fairs in the 1850s. On the streets and in nearby fields were the traditional oxen pulls, livestock displays, and plowing matches. Milling through town hall to admire displays of local produce and handicrafts were the crowds of fairgoers willing to pay admission. Outside on the Greenfield streets were other visitors who stopped in the local stores to buy and look at merchandise, gawked at the crowds, and celebrated with family and friends a day away from everyday toils on the farm or in the shop. This emphasis on business was a sign of how important commercial motives had become in gauging the success of a community event. It would have been hard to imagine such a gathering in Franklin County in 1770.

Inside the Second Congregational Church local dignitaries and agricultural society members gathered at the appointed hour to hear a distinguished speaker reaffirm the values of progressive agriculture: self-discipline, frugality, temperance, and productivity. At one meeting in the 1830s, Henry Colman listed several characteristics of successful farmers, rhetorically asking, "Now what are the causes of such success? Persevering industry; the strictest and most absolute temperance; the most particular frugality and always turning everything to the best account; living within his own resources; and above all things, never in any case suffering himself to contract a debt, excepting in the purchase of land, which could be made immediately productive, and where of course the perfect security for the debt could neither be used up, nor wasted, nor squandered." Similar exhortations were recurring features in the speeches of distinguished authorities who addressed local agricultural societies. The emphasis was on self-sufficiency, frugality, and virtuous living. Speaking for one of the most popular myths of the age, Colman cautioned that " . . . in the resolute habit of hiring within one's own means and depending mainly on one's own exertions, there is moral gain, which can scarcely be overvalued."[30]

This rhetoric of independence, of discipline and personal responsibility, of supporting one's family through one's own resources, touched a chord in the reformers and citizens of republican America. These values were powerful mythic symbols that helped to unify a culture that had a multiplicity of goals. Yet no community or family was truly independent or self-disciplined. The traditions of farming, the unending routines of days and seasons, the cognitive processes of men and women living on farms moved to a symphony of natural rhythms. For most people the commonplace things that surrounded them seldom merited much attention. Letters among family in rural areas like Franklin County sometimes described the homecomings and dramas of small town life, but more frequently they reported that not much was new. Most letters emphasized well-regulated rhythms, structure, order, and discipline, modulated only by an occasional variation in the day's routine—a variation that often depended on simple things. Hannah Hoyt affectionately wrote to her husband in 1807, "Here we are seated around a good wholesome fire, I mean a saturday night sit down each stocked with a book so that we have now the appearance of a peaceable well-regulated family."[31] Around books, sleigh rides, family visits, Sunday meeting, occasional parties, the arrival of the newspaper, and similar events families ordered their well-regulated lives.

In the span of ninety years the cultural history of Franklin County changed considerably. Few consciously reflected on changes as they happened, but looking back the sense of passage was striking to the participants and their descendants. Families expanded use of temporary wage labor, more people experimented with improved agricultural techniques and crops to expand market production, and progressive farmers and businessmen institutional- ized an agricultural fair as a forum for education and entertainment. Many traditions endured. The form and shape of agricultural tools, the layout of farmland, and the kinds of commodities farmers raised did not shift very rapidly. For in the world of well regulated families, where life revolved around an agrarian system of structure, rhythm, and human relationships, people continued to reshape the landscape and their lives in a dialogue of human consequences.

Chapter 4

Lowlands

In late May of 1771, John Adams set out on a journey from his home in Braintree, Massachusetts, to see the Connecticut Valley. While taking his midday meal in Waltham with acquaintances, he was interrupted by a vast drove of Connecticut Valley cattle that passed by outside, heading for the market in Brighton, just outside of Boston. After dinner he rode on, stopping in the evening at Benjamin Munn's tavern in Sudbury to spend the night. Over tea he talked with the proprietor of the establishment about the valley's agriculture, especially the region's livestock business. Munn knew about the valley's beef trade from personal experience. Born in Deerfield in 1738, Munn lived in Northhampton prior to his removal to Sudbury and knew the area and its farm practices well. As he told Adams about the livestock trade, Munn described the crops, feeding practices, and marketing strategies used by farmers in the river valley, outlining for his guest a commercially oriented agriculture that was already well established by the time Adams made his trip.[1]

Many lowland farmers in Franklin County earned a competency by marketing fattened livestock in the urban markets of Boston and New York. The practice reached its height in the period between 1800 and 1830, but it had roots that stretched back to the seventeenth century and the entrepreneurial skills of William and John Pynchon, the father and son who dominated the politics and economy of Springfield and the Massachusetts portion of the valley between 1636 and 1701. By the late eighteenth century, farmers in several of the lowland towns had become proficient at raising cattle for market, establishing practices that would dominate the agricultural strategies of lowland towns for nearly a half century and that would influence uplanders. The "fat cattle" business provided local farmers with an excellent opportunity to use the market to increase income by sending agricultural surpluses to market in the form of grain-fed beef that moved under its own power. Rather than transporting surplus grain overland with a team and wagon or via boat down the Connecticut River, several drovers could move herds to market for what was largely a one-way expense, thereby reducing the farmers' overhead costs. In return the farmer earned money from the sale of cattle and collected manure as a by-product with which to improve or maintain fields.[2]

Market-oriented agriculture was one of the engines that powered the transformation of the valley's landscape. It was a dynamic process that is difficult to reconstruct accurately from surviving sources, but to understand why the material landscape was shaped the way it was—why large New England–style barns and cowhouses were built, for example—it is essential to understand the details of a social and economic system that prepared the way for other commercial activities that followed. Agricultural patterns in the lowlands were different from those followed in the uplands, but there were important relationships that bound the two areas together. Before we can appreciate the structure of upland living, we need to examine the agricultural practices of lowlanders.

The system of stall feeding oxen evolved into a highly complex, thoroughly specialized pattern of work. The general procedure was to raise surplus grain and fodder crops on the extensive interval lands of the lowland towns, pen cattle up in November or December, feed the cattle until the fodder ran out or the animals reached a marketable weight, and then send them to market in Boston or New York with drovers. What made the system work for lowland farmers was a combination of highly developed farming practices and the fertility of valley soils. Many Sunderland, Whately, Deerfield, Montague, Greenfield, Gill, and some Northfield farmers used the stall-fed oxen system. By the early 1800s, the practice was spreading to prosperous farmers living in the more fully developed upland towns (Fig. 4:1).

The great age of stall feeding, roughly 1770 to 1820, depended upon the settling of upland communities. Farms in the hill towns provided two essential services to the livestock raisers in the valley: a cheap source of cattle to fatten and a place to pasture cattle during summer months. Until upland farms became well developed, it was difficult to raise enough fodder to keep many animals through the winter, and hay-fed beef fattened more slowly than animals fed on a grain diet. Some surplus animals had to be sold or they would starve. Upland farmers normally culled their herds between October and December. The need to sell seems to have kept prices down. Lowland farmers were therefore able to purchase cattle for fattening at favorable local prices without the need to provide large herds of young stock with summer pasture.[3]

While the system appears exploitive, there were reciprocal benefits. Once developed, upland farms contained a higher proportion of pasture land than did lowland farms. Many lowland farmers rented pasturage from upland farmers during the growing season to free fertile bottom lands for haying and

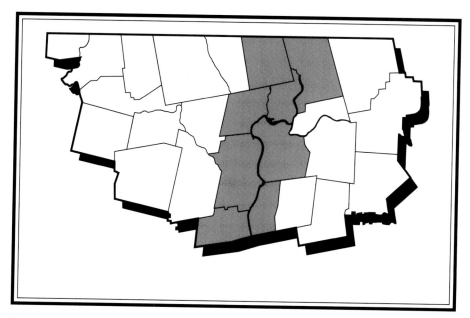

Figure 4:1. Towns with Stall-Feeding Operations, Franklin County, Massachusetts. (Drawn by the author.)

tillage. Jonathan Hoyt noted in his diary on May 14, 1805, that his son Cephas "Drove out cattle to Shelburne Pasture." Later that summer, on July 8, he wrote: "I went to Shelburne to salt our Cattle & to see that our Cattle kept Orderly in the Pasture." Such rituals continued for decades. Solomon C. Wells of Montague wrote in his diary in 1833 that on April 23 he put two cows, a yearling, and a colt in the Wendell Pasture.[4] This system of using upland pasture in the summer and of purchasing upland farmers' surplus cattle met the needs of farmers in both areas but it also created networks of exchange that went well beyond the boundaries of town and community (Fig. 4:2).

On lowland interval lands, three crops dominated the stall-feeding system. The first was hay, a crop that grew abundantly on lowland mowing lands. Yields of two tons an acre were normal; three tons an acre were somewhat common, and harvests of up to four tons an acre were known. The dominant field crops were Indian corn and "peas 'n' oats." The latter two were sown together in broadcast fashion and harvested by scythe when ripe. The corn and the peas and oats combination were mixed in a ratio of one to one, ground at a grist mill, and fed to the cattle together with quantities of choice hay. The mixture of grains, called "provender," was stored close to the feeding stalls in large bins with lids to keep out rats and mice. Grinding the mixture was an exacting process, for stockmen insisted the oats could not be too coarse or fine. The grains were readied for the mill in the slow periods of late fall and winter when farmers thrashed the corn and the peas and oats with hand

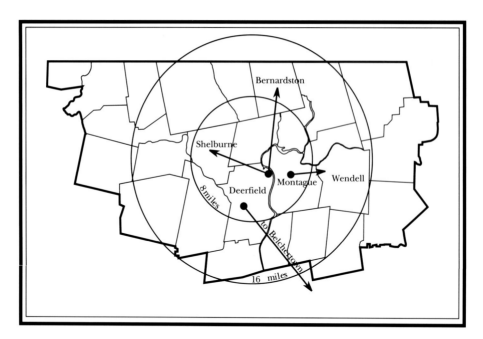

Figure 4:2. Upland Pasturing Relationship, Franklin County, Massachusetts.
(Drawn by the author.)

flails. (See Fig. 3:4.) Jonathan Hoyt reported in his diary on January 21, 1800, "We are thrashing Oats, Corn & . . . we do but little business, but we live enough all matters go on peaceably."[5]

During his conversation at Munn's tavern, John Adams had learned that fattening cattle was a demanding responsibility. He reported that "it is the whole Business of one Man to take care of em — to feed, Water, and curry them. They give an Ox but little Provender at first, but increase the Quantity till an Ox will eat a Peck at a time, twice a day." According to Adams's record of the conversation, it would appear that fattening one ox took nearly two bushels of provender a week. For farmers who fed a modest number of animals, four to six, feed grain consumption would have ranged from eight to eleven bushels a week, equivalent to about a third of the quantity Bettye Hobbs Pruitt has estimated would have been a yearly minimum for a normal family. Only substantial surpluses in grain production would have sustained such large-scale consumption. Pruitt found no clear differences between uplands and lowlands in livestock ownership in the Massachusetts Valuation List of 1771, but she did discover substantial grain production, well beyond what was necessary for household food needs. Her findings showed that grain production in the valley ranged from forty to eighty-six bushels per poll. Judging from account book evidence, some grains clearly were exported down river, but the substantial grain surpluses indicated in the valuation lists also enabled farmers to sustain livestock feeding operations using grain. In this case the valuations do not reflect the actual number of cattle in the feed lots because the lists were made in September, *before* cattle were purchased from the uplands for feeding in the lowlands. Similarly, local valuations were made in the spring, *after* most of the cattle had been sold to the drovers and been taken out of town. Because the feeding business was a dynamic process, the valuations do not pick up the true number of cattle fed in valley feed lots and are unreliable for estimating the nature and extent of commercial livestock feeding.[6]

While there is no way to prove the theory, it is tempting to see in this behavior a calculated attempt to bypass tax liabilities, since cattle were among the few items of personal property enumerated on the local valuations. While the tax rolls do not permit us to calculate precisely how many cattle moved through lowland lots, we can make an educated guess at the number of lowland farmers engaged in feeding beef. Only farmers in the top half of lowland tax lists had the necessary land and resources to consistently sustain cattle feeding. The wealthiest 10 percent were most likely to fatten cattle on a large scale — ten to sixteen animals a season. Farmers who were lower down the valuation scale generally fed fewer cattle, perhaps two to four. Not all of these farmers fattened animals for market every year, and, as the letters of Elihu Hoyt make clear, many of them lacked sufficient grain surpluses to fatten the animals completely even when they did feed cattle. Nevertheless, the livestock business was an important market venture for the middle-aged farmers who made their livelihoods principally from farming and controlled the lowlands' better-equipped farms.[7]

November was the usual time to bring the cattle down from the upland towns to the feeding stalls. So ingrained was the habit of purchasing from upland farmers that on occasion local cattle were passed over. A discouraged Deerfield farmer, Henry King Hoyt, wrote to his father on March 11, 1831: "I have not yet sold the cattle for I have not had an offer for them. our folks have sold a considerable number of cattle and are filling up again but they seem to prefer to go out of town for them for some reason or other." It is possible the Hoyt cattle were unsuitable, but account books, descriptions of the trade, and family correspondence support the observation that lowland raisers generally went out of town to purchase animals to fatten. Seth Sheldon's accounts noted the purchase price of cattle and their source. His records make clear that in his case animals were most often purchased from upland farms, quite often from people that he seems to have had limited acquaintance with. These transactions were commercial in nature and emphasized the specialized characteristics of the beef trade during the 1820s and 1830s. Eighteenth-century account books indicate, however, that the practices of men like Sheldon had roots in an earlier period.[8]

The best description of the stall-feeding system was provided by George Sheldon, who as a boy in Deerfield grew up with the beef trade. Late in the nineteenth century, he recalled the characteristics of the oxen who were brought to his family's lot for feeding. Normally, oxen were purchased in pairs and each pair had a temperament that made them distinct. When new cattle were gathered for their winter quarters, the farmers established them, in a ranked order, or, as Sheldon more colorfully described it, they began "seating the meetinghouse." Rank was determined by strength and skill. The feeders had to insure that yokes of cattle rather than individuals were arranged in a hierarchial sequence as yoke mates normally were trained together from the time they were very young and maintained a close relationship throughout their lives. To break up that relationship would cause problems among the herd. Most feeders, therefore, had to intervene judiciously during the ranking process to make certain that teammates were fed side by side. Once ordered, the ranking was seldom altered and contentment reigned. Contented cattle fattened better. Feeders worked carefully, then, to get their cattle organized and to minimize conflicts among the animals right from the start of the feeding process. If they did not, they risked a goring from a disgruntled beast, fighting among the herd, and lower profits.[9]

Sheldon's description of feeding stalls corresponds to the evidence surviving in some of the region's barns. A stall was usually about three feet wide and was separated from others by strong studs on the stable side of the manger. The studs were boarded up about thirty inches and a stout pole was fixed at the level of the oxen's necks to prevent them from stepping into the feeding area, a large trough extending across the length of the stalls. The oxen were held in their stalls by a rope that was fixed about their horns and tied to the stud next to them. The rope prevented the oxen from getting the meal of lesser companions and fear prevented them from contesting the territory of an ox further up on the herd hierarchy. The leader entered the stall first and was secured. He was followd by his mates each in their turn in descending order. After nearly a week of feeding, all but the most recalcitrant oxen had learned the system and would docilely pass to the proper stall.[10]

The first few weeks of stall feeding were the most difficult. Some animals grew homesick in their new situation, making sturdy gates and fences even more important than usual. Feeders had to keep a watchful eye on their herd to prevent runaways. Despite all precautions, some animals were so incorrigible that fences proved ineffectual. George Sheldon recalled one incident during his younger years: "One day I had turned into my well fenced barnyard a large pair of oxen just down from Vermont. Not long after I happened to see one of the strangers, with a spring as light as a deer, clear the top bar at a bound. The mate did not feel equal to this feat, but he proposed to show that some things can be done as well as others; so after giving one look around for a vulnerable point, he walked up the bars, bent his head deliberately down, adjusted his horns carefully to the rails and lifted both posts bodily out of the ground, quietly laid the whole down flat without misplacing a bar and walked out over the prostrate structure. But with all their active determination and prodigious power they acknowledged the mastership of man. I had no difficulty in stopping them in a lane leading to the highway, and so saving a world of trouble to all concerned." To bring the pair around, Sheldon confined them to close quarters. Several weeks of pampering and lavish feeding made them obedient and they grew accustomed to the routine.[11]

This routine almost never varied. Feeding began at daybreak with provender. When the ration was gone, hay was taken from the mow and fed by hand to each animal until they could or would eat no more. When the oxen had had their fill, the feeders took them out a pair at a time to drink from a trough filled with freshly drawn water. Afterward, the animals were bedded down in an open south-facing shed or cowhouse to rest. No interruptions were permitted. Children and women were kept away to prevent anything from arousing the animals' curiosity. Feeders believed that few things were worse than upsetting feeding routines or the animals' rest. A well-run feeding operation was characterized by neatness. Anything less was regarded as a sign of poor management. While the oxen rested, the barn was cleaned up. Excess hay was raked up and fed to the ordinary cattle. The manger was swept clean. Among stall feeders a spirit of competitiveness was commonplace and there was considerable peer pressure to keep the farm in good order. While this competitiveness seldom seems to have breached the code of neighborliness, peer pressure served to bind the community together in common habits even as self-interest laid the foundation for conflict.[12]

The eating behavior of the cattle was a source of constant concern and discussion. Although the basic diet of provender and hay seldom varied, farmers normally fed the cattle once a week with a large dose of roughage in the form of cornstalks, husks, or straw. This roughage not only promoted the digestive health of the animals, but it also served to preserve the oxen's taste for provender, the mainstay of the feeding system. Afternoon feeding occurred punctually at two o'clock, and few things were considered important enough to interrupt this schedule. When Major David Dickinson died in 1821, observers were witness to the rigidity of the feeding schedule. The funeral procession moved to the graveyard after midday dinner. One-by-one, as the procession passed by their doors, Dickinson's three surviving brothers slipped away to "put up" their cattle. By the time the procession reached the grave site, the ranks of the mourners had thinned noticeably. The body was lowered into the grave and, as custom dictated, the mourners paused to allow a close friend of the deceased a chance to eulogize the life of the recently departed soul and to express thanks to the participants in the funeral for their help and concern. On this particular occasion the pause was brief. Ebenezer Hinsdale Williams, whose presence as the conductor of the funeral was essential, "advanced to the grave with his peculiar emphatic ahem! and his accompanying kick with the heel of his right foot, sent the earth rattling down upon the coffin and exclaimed shortly, 'Cover him up! Cover him up! no friends here!' It is not clear whether he was the more vexed at the absence of the three brothers or of his own enforced presence after two o'clock." Farm rituals, then, were not easily altered by communal ones.[13]

Over the course of three to five months, stall-fed cattle gained a considerable amount of weight. Account books seldom provide much specific information about the weight of cattle before fattening, but a typical animal in the eighteenth century from the valley feed lots seems to have weighed 600 to 1000 pounds. By the early nineteenth century, animals were often purchased weighing 700 to 800 pounds and left the lowland barnyards 400 to 600 pounds heavier. A few extraordinary animals reached weights that exceeded 2200 pounds, but most animals went to market with live weights of 1000 to 1400 pounds. Much of this weight gain came in the form of fat, since the animals were discouraged from being active when they entered the feed lots. The high fat content contributed to the reputation of valley fat cattle as tasty and desirable beef. Before sending them off in a drove, the feeders typically had to exercise the animals for about a week to prepare them for the long walk to market. Although some of the weight gain was exercised off on the market drive, the loss was an accepted consequence of doing business.[14]

At night the cattle rested in their open sheds until roused for the morning feeding. Fed and pampered like spoiled children, they gained weight rapidly. Their manure enriched the land that provided their daily bounty, enabling the stall feeders to husband resources rather than mine them. Day in and month out this routine continued until the fodder gave out, the market conditions were right, and/or the cattle were ready. Ideally, the last two points would coincide, but often they did not, especially for the farmers with smaller holdings and fewer cattle. These more middling farmers seldom fattened more than four oxen compared with herds of ten to sixteen for the large feeders. As their resources were less, they sometimes ran out of provender and were forced to sell prematurely. Elihu Hoyt wrote home frequently in January and February during legislative sessions to inquire about the "barn affairs." While the answers he got were seldom detailed enough to satisfy his curiosity and concern, they reveal much about the affairs of a farmer with limited resources. Typical of these letters was one written by his nephew, Charles Hitchcock, on February 3, 1806. Hitchcock worked for Hoyt on contract during the legislative sessions. He dutifully reported to his boss and uncle; "yes Sir there is some hay left yet but I think the povinder works off pretty fast there is a grat many month stand waiting. I tried all I could to make the old gentlemen sell the steers, but he declined for he did not like to give him any more than they offered you but I wish they were gone." The old gentleman was Elihu Hoyt's father, whose opinions still mattered very much even if his son was supposed to be running things. Since the feed was running out, Hoyt was forced to sell sooner than he wanted to and the profit was less than he had hoped. The Hoyts simply lacked enough tillage and mowing land to operate an effective stall-feeding operation. With profits depending on so few animals in a capricious market, things could and often did go badly.[15]

Marketing fat cattle was a complicated affair and often was human drama of a relatively high order in rural areas. Normally, the cattle were purchased by drovers, middlemen who made a living driving cattle overland to the market in Brighton or even to the market in New York City. Often the transaction between cattlemen and drover occupied considerable time and included much haggling over price. The drover was speculating on the future price of the animal in the market while the farmer was anxious to make more than his costs. Both contestants employed an informal but extensive and well-developed network of news and rumor to project market conditions. From teamsters, travelers, relatives and friends of relatives who lived near the market centers, information on prices and demand made its way out to the hinterlands. Indeed, one of Elihu Hoyt's responsibilities while he was in Boston on legislative business was to keep his family and constituents back home posted about what was going on in the Boston market. He kept up a steady flow of letters, Boston newspapers, and market analysis to his home and community. He advised his wife on February 27, 1805: "Tell Charles to make the hay and corn hold out as long as possible for the prospect of beef is very good indeed. . . . I am told that there is not half as many cattle in the County as there generally is this time of year. I think we should do well if we can keep our cattle a month or two longer." By sundry means—the mail, a teamster back with provisions, a neighbor home from visiting relatives, the Boston paper, or even the Greenfield paper by the 1820s—the news was brought back, digested, evaluated, and decisions made (Fig. 4:3).[16]

With market information for a background, bargains were struck and cattle sold. Most often cattle were sold at a fixed price per head. Alternatively, the oxen were consigned to the drover at a fixed price per hundredweight, with settlement made after the drover returned with a bill of weight. Sometimes cattle were sold "on drift," with the drover peddling the cattle in the mar-

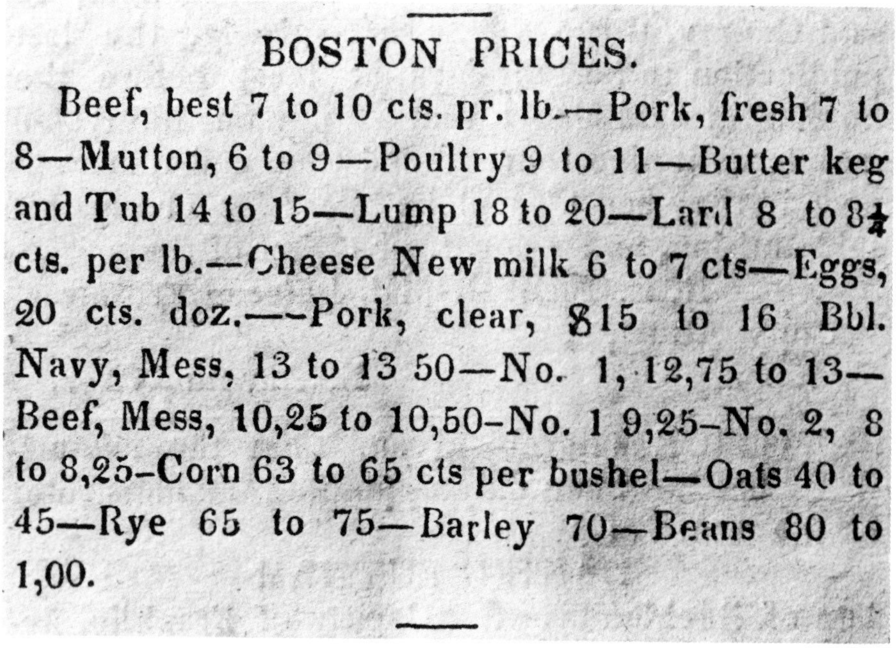

BOSTON PRICES.

Beef, best 7 to 10 cts. pr. lb.—Pork, fresh 7 to 8—Mutton, 6 to 9—Poultry 9 to 11—Butter keg and Tub 14 to 15—Lump 18 to 20—Lard 8 to 8¼ cts. per lb.—Cheese New milk 6 to 7 cts—Eggs, 20 cts. doz.—Pork, clear, $15 to 16 Bbl. Navy, Mess, 13 to 13 50—No. 1, 12,75 to 13—Beef, Mess, 10,25 to 10,50–No. 1 9,25–No. 2, 8 to 8,25–Corn 63 to 65 cts per bushel—Oats 40 to 45—Rye 65 to 75—Barley 70—Beans 80 to 1,00.

Figure 4:3. Boston Prices, *Greenfield Gazette,* June 14, 1829.
(Courtesy, Historic Deerfield Library.)

ket for the best price he could get. Once in a while, the feeders drove their own cattle to market. This practice eliminated the middleman but exposed the feeder to the problem of dealing with the Brighton butchers, who were always willing to take advantage of novices, and who worked within what was in some respects a closed corporate system. Butchers and drovers sometimes conspired against feeders who brought their own stock to market. One common tactic was to inform the farmer that the market was glutted and that prices had fallen. Another technique involved rings of butchers who might approach the feeder at different times, each offering a price lower than the last in an attempt to unnerve the inexperienced farmer and force a hasty sale. The only defense was to find a butcher not in the game or to withdraw the cattle from the market.[17]

The fact that there were a variety of marketing strategies limited the kinds of market exploitation that some drovers and butchers tried to practice. Farmers were not restricted to one market, although the Brighton market seems to have been the most common destination. Local butchers also received the area's cattle for slaughter. Before the railroad came, merchants in Greenfield and Cheapside — the central marketplace in the county — advertised for beef and pork to be barreled and shipped down river. On September 8, 1796, the *Greenfield Gazette* carried advertisements by two merchants seeking livestock and produce for export. Beriah Willard, a Greenfield merchant, advertised for 500 bushels of rye, 400 bushels of wheat, and 200 head of cattle. In the same paper, J. Chandler and Brothers, a Colrain mercantile establishment, sought 100 cattle to market. Most of these advertisements appeared in September and October, coinciding with the agricultural seasons. Some were ill-disguised attempts to persuade farmers to pay up their store debts. Others were posted in the clear hope that at least some of the county's agricultural surplus could in some way be channeled through the hands of local merchants. These merchants did in fact act as middlemen for a considerable quantity of the region's products. Horses, barrel staves, lumber, beef cattle, hogs, butter, cheese, poultry, honey, grains, flax seed, cider, beans, and other goods were some of the items taken in trade and exported.[18]

Upland farmers participated in the fat cattle business in several ways. Most upland families were more dependent on a mixture of marketing strategies to pay their bills than were the cattlemen of the lowlands. Since hill farm soils, growing seasons, and climate were less conducive to field crops, farming strategies there emphasized grazing and hay production. But it took time to develop the uplands by expanding pasturage and mowing lands. In the late eighteenth and early nineteenth centuries, as upland farmers were still developing their farms, many had to manage the size of their herds to conserve the winter feed for the cattle they intended to keep. While surplus cattle could be sold to the urban butchers in the fall, the large supply of cattle entering the market at that time of year tended to depress prices; lowland stall-feeders offered ready buyers closer to home. Relationships between uplanders and lowlanders involved with the stall-feeding trade lasted for decades.

Despite the commercial advantages of selling stall-fattened cattle in the spring when there were normally fewer animals to slaughter and when few hay-fed animals in the markets compared favorably with the grain-fattened livestock, the cattle business could be risky. Prices were generally strong between 1798 and 1807, but the good years were only part of the picture. When Thomas Jefferson imposed an embargo in 1807 as a tactic to win concessions from Britain and France and to try to protect American shipping, he dealt a severe blow to New England commerce. Although popular imagery has emphasized the New England merchant fleet rotting at the wharves, the Embargo and Non-Intercourse Acts which shut down legal trade with Europe were also highly unpopular in most parts of the New England countryside. When the embargo took hold in 1807, the prosperity generated by shipping foodstuffs to warring European nations ceased abruptly. By July 1808, as economic depression deepened, a local newspaper article lamented "our consumption is condemned by the government to rot and perish." A more poetic wit wrote to the tune of "Yankee Doodle":

The present times are duced bad,
　　And still worse they are getting.
Father and Mother's very sad,
　　and wife and children fretting.

Yankee doodle-devil's to pay,
　　Ships and produce rotting.
Can't get work by night or day,
　　Mischief sure is plotting.

The frustration generated by the Embargo and Non-Intercourse Acts was directed politically at the Republicans in general and Thomas Jefferson in particular. Unlike the participants in Shays' Rebellion in 1786–87, the farmers in rural New England did not respond with armed insurgency but sought instead to deal with the problem through political channels. They prepared petitions, resolutions, and letters, but their rebelliousness was limited to rhetoric.[19]

By contrast with the preceding years of prosperity, things looked bad indeed. An editorial from the Springfield newspaper, reprinted in Greenfield, summarized the problem pointedly: "In this place wheat is at one dollar pr bushel, and few or no purchasers even at that rate. Rye, Corn, Beef, Butter, Cheese, Beans, Peas, Pot and Pearl Ashes lumber, and almost every article which has supplied farmers and others with the means of clothing their families and paying their debts and taxes are going down! down! down!"[20] To many farmers in the country, the embargo was absurd, a massive overreaction to problems that did not directly affect them, and an ill-conceived action doomed to fail. Impressments and maritime violations were galling but acceptable business costs in view of the widespread benefits from expanded trade.

While the newspaper and politicians thundered about the stagnation of commerce, the rising cost of imported goods, and the collapse of produce prices, the human costs of economic dislocation were played out in debt executions. Many farmers had anticipated that the years of prosperity would continue and had willingly taken risks by going into debt. Notice of estate auctions to satisfy debts increased. Merchants scrambled to call in back debts, and some firms, like J. Chandler & Brothers in Colrain, announced that credit would be extended for only sixty to ninety days. As the depression worsened in April of 1809, the *Greenfield Gazette* observed: "Beef and Pork are staple commodities of New England. The price of these articles is nearly fifty percent less than before the embargo; and every other kind of produce is much less than it has been for years past. No kind of produce affords a quick and ready market." The lifting of the Non-Intercourse Act in 1809 eased the financial crisis, but ripple effects of the depressed market continued for some time. Foreclosures on mortgages extended into 1810. On July 10th alone, the *Green-*

field Gazette published notices of three sheriff's sales including that of a 130-acre farm in Rowe, 37 acres of land in east Deerfield, and 15 acres of land in New Salem. While the depressed years of 1807–1809 proved the undoing of many family farms, others survived the hard times to see prosperity return with the harvest of 1810. Prices of beef and most other kinds of agricultural products rose and remained steady until the War of 1812 once more plunged the area's farmers into a depressed market.[21]

Despite the economic dislocations brought on by the war, beef production continued. Profits fluctuated, but in general lowland farms continued to make a significant income from the business. Even in 1815, following the War of 1812, Rodolphus Dickinson's survey of Deerfield noted:

> It may be safely estimated, that the crop of Indian corn during the present season, is not less than 37,000 bushes; and that the average produce of other years considerably exceed 30,000, one half of which is probably raised by the inhabitants of the village; and by the latter 400 of the finest cattle, mostly purchased from the farmers in the upland towns, are annually fed, in the best manner, from the beginning of December to May, the weight of which may be computed at 440,000, and proceeds of their sale in the market, at $31,000 with a profit of about one half that amount.

Dickinson was born in Deerfield and undoubtedly had loyalties there, but he certainly knew about the town's economic conditions. Clearly, the cattle business in lowland towns like Deerfield was well beyond the point at which it could be characterized as household production. If anything, the depressed market may have encouraged families to greater cattle production to maintain the same income in a depressed economy.[22]

Following the war, prices for beef fluctuated. By 1819, upland farmers had developed their lands to a point where they offered serious competition to lowland stall feeders. Elihu Hoyt reported to his family as early as 1814 that "Col Nowell of Conway sold two pair very fat for 100 p head laid them at 5000 lbs." Nowell was not the only example of an upland farmer entering the cattle business, and over time the prices of oxen sold to lowland cattlemen rose. In addition, upland cattle swelled the numbers of livestock in the market at all times of the year, holding down prices and therefore profits. The problem seems to have accelerated in the late 1810s. On June 7, 1819, Elihu Hoyt grumbled in a letter to his wife: "I understand our cattle are in market today much to my regret, for tis said there are many more than are wanted, some say 150 head. If so we cannot expect to get much for feeding them, this you know is my usual luck. I know of no other way but to submit to it, & be at rest. I am sure no man wants the money more than myself." His information about the market was correct. A few hours later, he lamented that the cattle he had ordered sent on drift sold for $120.16. Following some quick calculations, Hoyt concluded that " . . . after paying for the cattle & interest, to this time & the drift, will leave me a clear profit of 42 cents. this is another lesson which goes to confirm me in my former opinion that I ought not to try to get money by fating cattle." His grumbling did little good. Beef prices and profits continued to be depressed and Hoyt concluded pessimistically that there were few prospects for improvement.[23]

Hoyt's letter is solid evidence of how far the market process had penetrated the experience of valley farmers. Throughout much of the eighteenth century, valley farmers would not have expected to pay interest on cattle that they bought on credit to fatten. They anticipated paying the original owner back after the animals were sold on the market. Seasonal rhythms of farming forced almost everyone to live within a system of credit, but after the Revolution interest payments became increasingly common. Credit cost money, and interest payments became a fact of life for farmers who had to compete in the market for capital. Wealthy farmers had enough resources to buy outright the beef they would fatten, but farmers of middling prosperity like Hoyt depended upon credit to participate in the system. As interest charges became more common, middling farmers were further squeezed between the prices they received for their cattle and the costs of doing business.[24]

Despite the declining profits, a number of farmers in the lowland towns continued to fatten stock. Against the advice of agricultural reformers like Henry Colman or Isaac Bates, against the judgment and experience of farmers like Elihu Hoyt, some farmers right up to the opening of the Civil War and beyond stubbornly clung to the traditions of fattening beef. Hoyt wrote in a letter in 1821 that " . . . the people of Deerfield are giving more for cattle than they fetch in this market." Colman bluntly quoted a local farmer's opinion in 1841 that the "fattening of cattle has not been a good business for years." Echoing Hoyt's earlier observations, Colman added that the purchase price of cattle was too high, that the market was capricious, and that the meat packers in Brighton conspired to keep cattle prices down in order to gain a larger share of the profits. If the fattening business was so poor, however, why did so many farmers continue in the feeding business? Surely continued losses or poor profitability would have forced them to seek alternatives.[25]

In a way, Colman provided an answer to why the beef trade continued. Some farmers, particularly those who had money, who owned good lands, and who farmed efficiently, continued to turn a profit from fattening cattle. So long as the farm was not encumbered by large debts, could produce sufficient fodder, and was managed effectively, the beef trade could turn a profit. Colman put it somewhat differently, but the point was the same, when he observed that "it is better for a farmer to use his hay on his farm, though it will produce him when thus fed to fattening cattle, but six dollars per ton, than to carry it even a short distance to market and obtain eight dollars for it. There are in the latter case the loss of the manure, which the hay would furnish, the waste in removing the hay, and the wear-and-tear and toil of carrying it to market." So long as fattening beef was managed within the limits of a farm's resources and so long as cattle yielded manure as a by-product of the fattening process, farmers could expect a profit in most years even if it was marginal.[26]

The hard lesson for men like Elihu Hoyt, who lacked sufficient resources to fatten beef for the market and make a decent return on their work, was that the beef business was increasingly left to rich farmers who could command the resources to compete. Men like Seth Sheldon, who fattened more cattle and whose farms were better situated, continued to turn a profit for decades, even if the profit in some years came principally in the form of several tons of rich manure that could be spread on the fields to keep up yields. So the fat cattle system survived as an agricultural strategy among wealthy farmers who could take risks in a capricious market or who could manage their business effectively enough to compete with the growing volume of western produce.[27]

The stall-fed oxen trade bridged the gap between the general mixed agricultural traditions of the eighteenth century and the specialized agriculture of the nineteenth century. The system worked well within the constraints of seventeenth-century nucleated village plans, and it husbanded farm resources by returning a portion of the soil's nutrients in the form of animal wastes. Finally, it was a system that was built on the complex network of relationships between upland farms, lowland stall feeders, and the marketplace. Not everyone benefited equally from that network, but one way or another the system touched the expectations and informed the strategies of many farm families in the area.

Falling profits from the beef trade eventually encouraged lowland farmers to seek alternatives. The first important commercial change in the lowland agricultural economy was the development of the broom corn business. Broom corn was a significant crop in the region's lowland towns for about fifty years. As an elderly man, Charles Jones, a Deerfield broom corn grower, recalled: "It became a staple crop about 1825 in the river towns, and the amount raised increased steadily until about 1842, after which it became unprofitable, and since 1855 but little has been raised in Deerfield. It was at one time a leading crop in the towns of Deerfield, Whately, Hatfield, Hadley, North Hadley, Sunderland, and to some extent raised in Northfield and Montague, and was largely depended upon as a ready money crop." Broom corn was hard on soil and required good land and careful fertilizing. Farmers grew it because it provided a cash income and because it gave them winter work making brooms. "Almost every farmer raised more or less of a crop," Jones recalled of Deerfield, "and very many manufactured brooms."[28]

Broom corn normally was raised only on the best meadow land. Each acre produced six hundred to a thousand pounds of brush, the tasseled stalk that was cut from the top of the plant and used for brooms. The crop was grown on well-cultivated land in hills spaced twenty inches apart and in rows that were separated from one another by three feet. Traditionally, the land was manured at the rate of seven cartloads per acre, but the rate obviously depended on how much manure was on hand. A shovelful of composted manure would serve for two or three hills. After the manure was set down, men with hoes and planting bags hoed earth over the manure, scattered fifteen to twenty seeds in the hill, and covered them with a half-inch of fine dirt. "It took a good smart man to plant an acre of broom corn in a day," Jones remembered. Once planted, the work was just begun. About the first of June when the plants were two inches high, the ground was hoed to keep down weeds. Two weeks later, the hills were thinned, leaving seven to ten stalks. During July, weeds were kept down by hoeing or by horse cultivation. Under ordinary weather conditions, the corn was nine to ten feet tall by early September and had long tassels with seeds.[29]

A trip down a farm road in a field of ripe broom corn was a journey in a mysterious world, a tunnel in a forest of green with the sky for a roof. George Sheldon, remembering the north meadows in Deerfield, wrote: "A bird's-eye view in August showed broad expanses of waving green turning to a reddish brown with here and there dark narrow ditches. These ditches were highways. We cultivated the land by general consent clear up to the wheel ruts. If teams met, care was taken to pass with as little damage as possible." In the pursuit of profit, there was pressure to plant crops to every inch of ground. No extra room was allotted beyond what was essential to accommodate farm work, but there were commonly understood rules in these common fields that preserved reciprocity among neighbors within a competitive system.[30]

One of the reasons broom corn was primarily a lowland crop was that it was ruined by frost. Even lowland farmers occasionally lost crops to early frosts. To harvest the broom corn, farmers broke the stalks about three feet above the ground and laid the tops and stalks diagonally across the opposite row. This procedure was known as "tabling." The tops of the broom corn were cut off about ten inches below the tassel and were dried on the table of stalks with the butt ends aligned in one direction. Depending on the weather, the brush would dry in three to four days, after which it was bound into small bundles and piled on a cart for the trip back to the farm yard. Generally, the brush was stored in a shed on an open scaffolding of poles in piles ten inches deep. There, the brush cured until it was ready for brooms.[31]

Once dry, the brush was "hetchelled" to remove the seeds. Hetchelling was done by hand in the early years of the broom corn business. Later, machines were developed to speed up the task. Hand hetchelling was very laborious. As Sheldon recalled it from his youth, a man held a handful of broom brush by the butt ends and drew the fibers through the sharp teeth of the comb-like hetchel.

> It was a low form of occupation. So far as the Deerfield Street was concerned the scraping of seed from the brush was principally or very largely in the hands of "Lance Loveridge" and Nels Burnham. . . . Lance would grasp a large handful of the brush and draw it through the hetchel with slow, steady strokes as those of a machine for 12 to 14 hours, probably not speaking as many words during the whole day. Nels, on the contrary, was an incessant chatterer. His motions were as jerky and as erratic as those of a chipmick [sic]. The seeds for Lance's hetchel fell in a pile; in the case of Nels it was scattered to the four winds.

Such idiosyncratic work habits were typical for farm communities, and Sheldon's memory of Lance Loveridge and Nels Burnham probably reveals as much about Sheldon's class-consciousness as it does about hetchelling broom corn. Although the broom corn industry was an important source of income for many farm families, its success frequently depended on laborers who often specialized in work that farmers did not want to perform, could not do as efficiently, or did not have time for.[32]

As by-products, a crop of broom corn produced quantities of stalks and forty to sixty bushels of seeds. Most farmers did not seem to have used these materials as effectively as they might have. Henry Colman recommended feeding the stalks to young cattle, but many stall feeders in the valley were suspicious of using either the seeds or the stalks. Seth Sheldon, a leading Deerfield cattleman, went so far as to insist that his grist of provender could not be ground on stones that had been used recently to grind broom corn seed. Some farmers such as Will Ross of West Deerfield fed broom seed to hogs, but many farmers were prejudiced against the use of the seed. Horatio Hoyt, Sr., fed his cattle and hogs with broom seed but insisted the results were unsatisfactory. Charles Jones recalled that Hoyt "said he fed broom seed to his hens until they ever after grew their feathers pointing towards their heads." Despite Hoyt's suspicions, other farmers used broom seed without any problems — either to their chickens or cattle.[33]

The broom corn market fluctuated but on at least one occasion reached seventy to one hundred dollars per acre of brush. The brush was marketed in a variety of ways. Much of it was sold in unprocessed form, but a number of farmers in lowland communities where broom corn grew well maintained broom shops with either their own or hired labor. Brooms were commonly manufactured for the Boston or New York markets. In Franklin County, Deerfield, Sunderland, and Whately led in the production of brooms, but some were also manufactured in Montague, Northfield, and Leverett (Fig. 4:4).[34]

Broom makers began by bleaching the brush with brimstone (sulphur). The load of brush was soaked in a tub of water and set, butt end down while still wet, on racks in a large box five feet square and eight feet high. The box was tightly closed, a red hot skillet was placed through a hole in the box below the racks, sulphur was dropped into the skillet, and the hole was sealed. A day later, the freshly bleached brush was removed and was brought to the broom shop for sorting. Jones considered it a day's work to bleach and make twenty brooms that each weighed a pound and three-quarters. Smaller brooms took less time. It was possible to make twenty-five pound-and-a-half brooms, thirty pound-and-a-quarter brooms, fifty clothes brushes, or fifteen half-handle fancy brooms in a day. George Sheldon remembered visits to the broom shops as a child. "Hour after hour," he recalled with obvious nostalgia, "the stifling brimstone atmosphere peculiar to the broom shop would be cheerfully endured while drinking in the old songs and ballads poured forth by the tuneful workmen." He occasionally got candy when visiting the broom shops, and the one owned by Dennis Stebbins was a particular favorite.[35]

Broom makers varied considerably in skill but the best of them specialized in the business and worked rapidly.

> At the shop of 'Uncle Dennis' the chief attraction besides the profit on candy, was to watch the deft workmanship and the mimicry of deaf and dumb black "Cab" (Calvin Salisbury). His manual dexterity in fiting on the 'outside' of a broom seemed marvelous. The lightning-like stroke of his sharp broom-knife with which he trimmed a handful of the stalks for fine braiding on the handle, three cuts to a stalk, each one which it seemed must take off a finger, then a swift turn of the wrist, and the whole was in place under the binding wire in a trice.

These specialists in broom making were most often valuable employees, people like Chet Loveridge "who could tie two days' work in one day, and keep it up for months." For most broom corn growers and makers, however, work was more likely done by youths, kin, or neighbors. In an agrarian culture, broom making provided an opportunity to expand income-producing activities at a time when profits from the beef trade were on the wane and when commercial growth was proceeding rapidly.[36]

While broom making was normally done under the auspices of individual farmers, making brooms required specialized machinery and several kinds of materials acquired from suppliers outside the shop or household. Broommaking machines were not especially complex or expensive but they were pieces of quite specialized equipment that it was necessary to obtain before

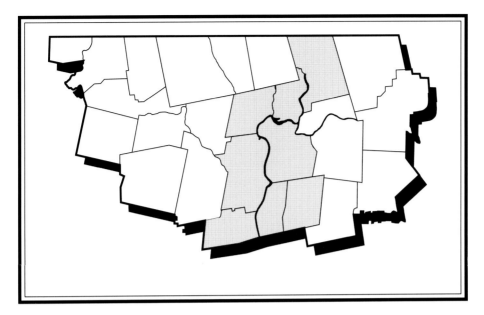

Figure 4:4. Towns Raising Broom Corn, Franklin County, Massachusetts.
(Drawn by the author.)

setting up a broom shop (Fig. 4:5). The brooms that were made in the valley were usually tied with wire manufactured in Hadley. A cheaper grade of brooms was tied with twine. As they were tied, the brooms were approximately round, but they were pressed flat and held in a sewing vice which simultaneously flattened the brooms and separated the bristles at regular intervals for sewing (Fig. 4:6). Brooms were sewn by wrapping two different strands around the brush and then locking together these strands by passing stitches back and forth between the bristles at approximately one-inch intervals. After sewing, the bristle end was trimmed flat, any remaining seeds were combed out, and the broom was ready for market. Sometimes broom handles were sanded, varnished, and decorated by stripping. Decorated brooms cost more, however, and were made infrequently.[37]

In terms of work discipline, the broom-making operation shared characteristics with industrialized production. Broom making was not custom work. The equipment and the process used in manufacture were designed to reduce variation in the product and to turn out thousands of brooms that all had more or less the same qualities. At the same time it was not a factory type of production. Most broom shops employed only a few workers, and a great number were seasonal operations designed to fill in the months between agricultural cycles with profitable and productive activity. Broom shops and equipment required relatively small amounts of capital investment and few farmers would have been prevented from raising start-up funds by the costli-

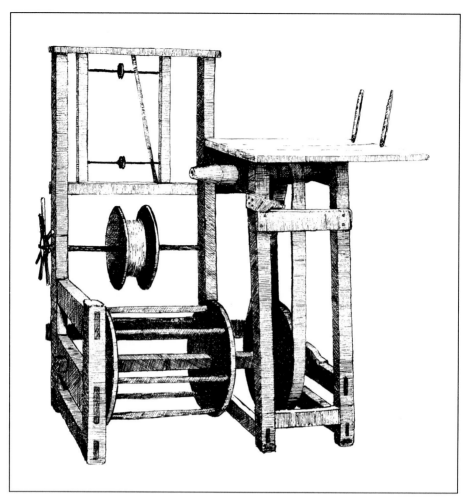

Figure 4:5. Broom Machine, Gill, Massachusetts, ca. 1830–60.
(Drawn by the author from the Collections of the Memorial Hall Museum.)

ness of the equipment. In short, it was a nearly ideal type of strategy for the agricultural systems of lowland farms.[38]

Like the farmers who raised fat cattle, broom corn growers frequently met at a convenient spot to discuss the market, talk politics, and socialize over a glass of flip. They reviewed old stories and argued the merits of different practices. During one of these convivial occasions, Dennis Stebbins, a leading Deerfield grower and broom maker, shared a letter from fellow townsman, Elisha Wells. At the suggestion of his agent, Wells had journeyed to New York to sand, varnish, and decorate his broom handles. The agent had notified him that the market was slow and indicated that the brooms might sell more briskly and at better prices if they were decorated. Rather than paying his agent to commission someone to do this work, Wells decided to do the job

Landscape and Material Life in Franklin County, Massachusetts

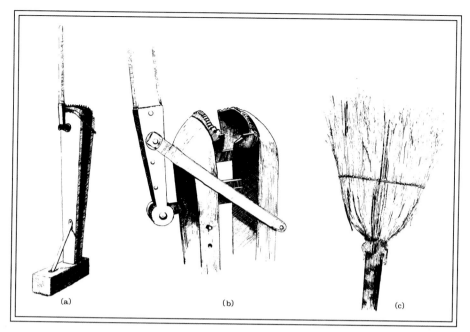

Figure 4:6. *(a)* Broom Press *(b)* Detail of Press *(c)* Broom, from Gill, Massachusetts, ca. 1830–60. (Drawn by the author from the Collections of the Memorial Hall Museum.)

himself. Upon arriving in New York, he discovered that his brooms were stored in a large warehouse high up on top of several large hogsheads of molasses. After buying sandpaper and varnish, he climbed up on top of the hogsheads and went to work, moving from hogshead to hogshead as he finished each lot. At one point while he was working, the head of the hogshead he was sitting on gave away and he fell into the container, soaking himself clear up to his neck. Fortunately, Wells had a sense of humor. After cleaning himself up, he wrote an account of his misadventures to Stebbins with the comment "that he had been in a sweet pickle," and directed Stebbins to gather up their friends at the usual spot "to make something" and he would pay the bill when he got home.[39]

Wells's account of his trip to New York to improve the market appeal of his brooms was an example of just how far commercial farming had proceeded. Sheep and cattle raisers had worked with markets for many years, but beyond timing the sale of their product in the marketplace and dickering with drovers, wholesalers, and butchers, their control of the exchange process was distinctly limited. The ability of broom makers to control the market process was equally limited, but there were additional variables. Brooms were not agricultural commodities in the same sense as an ox or a wether. Rather, they were marketable products prepared in agricultural villages but sold as finished goods. Thus in figuring their profits broom makers had to calculate the costs of raising the raw material, manufacturing, and marketing it. This did not mean that most of them made regular trips to New York to market stocks of finished brooms, but it did mean that the growers and broom makers became involved in manufacturing as well as farming.[40]

While men like Wells occasionally exercised their rights to alter their products to better suit the market, most farmers did not follow that practice. Charles Jones recalled: "Almost every farmer had a broom shop, and the product manufactured here went into all the large markets, and were sold all over the country. Many went to Canada. . . . I have also taken brooms to Springfield and Palmer, before the railroads came nearer to us, for shipment to the city markets. Nearly all the brooms manufactured in Deerfield found a market in New York City, and were generally sent to commission houses for sale for the benefit of the shippers." The use of commission houses separated farmers from the direct sale of their work, but the practice was the most convenient way of selling brooms. Few broom makers seemed as determined as Elisha Wells to compete by altering their brooms to meet new market demands. Most seem to have relied on their agents for information about the market and good prices for their products.[41]

Although only a few towns in Franklin County raised marketable crops of broom corn, the numbers were significant. In 1845, the count produced 237,817 brooms; a decade later the number had swelled to 399,600. Only one upland town, Leverett, raised significant amounts of brooms on a small area of lowland soils at its southern border. In 1845, Leverett manufactured a modest 13,725 brooms. Ten years later the number reached 15,000. By contrast, the broom makers in Whately made 160,087 brooms in 1845 and 107,000 a decade later (Fig. 4:7). Leverett excepted, upland farmers generally did not grow broom corn or make brooms in quantities that were marketable, but they did prepare the broom handles that broom makers used. Taken together, Conway, Charlemont, Hawley, Leyden, and Shutesbury produced more than 408,000 broom handles in 1845. Whately was the only lowland town to prepare significant numbers of broom handles for market. By 1855, uplanders had expanded broom handle production to 814,000, an increase of 99 percent in ten years (Fig. 4:8).[42]

The increase in broom handle production may well have represented an attempt by upland farmers to find a profitable product to market as the price of wool fell and flocks of sheep were cut back. Handle production expanded as the number of brooms manufactured in the region fell. The main reason for the decline in broom making was competition from the west. Not only was the broom brush of western broom corn larger and straighter, but it was of better quality than the brush grown in the Connecticut Valley. Although broom corn production continued for several decades more in the valley, particularly further south in Hadley, production declined after 1855 in Franklin County as competition from western growers overpowered local farmers. Upland handle makers apparently continued to find a market for their product, though it is unclear why handle production grew when broom making was in decline.[43]

The economic vacuum created by the decline of the broom industry set off a search for other cash crops, a process that had profound consequences for the area's farmers and the region's economy. For a time the profits of the broom business had eclipsed the old system of cattle feeding, but the features that distinguished broom corn from cattle feeding involved more than the differences between beef and brooms. Raising broom corn was an extractive process. Broom corn was hard on soil nutrients. These nutrients could be replaced by careful fertilizing, but unlike fat cattle, the corn did nothing to replenish the soil. So long as people ate beef, cattle raising had some use even if it was only for home consumption. Broom corn was inedible. Whereas the cattle trade was a profit-making activity that fit into the operating traditions of a mixed kind of agricultural production, broom corn was speculative. If the market for beef failed, farmers at least had the benefit of the manure, hides, and protein, but if the broom market failed, the business was likely to be a total loss. The fat cattle business had shown the way to a profit-oriented agriculture based on self-interest and market production. The broom corn business continued that commercial orientation without any of the safeguards built into the cattle trade. It also benefited those farmers who had the best kinds of land, operated with economies of scale, and were willing to accommodate their production to the market. Farmers might complain about capricious markets, the coming of an early frost, or the accelerating pace of change, but over the course of three decades, the broom business helped bind lowland farm families and hired labor ever more tightly to a commercial network in which producers, workers, and consumers were increasingly stratified into separate spheres.

While the decline of the broom corn industry was difficult for many lowland farmers, it was not an economic disaster. Few farmers were entirely dependent upon broom corn for economic and family security. Just as cattle raisers had mixed their economic strategies, broom corn growers do not seem to have relied on one crop. Inspection of farm journals makes clear that broom corn was only one of several crops that were grown. Moreover, the records suggest that at least some farmers continued to plant the crop after western competition had discouraged general production in the east. Augustus Fuller of the Bars section of Deerfield, sadly noted in his journal on September 15, 1859: "Our hope to be spared a frost was unavailing and this morning (15th

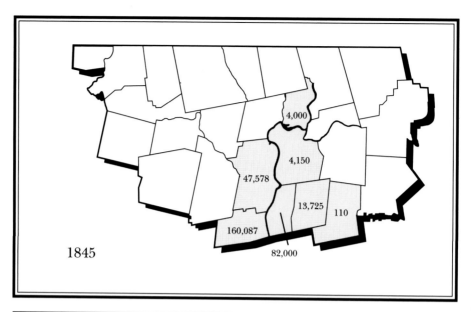

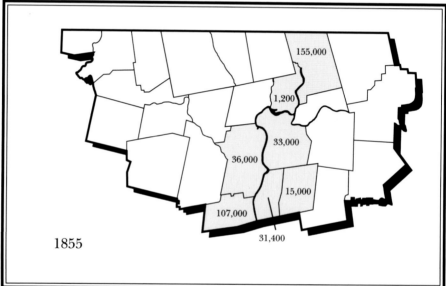

Figure 4:7. Broom Production, Franklin County, Massachusetts, 1845 and 1855.
(Drawn by the author.)

revealed its sad effects) our field of broom corn of 16 acres bore up bravely against the wind of the 14th but the freezing night has killed it all. I cannot estimate our loss at less than $1000. We shall save all that is possible and be resigned to inevitable fate." Although the loss was a severe setback, the Fuller family had planted other crops that were less susceptible to the early frost. They relied on these crops to help support the family.[44]

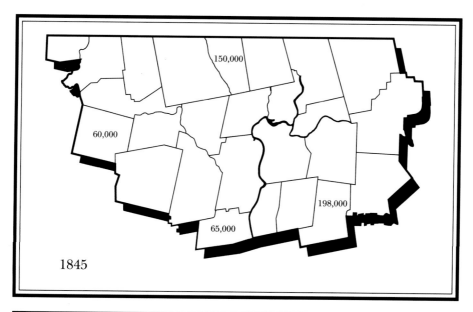

1845

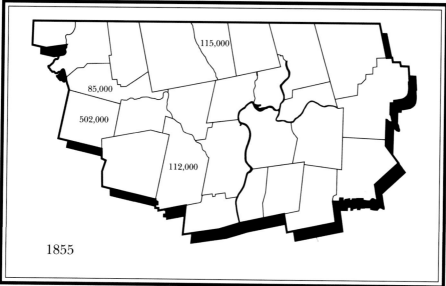

1855

Figure 4:8. Broom Handle Production, 1845 and 1855. (Drawn by the author.)

As early as 1851, the Fuller family had experimented with tobacco culture. In early May of that year, they drove their cattle southeast to Belchertown to put the animals in their summer pasture. On the way they must have passed through areas where tobacco was already under cultivation. Soon after, on May 13, Elijah Fuller wrote in his journal that his brother had gone to the neighboring town of Whately "to see Dickinson concerning cultivation

Figure 4:9. Detail of Stereoscopic View Showing Elisha Wells Farmstead, Deerfield, Massachusetts, 1868. (Courtesy, Pocumtuck Valley Memorial Association.)

of tobacco." By the middle of June, the family followed up their interest in tobacco by setting out three hundred fifty plants in three rows. During the next few years they would continue to plant tobacco, slowly expanding their acreage and commitment to the fussy and labor-intensive crop.[45]

Other lowlanders also began to experiment in the 1850s with field tobacco. Elisha Wells, of broom corn fame, planted tobacco in this period, drying it in the barn he built for it on the rear of his home lot. Erected in Deerfield between 1852 and 1868, the barn now survives as an implement shed, but an 1868 photograph and structural evidence permit a reconstruction of its original appearance (Fig. 4:9). At present it is probably the earliest tobacco barn surviving in the county. The Wells tobacco barn superficially resembled those built much later in the century. It was oriented with the long sides facing north and south along Wells's north lot line; it was originally eight bays (97–½ feet) long and two bays (23 feet) wide (Fig. 4:10). Framed like other mid-nineteenth-century barns with a mixture of hewn and sawn timbers, it was still a specialized building, carefully designed to dry the crop. On the north and south elevations, hinged doors made of 16-inch-wide boards opened outward to allow air to circulate amidst the tobacco hung up inside to dry. A louvered ventilator extended nearly the entire length of the roof, and the roof boards near the peak of the roof were blackened with soot, testimony to the small fires built on the barn floor to keep the tobacco drying in damp

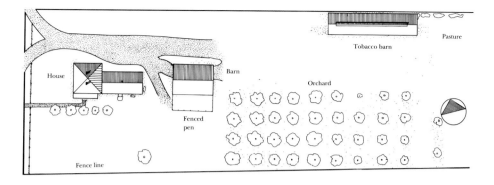

Figure 4:10. Reconstructed Plan of Wells Farmstead.
(Drawn by the author.)

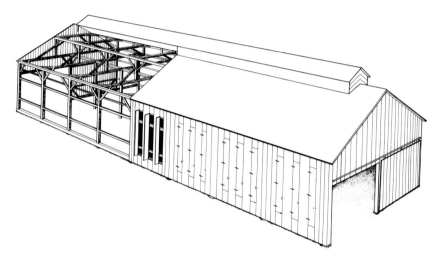

Figure 4:11. Tobacco Barn, Elisha Wells Farmstead, Deerfield, Massachusetts, ca. 1855–69. (Measured by J. Ritchie Garrison and Robert Paynter, drawn by the author.)

weather. Unlike later barns which had two hinged doors at each gable end, the Wells barn had only one door on the gable ends, suspended from a track that enabled Wells to slide it to one side. Mortises on interior posts suggest how the barn was originally used. After the tobacco leaves were harvested, they were tied up in bundles called "hands" and hung over laths, thin poles, that were set on top of the barn's girts. The Wells barn would have accommodated three tiers of lath between the ground level and the plates of the building. If the crop was big, a smaller tier could be hung off of the purlins under the roof. The north side of the barn was loaded first since the south side between the doors served as a runway. When these northern bays were filled, Wells apparently filled up the southern bays. To use the runway space more efficiently, he set removable temporary horizontal beams in place at a height of four feet above the dirt floor, working his way out to the door as the space filled up behind him.

Within a few years other Deerfield farmers built tobacco barns and expanded production of the crop. In at least one instance a farmer converted a hay barn for tobacco drying by replacing the barn's original siding with hinged doors, but such conversions were apparently rare. Most families built specialized tobacco barns to participate in a type of farming that in some years brought high profits. In spite of these profits, tobacco barns were expensive investments designed principally for a single crop that required special care. Unlike the big New England–type hay barns that were built to feed large numbers of cattle, tobacco barns contributed nothing directly to the family's food supplies. They were merely one more element in the cost of doing business.

While Wells, the Fullers, and others probed the commercial potential of tobacco, they raised other crops too. The Fullers were already growing a variety of vegetable crops by the time they began experiments with tobacco. Although many of these crops were grown in household gardens in the region, the Fullers grew them in fields on a commercial scale. Their most important market crops were onions, potatoes, cucumbers, and squash — produce that preserved well and was destined for sale in the expanding urban areas of the Connecticut Valley and beyond. This business was reasonably profitable. Not only did these market crops support the extended Fuller family, they also required additional farm labor. In August of 1851, Aaron Fuller hired "a Paddy" [an Irish worker] to help dig a ditch for draining a field that the family was struggling to improve. In September the Fullers raked cranberries from a bog the family had developed for commercial growing. As the crops came in, Aaron Fuller, the family patriarch, kept busy marketing the commodities. He filled an order from Springfield for 15 bushels of potatoes, sold 7400 pounds of squash in Greenfield, carted 130 bushels of onions to Shelburne Falls, brought 100 bushels of corn and onions to the railroad depot in South Deerfield, and marketed 10 barrels of cranberries in Hartford. These sales provided a considerable portion of the family's outside income, but the Fullers also raised much of the food the family would use.[46]

It is difficult to calculate how widely shared the Fullers' farming practices were. The family was in the vanguard of those who sought to exploit new markets, yet the strategies of these market-oriented farmers were still linked with many concepts that were quite conservative. Most of them grew traditional types of crops on a nontraditional scale and sometimes used new transportation technology such as railroads to get their produce to market. Equally important, these farmers took advantage of the region's expanding market communities, especially manufacturing centers such as Shelburne Falls, Green-field, and Northampton. Sometimes they traded with relatively distant centers such as Hartford, where Aaron Fuller was able to sell his cranberries instead of continuing south to market them in New York City. Fuller was perhaps unusual in his willingness to try new ideas and to undertake commercial risks, but only in degree. Countless other farm families followed similar patterns of work in a landscape much modified from the days of Benjamin Munn and John Adams.[47]

By 1860, the lowland landscape of villages and farms reflected the fluctuations of the region's economy. Hay barns and cowhouses survived from the great era of stall feeding, a few stock men continued to raise beef cattle, and some broom shops continued in business. But the signs of competitive market agriculture were palpable. Out in some fields and on some home lots carpenters were building tobacco barns. Elsewhere a few farmers had laboriously drained or modified swamps to make them suitable for crops like cranberries. Potatoes, onions, squash, and vegetables were in the fields where once only grains and hay were grown. And at certain times of the day smoke trailed a train heading up or down the valley, bringing manufactured goods and raw materials to the region's mills, villages, and consumers, and taking back to evolving urban centers the fruits and vegetables of well-worn fields.

Chapter 5

Uplands

John Williams of Conway was from an old and distinguished Connecticut Valley family. His grandfather was Israel Williams, one of the Connecticut Valley's most powerful political and military leaders in the mid eighteenth century. Self-conscious of his family's past glory, he was nevertheless caught up in the same cares and concerns of other rural youth who pondered their future in the 1780s and 1790s. Despite the head start his family background and traditions gave him, he grew up in difficult times. If his story was unique, there were still dimensions of his life that were quite common to others in Conway and the Connecticut Valley.[1]

Williams's father had met with a number of financial reverses just before and during the Revolution. To clear himself from debts, he had sold out his holdings in Hatfield and moved the family to Dalton, Massachusetts, a rural settlement near Pittsfield. Dalton was a raw and isolated town compared with the wealth and sophistication of Hatfield. Although Williams's father had bought the farm in Dalton as a speculative venture, his financial problems left him and his family with little choice except to work it. Years later Williams recalled, "I here pursued a line of business on the farm invariably and had been in general rather weakly, my Parents were disposed to put me to a mechanic." A brief stint with a hatter was unsuccessful, but family contacts were more effective. In 1784, after making a lengthy recovery from a smallpox inoculation, he was apprenticed to Epaphroditus Champion, one of the foremost merchants of East Haddam, Connecticut. While his apprenticeship was made possible by the wide-ranging network of Williams kin, young John began his duties like any other apprentice. Upon reaching the Champions' house, he set to work "in waiting upon his lady, selling goods, cutting wood, making fires, cutting and salting meat, taking care of his horse and cow and warehouses and occasionally hoeing garden and other duties." Content with his situation he noted, "My prospects were pleasing to the juvenile eye."[2]

Four years later, his apprenticeship completed, his future seemed less promising. At the end of his apprenticeship on February 22, 1788, he reckoned his personal estate. He calculated that he owned a total of £16.4.0 worth of clothing and a third of a share in a sorrel horse that his grandfather had willed to him and his brothers. Soberly, he wrote that he was "now left in a wide world on a fleeting ball to seek support in a way unknown to me. Many a long night I have had my head upon my pillow ruminating on schemes big with importance to the fate of millions, and of infinitely less consequence to myself—airy castles become of small comparative value when their true worth is entertained." Without capital and unable to secure help from his father, who was saddled with his own financial problems, Williams contracted with Champion for a year at a salary of £30. A year later he inventoried his estate and concluded that he owned £22 in clothing and a third of a horse. Once again he made a contract with Champion.[3]

This time his responsibilities increased. He accompanied Champion on a business trip to New York, traveling on a sloop carrying products from further up the river—potash and "one pair of excellent beef cattle of Elijah Colman's of Greenfield, Massachusetts." The increase in responsibility and a chance to make a sea voyage on one of Champion's ships persuaded Williams to stay on another year. In 1790, he embarked as a "cook, cabin boy and rawhand." The ship departed from East Haddam on June 17, bound for the West Indies with twenty-two oxen, thirty sheep and hogs, and about thirty dozen geese and other poultry. He returned in August with a cargo of rum, sugar, oranges, and pineapple. Although he was tempted to make a career of the sea, Williams abandoned plans to ship out again after receiving a letter from his father urging him to pass up a life under sail, to wait for a better opportunity, and to continue with Champion until prospects improved.[4]

Anxious to work for himself and frustrated by the thought of continuing with Champion, Williams returned home. Upon his arrival he learned of an opportunity to open a branch store in Williamstown, Massachusetts, in partnership with John Tryon of New Lebanon, Connecticut. He entered the business on trial, but it went poorly and Tryon backed out of the offer to incorporate. Back in Dalton Williams soon set out for Conway to investigate the business climate. "After I arrived there, I was suited with the Town and was informed by Uncle William and Elisha Billings that it was a tolerable place for business." The problem was he still had no capital. "With poverty staring me in the face I could not make a decisive declaration, but left things in the best posture I could and return'd to Dalton with the intention of going to see Capt. Champion." Back in East Haddam, he persuaded Champion to advance him the capital to start a store in Conway, secured by a guaranty from his father. In September 1791, he journeyed to New York to purchase supplies for his store; a month later he was back in Conway to open his business.[5]

The store prospered, and Williams remained associated with Champion

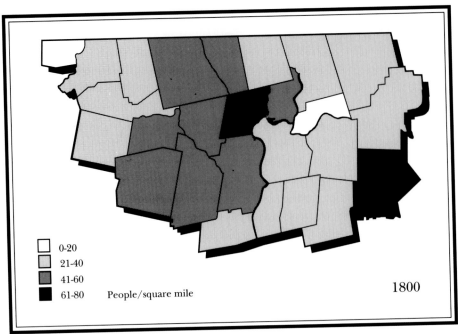

0-20
21-40
41-60
61-80   People/square mile

1800

Figure 5:1. Population Density, Franklin County, Massachusetts, 1800.
(Drawn by the author.)

for more than twenty-eight years and amassed a respectable fortune. In the panic of 1819, however, his prospects sank with the failure of his brother-in-law John Stoddard. Williams recorded in his memorandum book that he was forced to settle with Champion "by reason of my embarrassments occasioned by my being bound for brother John Stoddard by which means I lost over nine thousand dollars." While the story of his financial problems underscores the precarious nature of business for merchants in hill towns, it also points out that many families were able to prosper in the uplands. Williams's losses damaged his mercantile activities, but he was able to remain in Conway.[6]

Like Williams, many settlers contemplated a move in the 1780s and 1790s. The decision to move to a newly forming upland town was often prompted by a series of forces that pushed and pulled people in the direction of the frontier. As land was divided up and developed in older New England towns, opportunities to establish new farms for succeeding generations diminished noticeably. In Andover, Concord, the old valley towns along the Connecticut River, and in countless older towns in New England, young men and women found the opportunities to establish their own farmsteads were increasingly limited. Staying in the old hometown meant waiting and being dependent on the preceding generation. Moving to upland settlements was one alter-

Landscape and Material Life in Franklin County, Massachusetts

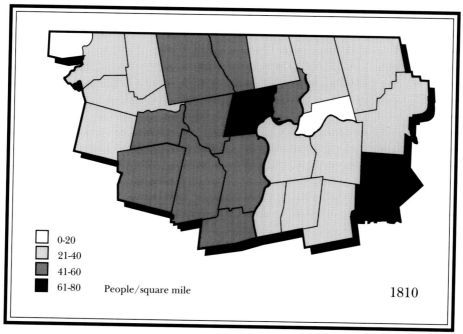

Figure 5:2. Population Density, Franklin County, Massachusetts, 1810.
(Drawn by the author.)

native open to young people. Some chose it because they had few prospects waiting on their parents' farms; others moved into the developing hill towns because there were good opportunities for work in construction and business as families built their farms. Some would move on once again, as this phase of building was completed.[7]

The movement to the hills encompassed a mixture of people—landless children of the old elite, families who had failed elsewhere and were trying again, and craftspeople who saw few opportunities to compete with the established tradesmen in older towns. Characteristically, the new settlers were young. Building a community was hard work and required a great deal of energy. Few settlers who initially moved to the uplands were older than forty-five and most were in their thirties or were younger. Not everyone who moved into the hill towns planned to farm. The uplands also drew a share of craftspeople and professionals. In the 1780s and 1790s, these families were starting out or just becoming established. Beginning in the early 1800s, the population of the older upland towns began to level off. Newly settled towns on the eastern and western fringes of the county continued to expand, but the rate of increase slowed. The county's population had jumped 325 percent between 1765 and 1790, and it increased another 21 percent between 1790 and 1800. During the decade 1800 to 1810, the rate slowed to 4-¼ percent (Figs. 5:1

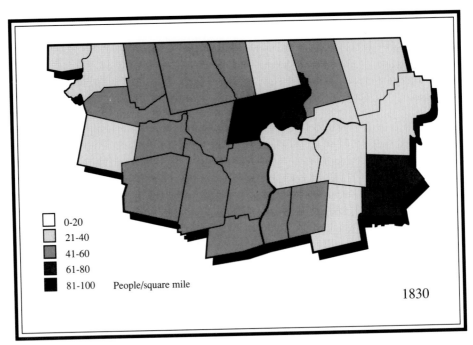

0-20
21-40
41-60
61-80
81-100   People/square mile

1830

Figure 5:3. Population Density, Franklin County, Massachusetts, 1830.
(Drawn by the author.)

and 5:2). In succeeding decades the population of the region continued to
grow, but only gradually. Moreover, in the grim economic years of the late
1830s, population actually decreased by almost 3 percent. Population figures
for the county obscure the fact that individual towns changed at different
rates (Figs. 5:3 and 5:4). Growth in the first half of the nineteenth century
was unevenly distributed. In general the more remote and rugged towns in
the county lost population, while valley towns, and especially the commercial
center of Greenfield, gained.[8]

A more accurate index of changing opportunities for farmers can be determined by calculating population density. Most towns reached a density of
twenty to forty people per square mile rather rapidly. In agricultural communities, however, population density was linked to the availability of land.
Despite differences in terrain, geographic size, and proximity to market, few
of the towns that remained primarily agricultural exceeded a density of fifty
people per square mile. Where commercial or manufacturing opportunities
existed, population density often surpassed that mark. For most towns, population growth slowed as available farmland was occupied and put under cultivation. Farms could be and often were subdivided, but, depending on the
quality of the land, farmers faced diminishing returns if their acreages became too small. Most towns with a substantial portion of workable farmland

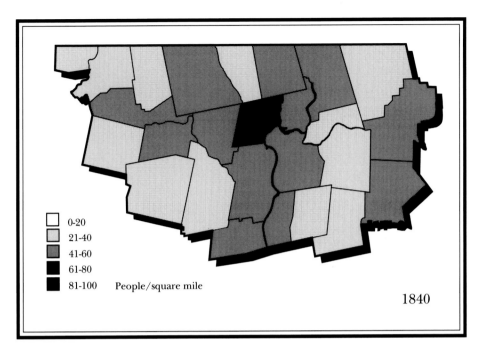

Figure 5:4. Population Density, Franklin County, Massachusetts, 1840.
(Drawn by the author.)

had reached a point of stasis by 1800. From then on, population density increases usually reflected changes in the industrial/commercial makeup of the community rather than changes in the agricultural landscape.[9]

The slowing of the growth rate and the flight from the region's farms by many youth were deeply troublesome to parents and observers. "Increase of population, and consequent demand for produce, originally gave and still give, value to land," said I.C. Bates in an address before the Hampshire, Franklin, and Hampden County Agricultural Society in 1823. He went on to examine the damage done to New England farming by westward migration: "I by no means wish ill to those of our friends who are interested in lands there, but, to the same extent as immigration prevails, the value of property is reduced here, to say nothing of the loss of capital and of men — the most valuable of all capital. It is this, among other causes, that has left farms upon the hills without tenants, without purchasers, and without price." Bates's lament covered the effects of migration from a business point of view — but not the cause. Westward immigration, flight from upland farms, occurred because the opportunities for the region's youth were unpromising and especially because chances for betterment seemed greater elsewhere.[10]

For many young men there were years of trial and error before settling down in the old home town. Stephen Fellows was born in Shelburne, Massachusetts, in December 1797. By his own account he received an "irregular" education. In 1814, when he was seventeen he set out on foot for western New York to look over the land. After reaching Sodus, New York, he headed for Long Point in Canada. When winter came he returned to Shelburne and remained at home for a year. Restless, he returned to Long Point, where he remained for several years before moving back to Shelburne to care for his aging parents. Finally, in 1832, when he was thirty-five, he bought a 150-acre farm nearby and began raising sheep, an occupation that he continued for many years.[11]

Nathan D. Newhall was the third son in a family of nine children when he was born in 1815. For a time he worked with his father on the family farm, but, with few prospects of inheriting sufficient land to set up on his own, he was apprenticed to Ira Barnard, a Shelburne carpenter who taught him the trade. Skilled with his hands, Newhall became one of the leading carpenters and joiners in town. In 1843, at the age of twenty-eight, he had accumulated sufficient savings to buy a farm. Newhall was never entirely dependent on farming, however, and he supplemented his farm income with his carpentry skills, gradually expanding his farm to 125 acres.[12]

Orsamus O. Bardwell was born in 1812 to a family that had roots stretching back to Shelburne's early settlers. He received the usual common school education and worked on the family farm until he was twenty-four, at which point he worked for himself, leasing land and hiring out his labor to make a living. When he was thirty-seven his father died, and Bardwell bought the old family farm from the other heirs. Bardwell's experience was like that of many others in the region. The long delay in acquiring land and a measure of financial independence was common for those who chose to stay and wait to inherit the family farm. For many, the old family farm was a symbol of continuity over the generations and a future that was worth waiting for.[13]

Although each of these men had different experiences, all ended up staying in Shelburne and all farmed to one extent or another. There was no simple or consistent path to becoming a farmer. Opportunities and limitations at home partially determined the range of choices, but personal traits were equally important factors. With countless variations, similar sorts of dramas were played out in other communities. The problem of passage, of one generation taking over from another was neither easy nor simple. The habit of dividing an inheritance equally among all offspring worked well only if there was sufficient land to break up into farms, or, as we saw in Northfield, if family members agreed to cooperate to manage the farm as a single unit. When there was not enough land or other siblings were not interested in husbandry, one son usually bought out the other heirs. While this practice preserved the farm, it also saddled the new owner with a large debt, weakening a family's ability to maintain the farm. Moreover, the siblings who held rights to the farm as part of their inheritance often did not live nearby. To buy out their rights often meant the buyer had to make payments in cash rather than kind and this in turn bound the farmer closer to the market. Title to a farm, then, was not in itself a guaranty of financial security for either upland or lowland farmers.[14]

The strategies of providing for a family in an upland town changed somewhat over time. Like lowland farm families, uplanders went through a kind of life cycle in which land was cleared, the farm was built, and stock was added. This process required a strong back, good health, determination, and considerable energy. As upland towns were developed in the late eighteenth and early nineteenth centuries, farmers marketed lumber, cordwood, livestock, palm leaf hats, and maple sugar to generate income. They also took advantage of regional exchanges by pasturing lowland cattle and sheep. As their farms matured, they competed with lowland towns. By the second decade of the nineteenth century, some farmers in the uplands were fattening their own cattle rather than selling them to lowlanders. Similarly, they worked to diversify their operations so as to minimize disruptions linked to seasonality, crop failure, and inadequate resources.[15]

Upland farmers may have lacked abundant quantities of good level tillage, but there were alternatives. When Rufus Saxton advertised his farm in the *Franklin Herald* on February 12, 1802, he noted that it contained 230 acres, a large dwelling house, two barns, a cider mill and corn barn, an orchard with 400 apple trees, and a sugar orchard large enough to produce 600 pounds of sugar annually. Claiming that his Colrain farm was "one of the best grazing farms in the County," Saxton estimated that his mowing lands could produce 80 tons of hay per year, a figure that if correct was greater than all but the very best lowland farms. True, Saxton's farm was also better equipped and much larger than all but the best farms in the upland region, but the advertisement emphasized general characteristics common to upland farms that exploited woodland and pastures and the description may be taken to some extent as typical of the region.[16]

Smaller upland farms had fewer resources but, when possible, uplanders followed the same principle of diversifying farm production by relying on a mixture of agricultural activities. Maple sugaring yielded income or met family needs in the spring; hay and pasture for lowland cattle supplemented the family budget in the summer; apples and cider added income in the fall; and, in winters, lumbering offered some assistance if the wood lot was large enough for commercial harvesting and the snow was not too deep. The variety of activities helped spread risks and income throughout the year. If one crop failed, a different product might bring success in another season. Reformers believed that an adequately developed farm should provide families with a competency and, if properly managed, add to the family stock, but the theory was contingent upon a number of variables. By 1800—earlier in some towns—the more fertile portions of the uplands were already occupied. Farms like the one Saxton advertised were beyond the reach of most young people. Increasingly, patterns of wealthholding in upland communities reflected the age stratification that had long been common in the older lowland towns.[17]

The ability to provide for family needs was recognized as an essential component in a well-regulated upland farm. One real estate advertisement in the 1810s described the hill farm of Elijah Herrick in home-grown doggerel that attracted attention if no poetic accolades:

> Of acres now methinks I own, including water land and stone, one hundred and twenty, I say. I think it will measure any day. I have pasture land thats very sweet, and mowing too that's very neat; that's fixed, I say, so very nice that every year I mow it twice. Likewise a lot of thrifty wood, which you will call most super good: an orchard to [sic] that doth produce a sort of spirit from the juice, which spirit, now I really know is called by some good Pupelow; which saves the money from the stores and keeps the cash within our doors. Wheat, rye, and corn now I can raise, as big as any in those days. . . . [18]

Such farms were touted as bastions of family independence and security, but the reality was somewhat different. Neither Herrick nor most others in the region could keep "the money from the stores" or keep "the cash within our doors," because they were always short of money and were tempted by the growing quantity of consumer goods that entered the marketplace. Herrick's upland farm was relatively typical: he had plenty of pasture, mowing, and wood lot, but lacked much tillage. In the 1810s in some portions of the county, he and other uplanders were still organizing the upland landscape.

Underdeveloped land—much of it very poor—remained in the remote uplands through the second decade of the nineteenth century. The *Greenfield Gazette* carried advertisements for proprietors' shares and notices of overdue proprietors' taxes throughout the 1800s and 1810s. Some speculators sought profits by selling land rather than settling it, and the line of settlement in the uplands was spotty. Settlers moved into the remote uplands of Monroe, high in the hills of the Hoosac Range, or into the rugged gore along the Miller's River known as "Erving's Grant," long after other areas of the county were established. This pattern of selective settlement on good agricultural land emphasized the close relationship between the intensive, mixed husbandry of European agricultural traditions and the quality of local ecosystems. Uplanders sought out good land first and adjusted their expectations to the possibilities.

Figure 5:5. Lumber Production, Franklin County, Massachusetts, 1845.
(Drawn by the author.)

While they often produced foodstuffs for their families, uplanders centered their market-oriented production on a landscape of forest and hilly pasture.[19]

The exploitation of forest resources coincided with first settlement. In the early eighteenth century, Deerfield residents responded to the wanton destruction of pitch pine trees for the production of marketable commodities like turpentine by restricting the tapping of trees on undivided land. By the early nineteenth century, many farm families relied on wood lots for cash or store credit. Caleb Alvord, Jr., a Greenfield merchant with business ties to Hartford, Connecticut, not only accepted forest products in trade but actively hired men to cut timber and make cooperage. By 1812, Alvord was contracting with Wendell, Shutesbury, and New Salem men to supply him with lumber, barrel staves, tierces, barrels, boards, and shingles for shipment down river. Greenfield also provided a market for firewood. Rodolphus Dickinson noted in 1815 that "from the woodlands of Deerfield, individuals are enabled to meet the principal part of the great and increasing demand for firewood in the village of Greenfield, where it is sold by the cord at two dollars and fifty cents, an advance of one dollar over the price in Deerfield." Twenty-five years later farmers on the border between Shelburne and Deerfield were still cutting timber for merchants and families in Greenfield. On March 26, 1840, Julius

Uplands   103

Robbins noted in his diary that he was "chopping timber for James Jones on Clark and Newcomb . . . to saw and wraft down the river."[20]

Robbins was only one farmer who cut timber for a neighbor's or his own account. Millions of board feet of lumber were shipped from Franklin County before 1860. Families in rugged upland towns like Hawley sometimes cut and milled more than a million board feet in a single year for export in the 1830s and 1840s, but even fertile lowland towns such as Whately, Northfield, and Deerfield shipped large quantities. By 1840, every town in the county had at least one sawmill, although logging was skewed to the eastern portion of the county (Fig. 5:5). There, the rough terrain, stony soils, and poor prospects for pasture encouraged families to concentrate on forest products for shipment down the river to expanding urban markets. By contrast, upland farmers west of the Connecticut River specialized in raising livestock, especially sheep.[21]

By 1837, there were 55,308 sheep in Franklin County, most of which were pastured in upland towns in the western half of the county. Ashfield, Colrain, Charlemont, Leyden, and Conway were the leading towns for sheep raising (Fig. 5:6). The boom in sheep raising began in the second decade of the nineteenth century with the widespread importation of merino sheep. Although the breed was developed in Spain, the sheep were generally unavailable to foreigners until the 1800s. Their outstanding attribute was a long staple wool fiber that was clearly superior to the wool from common sheep found on American hillsides. Prices for full-blooded merino sheep were exorbitant during the opening years of the nineteenth century. Few farmers — even wealthy ones — could afford them so long as the price of a superior ram approached $1500. After 1811, however, the prices began coming down as more merinos were imported.[22]

Newspaper advertisements of merino sheep appeared in Franklin County by 1814. On September 13, Thomas and Charles Shepherd offered their flock of merino sheep at auction in Northampton during court week. They modestly claimed that their flock was "called by judges of Merino Sheep the best in this state." By the 1820s, flock sizes were expanding steadily in the hill towns and for a time in the 1820s wool prices were high. Even lowland farmers sometimes got involved with sheep farming. John Wilson of Deerfield bought 250 merino sheep in November of 1823. Although he lost several over the following winter, he reported that 97 of the sheep had produced 454 pounds of wool after washing. Later that year he bought a flock of sheep from the estate of Clark Chandler of Colrain, remarking that they were "all pure Merino blood of the best stock — they were selected from Capt Williams' family of Noddles Island." Wilson's efforts to expand his flock were successful; he reported in 1825 that he had pastured his sheep in Shelburne and had sold

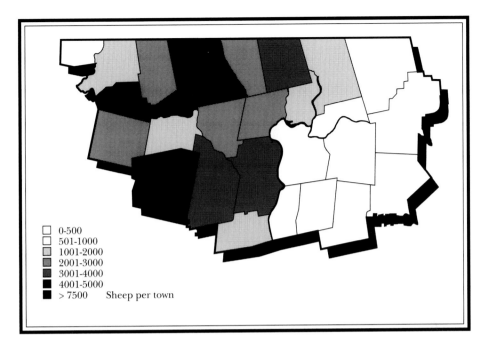

Figure 5:6. Sheep Distribution, Franklin County, Massachusetts, 1837.
(Drawn by the author.)

642 pounds of wool at 65 cents a pound for a total of $417.30.[23] Upland farmers in the 1820s realized similar profits and expanded their flocks.

By the 1830s, fewer and fewer sheep contained full-blooded merino heritage. Enthusiasm for pure-bred strains waned. The introduction of the Saxony breed in the 1820s created less of a sensation than the earlier fervor over the merinos. Part of the reason was the instability of prices. As Colman stated in 1841, "The hilly portions of the county are well adapted to sheep husbandry, though of late years the fluctuations in the prices of wool have discouraged it." Despite the decline in wool prices he noted that there was "a compensation for this in the low price of the fine wooled sheep compared with that which they formerly commanded." This decline made imported breeds more affordable, but raising imported sheep was not easy. Farmers found the merinos less resistant to native diseases, especially during lambing season. To improve their flocks, farmers bred them with common sheep. By 1840, nearly all the common sheep in the region had merino blood. While common sheep did not yield the same long fiber staple as full-blooded merinos, they had more meat, were resistant to diseases, and reproduced readily.[24]

The expansion of sheep grazing in the western portion of the county had important consequences for the area's landscape. Sheep were hard on the pastures because they had a tendency to eat grass down to the roots. Sound

Figure 5:7. View of Colrain, Massachusetts. From John Warner Barber, *Historical Collections*, 1839. (Courtesy, Pocumtuck Valley Memorial Association.)

management required farmers to move the animals to prevent overgrazing, and this in turn prompted them to clear more acres for pasture. John Warner Barber's views of upland towns in the late 1830s provides evidence of this change. His view of Colrain center shows the lower slopes of the hills behind the town were clear. The higher elevations and the hilltops were still wooded at this time. The view of Charlemont depicts the same story (Figs. 5:7 and 5:8). Gentler slopes were used for tillage and the more steeply graded portions of the landscape were reserved for mowing, pasture, and woodland. Although clearing was well advanced by the 1830s, farmers increased pasturage during the 1840s and 1850s due to expanded demands for lumber, continued sheep production, and the process of making land.

Some upland farmers found that fattening sheep was more profitable than raising beef cattle because the supply of stock was nearby, it took less time to ready the animals for market, and they required less feed. Fattened wethers (castrated rams) were preferred for market. "Our sheep, in general, are fed with hay, corn, or meal, oilcake, and potatoes; and if put up in good condition are in six weeks under judicious and faithful care, made fit for market." In the 1830s, Shelburne and Conway, two upland towns west of the Connecticut Valley lowlands, made a specialty of fattening sheep, sending many to the Brighton market. The "judicious care" that Colman referred to instilled many of the same habits of discipline that the lowlanders who fattened oxen learned, discipline that would become essential when the area shifted over to dairy production in the 1840s and 1850s. Profits on sheep did not last. The

Figure 5:8. View of Charlemont, Massachusetts, in John Warner Barber, *Historical Collections*, 1839. (Courtesy, Pocumtuck Valley Memorial Association.)

number of sheep in the county declined from 55,398 in 1837, to 52,239 in 1845, and plummeted to 18,412 in 1855 (Fig. 5:9). Several factors prompted the last decrease. In 1846, tariff protection of the wool industry ended and the railroad reached Greenfield. The first event eliminated the price protection that the farmers had enjoyed; the second increased competition. In addition, there was no important local market for wool, as few women in the region continued to spin and weave after 1840, preferring to buy factory-made yard goods in local stores. Like other southern New Englanders, Franklin County farmers, discouraged by low wool prices and poor prospects for improvements, sold hundreds of animals to slaughterhouses.[25]

For farm families who elected to stay on in the uplands, the decline in the sheep trade prompted a search for alternative market strategies. For some, beef cattle and dairying provided a measure of profit. Although the total number of beef cattle raised in the county fell 11 percent between 1845 and 1855, the raw numbers are deceptive. In some towns the ratio of cattle to people actually increased as population decline outstripped cutbacks in cattle production. This ratio suggests that the cattle market continued to be a viable farming strategy throughout the period. Beef animals met household food needs, and milk and butter production remained strong in several towns. Cattle and horses continued to have a market value locally and regionally. By contrast, sheep figures dropped 66 percent in the ten years between 1845 and 1855, indicating how sensitive upland farmers had become to changing market conditions.[26]

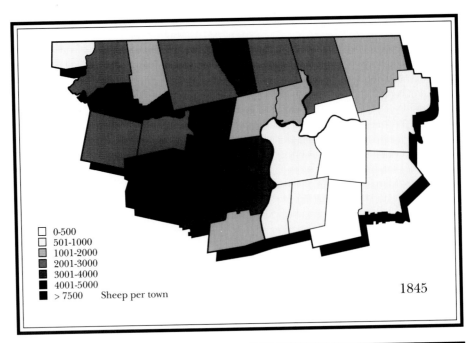

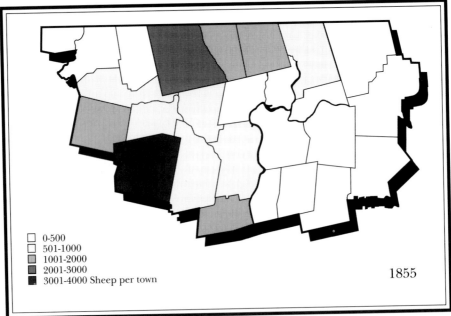

Figure 5:9. Sheep Distribution, Franklin County, Massachusetts, 1845 and 1855.
(Drawn by the author.)

Although the entire farm family became more involved with market production and was affected by shifting commercial demands, state census takers began to recognize women's contributions to the well-being of upland and lowland farms by collecting data on the outwork system. By the 1830s and 1840s, many women in the eastern half of the county braided and prepared palm leaf hats. The palm leaf was available in local or regional stores. In exchange for braid or finished hats, the women received credit at the store. In 1845 when Massachusetts first began to record palm leaf hat production in the Census of Manufacturers, much of the business in Franklin County was clustered to the east of the Connecticut River, especially in the upland towns of New Salem, Orange, and Warwick. While a few lowland communities also participated in the trade, they were located in the southern portion of the county—Whately, Deerfield, Montague, and Gill. The towns with the greatest production were located on roads that led to the major regional center of the industry, Amherst.[27]

The hat business initially seems to have served communities without important ties to the wool industry, augmenting family income in some of the poorer towns in the county. During the next decade, hat production in the western portion of the county grew. This was the region where residents had experienced a fall in the price of wool and where the search for alternative income evidently encouraged women to become involved in the outwork system. The growth of the hat business in western towns did not come at the expense of the eastern ones. Although production in towns east of the Connecticut River decreased somewhat in the 1850s, all towns east of the river reported hatmaking. The decline in some eastern towns, particularly New Salem, probably was caused by population losses. There were simply fewer women in these communities to participate in the trade (Fig. 5:10).

In addition to piecework and participation in the outwork system, farm women also made significant contributions to farm income through their management of poultry and dairying. We have already shown that dairying in certain sections of the county exceeded household needs, that the production of butter and cheese was one way farm women contributed to family income and sometimes earned their own money. Elihu Hoyt, for one, wrote to his wife Hannah on January 18, 1820: "I hardly know whether to advise you to send your butter here. I think not if you can get 7s. at home. poultry will not fetch anything for a month or two to come in this market." The income these women earned, then, contributed materially to the welfare of their families. It bought shoes and clothing, made possible the purchase of furnishings, carpet, and cloth for the house, and elevated the significance of women's contributions to the local economy. The importance of women's activities was increasingly recognized in the reshaping of the county's architecture to sep-

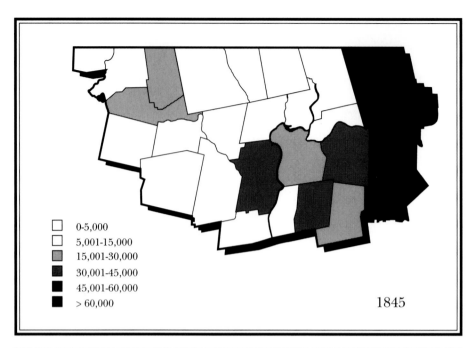

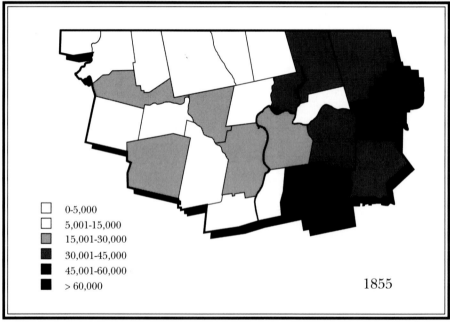

Figure 5:10. Palm Leaf Hat Production, Franklin County, Massachusetts, 1845 and 1855. (Drawn by the author.)

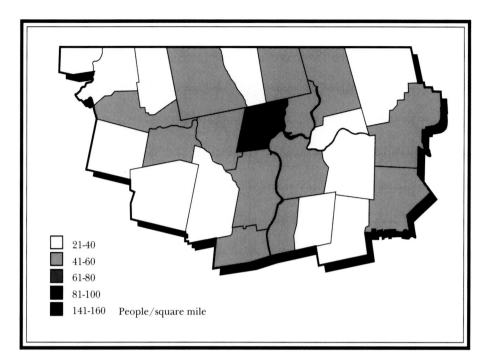

21-40
41-60
61-80
81-100
141-160   People/square mile

Figure 5:11. Population Density, Franklin County, Massachusetts, 1850.
(Drawn by the author.)

arate kitchen and work areas from the rest of the house, to adopt designs that
worked to the advantage of women. The progressive farmwives who wrote
into the agricultural press with designs for more efficient farmhouses were
the more articulate individuals who were reflecting widespread cultural change
already washing over northern households. Female outwork activities helped
pay for those changes.[28]

The rates of production for any of these commodities and products varied
according to the nuances of local discourse. Outwork systems functioned well
in communities where there were few alternatives to life on a family farm,
but they were generally less popular in towns where there was significant
manufacturing. By 1855, the region's economy had recovered from the tough
years of the late 1830s and 1840s. Factory work expanded in those communities situated on sources of water power and conveniently located near the
county's major transportation routes. Some of these factory sites were in lowland towns such as Greenfield and Deerfield, but the economies of Shelburne,
Buckland, Colrain, Erving, and Orange also quickened as manufacturing
developed. Population density in these towns grew noticeably in comparison
to the communities that surrounded them, accenting the differences between
farm and factory life (Fig. 5:11). For the first time in their histories Erving
and Orange attained prominence and modest prosperity in the 1850s as manu-

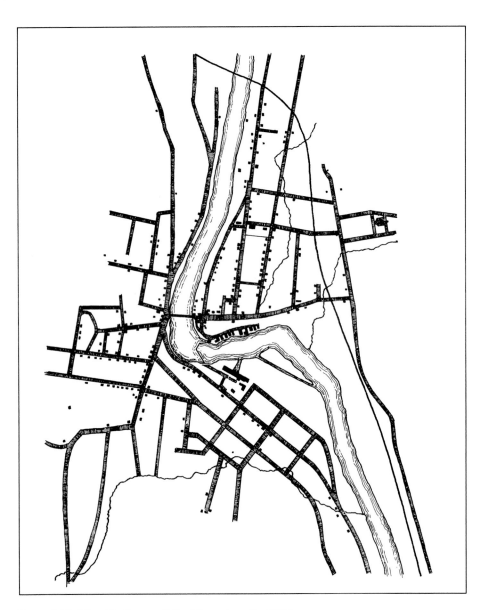

Figure 5:12. Map, Shelburne Falls, Massachusetts, 1858.
(Drawn by the author based on 1858 county map.)

facturing villages. While factory villages in the uplands were small by the standards of Lowell or Lawrence, they were less likely to be dominated by textile
production than the more famous mill communities on the Merrimack River.
Upland factories produced a variety of manufactured goods: cutlery, axes,
and scythe snaiths in Shelburne and Buckland; textiles, sash and blinds
in Colrain; piano cases and tools in Erving; pails and wooden items in Orange.
    The growth of industry was more than a shift in mode of production and

Figure 5:13. View of Lamson and Goodnow, Shelburne Falls, Massachusetts, ca. 1840. (Courtesy, Pocumtuck Valley Memorial Association.)

the use of labor. Factories created a need for industrial villages to serve the workers. By 1858, when a wall map of the county was published, communities like Shelburne Falls looked much different from only a decade earlier (Figs. 5:12 and 5:13). On the Buckland side of the river, there was a modest grid plan to serve the new cutlery factory of Lamson and Goodnow. Across the falls that provided the cutlery's power was the old village. On the new side streets, builders had put up houses for skilled factory workers, local merchants, mill owners, and professional people. Beyond these streets were the tracks for the railroad that brought in raw materials and workers for the factories and that sometimes carried young men and women away from parents and upland homes as they sought their futures in a wider world.

Despite population losses during the late 1830s and early 1840s, upland towns did not all wither and decline. The landscape of the uplands became more complex at midcentury as factory production vied with farmers for space and labor. Some communities drifted as the momentum of the national economy bypassed the hardscrabble farms of remote uplands. But in other towns families turned to the outwork system and reshaped the economic landscape by utilizing important sources of water power, hiring local people to labor in the mills, and/or supplying workers with foodstuffs and housing. In the process some of the uplands remained relatively homogeneous, and other places became more diverse as industrial production encouraged the immigration and concentration of new ethnic groups, wage laborers, and skilled tradespeople. Upland farm landscapes continued to exhibit traditional production strategies to provide for many family subsistence needs, but there were also differences between towns and families that were adjusted by exchanges with other households and communities. These differences were controlled by the kind and quality of dirt that was available, individual and family circumstances, climate, personal inclination, and opportunities for trade.[29]

Both men and women participated in the process of shaping an economic landscape focused on family survival within an increasingly specialized world. As in lowland communities there were winners and losers in this process. But the uplands did not collapse into a winter world of Ethan Fromes, of haggard men and women stubbornly trying to keep old ways going against the glacier of modernity. Beyond the sumac-filled cellar holes of abandoned farmsteads were the pastures of families who had accepted change, adapted their landscapes, and learned that there were benefits as well as the hardships in rural life.

Chapter 6

Farmsteads

In 1823, Timothy Dwight observed that the house lots of the valley lowlands fit a distinctive mode. On each home lot he found "a house is erected at the bottom of a courtyard (often neatly enclosed) and is furnished universally with a barn and other convenient outbuildings. Near the house there is always a garden replenished with culinary vegetables, flowers, and fruits, and very often also prettily enclosed."[1] Dwight's description expressed values he held dear—order, neatness, frugality, and convenience—but the image he conveyed was only partially accurate. By the 1810s and 1820s, the landscape of houses, outbuildings, and gardens that Dwight so admired largely obscured an older landscape, ruder and less orderly, that was being replaced. Just as families adjusted their economic strategies to accommodate new market conditions, they altered their house lots and outbuildings. This process was dynamic and powerful, for the yards around the dwellings directly mirrored farm families' daily lives, testified to some of their aspirations, and served as the complex stage on which family and community life took place.

Whatever the rural ideal may have been, few families in the region, or anywhere else in the United States, lived within a complex of buildings that was as self-sufficient or idyllic as the one Dwight described. Even in the comparatively wealthy lowlands the number of houses exceeded the number of barns. According to the 1791 tax valuation records, for example, 72 percent of the heads of household of Deerfield owned a house, but only 52 percent owned a barn. A careful study of the valuation list, however, indicates that a majority of Deerfield heads of household who farmed and who were between the ages of forty-five and sixty-five owned not only a house but usually two barns rather than one. Those heads of household who did not own houses or barns tended to be young, elderly, or engaged principally in a trade. While these numbers indicate that the composition of house lots was less uniform than Dwight's description, they tell little about how families used their house lots, how they modified them to respond to new opportunities or needs, or what they built.[2]

Farms are capital-intensive enterprises and a large percentage of family wealth was bound up in the physical assets of house, barn, outbuildings, and land. Probate inventories show consistently that real estate was by far the more valuable portion of a family's estate. Personal estates, even of wealthy people, were normally only a modest fraction of the total estate. On a small or large scale, farmland and buildings represented a considerable investment in modification to the landscape, in labor, and in equipment. The landscape around the farmhouse was an extension of the household space, and it mediated between the home and the barn, between humans and animals. The barn was the center of men's work, the house was the focal point for women, and the yard in between those two spheres met the needs of the entire family in many ways.[3]

Archaeological research has demonstrated that the few hundred square yards around the dwelling were the most intensively used portions of a farm's landscape. The area located in the general vicinity of a house's entries was known as the "dooryard" and was sometimes further subdivided with additional prefixes such as front or rear dooryard, or woodyard. Usually, the area was defined by the placement of outbuildings and fences, but not always. Often the rear or working dooryard was oriented to take advantage of a south or southeast exposure. The formal facade of the house normally faced the most prominent public view, but families frequently tried to take advantage of building forms to shield outside work from cold north or northwest winds. By the early 1820s, rear or side porches and sheds extending beyond ells helped protect those performing recurrent outdoor activities. This careful orientation of workspace made little difference in January, but in late fall or early spring the strategy was quite effective. Dooryard chores could be messy. Julius Robbins, a middling farmer who lived in West Deerfield, noted in his diary on Monday, March 23, 1840, that he was "drawing wood to door with sled, no snow, had C. Taintor for help." Firewood chopping, butchering, candle and soap making, occasionally laundry, and even some food preparation procedures took place in the rear dooryard near the cooking fireplace or stove, but outside where dirty jobs could be kept apart from clean interiors. Some jobs, like laundry, could be done indoors or out according to the weather, but for most of the year the area around the back door was one of intense human activity.[4]

By contrast front dooryards were places for public display of status and economic control. In village landscapes most front yards were fenced by the 1830s. In the eighteenth century, only the elite seemed to have been willing to undertake the expense of erecting picket fences around front yards. Thomas Williams put up a picket fence in front of his house before his death in 1775, but he was apparently ahead of most neighbors. Picket fences were forceful statements of power. Like all fences they enclosed land, signified ownership, and denied access to others whether animal or human. More importantly, they were ostentatious symbols of status; the sawn pickets nailed onto milled rails in precise rows represented a higher level of artifice than split rails or board fencing. We have no evidence of what Williams's picket fence was like, but in 1816, Calvin Stearns built a picket fence in front of the house he constructed for Isaac Mattoon. (See Fig. 7:16.) For a country dwelling in a rural village like Northfield, it was an elegant fence. Perhaps because he had never before built such an elaborate barrier, Stearns made a detailed record of it in his account book. Mattoon's was constructed entirely of sawn lumber, a considerable contrast to the riven posts and rails of most local enclosures. Stearns and his assistants spent several weeks setting the posts, attaching the rails, cutting and nailing up the vertical pickets, and hanging the gates. When it was finished he and his crew painted it white. Paint was a symbol of affluence since pigment, oil, and the labor to apply it to an intricate picket fence were relatively expensive. Equally important, white was a color that stood out against the green of trees and shrubs and emphasized the fence's artificiality.

Over time, other families on Northfield's main street and those in other villages in the region would also convey their status and power through the fences they put up. Most of the picket fences Stearns recorded in his accounts were built between 1819 and 1830. These fences were evidently similar to the Mattoon fence, but in 1819 he noted carefully that he turned "acorns" for the fenceposts in front of Thomas Doak's house, presumably inverted acorn-shaped finials that graced the tops of boxed gateposts. Stearns's work on Doak's fence coincided with a brief period of prosperity after the War of 1812 and before the Panic of 1819, but it also mirrored the social competition played out on village landscapes across New England, especially as the economy improved in the 1820s. Once the local elite began putting up picket fences, many other Northfield residents followed their lead. Like most improvements there was a price for raising local standards with a fancy enclosure. Mattoon's picket fence lasted for seventeen years before Stearns was called back to make repairs; he and his assistant George Smith spent seven and a half days in August 1833 fixing the gates and pickets.[5]

Mattoon's costly embellishment and those of his fellow townsmen were evidence of a new level of self-consciousness about the landscape and of a desire to engross the land in ways that excluded others. Like the entrances of houses that faced drives rather than public ways, picket fences guarded the front yards that distanced occupants from passersby, served to intensity human control over nature by establishing formal artificial boundaries, and extended the family's responsibility to organize and maintain the land in more intensive ways. This emphasis on control extended to other parts of the house lot. Fences symbolized the imposition of human order on the chaos of nature. Timothy Dwight and others of his generation might admire God's sublime handiwork in the natural landscape, but they nearly always preferred a landscape that was subdued by human beings. Fences signified human power to manage the environment. The absence of fences in the common fields of old nucleated villages surrounded by common fields, the stone walls of the uplands, and the brush fences that surrounded newly cleared fields were clues to cultural rules of land use in which individual families practiced an intensive form of mixed agriculture predicated upon private ownership. Fences denoted the boundaries between one farm and another, but farmers also depended upon them to manage fields that were used for different purposes. Even in the lowland towns where there were open fields enclosed by a common fence and where it was essential for a group to manage access to the entire field, individual lots were the property of their owners rather than the entire community. Hence, the "common" field fence was actually controlled by the select group of people who owned land inside the enclosure. Given the traditions of mixed agriculture in which farmers had to separate livestock from grains, then, it was not possible to intensify farm productivity or to keep control without fences, and farm families necessarily spent a great deal of time building or maintaining them.

The politics of fencing were less divisive in the region than they were in the southern uplands or in portions of Delaware. In the eighteenth and early nineteenth centuries, voters underscored the significance of proper enclosures by electing "fence viewers" at the annual town meeting. These men were charged with the job of checking to see that proper enclosures were maintained and that families secured their property against the ravages of wandering livestock. By the mid 1820s customs were changing. While the old common field system in place in the lowlands required fence viewers to properly manage the fields, elsewhere owners were now responsible for securing livestock. Some towns like Whately built public pounds for keeping strays, requiring owners to pay a fine to recover their animals. Unlike some sections of the country where such changes were met with outcries from the rural poor, there is little evidence of opposition in Franklin County, where the extremes of wealth and poverty were less pronounced, where few family diets relied on pork (the animals most likely to invade fenced land and cause damage), where wood for fencing was still inexpensive, and where families had a long tradition of intensive land management.[6]

The types of fences varied according to need and situation. Around gardens, orchards, hog pens, and some cattle yards, farmers usually used board fences. For gardens and orchards, this type of fence offered some protection from small animals such as rabbits or groundhogs. Around valuable tillage

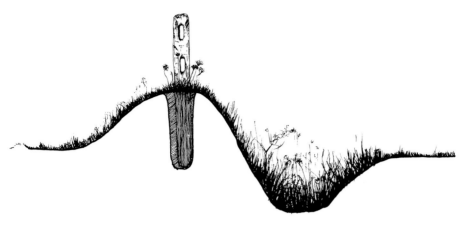

Figure 6:1. Reconstructed Cross Section, Common Field Fence, Deerfield, Massachusetts. (Drawn by the author.)

lands, post-and-rail fences were the most common type. Farm diaries were seldom specific about fencing activities, but there are occasional references to "holeing" fences (i.e., cutting mortises in the posts for the fence rails) and to splitting rails. In towns with common field systems, such as Deerfield and Northfield, farmers who owned land in the common fields frequently used a variation of the post-and-rail fence. The normal practice was to dig a ditch between two and three feet deep, pitching the excavated dirt in a mound on the inner side of the field they were enclosing. On top of this mound they set up a shortened version of the post-and-rail fence with only two or three rails instead of the four- or five-rail fences that were common. This type of barrier was relatively durable and discouraged all but the most determined livestock from breaching the combination of trench, mound, and rails (Fig. 6:1).[7]

Outside of the interval lands which were free from stones, farmers resorted to stone walls as a means of clearing their fields of unwanted geologic rubble. Despite the popular image of carefully laid stone walls, the surviving examples in Franklin County exhibit a mixture of sloppiness and precision. Some did neater work than others; some walls were carefully laid while others were haphazardly formed by tossing stones onto the edges of fields being cleared. The latter approach sometimes resulted in walls that were more like uneven strips of stone piled several feet wide rather than neatly laid up walls (Fig. 6:2). On stony pasture land where farmers were interested more in clearing the land of unwanted rocks than in spending much time in building walls, straggling fences were good enough. Around tillage fields or farmsteads stone walls were often neater. While building a stone wall was back-breaking work, the walls were virtually maintenance free once they were in place. Upland farmers could take some comfort in that fact as they heaved the stones into

Figure 6:2. Stone Wall, Warwick, Massachusetts. (Photograph by the author.)

place, but the rewards, like those for most farmers, were measured over the long haul. The miles of stone walls that still crosscross the uplands are the enduring tale of efforts to control property and to eliminate customary forms of use in which farmers left their stock to forage at will on unimproved land. By the early 1800s, the frontier phase of customary land use was nearly gone, replaced by a more controlled pattern of enclosed land.[8]

Wooden fences lacked the permanence of stone walls, but they were easier to construct. They also required constant maintenance. Jonathan Hoyt noted in his diary on September 17, 1810, "Our folks are making and mending fence up the hill to stop creatures from getting the rye." His brother, David Hoyt, recorded a tremendous thunderstorm one summer that did heavy damage in Deerfield, noting in a memorandum that "fences and apple trees were blown down." Most of the time fences were damaged by rot rather than winds. Despite the use of chestnut and locust fence posts—woods with somewhat greater resistance to rot—most farmers found that it was essential to spend time repairing fences.[9]

Aside from the wooden fences associated with the farmstead, there were two common types of wooden fences used with fields: post-and-rail fence, and the "Virginia" or snake-rail fence. Both types were widely used in the region, even in the uplands where stone walls were common. Post-and-rail fences reached a height of about four feet and generally had mortise holes for four or five rails. Farmers usually made posts by splitting a six- to eight-inch diameter log in half and cutting out mortises for the rails. They split rails from logs eight to ten feet in length and dressed the ends with an axe so that they would fit into the mortises of the posts. The posts were set into holes dug in the ground, then the rails were jockeyed into place and the post holes were backfilled. The system made sturdy fences with a minimum of tools and did not take up much space in valuable tillage areas. By contrast, the "Virginia Fence" (as it was known in period documents) used split rails that were piled up in a zigzag fashion. This fence could be built with an axe, wedges, and beetle (a large mallet), but it used up a considerable amount of timber and created triangular patches of ground between each section of fence (Fig. 6:3). These sections were wasteful in tillage areas but did not matter much on pasture or mowing lands because livestock could graze in the triangles or mowers could follow the line of the fence.[10]

There were other less sophisticated types of fencing that worked effectively. Jonathan Hoyt's farm was regarded by some as one of the best farms in the area, but even on this farm there were brush fences. Hoyt wrote in his diary in 1810, "Our folks are sledding down an old brush fence today & 20 five loads of wood out of it." Brush fences were formed by piling stumps, poles, brush and other wastewood around the perimeter of a field to enclose it and keep out livestock. As in the Hoyt's case, it was often an expedient type of temporary fencing used to set off a newly cleared field. Hoyt also noted in his diary that his son had made a log fence on November 5, 1804, perhaps referring to the process of fencing land by piling up logs on the edges of a clearing. As farmers steadily worked to improve or "make" land, fencing be-

Figure 6:3. View of Orange Center. From John Warner Barber, *Historical Collections*, 1839. (Courtesy, Pocumtuck Valley Memorial Association.)

came more regularized. Like the process by which wage rates converged over time, this regularity was symptomatic of growing pressures to improve agricultural practices and to compete effectively in an expanding market economy. Post-and-rail and Virginia fences increasingly dominated the open spaces of uplands and lowland. By the 1850s, the region was nearing the point where agricultural activities had cleared more than half the land of forest cover. In about six decades farmers had sectioned off the uplands with fences and transformed a forested wilderness into a pastoral landscape.[11]

Beyond the back dooryard of the region's better-developed farms stood a barn. While documenting barns is far more difficult than studying houses, enough have survived to test interpretations suggested by the dwelling houses. The earliest view of a barn in the region is in Dudley Woodbridge's sketch of Deerfield (See Fig. 7:1). It shows an English three-bay barn and a number of houses. This form was built throughout the eighteenth and nineteenth centuries and was used ubiquitously by rich and middling farmers alike. Most of these barns were modest in size during the eighteenth century. Few were larger than 30 by 50 feet. The size of barns was controlled in part by economics and in part by the form. English barns traditionally used a triparite system of bays in which a runway passed through the barn on the structure's long side. In Franklin County, the runway was usually off-center to allow one of the bays flanking the runway to be larger. The larger bay was generally used for hay storage and the smaller one frequently housed animals and had a haymow above. Hay was also stacked above the runway on poles and boards loosely laid across the girts.[12]

Like houses, the barns that farmers built in Franklin County were more varied than surviving examples of English-style barns generally suggest. The most common barn size in Franklin County was 30 by 40 feet. An analysis of the seventy-two barns surveyed in the upland town of Colrain in 1798 for the Federal direct tax census yielded a rather distinctive pattern. Thirty-nine of the seventy-two barns (54 percent) measured 30 by 40 feet, and seven (10 percent) measured 30 by 50 feet.[13] An analysis of Colrain barn sizes is shown in Table 6:1. The evidence for Colrain, which was not the most properous town in the county in 1798, suggests that upland farmers built moderately sized to large barns rather than small ones.

Real estate advertisements only reinforce what the tax census suggests. Although few real estate advertisements actually specified the number and size of outbuildings, the barn sizes that did appear most often reflected the median barn size in Colrain—30 by 40 feet. Micah Cannady advertised his seventy-one-acre farm in Hawley in the *Greenfield Gazette* on August 16, 1802. His farm had a "low, double house," probably similar to a fully developed

Landscape and Material Life in Franklin County, Massachusetts

Table 6:1.
List of Barn Sizes, Colrain, Massachusetts, 1798

No.	Size	No.	Size
1	18 x 20	1	22 x 26
1	20 x 30	1	25 x 30
1	26 x 30	1	30 x 30
1	26 x 36	1	30 x 35
1	28 x 38	1	30 x 36
1	30 x 37	1	28 x 40
1	30 x 38	39	30 x 40
1	30 x 43	2	30 x 45
7	30 x 50	5	30 x 60
1	30 x 65		

"Cape Cope" style dwelling, and a "40-foot barn." A Greenfield man, Oliver Hastings, advertised a farm on January 3, 1803, noting that it consisted of forty acres, a "convenient house," and woodhouse, a 30-by-40-foot barn and a separate fifty-acre woodlot. Toward the upper end of the economic scale, Shelburne farmer Isaac Martin advertised a very large (44 by 30 feet), three-story farmhouse but even this substantial farmer owned a 30-by-40-foot barn. Larger barns like the "50 foot" barn owned by Zephaniah Pitts of Gill were occasionally listed in the newspaper, but most real estate advertisements correspond to the evidence recorded in the 1798 tax census.[14]

We lack the same detailed records for lowland towns in Franklin County, but there is a surviving fragment of the 1798 Direct Tax Census for Deerfield that listed the houses and outbuildings owned by David Hoyt (Table 6:2). The Hoyt farmstead was large and well developed but it was not an exceptionally well-appointed farm by Deerfield standards. Other farms were valued at a higher level on the 1791 Massachusetts valuation records for Deerfield, and the Hoyts' holdings seem to have been similar to other substantial farms in town. The size and diversity of Hoyt's outbuildings undoubtedly reflected the fact that the farm was more than a century old in 1798 and was thoroughly developed, but the farmstead was also a product of the agricultural prosperity of the lowland farms. Only one Colrain barn approached the Hoyt barn in size, but there seem to have been barns in Northfield, Deerfield, Whately, and Sunderland that were comparable.[15]

Further down the valley in South Hadley there are more detailed records. In 1798 the South Hadley landscape had ninety barns. The smallest was a 20-by-18-foot structure and the largest was 54 by 70. The mean square footage of South Hadley barns was 1137 square feet, roughly the size of a 30-by-38-foot barn. The median size barn, and there were twelve of them, was

Table 6:2
List of David Hoyt's buildings, Deerfield, Massachusetts, 1798

House	2 story	42 x 21
Kitchen	1 story	42 x 13.5
Bedroom	1 story	15 x 14

(These measurements represent one dwelling: a two-story, central chimney house, a one-story kitchen attached to the rear, and a one-story bedroom ell. David Hoyt bought this house from the Sheldon Family [See Fig. 7:2].)

Horse house	25 x 11
Saddle house	10 x 9
Barn	62 x 32
Stable at end of barn	24 x 9.5
Cow house	64 x 12
Corn house	18 x 16
Barn	24 x 18

30 by 40 feet. Viewed in ascending order by square foot, the barn sizes are summarized in Table 6:3. South Hadley's landscape contained a much wider range of barn sizes than that found in Colrain, but there are a number of similarities between the two towns. Twenty-seven of the ninety barns (30 percent) in South Hadley were larger than the standard 30-by-40-foot type; a larger number were smaller, but not much smaller. The list also contains several structures listed as barns that were clearly very long and narrow — 16 to 20 feet wide and 30 to 50 feet long. It also includes twenty-one other structures listed as "cow house" which have similar dimensions. As the assessors went about town making up their lists, what distinguished a barn from a cow house? The lists do not tell. Although it is easy enough to conclude that barns were large and significant structures on the late eighteenth century landscape of the Connecticut Valley, the sizes by themselves do not reveal much about how such structures functioned or what the different sized buildings looked like.

Only a few existing barns in the region seem to date to the eighteenth century. Most of them stand in the lowlands where agriculture has continued and where they remained useful. Partly because of this selection process, standing barns are either large or they have been added on to. Most are in poor repair and have been changed many times by former owners as their needs changed. To analyze these barns requires some educated guesswork and the careful reading of mortise holes for evidence of where earlier partitions, stanchions, or framing once went. What does remain is instructive in many ways. One of the earliest barns in the lowlands is the Mattoon barn

Table 6:3
Number of Barns by Size, South Hadley, Massachusetts, 1798

No.	Size	No.	Size	No.	Size	No.	Size
1	20 x 18	1	22 x 18	1	20 x 20	1	30 x 18
1	30 x 20	1	40 x 16	1	26 x 26	1	28 x 24
3	30 x 24	1	40 x 20	1	32 x 26	3	30 x 28
1	34 x 26	1	42 x 22	3	36 x 26	1	38 x 25
1	50 x 20	5	36 x 28	6	38 x 28	5	40 x 28
2	38 x 30	1	41 x 28	1	39 x 30	12	40 x 30
1	44 x 28	1	42 x 31	1	44 x 30	2	45 x 30
1	45 x 32	4	50 x 30	1	40 x 38	1	56 x 28
1	52 x 31	1	45 x 36	1	50 x 34	1	45 x 38
2	46 x 38	1	62 x 29	1	60 x 30	1	73 x 26
1	66 x 30	1	56 x 36	1	70 x 30	1	70 x 40
2	70 x 54						

in Northfield (Fig. 6:4). Built with shouldered posts and very large braces, it follows the general construction practices of domestic architecture, adjusted to hold down the costs of framing. The Mattoon barn (ca. 1760–90) uses two horizontal rails between bents for bracing and for holding the vertical board sheathing on the exterior. Unlike barns surveyed in other New England towns, this barn apparently did not originally shelter animals. There are no mortises on the inner bents that flank the runway, no evidence that there were originally any stanchions for animals and no intermediary supporting posts for the massive girts that span the entire 32-foot width of the barn. Evidently, this barn was used for hay and fodder storage on either side of the runway and animals were kept elsewhere, probably in a cowhouse. It is possible that this barn is an exception, but high up on the hill that overlooks Northfield, on the old road to Warwick, is another barn with similar construction features.

Although it was built later than the Mattoon barn, the Janes/Field barn (ca. 1790–1810) has the same system of shouldered posts, large braces, and massive girts flanking the runway. There is no evidence of any original partitions to accommodate animals (Fig. 6:5). Measuring 30 feet by 41 feet 7 inches and 14 feet 8 inches (to the top of the plate), its massive collar beams are 13 inches thick in the center and taper to 9 inches on either end. The roof construction is later than the Mattoon barn. The Janes/Field barn makes use of a ridgepole with unhewn poles for rafters, a form of roof framing that was common throughout the county in the nineteenth century. Despite these differences, it served the same function as the Mattoon barn, the storage of large quantities of hay and fodder for livestock.

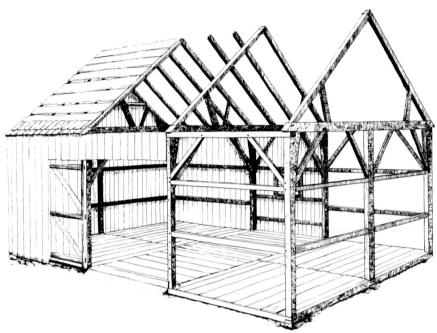

Figure 6:4. Mattoon Barn, Northfield, Massachusetts, 1750–1800.
(Measured and drawn by the author.)

Cattle were located in the cowhouse next to the barn. The cowhouse is 16 feet 4 inches by 48 feet 9 inches and of lower height than the barn, 11 feet 8 inches (to the top of the plate). It contained an enclosed bay with a door opening to the south, and three bays to the west which were open to the south (Fig. 6:6). It may be that the distinction between cowhouses and barns noted previously was that cowhouses were open on one side while barns were enclosed. The Janes/Field cowhouse was oriented to take maximum advantage of the southern exposure and works with the barn to form a sort of courtyard, blocking the cold northern winds from the barnyard. Above the animals was a loft. This area was probably used as storage space for straw or provender and was floored over by laying boards on top of joists made of peeled poles. The foundation consisted of a few fieldstones set directly on the ground underneath the main supporting posts, leaving almost no footprint for future archaeologists to find after the building is gone. The enclosed shed space was probably for young stock, but its use must remain conjectural. Similar long and narrow shedlike structures appeared in later nineteenth-century photographs in other parts of the county, but most of them were demolished or have been altered beyond recognition.[16]

Both the Mattoon and Janes barns were large, similar to the sizes listed as most common on the 1798 Direct Tax. Some smaller barns similar to the sizes that were recorded on that list have also survived. Nathaniel Stearns's

Figure 6:5. Janes-Field Barn, Northfield, Massachusetts, 1790–1810.
(Photograph by the author.)

barn in Warwick was moved across the street from the field where it once stood to a position closer to the house. Originally, it was a bay/runway form, 30 feet 8 inches square and 15 feet high (to the top of the plate) (Fig. 6:7). Now much altered and expanded, it shows no evidence that it originally had provisions for sheltering animals in the bay. Like the preceding barns it was probably used for hay storage, while animals were kept in another building. Some English-style barns have survived that were smaller and maintained the traditional pattern of integrating animals and fodder into the same space. Samuel Stearns, Nathaniel's son, built a barn on his Northfield property in 1825, the year after he completed the work on his new house (Fig. 6:8). The Stearns barn was 26 by 36 feet and 14 feet high (to the top of the plate). Each bay was equal in length. The Stearns barn was too altered to recover much information about the bay used to house the animals, but the family of carpenters built one about fifteen years later for a prominent Northfield merchant, Benjamin B. Murdock, that was nearly identical. This barn is worth a closer inspection for what it reveals about barn construction of the 1840s (Fig. 6:9).

The Murdock barn was a standardized plan like others, that differed in size but not in detail. In the 1840s in rural towns like Northfield, the main framing members of a barn were still hand hewn, but all of the boards, braces, nailing rails, and smaller-dimensioned stock were cut in an up-and-down-type sawmill. Rafters and floor joists were peeled poles with each end shaped

Farmsteads   127

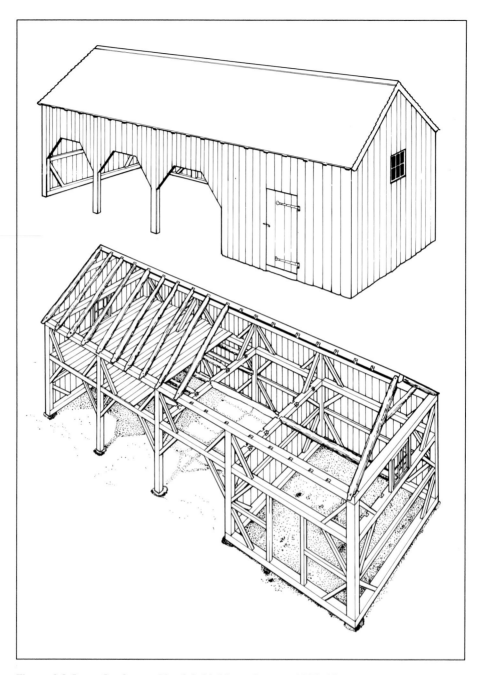

Figure 6:6. Janes Cowhouse, Northfield, Massachusetts, 1815–40.
(Measured and drawn by the author.)

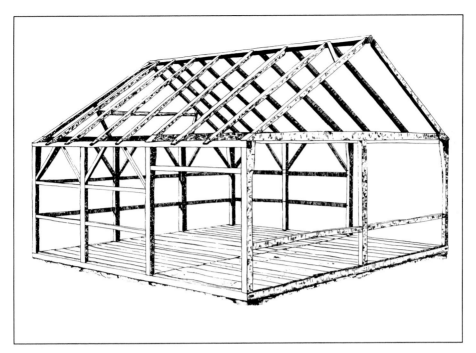

Figure 6:7. Nathaniel Stearns Barn, Warwick, Massachusetts, 1790–1815. (Drawn by the author.)

Figure 6:8. Samuel Stearns Barn, Northfield, Massachusetts, 1825. (Photograph by the author.)

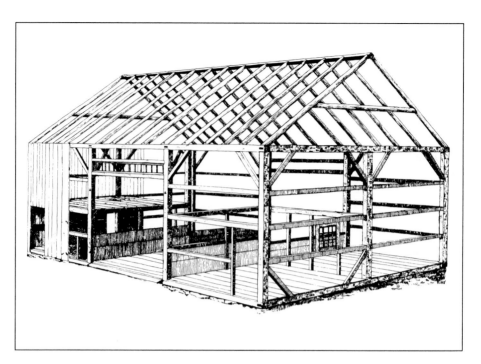

Figure 6:9. B. B. Murdock Barn, Northfield, Massachusetts, ca. 1840–45.
(Drawn by the author.)

to fit into the framing. Braces were standardized as the hypotenuse of a three-foot equilateral triangle, posts were square up their entire length rather than shouldered as in the eighteenth century, and there were three nailing rails rather than two. The Murdock barn also had a basement, an improvement that reformers had recommended to New Englanders for years but that few had adopted (Figs. 6:10 and 6:11). In the Murdock barn, animals were housed on either side of the runway, but only in the east half of each bay. Horses were on the north side of the barn; cows were on the south side. Above the animals and in the western half of the bays was hay storage. A low 28-inch knee wall kept hay from the bays out of the runway. Doors on the front and back of the runway provided access to the front drive and the fields out back. Horses entered their stall only through a door on the northeast corner of the front facade, but cows could enter through a door on the southeast corner or through a door that opened on the south facade. Evidence of wear and nail patterns on the floor of the Murdock barn was analyzed in the stall areas. Only the cow side of the barn had stanchions, with a manger that was 2 feet wide. The manger was created by nailing up two, 14-inch-wide boards on the runway side of the manger — the same height as the knee wall on the hay portion of the bay to the west. There was no means of closing up this area to

Figure 6:10. West Elevation, B. B. Murdock Barn. (Photograph by the author.)

Figure 6:11. Basement, B. B. Murdock Barn. (Photograph by the author.)

the elements; only after the Civil War did farmers begin to install hinged shutters that folded up and latched to cover these manger areas.

These kinds of barns served the needs of different families quite well and they were built by middle-class and wealthy farmers alike, but they were not necessarily markers of traditional values. The Murdock barn was owned by a merchant who seems to have done little serious farming and who had quite limited needs for a barn. Samuel Stearns was a carpenter, and he used his barn to store lumber. It seems clear that by the early nineteenth century the more prosperous farmers of the lowlands and some in the uplands, people like Elijah Mattoon or Nathaniel Stearns, were likely to place their livestock in separate buildings and to use their barns only for storing animal food. This specialization had antecedents in the colonial period but it was to become widespread in the nineteenth century in Franklin County and elsewhere as more farmers became attuned to increased production for the market. The bank barns of Pennsylvania and the Valley of Virginia were different manifestations of related phenomena. Increased herd size and larger numbers of acres put into production encouraged farmers to build larger barns or barn complexes to earn higher profits. Bank barns were not used in Franklin County until after the Civil War. Instead progressive farmers in the valley lowlands began to build what Thomas Hubka has called the "New England–type barn."[17]

The New England barn was distinguished by the arrangement of the runway on the gable end of the building rather than on the long side. The form was known in the valley by the end of the eighteenth century, although it is difficult to prove this conclusively. One key bit of evidence is that New England barns are simply wider than traditional English barns—they have to be to accommodate the runway. The Alexander barn in Northfield Farms is 32 feet 10 inches wide, about as narrow as these barns get. This works out to a hay bay 12 feet wide, a runway of 11 feet 6 inches, and a stable of 9 feet 3 inches (Fig. 6:12). Most New England barns are at least 40 feet wide and many are wider. Of the barns listed on the 1798 South Hadley list, only nine were large enough to meet the size requirements for a New England barn, and, of these, only two or three were probably built in this fashion. There is little reason to think that this pattern was different further up the Connecticut River. In a letter to his brother-in-law, Elihu Hoyt, written in 1810, Justin Hitchcock of Deerfield passed on the news that "Last Thursday we raised Mr. E. H. Williams' barn. It is an enormous sized barn and covers more ground I believe than any building in town." Williams was an important cattle raiser and the son of wealthy landowners in Roxbury, Massachusetts. The commercial needs of the cattle business required storage of large quantities of hay and grains; Williams's barn was 40 by 90 feet. Clearly, it was big enough to merit Hitchcock's notice, but it would not remain the largest barn in town. By the mid nineteenth century, farmers like Rowland Stebbins of Deerfield owned barns that were even larger. In May of 1848, the Deerfield correspondent reported in the Greenfield newspaper, "Rowland Stebbins has raised the largest barn in our town." The Stebbins barn was 40 by 100 feet and dwarfed everything nearby. Despite its large size, it was not built in the form of a New England barn. Instead, Stebbins had his carpenters construct an English-

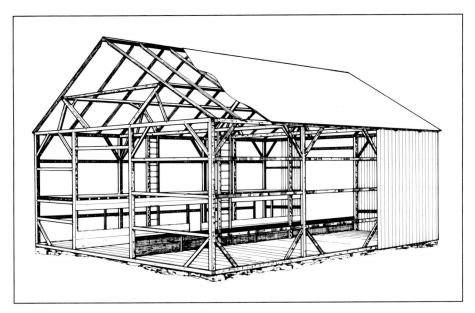

Figure 6:12. Alexander Barn, Northfield Farms, Northfield, Massachusetts, ca. 1830–50. (Measured and drawn by the author.)

type barn with two runways. Because we know barn sizes from documents, we cannot assume, then, that size alone is a clear indication of a barn type; we must go and look for surviving examples before we can interpet them.[18]

Since they were rare to begin with, very few eighteenth-century New England–type barns have survived. The Joseph Stebbins barn was probably one of the earliest examples in Deerfield (Fig. 6:13). Stebbins was one of that community's wealthiest farmers and he owned one of the biggest houses in town. (See Figs. 7:7 and 7:8.) Like other early barns in the region, the Stebbins barn had shouldered posts. While this construction detail was not proof that it was an eighteenth-century building, Stebbins had the means and, as a wealthy cattle raiser, the need to undertake the construction of a very large, 42-by-60-foot barn. The barn was located to the northwest of his house, separated from human space by a little more than a hundred feet. To the south of the barn in the former stockyard, archaeologists recovered the outlines of the well that was once used to water Stebbins's fat cattle (Fig. 6:14). The drive ran along the north side of the house to the barn runway. Through the runway and down the farm lane that ran west of the barn were tillage fields, mowing, and pasture. The Stebbins barn mediated between the public street in front of the house and the farm fields behind. Somewhat like a factory, Stebbins's barn was the collection and processing point for raw materials that entered at one end. Out the other end emerged the product in the form of fat-

Figure 6:13. Joseph Stebbins Barn, Deerfield, Massachusetts, ca. 1790–1819. (Drawn by the author.)

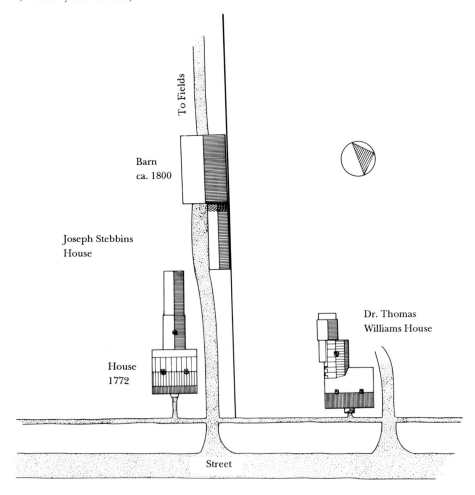

To Fields

Barn
ca. 1800

Joseph Stebbins
House

Dr. Thomas
Williams House

House
1772

Street

Figure 6:14. Site Plan, Joseph Stebbins Farmstead, Deerfield, Massachusetts, ca. 1790–1819. (Drawn by the author.)

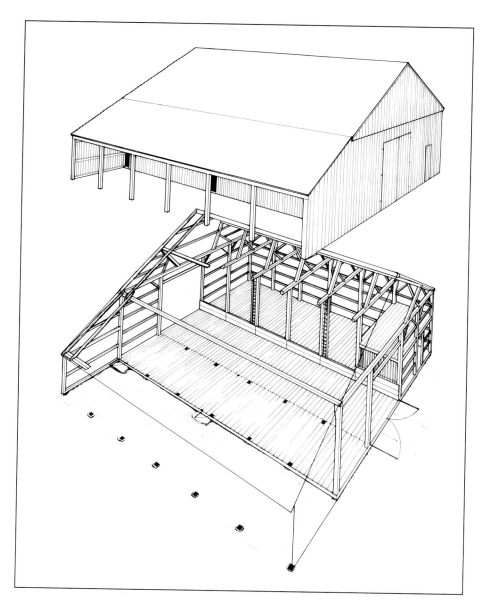

Figure 6:15. Walter Field Barn, Northfield, Massachusetts, 1795–1810.
(Measured and drawn by the author.)

tened beef bound for market. It was this systematic, specialized use of the landscape that was the key to progressive farmers' improving productivity.

A more complete example of an early New England–type barn is the Walter Field barn in Northfield (Fig. 6:15). The original section of the barn is 42 by 60 feet; in the fall of 1836, several decades after the first period of construction, Samuel and Calvin Stearns recorded building a shed onto Walter Field's barn and repairing the barn roof. The original section of the barn was framed up with shouldered posts and was very heavily constructed, a fact that contributed to its long life. The bents were only 10 feet apart. Later New England–type barns in the region were consistently built with bents spaced 12 feet apart. The carpenters who framed the Field barn created an unusually complex joint to hold the girts and plates together and lock them onto the tops of each post (Fig. 6:16). No other barn of this type in the county is known to have this complex framing feature. The heavy construction suggests an early date because, without traditional experience or known load factors, the carpenters who worked on the project built very cautiously. Other features also imply an eighteenth-century date for the structure. The hay bay has one extra supporting post on either end of the building—a detail that is known on eighteenth-century English-style barns in the region but which builders did not retain in the nineteenth century. Beneath the south-facing shed the Stearnes probably added in 1836 is some of the original vertical board siding, heavily weathered. Clearly this siding was exposed to several decades of sun and rain before the shed addition covered it up. The circumstantial evidence points logically to a date of 1790–1810, but all of the siding under the shed is attached with machine-headed cut nails. There is no other evidence that hand-wrought nails were used. Nail chronologies have generally indicated that cut nails with machine-made heads were not available until the 1810s, but recent research suggests that they were made much earlier in New England, probably by the late 1780s or early 1790s. In any case there is no documentary information to unequivocally establish the date of this barn. The best estimate is that it was built sometime between 1795 and 1807, years when the New England economy was strong from overseas demand and before the economic shocks that began with the Embargo Act of 1807 took hold.[19]

Although the Field barn was thoroughly remodeled to accommodate twentieth-century health codes for dairy farmers, enough evidence survives to reconstruct some elements of the structure's early appearance, particularly for the hay bay. By comparing this evidence with that of later barns, we can recreate a picture of how the structure functioned. The barn was oriented roughly east-west, with the runway off-center toward the south side. The hay bay was 17 feet wide and extended the length of the structure, except for a horse stall in the northeast corner of the barn. Ladders attached to two of the posts afforded access to the loft over the runway. A 31-inch-high knee wall helped keep hay from falling into the runway. On the south side was the stable for the cattle. It was 12 feet wide, extended the length of the building and also had a ladder to the loft. There was a floor over the stable that provided support for additional hay storage above. Two doors opened from the cattle bay to the barnyard on the south side. The shed that the Stearnses built

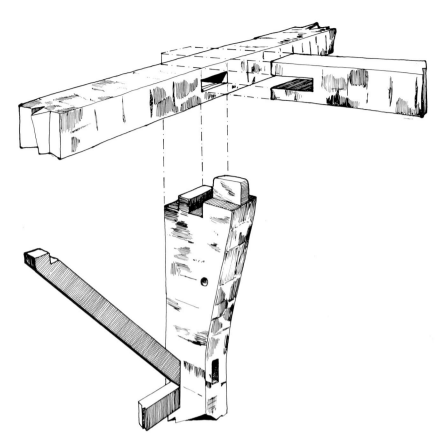

Figure 6:16. Framing Detail, Walter Field Barn. (Measured and drawn by the author.)

was added to provide shelter to the stock when they were not in the barn feeding or being milked. These barns were carefully designed to integrate the functions of storing fodder, sheltering stock, and fattening them for market. Hay was located over and opposite the mangers where the animals were fed. The cattle bay was large enough to hold more than a dozen animals with room to spare, far more than a family needed for household food supplies. By regional standards, the Field barn was as sophisticated a scheme for fattening and caring for livestock as existed in late eighteenth-century New England.

Although the New England barn was initially a specialized form built by a few elite farmers, many of whom were in the cattle-fattening business, it became more common by the 1840s when middling farmers like Stephen Alexander were building them (See Fig. 6:12). These middling barns were generally smaller—the Alexander barn was 32 feet 10 inches by 36 feet—but they incorporated the same features that the Walter Field barn had tested forty years before. By the 1850s few of the area's commercial farmers con-

Figure 6:17. Elisha Wells Barn, Deerfield, Massachusetts, ca. 1852–60.
(Photograph by the author.)

tinued to build English-style barns and many older barns were altered to
include an opening in the gable end. One common conversion was related
to the gable-end barn type. The basic plan used a two-bay-wide bent system
which meant that the barn's runway extended from one side of the gable end
to the back of the barn. Usually, this runway was oriented to the southern
or warmer side of the barn. On many of these barns, farmers added a lean-to
in order to expand the barn to a bay-runway-bay form, a practice that created
an asymmetrical barn with the roof ridge distinctively off-center. Some of
these barns were built with integral lean-tos; in other cases the lean-to was
clearly added later. It is not clear why these barns were built the way they
were, nor is it known where the tradition began. They appear in both upland
and lowland towns (Fig. 6:17).[20]

Another type of barn was not so much a different barn form as it was
an alternative arrangement of house and barn. Known to cultural geographers as the "connecting barn," the plan joined house and barn with a series
of sheds. While many of these barns were originally built separately from the
house, over time the number of sheds increased to a point at which house
and barn were joined. Not all of these structures were evolutionary. A few
wealthy farmers like Zebina Stebbins seem to have connected barns and houses
in one large construction project, but few farmers probably had the capital
to emulate this approach to building (Fig. 6:18). In Franklin County, the con-

Landscape and Material Life in Franklin County, Massachusetts

necting barn tradition appears to have begun in the 1830s when farmers began to employ Greek Revival styles in their house plans and, as we will see, experimented with a wider variety of house forms. Very few eighteenth-century houses in the region were modified into connecting barn units. The connecting barn tradition violated, at least visually, the long-standing New England resistance to mixing animals and humans in the same structure. That resistance remained inviolate in the oldest sections of the county where the established tradition was to separate house and barn. In the more recently settled areas, however, where land was organized in dispersed farmsteads rather than in nucleated villages, connecting barns were more common. It may be that the newer settlements had fewer established traditions and a greater willingness to venture new ideas. It may be that the more recently settled areas were going through a period of refining farmstead structures at a point when the connecting barn pattern was current. Older towns already contained well-developed farmsteads by this point and had fewer reasons to undertake much new construction. Whatever the reason, the tradition certainly existed by the late 1830s, when John Warner Barber was preparing to publish his views of New England towns. In a view of Turners Falls, he illustrated a farm on a distant hillside with a house and connecting barn. Similarly, in his view of Shelburne Falls, a manufacturing village, he depicted at least one house with a connecting barn (Fig. 6:19).[21]

Whether separated or connected, houses and outbuildings defined the immediate locus of household operations. Numerous real estate advertisements in the nineteenth century mention farms "with convenient outbuildings," but documentary information on these structures is difficult to find. Wealthy fami-

Figure 6:18. Zebina Stebbins Farm, Deerfield, Massachusetts, before 1852. This view is from a wall map of Deerfield published in 1852. (Courtesy, David R. Proper.)

Figure 6:19. View of Shelburne Falls. From John Warner Barber, *Historical Collections*, 1839. (Courtesy, Pocumtuck Valley Memorial Association.)

lies had more outbuildings than middling and poorer sorts and their barn yards were evidently more specialized, a pattern that persisted throughout much of the nineteenth century. By the 1850s Julius Robbins's property in West Deerfield was similar to many middling farms in the region. He owned a house with a kitchen ell and an English-type barn (Fig. 6:20). The farm was across the road from his parents' place and up the road from the district schoolhouse. He apparently owned no other buildings, and his barn followed the traditional pattern of housing his stock, fodder, and tools.

By contrast, a mile and a half away, Cephas Hoyt owned a farm with two houses and a number of outbuildings. In 1831, the year Cephas Hoyt died, the farm consisted of two hundred acres, fifty of which were rich meadowlands extending from the Deerfield River to the road that led to Greenfield. In a letter to Henry Colman, who had inquired about the farm, cousin Elihu Hoyt wrote that these meadows were

> manured by the backwater of the Connecticut River (about 1 mile distant) annually. — nearly all this tract is used for mowing produced the best of hay in abundance, sometimes 100 tones [*sic*] in a year. — there is a balance between twenty and thirty acres of tillage land on the banks of the Deerfield river & near the connecticut, which lies above high water mark — which is well suited to corn, oats, rye and the residue is situated still higher, consisting of pasturing, orcharding & rye tillage & woodland, there is from seventy to eighty acres of the latter. — The buildings are from forty to fifty years old, there are two dwelling houses, two barns & some small outbuildings, one of the houses is small, & only one

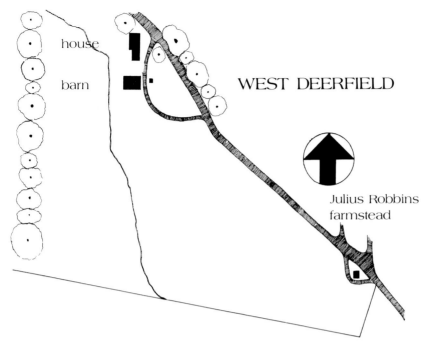

Figure 6:20. Julius Robbins Farmstead, West Deerfield, Deerfield, Massachusetts, ca. 1850–80. (Drawn by the author.)

story high, the other is two stories and probably about forty feet by thirty, with a kitchen, woodhouse & adjoining.

This landscape represented the rarest type of farm in the county, owned by the smallest percentage of wealthy farmers, whose ancestry frequently dated back to the area's first settlement. Creating landed wealth took time. The Hoyts, Jonathan and his son Cephas, constructed the farmstead over two generations. It is not surprising that among the Hoyts' outbuildings there were still impermanent structures in the first decade of the nineteenth century. On November 22, 1810, Jonathan Hoyt recorded in his diary that a carpenter was framing a new cowhouse to replace the "Old slab hovel" that his son and a hired man had torn down the day before. The structure was finished in five days and the cows were put in.[22]

These examples illustrate the difficulty of describing "typical" patterns of farmsteads, for wealthy farmsteads like the Hoyt estate had ephemeral elements that were common to farms elsewhere in the region. While cowhouses were fairly common buildings by the 1800s, especially in lowland communities, we know far less about hovels and corn houses, two of the outbuildings recorded in documentary sources. The Direct Tax List of 1798 listed six hovels in South Hadley. They were probably simple shelters for animals sup-

Table 6:4

Number of Hovels by Size, South Hadley, Massachusetts, 1798

No.	Size	Sq. ft.	No.	Size	Sq. ft.
1	20 x 15	300	1	28 x 12	336
1	20 x 18	360	1	40 x 15	600
1	40 x 20	800	1	38 x 28	1064

Table 6:5

Number of Corn Houses by Size, South Hadley, Massachusetts, 1798

No.	Size	Sq. ft.	No.	Size	Sq. ft.
1	14 x 12	168	1	16 x 12	192
1	20 x 10	200	3	18 x 14	252
1	18 x 15	270	4	18 x 16	288
3	20 x 16	320	1	21 x 17	357
1	24 x 20	480			

ported by posts set into the ground, but they were not particularly small as Table 6:4 shows. The examples that are listed were usually owned by prosperous farmers or merchants. None of these buildings has survived; they were not meant to. The impermanent nature of construction did not signal poverty or marginality, an interpretation often associated with earthfast construction practices. When Cephas Hoyt tore down his slab hovel and replaced it with a framed cowhouse, a more permanent type of structure, he was completing a cycle of building that grew out of a rational strategy to meet his needs. Like other farmers he built permanent buildings when it made sense. The pattern for outbuildings is consistent with that of dwellings; families in the region generally sought to erect durable buildings—whether for cows or humans.

Like hovels, corn houses were also uncommon, probably because most families did not need a separate building to store grains. Again the 1798 South Hadley list is instructive. The town had only sixteen corn houses in that year. They were smaller than most of the hovels and probably better built to protect the grain from infestation with vermin (Table 6:5). While outbuildings for livestock tended to be long and narrow, corn houses were more nearly square in proportion. The corn barn built by Calvin Stearns for Lyman Gilbert in Northfield Farms in 1835 is one of the few surviving examples that can be precisely dated (Fig. 6:21). It was nearly square, 16 by 16 with a porch in the front of the building that provided shelter. Without the porch the build-

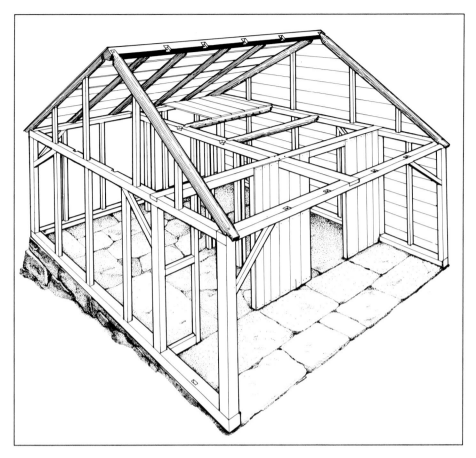

Figure 6:21. Corn Barn, built by Calvin Stearns for Lyman Gilbert, Northfield Farms, Northfield, Massachusetts, 1835. (Measured and drawn by the author.)

ing would measure 12 by 16 feet, the size of a corn house on the South Hadley list. Two doors gave access from the porch into two separate cribs. An attic loft extended over the porch, but storage space was limited. None of the interior partitions has survived but the mortise holes for the stud partition that separated the two sides of the building are still visible. The building had a massive stone floor of cut granite slabs set on a susbstantial stone foundation; the floor sealed the building from stray mice, rats, chipmunks, squirrels, and birds that would flourish on the contents stored there.[23]

For most farm families, dwellings and barns met most storage needs, but when they needed space, they could attach a shed to either the house or the barn. The Sheldon family of Deerfield expanded their storage areas by attaching sheds to their eighteenth-century barn (Fig. 6:22). One shed held tools, another housed the horses, another sheltered the oxen for the family's stall-feeding business, and another held grain. If the need was great enough,

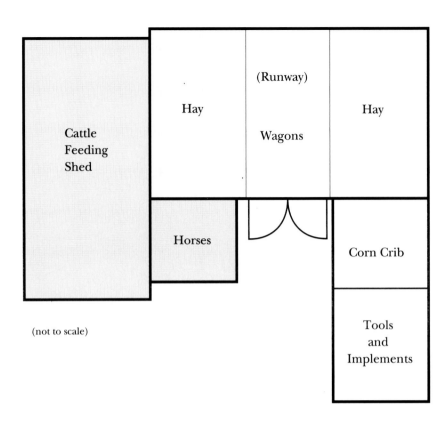

Figure 6:22. Reconstructed Diagram of the Sheldon Barn, Deerfield, Massachusetts, built over time between 1770s and 1850s. (Drawn by the author.)

it was possible to move most farm structures, but it is hard to learn how frequently this was done. Judging from documentary sources and surviving structures it is clear that people sometimes moved buildings, but it would be a mistake to assume that farmers were constantly moving buildings over the Franklin County landscape before the Civil War. In the five decades after 1800, Calvin Stearns, Northfield's most prominent antebellum carpenter, moved fewer than a dozen buildings. His accounts typically were filled with contracts to tear down older structures or frame new ones. The sheds, lean-tos, and barns Stearns built were intended to last under normal conditions, but the pressures to modify the landscape were great enough to justify the demolition of older buildings that were in poor repair or that no longer served family needs. Despite their predilection to build durable buildings, then, men and women in Franklin County created a landscape of steady change.[24]

Near most of the region's farmhouses was a place for a garden. Often these gardens were situated to take advantage of a southern exposure, for

Table 6:6

List of Garden Seeds Available in Greenfield, Massachusetts, 1820

Asparagus	Endive	Peas
Beans	Indian Corn	Pumpkins
Beets	Sweet Corn	Rhubarb
Broccoli	Lettuce	Radish
Cabbage	Melons	Spinach
Cauliflower	Onions	Squash
Carrots	Parsnips	Turnips
Celery	Parsley	Tomatoes
Cucumbers	Peppers	

with careful planning the sunlight would warm the soil faster in the spring and reduce the risk of frost in the fall. Gardens varied in size and usually were enclosed by some kind of board fence to exclude small animals. Root crops, squashes, peas, beans, and other vegetables that kept well were staples in most family gardens, but herbs, salad greens, and seasonal vegetables were also popular. Garden seeds were readily available from merchants in the region by the 1790s, and newspapers carried many advertisements recording the variety of types available. By the 1820s the seed business was well developed (Table 6:6). Many seeds came in several varieties. Not all families planted extensive gardens, but most people in the region had gardens with a number of these fruits and vegetables. A few were avid horticulturalists, interested in experimenting with a wide variety of fruits and vegetables. Dr. William Stoddard Williams left a detailed description of his 1823 Deerfield garden that permits a visual reconstruction of its appearance (Fig. 6:23). Williams's garden was not typical in its scale or variety. His horticultural interests were well known locally; he was a talented amateur scientist, and he used his plant knowledge professionally as a physician. Williams laid out his garden in beds. He seems generally to have planted his seeds in rows spaced a foot apart, but the arrangement depended upon the type of plant. There were at least seventeen beds devoted to vegetables. Two were for parsnips, two contained beets, two held cultivars of the cabbage family, another held salad fixings, and in a few places there were herbs such as parsley and sage. He also devoted one bed to melons including muskmelons, watermelon, and cantaloupes. Williams's garden was designed for family needs. It emphasized root crops and vegetables that stored well, but it also included salad greens for seasonal variety. Like the location of the house and outbuildings, this was a carefully planned landscape feature located behind the house, close to the family kitchen and dining table.[25]

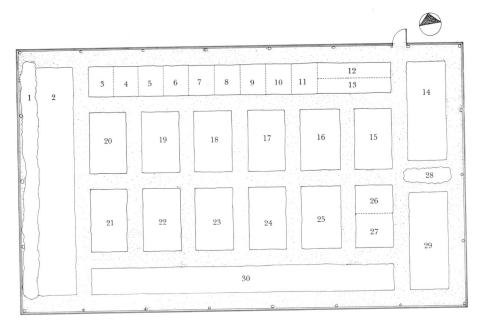

1	Bayberries	21	Pole Beans
2	Marrow Fat Peas		(Goose Bean)
	Chesterfield Peas		(White Cranberry)
	Vermont Peas		(Thousand for One)
3	Early Frame Purple Radish	22	Sweet Marjoram
4	White Cabbage Lettuce		Parsley
5	Early Frame Salmon Radish		Sage
6	Imperial Cabbage Lettuce	23	Blood Beets
7	Short Top Scarlet Radish	24	Red Beets
8	Peppergrass	25	Carrots
9	London Scarlet Radish	26	Red Cabbage
10	Peppergrass	27	Turnip Cabbage
11	White Turnip Radish	28	Currents
12	Leeks	29	Early Cucumber
13	Tennis Ball Lettuce		Long Cucumber
14	Asparagus		Cantalope
15	Fox Glove		Watermelon (Seed from Virginia)
	Savoy Cabbage		Watermelon
16	Carrots		Musk Melon
17	Carrot Parsnips		Mandrakes
18	Carrot Parsnips	30	Blue Potatoes
19	White Onion		
20	Lazy Beans		
	Pole Beans		
	(East Arlington)		
	(White Pole)		

Figure 6:23. Diagram of William Stoddard Williams's Garden, 1823.
(Courtesy, Pocumtuck Valley Memorial Association.)

Many families also supplemented their diets and incomes with orchards. John Wilson also recorded some of his planting experiments in his memorandum book and sometimes noted the page numbers of the magazine he got his ideas from. The diagram of his Deerfield orchard illustrates his bent toward careful organization and scientific experiment (Fig. 6:24). Only a small minority of individuals approached horticulture with such intellectual or scientific zeal. Most families planted gardens to augment household food supplies, and in most cases women seemed to manage them. Like Wilson's plan, most orchards in Franklin County contained apple trees. Some farmers grew pears, cherries, and peaches, but not as successfully as apples. Epaphras Hoyt wrote in May 1806, "Apple trees put forth their leaves the 6th of the month; peach trees were in full blossom the 13th; cherries and pears the 19th; apple blossoms began to appear the 17th, and on the 20th they were in full bloom. Much of the peach trees on our old intervale and houselot lands in this town, are nearly dead: these trees for several years past have flourished and produced fruit plentifully; but the soil of our lowland does not seem to be congenial to them, they are apt to winter-kill." Apples and pears also flourished in the uplands. William Cobb of Warwick commented in the same year as Hoyt, "We have had pears and fruit of the stone kind in great plenty. The quantity of apples in proportion to our orchards will be very moderate." Despite variation in yields, apples dominated because the trees withstood harsh winters and the fruit could be preserved in the form of cider.[26]

Cider making was a fairly common business in the area. During the years of temperance reform in the 1830s, when some apple orchards in New England were cut down, Franklin County farmers continued to produce. It was possible to make cider at home, but most farmers seem to have taken their apples to mills that had specialized equipment. Some cider mills were associated with distilleries that converted the cider to brandy. A description of Christopher Tyler Arms's early nineteenth-century distillery noted: "Apples from the county round were sent to the mill, and barrels of cider lined the street on either side for a considerable distance. As the cider was needed for distilling, it was drawn from the barrels through a trough into huge vats, which stood on a floor of the building that was below the level of the street. There were about twenty of these vats, and each held from thirty to forty barrels of cider." As it was needed, cider was pumped from the storage vats to a still which distilled the cider into a substance called "low wine." This liquid was distilled again to make cider brandy. The distillery often ran on a twenty-four-hour basis and required constant watching, for the heat had to be kept even to prevent cider from boiling over and ruining the process. The brandy was either used at home or sold for ready cash. Few farmers, however, seem to have had large enough orchards to specialize in fruit production for market

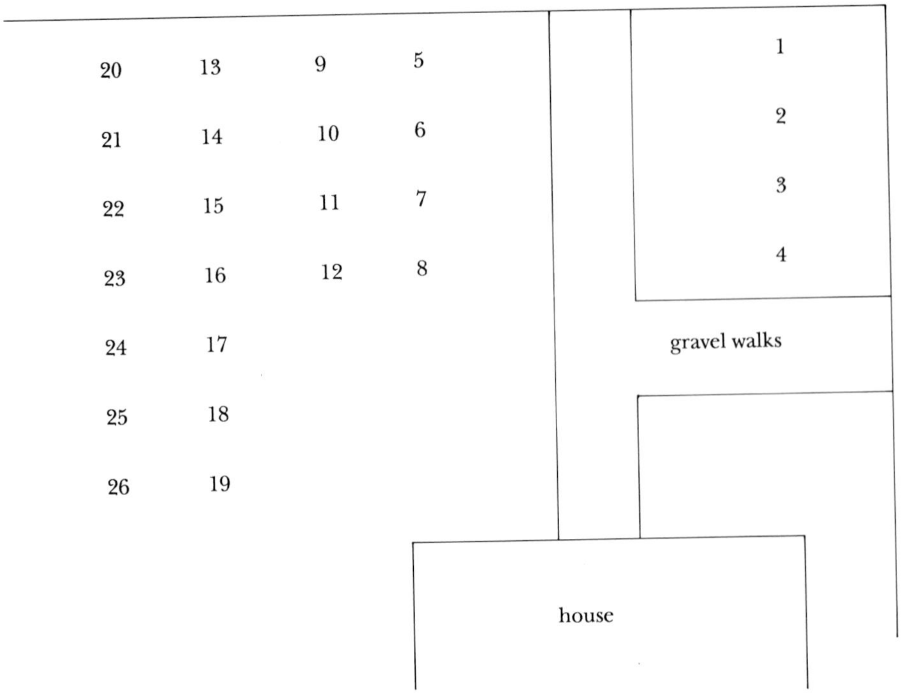

20   13   9   5

21   14   10   6   1

22   15   11   7   2

23   16   12   8   3

24   17   4

25   18   gravel walks

26   19

house

List of Trees in John Wilson's Orchard

1. French Rinette	14. Red Melacaton
2. Red Melacaton	15. Quince (Apple Shaped)
3. O [unreadable]	16. Hop Tree
4. Grey [unreadable]	17. Red Melacaton
5. Golden Pippen	18. Standard Peach
6. Peach (autumn)	19. Royal Peach
7. French Apple Dwarf	20. Catalpa
8. French Apple Dwarf	21. Red Melacaton
9. Roman Nectarine	22. Red Melacaton
10. Large Bogardus Bud (Fine Peach)	23. Red Melacaton
11. [unreadable]	24. ? Cherry
12. Roman Nectarine	25. Madeira Nut
13. Standard Peach	26. Large Holland Plum

Figure 6:24. Diagram of John Wilson's Orchard, Deerfield, Massachusetts, ca. 1845. (Courtesy, Pocumtuck Valley Memorial Association.)

purposes. Most people kept their gardens and orchards for home use, and there is little indication in period documents that fruit and vegetable growing expanded very much before 1850 when the railroad made it easier to ship perishable produce rapidly.[27]

Considered as a whole, the yards around farmsteads were organized to take advantage of specific site problems or opportunities. They were arranged in hierarchic fashion with the more formal and ornamental yards out front and the messier working areas to the south side of structures or to rear door yards. The region's farmsteads, like family production strategies, contained features that provided security for the household unit and simultaneously augmented commercial choices. The property around the region's farmhouses extended the notion of domestic control to the wider landscape and established disciplined hierarchies of space. To the front was a formal statement of public etiquette and prestige that operated in much the same way that a formal parlor inside a house conditioned social responses. To the rear of the house were the barns and outbuildings. Their size and state of repair conveyed much information about the financial well-being and aspirations of the owners. Farm families moved impressive amounts of dirt with scrapers and hand tools in this intensively used zone to create a smooth, graceful setting. Hillocks were cut down and hollows were filled in. Slopes were often terraced near the house to enhance its artificial context, distancing the occupants further from the more chaotic reality of the natural world. During the ninety years preceding the Civil War, then, families in Franklin County not only acquired work discipline, they imposed it on their landscape.

Chapter 7

Dwellings

As he rode through the Connecticut Valley lowlands in 1789, George Washington recorded his observations on the region's architecture. He noted that there was a "great similitude in their buildings—the general fashion of which is a Chimney (always of stone or brick) and a door in the middle, with a staircase fronting the latter—two flush stories with a very good show of sash and glass windows—the size generally in from 30 to 50 feet in length, and from 20 to 30 in width, exclusive of a back shed, which seems to be added as the family increases." He was clearly impressed. Although Mount Vernon and the great plantation houses of Washington's social peers were very large, most middling planters in Virginia and the Chesapeake region lived in small one- or two-room houses. Many of these houses were built of log or light timber framing, quite a few were in poor condition, and only the best plantations had the equivalent of a "very good show of sash and glass windows." Understandably, then, he was conscious of the differences between the housing stock of the two regions.[1]

What Washington described with considerable precision was a central chimney house, a form that settlers had brought to New England during the Great Migration. Local carpenters modified the details over time, but they continued to build central chimney houses in the Connecticut Valley and elsewhere until the 1840s or 1850s, when other styles became more fashionable. They also built other house forms that Washington did not see or else did not bother to record. Like the landscape of farmsteads, the area's domestic architecture narrates a rich tale of variations in agricultural wealth, age of settlement, class distinctions, and individual aspirations. What Washington and most of his contemporaries wrote descriptions of—what have usually survived from the eighteenth and nineteenth centuries—were buildings that represented the upper strata of the built environment and that were more characteristic of lowland communities. Up in the hill towns on either side of the lowlands, houses were usually not so large nor so old. Many of these upland farmhouses are gone, abandoned in the late nineteenth or the first decades of the twentieth century to decay and collapse. The present terrain, then, is an archaeological fragment of a landscape that changed many times. It underrepresents the number of middling dwellings that once were the most common forms in Franklin County and overrepresents elite structures. We can best learn how people lived, not by conjuring the past entirely through the present landscape, but by merging information derived from documents and from standing structures to reconstruct what the domestic landscape was like.

Dudley Woodbridge was a Harvard classmate of Ebenezer Hinsdale, a Deerfield youth who was the son of the town's largest landholders. In 1728 both of them set out on horseback from Cambridge, heading for the Connecticut Valley. Upon their arrival they tarried in Deerfield for several days and Hinsdale took his friend around to see local sites and meet important people: the monument of stones at Bloody Brook where valley troops were ambushed during King Philip's War in 1675, the Sheldon house where the front door still bore the scars Indian tomahawks had made on the night of February 29, 1704, and Deerfield's most distinguished citizen, the Reverend John Williams, whose account of the Deerfield massacre on that famous night became a New England best-seller. Woodbridge kept a small journal during the trip and on the back flyleaf he sketched some buildings. One of them was clearly the John Sheldon house, for the drawing closely resembles the image captured by a photographer in 1848, the year the building was taken down (Figs. 7:1 and 7:2). Woodbridge also sketched three meetinghouses, although only one was standing in 1728, labeling them "Deerfield Meetinghouses." Elsewhere on the page, he added a barn, a horse, a tree, a well sweep, and several houses. This sketch is the best visual evidence we have for the appearance of early eighteenth-century dwellings in the Massachusetts part of the valley.[2]

What is significant in the drawing is the variety of structures Woodbridge recorded. The house form Washington observed in Connecticut was one of the buildings he drew. So were smaller structures of one or two rooms without central chimneys, with what may have been diamond-paned casement sash rather than sash with rectangular panes. None of these smaller houses survives, but they illustrate the diversity of the town during its third rebuilding—a painful gestation period occasioned by two major periods of Indian warfare. This early landscape was not as regular as the one currently visible. In 1986 archaeological researchers working on the Nims lot in Deerfield uncovered a late seventeenth-century foundation of a structure that was approximately 15 by 20 feet. The building lined up with magnetic north placing it at a 23° angle to the town street. By the middle of the eighteenth century, the family had replaced this structure with a large two-story New England square-plan

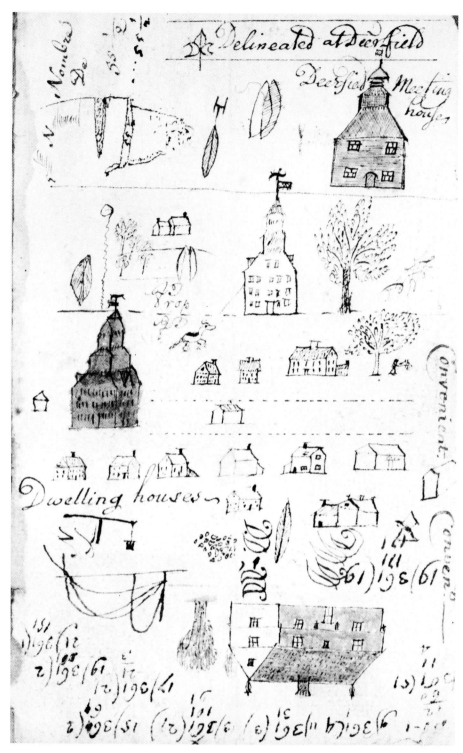

Figure 7:1. Dudley Woodbridge, Sketch of Deerfield, 1728.
(Courtesy, Massachusetts Historical Society.)

Figure 7:2. John Sheldon House, Deerfield, Massachusetts, 1848.
(Courtesy, Pocumtuck Valley Memorial Association Library.)

house that, like most other dwellings in town, lined up parallel with the town street. (See Fig 7:11.) Thus, by the 1750s, Deerfield's architecture would appear more uniform, highly decorated, and formal than it had looked in the 1710s and 1720s.

Some of the early diversity reflected the town's relative instability as a new community rebuilding after the 1704 massacre. Analysis of the town's politics in the seventeenth and early decades of the eighteenth centuries indicates that office holding was widely distributed among males and that most men over twenty-one participated in the community's political life. At a period when political life was more egalitarian and people were poorest, then, the domestic architecture along the town street was more diverse. Beginning in the 1730s, as class lines sharpened, politics became more stratified, and the community became wealthier, architectural *forms* on the old village street became, paradoxically, more alike. In a village setting, where neighbors' judgments were close at hand and where competition to maintain standards of material respectability was most visible, the reduction of sharp differences in building forms encouraged families to organize their lives in similar, more predictable ways. Evidently, the voters of Deerfield granted unequal social and political power to the elite without giving away their rights to assert personal equality through building form.[3]

Dwellings   153

Figure 7:3. Ebenezer Wells House, Deerfield, Massachusetts, ca. 1743–51. (Photograph by the author.)

Local attempts to build houses with somewhat similar forms did not mean that differences in status or wealth were unapparent or that the gentry did not attempt to imply their superiority by means of their buildings. During the 1740s to 1770s, many of the town's elite families rebuilt or constructed mansion houses in the Georgian style (Fig. 7:3). The majority were built with central chimneys. A smaller number of gentry houses, particularly those owned by members of the Williams family or their kin, had central passages. As Kevin Sweeney has shown, central passage houses with elaborate doorways and gambrel roofs became both a status symbol and a statement of power that entwined the local gentry and their regional kinship networks in a competition for identity and prestige. Yet these elite architectural statements represented choices that were logical, albeit expensive, elaborations of traditional forms. For the most part they did not violate the basic design logic of two-story, five-bay, single-pile design that increasingly dominated the landscape of the lowland villages in the Connecticut Valley and that Washington or others noted. Thomas Anburey, journeying through Enfield and Suffield, Connecticut, in 1778 observed that he "could not help remarking that these houses are all after the same plan." Anburey was wrong. The houses in the valley's lowlands were not all of the same plan, but to outsiders like him or

Washington the similarities outweighed the differences. To local residents, the variations in size and detail reinforced the status and aspirations of local families, for neighbors understood architectural nuances in ways outsiders could not.[4]

The most impressive feature of lowland architecture was the number of large two-story houses. Along the main streets of lowland villages like Enfield, Suffield, Springfield, Northampton, Hadley, Hatfield, Sunderland, and Deerfield, the majority of families lived in two-story structures by the 1770s. Although the scale and proportions of these buildings were generally similar, architectural details set them apart. Across the road from the fourth Deerfield meetinghouse, Elijah Williams's dwelling (1755–56) represented the gentry's vision of a mansion house. Its wide central passage, window seats in the parlors, and elaborately detailed door established a standard that others in the community could and did look to for inspiration and as a measure of status (Figs. 7:4 and 7:5). In the pantheon of the "River Gods"—a period term applied to the Connecticut Valley gentry who dominated the region's political, social, and cultural life before the Revolution—Elijah Williams was a relatively minor deity. Others in town soon surpassed the stylistic challenge his house posed.

Maintaining cultural hegemony with buildings was difficult because competition was expensive. The architectural monuments that the region's political elite erected at such great cost in the 1750s and early 1760s were challenged by other elites whose concern with their own status rivaled or eclipsed the River Gods. By the 1770s wealthy families in the valley who were not tied in with the Williams patronage system outbuilt the River Gods and simultaneously challenged the Williamses' control of the valley's political affairs. While all of this building activity coincided with changes in the River Gods' political fortunes, it was also part of a broader pattern of change in the valley's architecture. These changes showed up first in the lowland towns established in the seventeenth century, towns that had prospered by a combination of agricultural wealth, steady population growth, and royal political patronage during King George's and the Seven Years' Wars. Within thirteen years Williams's innovations paled in comparison to the house Joseph Barnard built on the other side of the common. After inheriting a substantial fortune from his Salem merchant uncle, Barnard hired a local joiner, Benjamin Munn, to build a new house in 1769. The classically inspired segmental arched doorway, quoins at the corners of the clapboarded walls, double-hipped roof, and five-bay, double-pile floor plan made it the largest, most elaborate, and expensive dwelling built in the town to that time. The house reflected architectural modes that were fashionable in eastern New England and further south in the Connecticut Valley, and it solidified Barnard's position in town as a man of sophistication, wealth, and influence (Fig. 7:6). Several years later, Joseph

Figure 7:4. Elijah Williams House, Deerfield, Massachusetts, 1755–56.
(Photograph by the author.)

Stebbins built an even larger house several rods up the street that combined stylistic elements from the vocabulary of the River Gods' mansion houses and the pattern book–inspired doorway on Joseph Barnard's house (Figs. 7:7 and 7:8).

These two very large gentry dwellings were only the most conspicuous examples of the reorganization of the community's domestic architecture—a reorganization that extended to other less pretentious houses in the old village area. By the end of the Revolution, outsiders took note of this impressive rebuilding. Salem's distinguished minister, the Reverend William Bentley, traveling through town in the winter of 1782, noted: "The School is on the open square in which the church stands &n the side of it is the Burying ground. Back stands an elegant House belonging to Mr. Williams. There is a gate at each end of the Street, & about 60 houses in the Street in better style, than in any of the towns I saw." Bentley's description was testimony to the thoroughness with which Deerfield's residents modified the landscape that Dudley Woodbridge had recorded little more than half a century earlier. It is this rebuilt landscape, not the earlier one, that survives for modern tourists to admire.[5]

After 1800, this rebuilding was largely complete and Deerfield families in the old nucleated village center seemed relatively content with the way the

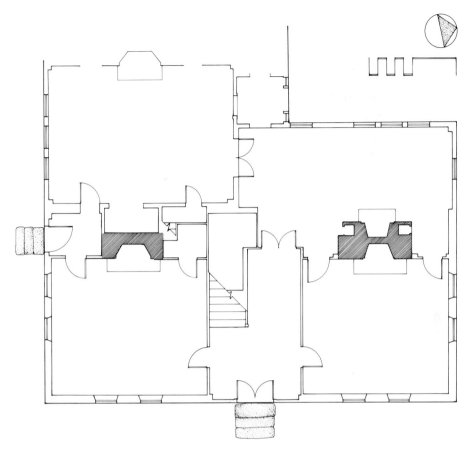

Figure 7:5. Plan, Elijah Williams House. (Redrawn by the author from Historic American Building Survey, National Park Service.)

town looked. Few houses in the Federal style and even fewer in the Greek Revival style were erected. But outside of the village in the areas settled in the 1750s, Deerfield farmers and mechanics rebuilt the landscape much later, and their dwellings consequently reflected newer styles. The same transformation took place seventeen miles upriver in Northfield. Although that town was first settled in the seventeenth century, the reorganization of Northfield's landscape took place a decade or two after Deerfield's. Similarly, after Greenfield (settled in the 1730s) blossomed into the region's leading community and central marketplace in the 1790s, talented architects and carpenters reshaped that town's buildings. Thus the patterns of stylish details that adorn the county's houses reflected the timing of economic tides and the maturation of landscapes. While the pattern is uneven, it appears that after the first permanent settlement in each town, the region's families generally took about two generations to create durable standards of housing that consistently survive. The earliest towns matured sooner and have the greatest density of surviving early

Figure 7:6. Joseph Barnard House, Deerfield, Massachusetts, 1769.
(Photograph by the author.)

Figure 7:7. Joseph Stebbins House, Deerfield, Massachusetts, 1772.
(Photograph by the author.)

buildings. Many of these houses persisted because they were large and well built, were owned by the same family for long periods of time, or met the needs of later occupants regardless of changing architectural tastes. Because of these factors, the material evidence from the present landscape favors the larger dwellings of substantial citizens (though not necessarily elites) rather than smaller inexpensive houses built for poorer families.

Some small houses from the eighteenth century have survived in lowland towns. Most of them have been greatly altered. One example built in Deerfield in the 1760s or 1770s is nearly square in configuration. It represents a variety of house that scholars have only recently recognized as a common New England house type, and which we might call the "New England square plan." The plan has an asymmetrical facade and a massive chimneystack set

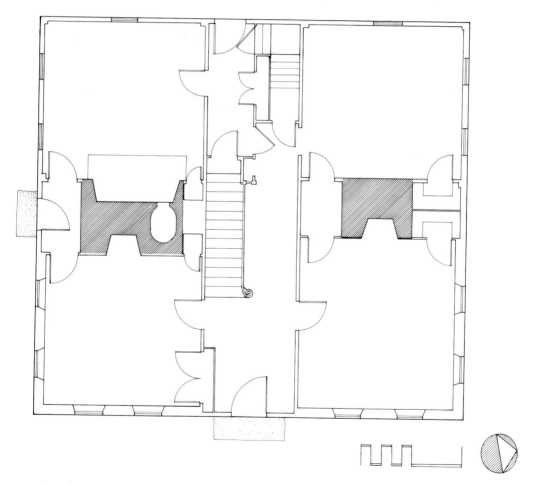

Figure 7:8. Plan, Joseph Stebbins House. (Redrawn by the author from plans by F. A. Loomis, Pocumtuck Valley Memorial Association.)

Figure 7:9. David Saxton House, Deerfield, Massachusetts, ca. 1761.
(Photograph by the author.)

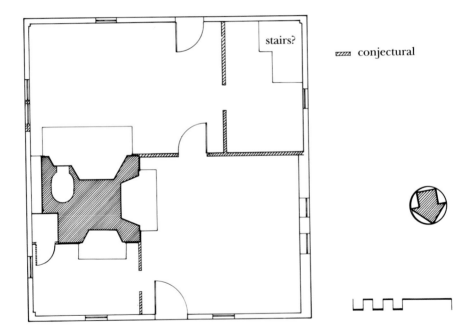

stairs?

conjectural

Figure 7:10. Reconstructed Plan, David Saxton House.
(Measured by J. Ritchie Garrison, Kevin M. Sweeney,
Amelia Miller; drawn by the author.)

off-center (Figs. 7:9 and 7:10). The front door opened directly into a parlor; the kitchen was in the rear. A pantry/storage room was located to the right of the door from the parlor to the kitchen on the west side of the structure. It probably contained the stairs that once led to an unfinished attic. To the left of the front entrance was a small heated room. At some point a lean-to addition (now removed and replaced with a modern ell) was added to the rear, but originally the house contained approximately eight hundred square feet, a significant proportion of which was taken up by chimney and fireplaces.[6]

This New England square plan also came in a two-story version (Fig. 7:11). The Nims house (ca. 1739) in Deerfield is the only surviving example of this form currently known in the county, but documentary records and photographs indicate that others existed. George Sheldon, Deerfield's town historian, believed that this type of square plan and the central chimney, hall-parlor plan were the two early forms local residents commonly built. Although the Nims family remodeled the parlor and changed the roof from a pitched to a gambel form sometime in the 1780s or 1790s and later added an ell in the nineteenth century, they did not modernize the original form by building an intervening passage or entry that barred visitors from the family's personal space. It is tempting to see in this arrangement a continuation of seventeenth-century practices of open rather than closed architecture, of direct public access to intimate family space, but appearances can be deceiving. In both the one- and two-story versions of the square plan, the public entry brought visitors to the most formal parlor. Work spaces such as the kitchen and the pantry were placed to the rear where family and close friends had direct access from the dooryard through side or rear doors. Thus the builders of these types of houses in Franklin County were already arranging rooms in a hierarchical manner by the mid eighteenth century. In two-room-deep houses, whether single-story, two-story, or lean-to form, builders put the most formal rooms up front near the public way, and the more chaotic work areas to the rear. In one-room-deep houses, work areas such as kitchens were often located on the south side of the house, frequently with a direct outlet to the dooryard nearby. Although New England square plan structures lack the formal bilateral Georgian symmetry that Henry Glassie and James Deetz have argued was the symbolic watershed between a seventeenth-century organic lifestyle and the rationalized patterns of Georgian Enlightenment thought, these structures represented a rational post-Newtonian reorganization of space into more specialized zones. This rational hierarchy of specialized functions, like the appearance of bilateral symmetry, embodied the architectural language of Enlightenment thought and marked the transformation from seventeenth-century lifeways to those of the nineteenth century, from organic forms open for public involvement in family domestic life to those that regimented and

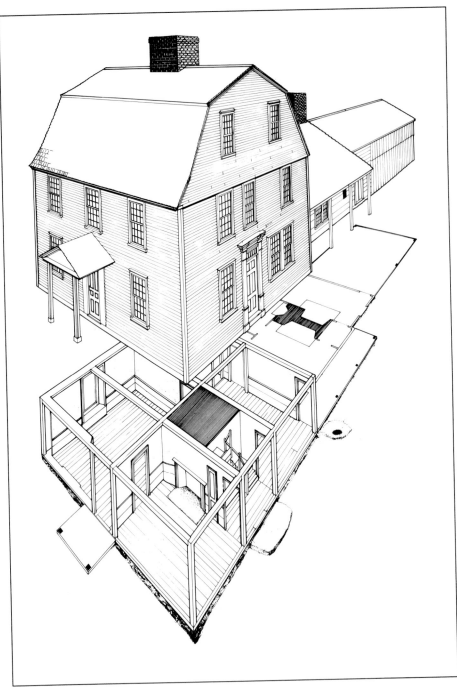

Figure 7:11. Nims House, Deerfield, Massachusetts, ca. 1739. (Drawn by the author.)

controlled access, directing visitors and family to portions of the house where certain behaviors were deemed appropriate.[7]

The most important spatial reorganization in the region's domestic architecture amplified these patterns by leaving intact much of the eighteenth-century house form but dramatically altering work patterns. In the last two decades of the eighteenth century builders increasingly added ells to earlier houses, or built new houses with the ells already attached. Previously, the principal means of adding space in most valley houses throughout the eighteenth century was to add a one- or two-story lean-to onto the back of the structure. These lean-tos might extend all or part of the way across the house. (See for example, Fig. 7:4.) Like most other architectural innovations, ells were first built by the area's gentry. One of the earliest was attached to the house of Dr. Thomas Williams of Deerfield, who added an ell sometime between 1748 and 1775 (Figs. 7:12 and 7:13). There were other early examples elsewhere in the region, but they were uncommon. The ell, like central passages, changed how people organized space and how they moved through the house. Most ells were in the rear of the house's main block and continued in a linear fashion toward the rear door and barnyards. Almost always these ells contained a kitchen — new ones in the case of additions to earlier structures — and many included a dining room. Beyond or next to the kitchen were spaces for a pantry or buttery, a woodshed, and, in the very rear, a privy. Pantries and butteries were known in earlier house forms, but the attachment of a wood shed and privy brought inside the dwelling house tasks that formerly had occurred outdoors or in separate structures. Archaeological research suggests that, prior to the Revolution, privies in the region were small separate structures located about sixty to one hundred feet from a back door. After the Revolution, families who constructed ells increasingly located a privy at or near the back of the woodshed, where its users could escape notice.[8]

It is hard to learn precisely when the implications of building an ell first became clear to middling farm families, but the advantages were clearly understood by a variety of people in the eighteenth century, even if they could not immediately afford to hire a carpenter. The evidence from the accounts of Calvin Stearns, a carpenter in Northfield, Massachusetts, helps define the timing more precisely. His accounts between 1800 and 1811 document the usual round of odd carpentry jobs and the building of sheds and ells. Stearns's own home, begun in 1805, included an ell and served as a model for the community (Figs. 7:14 and 7:15). There were two general patterns of constructing ells recorded in Stearns's account and daybooks. The first pattern, which lasted approximately from 1800 to 1820, generally involved an addition to an older building. After 1811, when he secured his first important building con-

Figure 7:12. Dr. Thomas Williams House, Deerfield, Massachusetts, 1748–75.
(Photograph by the author.)

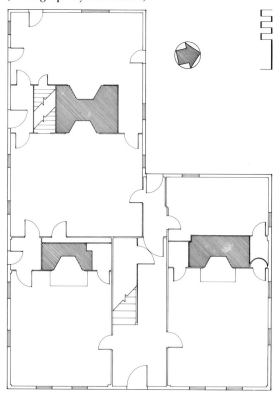

Figure 7:13. Reconstructed Plan, Dr. Thomas Williams House.
(Redrawn by author from plans and measurements by Kevin M. Sweeney.)

Figure 7:14. Calvin Stearns House, Northfield, Massachusetts, 1805.
(Photograph by the author.)

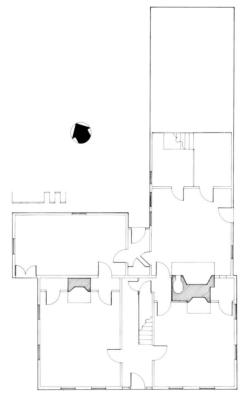

Figure 7:15. Reconstructed Plan, Calvin Stearns House.
(Measured by J. Ritchie Garrison and Rosa Johnston, drawn by the author.)

tract and became a recognized master carpenter, Stearns began to design and build houses with the ell already in the plan.[9]

The pattern was more varied than Stearns's experience suggests, for carpenters added ells to older houses and built new houses without ells throughout the nineteenth century. Nevertheless, the trend to build domestic structures with integral ells became well established between the 1800s and 1830s, particularly on larger houses erected by those ranked in the top three deciles of tax valuation lists. Isaac Mattoon's house on Northfield's main street, which Stearns built in 1816, illustrates the form of many large houses with ells. The plan followed a pattern that Stearns repeated at least four more times. The front section of the house was a standard central passage, five-bay, single-pile plan. The form harked back to the seventeenth century, but the details were distinctly modern. Stearns built it with a hipped roof, an elaborate neoclassical cornice, and a fanlighted doorway protected by a columned front "portico," marking Mattoon's prominence in the community and his acquaintance with fashion. Centered on the back wall was the ell. The first room in back of the front section was a dining room. Beyond was a south-facing entry, a chimney, and a pantry, and behind all of that was the kitchen, a buttery, and the back stairs to the second floor. Further back was shed space (Figs. 7:16 and 7:17). Like most people who lived in a region with cold winters, Stearns was conscious of the importance of building orientation. He placed the kitchen to the south of the buttery and pantry. Similarly, most of the surviving ells in the region are situated to take advantage of a warmer southern or eastern exposure, and many had sheds or porches that faced south. Once his new house was finished, Mattoon had Stearns demolish his old dwelling, eliminating the past from the new landscape he had made. In similar processes, step by step, people steadily changed their domestic landscape.[10]

Not all ells extended to the rear of the house. Stearns radically altered Lyman Gilbert's central chimney, story-and-a-half house in the Northfield Farms section of town in 1832 (Fig. 7:18). He tore off the old roof and raised the house to a full two stories. On the south side of the house, adjoining the original kitchen, he erected a wing for Gilbert's new kitchen, pantry, laundry, shed, and privy. This wing ran parallel to the road, partly because Gilbert had enough frontage to build it that way and partly because Stearns had to keep clear of the stream and low-lying land that ran several hundred feet behind the house. In any case houses in rural locations like Northfield Farms were more likely to have a wing that ran parallel to the road than houses in village centers where lots customarily were narrower and where the proximity of neighbors probably prompted more circumspection about where you hung your laundry, chopped wood, and slaughtered hogs. In the village centers of towns like Northfield, where the architectural and landscape expecta-

Figure 7:16. Isaac Mattoon House, Northfield, Massachusetts, built by Calvin Stearns, 1816. (Photograph by the author.)

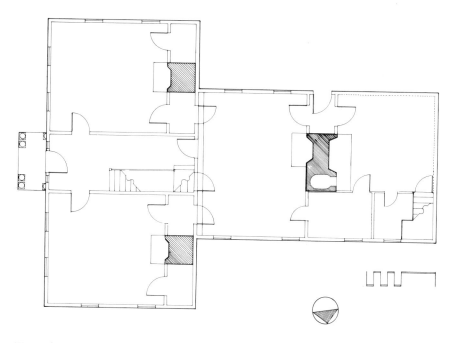

Figure 7:17. Reconstructed Plan, Isaac Mattoon House. (Drawn by the author.)

tions were more genteel, the ells and the messy tasks they contained were almost always located out back, away from gossip and the probing eyes of passersby on the town street. This pattern of seeking privacy was less important in rural locations where distances between families provided a measure of isolation, but even in these areas there were hierarchies of work that dictated room arrangement. The Gilbert house was arranged so that wet and dirty farm and household chores were located in back of the house or to one side where they were less prominent.[11]

As the region's families restructured their work and dwelling space with ells they also began to modify old housing forms. One early variation on an old theme was the side entry house, which carpenters developed during the first decade of the nineteenth century. Joseph Stebbins, Jr., built a brick house in this form in Deerfield in 1811 (Fig. 7:19). Another example with better documentation is the Samuel Stearns house in Northfield. Calvin and Samuel Stearns began framing the building in 1819, finishing it in 1824. Like other examples in the region, the Samuel Stearns house looks like a typical central chimney dwelling from the south side, but this elevation is secondary to the east facade which faces the town street (Figs. 7:20 and 7:21). On this side

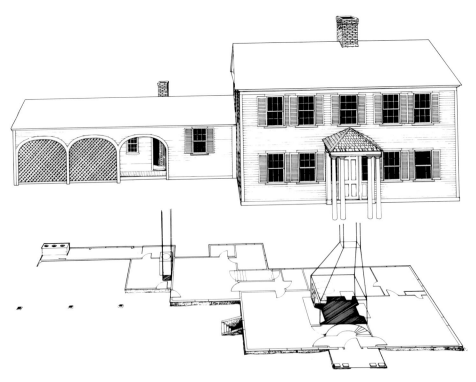

Figure 7:18. Lyman Gilbert House, Northfield Farms, Massachusetts. Enlarged by Calvin Stearns, 1832. (Drawn by the author.)

Figure 7:19. Joseph Stebbins II House, Deerfield, Massachusetts, 1811.
(Photograph by the author.)

Stearns built a three-bay facade with a fanlighted front door. To Northfield residents who were unaccustomed to either the form or the interior embellishments, such as the circular front stairs that curved upward to the second floor in a quarter circle, the original effect must have seemed most impressive even before the portico and four columns were added two or three decades later (Fig. 7:22).[12]

The introduction of these side entry houses to Franklin County clearly antedated the Greek Revival style of architecture and emphasized the progression of domestic space from a more formal front unit to a less formal, more utilitarian ell. The form reoriented a familiar building tradition to create a new order of domestic architecture from a familiar and safe design vocabulary. In turn this reorientation was to prepare the way for other forms that were less traditional but that reused the hierarchic design imperatives seen in the side entry house. What emerged was a sense that domestic space ought to be organized to nurture social rituals, family life, and work, a notion widely shared several decades before the literature of reform got around to writing about ideal housing design. In a crude way, then, houses increasingly rationalized these goals into a linear domestic taxonomy with social ritual located near public ways, family life centered in the middle, and kitchen/work

Figure 7:20. Samuel Stearns House, Northfield, Massachusetts, 1819–24.
(Photograph by the author.)

Figure 7:21. South Elevation, Samuel Stearns House, Northfield, Massachusetts, 1819.
(Photograph by the author.)

Figure 7:22. Circular Stairs, Front Entry, Samuel Stearns House.
(Photograph by the author.)

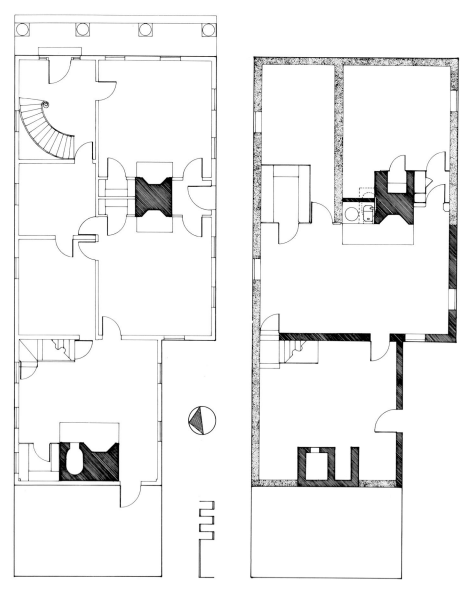

Figure 7:23. Plan of Basement and First Floor, Samuel Stearns House.
(Drawn by the author.)

space to the rear. This taxonomy was retained even after Victorian fashion and style modified or departed from traditional architectural forms.[13]

These developments in the countryside did not evolve in isolation from urban areas nor were country folk as conservative as reformers and innovators of the period charged. Stearns's innovations, for example, were not limited to surface decoration. In the basement he constructed a full kitchen with sheathed whitewashed walls, storage rooms, and access to the dooryard, which sloped down from the street. While this kitchen might have been the primary food-preparation site, it seems likely that it was a secondary kitchen that supplemented the one on the main floor of the ell (Fig. 7:23). The Stearnes built at least three other basement kitchens in Northfield, but all those that survive were in houses owned by family members. They were not common in the county and the examples in Northfield appear to represent a conscious adoption of urban forms. Basement kitchens were well known in cities, where space was at a premium and real estate was too expensive for kitchen ells (Fig. 7:24). As a young man, in 1806 and 1807, Calvin Stearns had worked in Boston for the noted architect Peter Banner. He may have picked up the model for a basement kitchen while there, or he may have read about them in some of the periodical literature that circulated in the early nineteenth century. In any case urban areas did not have barriers that prevented the import or export

Figure 7:24. Basement cooking hearth, Samuel Stearns House. The stone lintel on the right side of the photograph shows the extent of the original cooking hearth. To the left is a masonry range with a steamer in the center and a boiling kettle on the left. Openings, now bricked in, beneath the steamer and kettle were used to build fires. The steamer is a later replacement. Originally, this was the location of a brick bake oven. (Photograph by the author.)

of ideas and rural people were often acquainted with what was happening in cities. Rural families consciously accepted some of these ideas and rejected others as frivolous or impractical. While several local families in Northfield adopted the side entry form of architecture, none seems to have accepted basement kitchens as a practical alternative to one located on the main floor.[14]

Local willingness to innovate within the comfortable confines of traditional forms was not limited to those who constructed side entry houses. A more typical manifestation of design innovation was a house that was probably built for Stephen Alexander about 1843 in Northfield Farms (Figs. 7:25 and 7:26). Decorated in fashionable Greek Revival style, hidden now under layers of asphalt siding, the plan of the building is clearly related to New England hall-parlor-plan designs of a century earlier. By the mid 1840s, stoves had eliminated the need for massive central chimneystacks in most new construction. In the Alexander house this technological change resulted in a warmer house and space for the stairs to run in a straight flight up from the front entry. The kitchen was located in the ell that extended west in a line with the south wall of the house. This kitchen ell was not an afterthought but was integrated into the design from the beginning. In eighteenth-century plans the rooms to the rear of the front parlors were typicaly rather narrow, generally ranging from ten to fourteen feet. To make the Alexander kitchen bigger, the builders incorporated this rather narrow space into a larger kitchen that stretched to the west. From the beginning this kitchen contained a cookstove, a sink, and running water. Until the mid twentieth century, water ran down through pipes from a spring on the hill to the east. Near the drive this pipeline split, one line going into the kitchen, and one line continuing west to the barnyard where it fed a watering trough for the stock. The line that entered the kitchen emptied into a wooden barrel next to the cookstove. From the barrel the cook used a dipper to transfer water to the stove for warming or, one step away, to the sink which faced a window looking north. To prevent a freeze-up in the winter, water ran continuously, and the overflow from the barrel next to the stove was piped down to another barrel in the shed behind the kitchen, after which the waste was carried off via a wooden trough to the dooryard on the north side of the ell.[15]

How common were these kinds of technological innovations in rural areas of the north in the nineteenth century and when did they begin to become common? The Alexander house was not a gentry house by Northfield's standards, but it was a substantial middle-class dwelling, better than most in the area where it was built. Extensive archaeological work at the Stratton Tavern down the road from the Alexander house revealed a similar but earlier system of water supply, suggesting that these kinds of innovations were known before the first two decades of the nineteenth century. The Stratton tavern was the

Figure 7:25. Stephen Alexander House, Northfield Farms, Northfield, Massachusetts, ca. 1843. (Photograph by the author.)

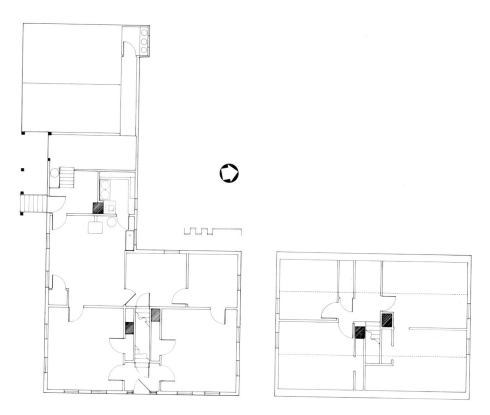

Figure 7:26. Plan, Stephen Alexander House. (Measured by Agnes Hammond and J. Ritchie Garrison, drawn by the author.)

property of one of Northfield's most prominent families, and it was thoroughly rebuilt between the late 1790s and the 1820s (Figs. 7:27 and 7:28). Among the improvements were an ice house, a large ell, a woodshed, terraced gardens, and a wooden pipe system that brought water down from a spring on the hill. The pipes were made of ten-foot-long logs with a two-inch hole bored down the middle. One end of the log was tapered to fit into the hole at the end of the next log and as each section was laid, the joint was sealed with clay to prevent leaks. Just beyond the house, the water line branched. One section ran on in a straight line to what archaeologists believe was a cistern or part of a still house. The other section ran to the wing of the house where it filled a wooden tub with continuously running water. Overflow from this tub was routed over a "French drain" to the west of the structure, where it watered ornamental shrubbery. For family and hired help the Strattons hung mugs or cups from the needleless top of an evergreen tree that was set into a pile of white rocks in the bottom of the tub. The pipe that fed this tub continued on to the south to a privy. By turning a valve, the Strattons could divert water from the tub to the privy where the running water would flush out the privy wastes down a normally dry gully toward a hog pen.[16]

The Stratton's sophisticated hydrological system was evidently in place by 1800. Eventually other families would incorporate water systems directly into their houses instead of into wings. Calvin Stearns's accounts indicated that carpenters were adding these improvements in the 1820s and 1830s. In 1835 Stearns noted that he worked at Walter Field's house where he made "one cink and 2 tubes for water $2.00." Stearns also recorded constructing sinks in other houses during this period. Clearly the introduction of sinks began in the ranks of the rural elite, but it filtered down to the middle class who laid pipe and installed "tubes," "cinks," and pumps when they could afford them. We know far too little about how these technological systems affected rural family life. What is clear is that these improvements especially benefited women and may have contributed to the expansion of female productivity in the outwork system. With running water, women no longer had to lug well water into the kitchen and they could more conveniently improve standards of family cleanliness and hygiene. To some degree the water tub in the shed may have kept men with dirty hands and clothes away from the kitchen, but it also facilitated the washing of clothes and floors, bathing, and food preparation and cleanup. As Ruth Schwartz Cowan points out, however, the convenience of running water had a trade-off. Higher standards of cleanliness meant more work for mother.[17]

Around the same time they were building water systems into homes, Franklin County families also began to adopt cookstoves. The earliest advertisement for a cookstove in the Greenfield newspaper occurred in 1812, but

Figure 7:27 Stratton Tavern, Northfield Farms, Northfield, Massachusetts. Photograph ca. 1880–1900. (Courtesy, Northfield Historical Society.)

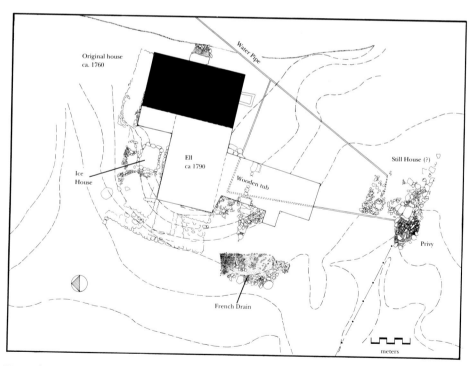

Figure 7:28. Site Plan, Hezekiah Stratton Tavern, Northfield Farms, Northfield, Massachusetts, ca. 1792. (Courtesy, Old Sturbridge Village.)

New York
Stove Warehouse.

A BRANCH of this establishment is opened at this place, where an extensive assortment of *COOKING, PARLOR & BOX STOVES* may be found, viz : Lewis's Patent, cast and elevated oven, hot air, four boiler, which possesses superior advantages over the elevated ovens now in use. Four boiler Stoves, with cast iron ovens, as low as $18; Union and Premium, with apparatus complete, for $12; Norton Furnace, four boilers, with an improved draft plate;—with a great variety of approved patterns now in use.

For Parlors.

The Harp,
Minerva, Grecian,
Vermont, &c. &c.

at very low prices.

Russia and English Pipe, Sheet Zinc and Tin Ware.

CHAUNCEY FOWLER, Agent.
Greenfield, Oct. 14, 1840.   1

Figure 7:29. Cookstove Advertisement, *Greenfield Gazette and Franklin Herald,* October 14, 1840. (Courtesy, Historic Deerfield Library.)

the fifty-dollar price tag for an object that did everything cooks could do before an open fire was too high for all but the region's most prosperous families. By the 1830s the price had dropped to twenty-five to thirty dollars, the stoves worked better, and more families began installing them. Only after the early 1840s, however, did the price of a good cookstove fall low enough, twelve to eighteen dollars, for large numbers of middling families to afford them (Fig. 7:29). Most households had cookstoves by the mid 1850s, when competition and manufacturing improvements combined to lower the prices of the stoves, women became accustomed to cooking on them, and fuel expenses rose. Manufacturers promoted cookstoves to men and women differently; for men they stressed how fuel efficient a good cookstove was and how much warmer they were than fireplaces. For women they emphasized how convenient it was to cook and bake food on a stove instead of before a fire. Cookstoves did cook foods conveniently and they undoubtedly made baking more frequent since women could bake anytime the stove was fired up, but the biggest change the stoves brought was in keeping the kitchen warm even on very cold days during the long months of winter. Family space was now not just emotionally comforting but physically warm to the corners of the room and sometimes to adjacent rooms. Mid-nineteenth-century sentimentalized attitudes toward the home and family were nurtured in part by these technological innovations, as dining rooms, kitchens, and ells — the family and work spaces of rural houses — presided over by women became havens from the often cold world outside.[18]

Technological innovations in dwellings were only part of a larger picture. By the late 1830s, builders working on commission for rural elites began to accelerate the pace of architectural change. In the village centers of Greenfield, South Deerfield, Shelburne Falls, and Montague, Grecian-style dwellings became fairly common. The concentration of these structures in villages served to distinguish such places from the rest of the countryside, but a number of Greek Revival–style dwellings were built in rural areas too. The style was particularly popular after 1835. Many of the houses built during this period were rather conventional side entry structures with rear ells, decorated with the massive moldings that made the style so distinctive, or, like the Alexander house, were older Georgian forms in Grecian mode. More and more, however, these houses broke with long-established design traditions.

George Stearns's house, constructed in 1843, represented one example of the type of innovations some were choosing. George was the son of Calvin Stearns and took over the family carpentry business after his father retired in 1841. George's dwelling was a Greek Revival–style cottage that faced the town street of Northfield. It was placed on an artificial earthen platform created by grading the dirt that was thrown out when the cellar hole was dug

Figure 7:30. George Stearns House, Northfield, Massachusetts, 1843–46. (Photograph by the author.)

Figure 7:31. Side/Main Entry, George Stearns House, Northfield, Massachusetts. (Photograph by the author.)

Landscape and Material Life in Franklin County, Massachusetts

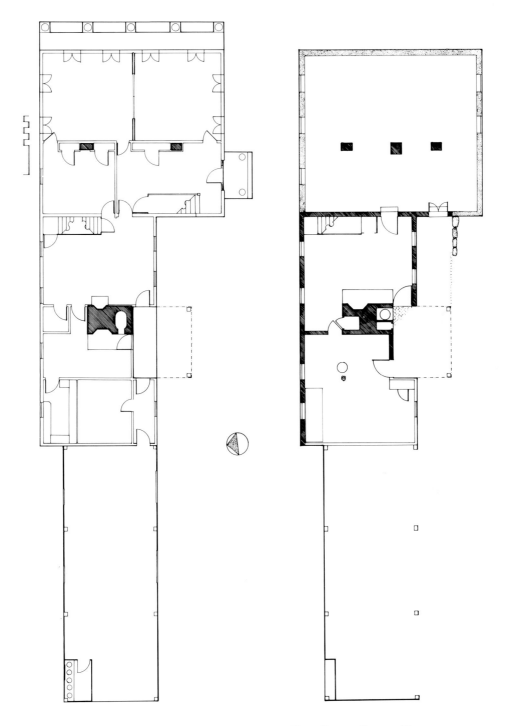

Figure 7:32. Reconstructed First Floor and Basement Plan, George Stearns House. Northfield, Massachusetts. (Measured and drawn by the author.)

(Fig. 7:30). The plan of the main part of the house was similar to the townhouse plan that Asher Benjamin published in *The American Builder's Companion*, except that Stearns turned the plan ninety degrees. Calvin Stearns owned the 1827 edition of Benjamin's book. George may have developed his design from this model or from contact with urban styles picked up from his many trips to eastern Massachusetts or on a longer journey in 1840 when he taught school in Wilmington, Delaware.

The principal entry of the George Stearns house was to the south side of the structure and was set off by a small Grecian porch (Figs. 7:31 and 7:32). The east, or street facade, consisted of a one-story portico of five Doric columns set on a granite base. Behind the porch and visually framed by the columns, Stearns placed four full-length French doors, which swung into the two front parlors. The columns supported the portico that contained upstairs bedrooms. Behind the main block of the house Stearns added an ell in 1846. The basement of the ell contained a cellar kitchen with direct access to the south dooryard, and Stearns's shop and workbench. Above the cellar kitchen was a dining room, and above the shop was the main kitchen, pantry, and workroom. The rear sheds stretched back for three bays. In the northwest corner of the shed was the privy, an island of civilization with its plastered and papered walls, and, to preserve modesty, a curtain over the window.

From the two formal front parlors separated by sliding pocket doors to the privy 120 feet to the rear, Stearns's house was a carefully refined and articulated statement on domestic order. The house presented a genteel, ordered world to the public street whose most immediate access to the intimate life of the Stearns family was the view through the glassy expanse of the front windows. Public entry from the street was no longer so direct as in the earlier dwellings. Visitors had to enter via the side of the house and only then after climbing up a set of steps to mount the terrace. Past the front door and to the right were the front parlors. Charity Richardson Stearns's piano, valued at more than forty dollars at the time of George's death in 1859, was here. Much of the family's daily activities took place on the first floor, most of it centered in the middle of the house around the kitchen and the dining room. Storage and messy work routines took place downstairs in the cellar. Sleeping was segregated to the second floor. This was a different world than that of Joseph Stebbins, whose enormous Deerfield mansion house of 1774 included a wide closet in the southeast parlor for a turn-up bedstead (Fig. 7:8). Stebbins's home was of the eighteenth century, of a world in which the spatial order of everyday life was less programmed. Stearns's house, by contrast, was built by someone living within a competitive, increasingly specialized society in which landscape and dwelling space often echoed the rationalization of economic and cultural life. Reputations of calculating Yankee shrewdness were built on foundations such as these.[19]

The Stearns's later work in Northfield remained largely within the tradition of the Greek Revival. In the late 1840s and the 1850s, other county carpenters also built in that fashion. These forms were associated with prosperous agricultural towns in which families were replacing older structures with new forms, and they were even more common in the new factory areas. While the Greek Revival style was very popular at a variety of aesthetic and class levels, few people in the region built in Italianate or Gothic styles until after the Civil War. Italianate house forms first emerged in the late 1840s and early 1850s in Deerfield and in the county seat of Greenfield. Many of these houses were variations of Greek Revival forms. In Deerfield the first Italiante-style house was built in the late 1840s as a parsonage for the orthodox Congregational Church. In plan it is similar to central-passage, double-pile dwellings dating back to the eighteenth century, but the Italianate details such as the front porch with Egyptian revival columns followed more fashionable trends (Fig. 7:33). The style in Franklin County typically featured rather boxy plans with large window sash, shallow roof slopes, and broad overhanging eaves.

Another Italianate form built in these two towns was the cross passage, or upright-and-wing plan, a style that was built to Greek Revival, Italianate, and Gothic designs. Most of these structures initially were built for the local elite and were rather large, and most were built in villages rather than in the countryside. The Edward W. Stebbins house is a case in point; it was built in 1849 in an Italianate mode, with broad overhanging eaves, a bay window, and a decorative band of snowflake-like motifs at the second floor level (Figs. 7:34 and 7:35). Stebbins was the son of a wealthy farmer and businessman. His dwelling reflected a knowledge of and interest in popular architectural fashion, but Stebbins's tastes were not widely shared before the Civil War. Only after the war did builders commonly build this form for non-elites.[20]

The growing variety of house forms in the county during the late antebellum period carries several implications. Although new fashions were usually adjusted to traditional conceptions of what constituted a proper house, these traditions were not static. Families could and did adjust their expectations of proper house design as they saw innovations that made sense. Often this adjustment meant altering older buildings by adding an ell in which domestic chores were reorganized structurally and placed alongside of or behind the main section of the house. New dwellings often encoded these ideas of domestic efficiency and convenience directly into the built landscape. Whether by new construction or adaptation this reorganization reflected a more specialized view of tasks that were appropriate in different areas of a dwelling. The

Figure 7:33. Orthodox Parsonage, Congregational Church, Deerfield, Massachusetts, 1847. (Photograph by the author.)

Figure 7:34. Edward W. Stebbins House, Deerfield, Massachusetts, 1849. (Photograph by the author.)

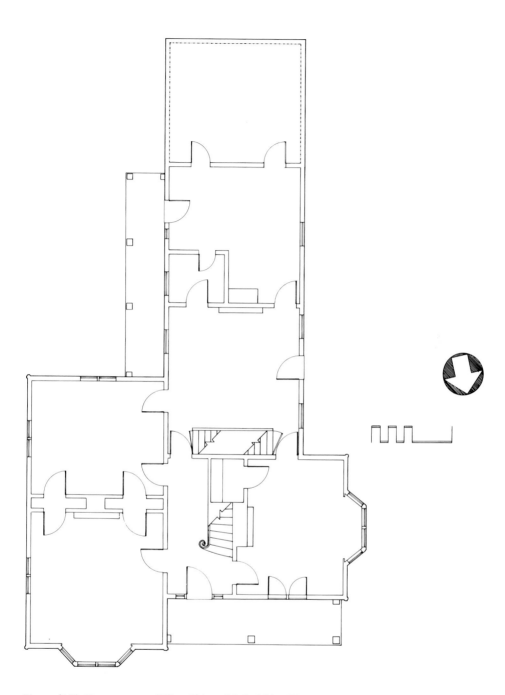

Figure 7:35. Reconstructed Plan, Edward J. Stebbins House.
(Measured by Kevin M. Sweeney and J. Ritchie Garrison, drawn by the author.)

Dwellings   185

reorganization of space on the region's farmsteads also took place outside of the older and more prosperous lowlands where large two-story houses persisted. But to interpret these lowland houses as typical of an entire area for a particular time distorts the more complex reality of the region's domestic landscape. If we are to recover the meaning of dwellings in the antebellum period, we must thicken our description with documentary sources.

In the uplands, small houses were common. Most of these houses were one- or one-and-a-half story dwellings with central chimneys flanked by a hall and parlor or kitchen and parlor. Often the room behind the chimney was a bedroom or kitchen. Several examples of these houses survived to the twentieth century. Samuel Kendrick's house in Heath, built ca. 1815, is typical of a form owned by a middling farmer (Figs. 7:36 and 7:37). The Herrick house in Conway was a bit bigger and better finished, but it was also a common form (Figs. 7:38 and 7:39). The 1798 Federal Direct Tax census is not very detailed for most of Franklin County, but it yields some documentary material to help place in perspective the evidence from these standing structures. Records for New Salem, located on the southeastern corner of the county, are the most complete. Established in the 1740s and 1750s by settlers moving up the Swift River valley, it had become by 1820 the most densely settled and prosperous town in the eastern uplands of Franklin County. It compared favorably with the upland towns west of the Connecticut River, towns like Conway, Buckland, Colrain, and Leyden. Of the 175 houses in New Salem listed on the 1798 tax census, 145 (83 percent) were of one story.[21] While there is insufficient data to determine if this pattern held precisely in other upland towns, the surviving evidence suggests that it probably did.

The New Salem census also permits some comparison of house size, although the list does not contain exact dimensions. Most dwellings in the town were fairly substantial. Sixty-eight percent of the houses were larger than 800 square feet—representing roughly a 20 by 40 structure. Slightly less than half the home owners (46 percent) lived in houses of more than 1,000 square feet. Broken down by square footage, the housing stock of New Salem is listed in Table 7:1. The vast majority of these houses were owned by those who lived in them. Seven of the 175 houses (4 percent) were occupied by nonowners and four houses were jointly owned by occupants with two different surnames. Given the variations in value of houses with similar square footage, it seems likely that the interiors of many houses were not completely finished in the 1790s or were in poor states of repair. Despite the differences, the majority of houses in New Salem were roughly 24 by 34 feet or larger and some were bigger than 30 by 40 feet. Few of the town's houses were small; all but three or four had more than one room. By the standards of

Figure 7:36. Samuel Kendrick House, Heath, Massachusetts, ca. 1807–15.
(Courtesy, Michael D. and Sophie Coe.)

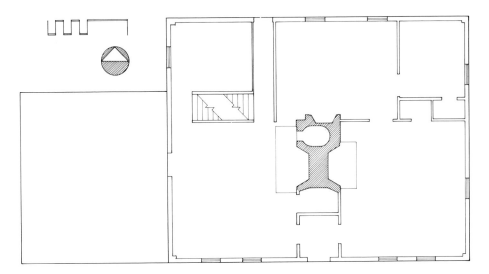

Figure 7:37. Reconstructed Plan, Samuel Kendrick House.
(Drawn by the author from a plan by Michael D. Coe.)

Figure 7:38. Elevations, Herrick House, Conway, Massachusetts, 1775–1800. (Redrawn by the author from originals by the Historic American Building Survey, National Park Service: original drawing by James R. Hanlon.)

other regions, such as Sussex County, Delaware, where an estimated 80 percent of the dwellings were of one room, New Salem residents seem to have attached considerable value to the task of building or acquiring houses that were relatively large. This general picture appears to hold for a number of the region's upland farm houses.[22]

Similar evidence for lowland communities in the county is unavailable, but further down the Connecticut River in South Hadley, one census schedule includes the dimensions for all houses valued at less than $100. Table 7:2 summarizes the variety of inexpensive structures that existed in South Had-

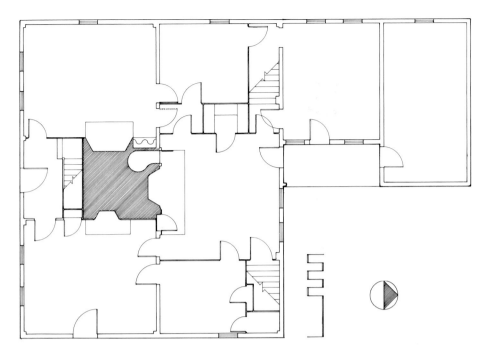

Figure 7:39. Plan, Herrick House. (Redrawn by the author from originals by the Historic American Building Survey, National Park Service: original drawing by James R. Hanlon.)

ley in 1798. Six or seven of these structures may have been one-room build-ings. The smallest was a 10-by-12-foot "hutt," but of the thirty houses listed in this sample, twenty-one (70 percent) were larger than 500 square feet. The median size of these inexpensive homes was 20 by 30 feet, and the mean floor plan was slightly larger at 652 square feet. We know little about what these kinds of houses were actually like because most of the smaller ones have disap-peared long ago, or have been so altered that they are now unrecognizable. One rare example of a hall-parlor-plan house built in Greenfield survived in-to the 1930s, however, and was recorded by the Historic American Building Survey. Probably built between 1770 and 1800, the hall-parlor-plan structure contained just over 640 square feet, slightly less than the median size of the South Hadley schedule for houses valued at less than $100 (Fig. 7:40). It was this type of dwelling that was common on the late eighteenth-century land-scape in both upland and lowland towns. Larger houses that were listed in the tax census, 840 to 1140 square feet, represent forms, such as an example in Gill, that are still useful and frequently survive (Figs. 7:41 and 7:42). In other cases the low valuations of these structures reflect condition or finish more than the size of the structure. Some South Hadley buildings, particu-larly the larger ones, were either in bad repair or were not finished when the census was taken.[23]

Table 7:1

Size and Number of Houses, New Salem, Massachusetts, 1798

No.	Sq. Ft.	No.	Sq. Ft
6	0-500	16	501-600
19	601-700	15	701-800
23	801-900	30	901-1000
30	1001-1100	31	1101-1200
6	1201-1300	6	over 1300

Table 7:2

Size and Number of Houses Valued below $100, South Hadley, Massachusetts, 1798

No.	Size	Sq. Ft.	No.	Size	Sq. Ft.
1	10 x 12	120	1	16 x 18	288
1	15 x 20	300	3	18 x 20	360
1	16 x 26	416	1	20 x 22	440
1	20 x 24	480	1	18 x 28	504
1	22 x 23	506	1	23 x 23	529
2	24 x 24	576	4	20 x 30	600
2	18 x 36	648	1	20 x 36	720
1	20 x 38	760	1	22 x 36	792
1	24 x 35	840	1	20 x 45	900
3	24 x 38	916	1	30 x 36	1080
1	30 x 38	1140			

A second schedule for South Hadley ranked the houses valued at more than $100 (Table 7:3). There were seventy-nine houses in town, 73 percent of the total housing stock, valued in this category. Of these seventy-nine houses, fifty-one had two stories, and all of them were of frame construction. The mean size of these houses' first floors was 1185 square feet (for all 109 houses in town the mean is 1000 square feet). The biggest and most expensive house in town belonged to Ruggles Woodridge, a merchant, whose two-story house contained thirty windows and was valued at $1550. At the bottom of this schedule was Noah Taylor whose 502-square-foot house had only four windows, one story, and was valued at $105. Presumably, Taylor's house was better finished than those in town valued less than $100. Analysis of the values of these buildings is revealing; only four of South Hadley's houses were valued at more than $1000, and only four more were rated at more than $500. By con-

Table 7:3

Size and Number of Houses Valued above $100, South Hadley, Massachusetts, 1798

Sq. Ft.	No. Windows	Value ($)	Sq. Ft.	No. Windows	Value ($)
1064	14	burned*	1200	16	n.a.
1280	28	minister**			
502	4	105	1008	12	105
504	6	105	600	4	105
1008	4	105	1200	6	110
1200	9	110	760	4	110
1110	5	110	1008	5	110
528	5	115	1008	3	120
1140	8	120	1080	6	120
564	7	120	808	6	120
1064	9	120	936	7	120
492	6	125	720	12	130
840	8	130	884	4	130
1280	8	130	728	9	130
900	7	130	934	12	140
1200	14	145	720	7	145
494	5	150	1200	12	150
1148	13	160	936	11	160
1280	16	170	960	14	170
1080	7	170	1140	3	170
1240	16	170	1140	12	170
848	14	175	1200	18	180
1143	16	200	1008	12	200
1110	12	200	1200	12	200
841	9	200	1280	19	200
1200	11	205	1164	9	215
1200	16	220	1116	12	230
1200	16	230	1102	14	230
1200	16	250	1065	8	250
1436	11	260	1512	14	280
1520	21	300	1690	6	300
1140	13	350	1064	11	350
1280	13	370	1640	20	400
1288	17	400	1530	19	450
800	13	500	2192	18	500
3132	18	500	1844	22	500
1280	18	500	1200	19	520
1656	25	750	1828	24	800
1932	27	1000	2214	32	1350
2468	31	1500	2400	30	1550

*Evidently, this house burned before the valuation was completed.

**By Massachusetts's law at this period, a minister's house was exempted from taxation.

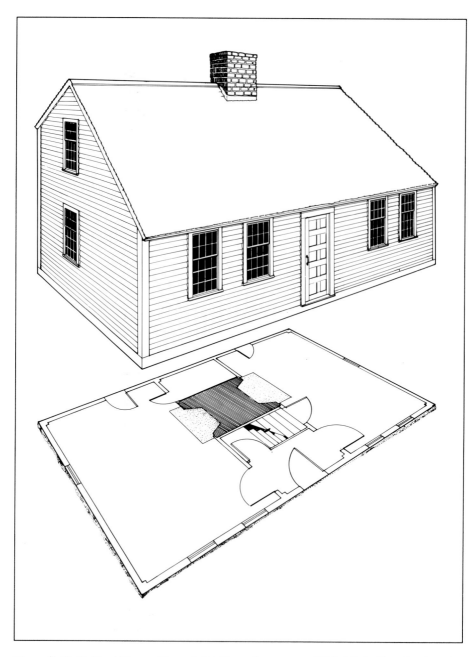

Figure 7:40. McHard House, Greenfield, Massachusetts, ca. 1765–1820. (Drawing based on plans by the Historic American Building Survey, National Park Service: original drawing by Edmund P. Lynch.)

trast thirty houses were valued between $200 and $500, and forty-one between $100 and $199. The evidence sustains the interpretation that middling wealthholders represented the largest group in the valley's landscape, that the lowland towns had a much higher density of two-story houses, and that on the average lowland houses were a bit larger than those in the uplands.[24]

While documents and surviving structures indicate that most upland houses in the county were one story high, there is also some evidence that there were qualitative differences between the eastern and western parts of the county. Housing stock of the western uplands was generally better than the dwellings in most of the eastern half of the county. Some of these structures rivaled or surpassed the houses of prosperous lowland farmers in terms of size and elaborateness. Joseph Griswold's large brick home in Buckland center (Fig. 7:43) was an example of gentry architecture as elaborate as the best homes in lowland towns like Deerfield or Northfield. (See Figs. 7:8 and 7:9.) By contrast, the elites in Wendell, Warwick, or Orange were not as prosperous. When passing through poor towns in the region like Shutesbury, Dwight recorded, "we rode through a country, rough, lean, and solitary lying principally on the range of Mt. Toby. . . . The inhabitants are few and thinly scattered. Generally, also, they were in poor circumstances, and without any apparent hopes of advancing to better. Their houses were bad in most instances, their enclosures imperfect, and their cultivation wretched." The poverty of Shutesbury that Dwight observed was mentioned by others who noted, sometimes derisively, that the towns in the rough terrain of the eastern uplands were generally poor. Apparently much of the housing was also.[25]

Architecture in the region's core town, Greenfield, only emphasized the comparative roughness of housing in the uplands. Timothy Dwight observed that in Greenfield, "The houses are generally good; a few of them may be termed handsome. It is said that there is more business of various kinds done in this town than in any other in this county except Northampton and Springfield. The number of the traders and mechanics is considerable and the town exhibits a general aspect of spritliness and activity." When Franklin County was set off from Hampshire County in 1811, Greenfield would become the county seat. The stong business climate that Dwight sensed in the early nineteenth century continued for much of the antebellum period. There were recessions during the embargo years of 1807–1809 and during the War of 1812, but over the long term the town made steady if not spectacular progress. This improvement was apparent by the late 1830s when John Warner Barber published a view of the town center showing the county courthouse, stores, and Second Congregational Church (Fig. 7:44). Many of the commercial or public structures were of brick, conveying an urbane sense of style in a landscape where buildings were almost always made of wood. Most were consciously

Figure 7:41. House, Gill, Massachusetts, ca. 1750–1800. (Photograph by the Historic American Building Survey, National Park Service.)

embellished with symbols of prestige and power. Situated on a rise overlooking the Green River, Greenfield's common commanded a view down the valley toward the parent town of Deerfield and beyond. By the early 1800s, though some in Deerfield thought otherwise, it was clear to most people which community had the upper hand. No other town between Northampton to the south and Brattleboro, Vermont, further north, maintained the same appearance of urbanity and sophistication.[26]

Greenfield became dominant because it was situated at the confluence of transportation routes and because its leaders were very aggressive entrepreneurs who in the 1790s reoriented the local economy to business and commerce. The central location of the town and its encouraging economic climate caught the attention of Jonathan Dwight, one of the principal merchants in Springfield, who advanced capital to son-in-law Lyman Kendall to establish what became for a time the principal business in the town. Kendall was merely one member of a growing community of merchants and lawyers, whose ambitions and political connections set Greenfield apart from other parts of Franklin County. Some of these people, like the lawyer William Colman, who helped set up the first newspaper in the county in 1792, and fellow bar member Jonathan Leavitt, erected monuments to their status and taste in the form of Asher Benjamin–designed houses that incorporated modern neoclassic designs (Figs. 7:45, 7:46, and 7:47). At the time they were constructed, these houses were dramatic and forceful departures from the local

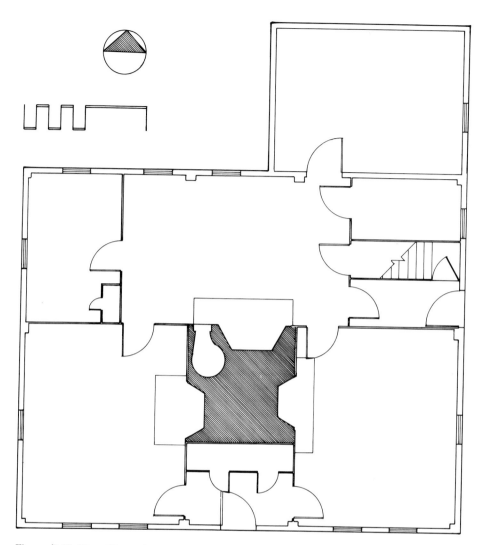

Figure 7:42. Plan, House in Gill. (Redrawn by the author from originals by the Historic American Building Survey, National Park Service: original drawing by Thomas M. Stetson.)

traditions of eighteenth-century gentry architecture. The large scale, the vaulted ceilings of the central hallway, the flowing sweep of the circular stairs to the side of the hallway, the glazed fanlight over the front door, and the two-story engaged pilasters gracing the front facade of the Colman house not only connoted wealth and power but reflected the penetration of modern European design into the valley. Jonathan Leavitt's house with its five-part Palladian plan was equally imposing if less embellished. Together the two houses testified to the region's growing connections with the outside world and the desire

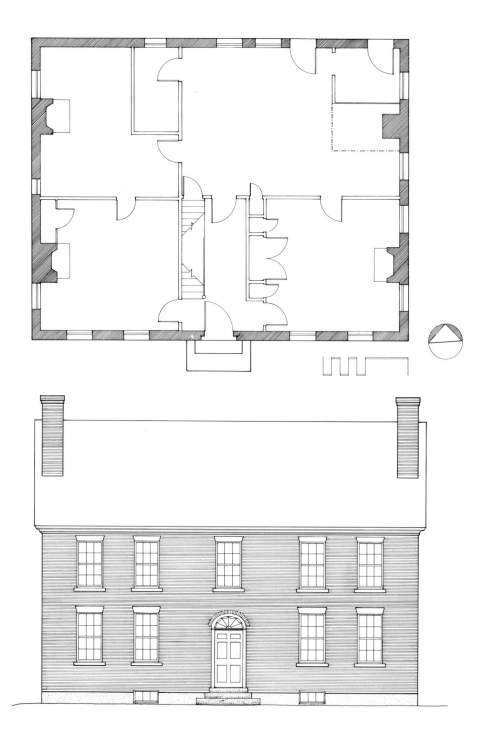

Figure 7:43. Joseph Griswold House, Buckland, Massachusetts, 1818. (Redrawn by the author from originals by the Historic American Building Survey, National Park Service: original drawing by Henry Slocum.)

of some local gentry to discourse at a material level that rivaled urbane centers of commerce.

Benjamin's flashy architectural designs also signaled a desire on the part of the county's leaders to establish a separate cultural core that could rival the dominance of coastal elites to the east, and valley elites to the south in Springfield and Hartford. During his two-year stay Benjamin designed an academy for Deerfield and prepared a carpenter's guidebook which he proclaimed as the first edition prepared by an American for American carpenters. Superficially, the book implied a model of stylistic diffusion from a metropolitan core out to its periphery—in this case, from Europe (especially England), to an entrepot on the Atlantic coast (Boston), to regional centers in the hinterlands (Greenfield), to the back country. Information was passed by consumers who traveled and who saw acceptable variations, by craftsmen who tramped from job to job picking up and diffusing new ideas, and by spoken and printed words and pictures that spread ideas widely. Buildings were not just statements of cultural competition over prestige and power, although they mirrored some of those issues. In an elemental sense they were working hypotheses by which people sought to manage their world and provide for the security of their loved ones. We need to step back to a broader level of perspective and interpret the meaning of changes in the domestic architecture of Franklin County.

Judged by the architecture of their houses, most people in Franklin County followed rather conservative cultural patterns until the Civil War. Few houses conveyed the sense of architectural self-consciousness to be found in the pub-

Figure 7:44. View of Greenfield. From John Warner Barber, *Historical Collections*, 1839. (Courtesy, Pocumtuck Valley Memorial Association.)

Figure 7:45. William Colman House, Greenfield, Massachusetts, 1796.
(Photograph by Historic American Building Survey, National Park Service.)

lic buildings or elite homes in Greenfield, and house form changed slowly throughout the first half of the nineteenth century. There are enough Gothic and Italianate style houses in the area to clearly demonstrate that the lessons of popular fashion had penetrated rural areas by the late 1840s, however. People were not ignorant of new architectural fashions; they simply did not choose to follow them until they were proven, preferably by someone else willing to take the risks. From the 1800s to the 1860s, the neoclassic style dominated the vocabulary of architectural detail and embellishment on most types of upper-class architecture in Franklin County. It was a style that worked within the traditions that reached back into the colonial era, yet it allowed for innovations, modest though they often were. At times monumental and pretentious, it was more often simple and straightforward. Despite the conservative tone to the county's buildings, architecture in Franklin County was not stagnant. The choices that the majority of the population made over time speak eloquently of their opportunities and values. It is essential to understand in a general way what they selected or rejected.

One of the most obvious and deeply felt values held by people in the county was that home ownership and durable houses were important. Although tenancy was known, was practiced by people of varying classes, and increased during the later antebellum period, the evidence suggests that the

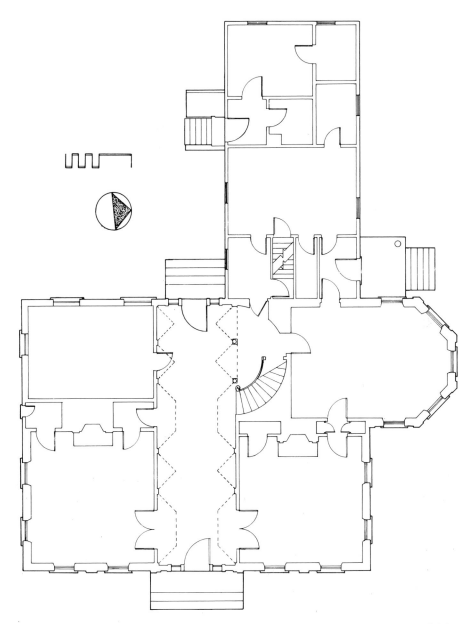

Figure 7:46. First Floor Plan, William Colman House, Greenfield, Massachusetts, 1796. (Redrawn by the author from originals by the Historic American Building Survey, National Park Service: original drawing by Fred Sawyer.)

majority of the families in the region formed nuclear households and lived in houses that they owned, even when these households did not possess much additional land. In rural New England, family status and standards of living were strongly influenced by the belief that one's housing was an important statement of economic and personal aspirations. Size was a criterion critical

Figure 7:47. Jonathan Leavitt House, Greenfield, Massachusetts, 1797.
(Photograph by Historic American Building Survey, National Park Service.)

to social status, and many farmhouses in the area became larger during the first half century of the 1800s as families added ells, wings, sheds, and lean-tos to expand living and working spaces. Perhaps because the probate inventories historians have used for data are unreliable sources for examining the size and quality of buildings, few scholars have paid serious attention to the varying modes of housing when comparing eighteenth-century wealth and standards of living in the New England, Middle Atlantic, and Southern regions. While personal estates were often modest and houses were in a poor state of repair throughout the United States in the 1790s and 1800s, northern farm families seem to have built larger and more durable buildings than their counterparts further south. By the 1850s the majority of homeowners in Franklin County could boast about a coat of paint on their dwelling's exterior and of tidy dooryards, visual evidence of a sustained drive to use the landscape more intensively and of reformers' determined calls to improve the conditions of the region's domestic landscape.[27]

These improvements were linked to the moral virtues of hard work, cleanliness, and family sanctuary that preachers and reformers called for, but they also reified the increasing rationalization of domestic space. Family size decreased in many parts of the Northeast at the same time that the size of dwellings increased. Beds were moved out of parlors, rooms were assigned for dining, kitchens were moved back into ells, and porches and shed space more often sheltered the messy tasks of household production. Stoves, whether for warming or cooking, dramatically reduced fuel consumption and increased warmth, opening more domestic space to comfortable everyday use in the winter months. Paint, wallpaper, and sometimes carpets, appeared in more and

Figure 7:48. Mill Worker's House, Greenfield, Massachusetts, ca. 1852.
(Photograph by the author.)

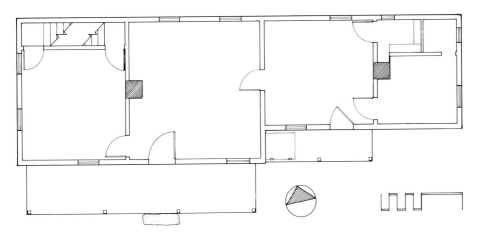

Figure 7:49. Plan, Mill Worker's House, Greenfield, Massachusetts, ca. 1852.
(Measured and drawn by the author.)

more dwellings, new and old. These amenities transformed visually and practically the lifestyle of the region's inhabitants.[28]

While fashion was surely an important influence in this transformation, the word that was used consistently to advocate and market these changes was not morality or virtue but "convenience." Cookstoves, sinks, piped water, and ells were touted as "convenient," likely to make life easier, particularly for

Figure 7:50. Gould-Clapp House, Greenfield, Massachusetts, Elijah T. Hayden Architect, 1827. (Photograph by the author.)

women. A "convenient" dwelling promoted domestic harmony by improving cleanliness and domestic comfort, saved time which might be profitably used for other pursuits be they economic or spiritual, and in the long run helped save money. In the 1790s many of these conveniences were accessible only to the rich or industrious, but by the 1850s most people in the county shared the material fruits of at least some of these innovations. Taken day by day, the pace of change was slow and uneven, but the long term drift was clear; architectural space was becoming increasingly specialized with an emphasis on disciplined efficiency of production amid romantic concepts of virtue.

This specialization simultaneously represented a form of withdrawal as families enhanced privacy by closing some spaces to public scrutiny, and a form of reaching out as the spatial reorganization of dwellings accommodated increasingly efficient forms of household production and encouraged more men and women to buy and sell things in the marketplace. Beginning in the 1820s some families moved the public entry to the side of their dwellings, away from public streets. Others shifted family life into ells or wings where the warmth of stoves expanded the zone of comfort during long months of cold weather. In either case the movement was away from the road or street toward the back of the house and rear dooryards. To a degree these changes transcended class and occupational lines. Some of the small, inexpensive houses built for the skilled English and German cutlers who worked in John Russell's factory in the 1850s had no front doors facing the street (Figs. 7:48

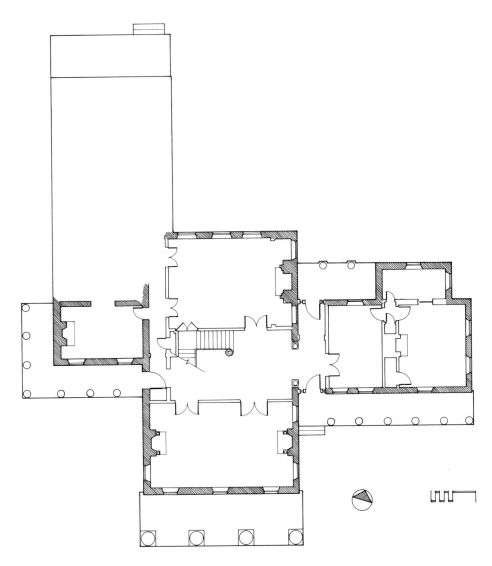

Figure 7:51. First-Floor Plan, Gould-Clapp House. (Redrawn by the author from originals by the Historic American Building Survey, National Park Service: original drawing by S. J. Lebowitz and R. V. Keune.)

and 7:49); neither did the brick mansion house of Henry Clapp (Greenfield's wealthiest landowner and entrepreneur), the county's most elegant dwelling before the Civil War (Figs. 7:50 and 7:51), or the temple style cottages in Northfield that George Stearns and his brothers built for several clients. These dwellings were most often located in the industrial villages or lowland towns of the region where the population was the most densely congregated, class differences were more sharply etched, and market production furthest advanced. This was a world where admission to the family core proceeded in measured steps—up a drive or walk, beyond a porch, into a hall or entry, through a door to the parlor, dining room, or sitting room, and eventually to the kitchen— through layers of fashion and formality, until you eventually reached the working core of the family's world where food storage and preparation, bathing, sewing, laundry and similar tasks occurred. Such spatial ordering of family life upheld certain values—tidiness, neatness, frugality, modesty, and convenience— canons of gentility that identified the practitioner with middle-class dignity and Christian virtue. Mill owner and mill hand acceded to these idealized standards in varying degrees. To fall behind was to risk loss of membership in a tacit but powerful system of social competition in which individuals and families sought to develop their capabilities and belong to a community that shared similar values of respectability. By organizing their houses in ways that derived from shared goals, yet preserving the decisions made by individuals and families in a variety of idiosyncratic architectural detail, the people of Franklin County used the language of material objects in ways that paradoxically separated families by class yet subtly bound them in the structural myth of common cause.[29]

The danger of studying houses and interpreting their meaning, of course, is that they tend to homogenize real life, to isolate it from broader cultural experience. We can analyze documents to gain perspective on variations in the region's housing, or study and measure surviving buildings to cross-check and give three-dimensional form to the documents, but dwellings were only a part of the rural landscape. Studying houses or the domestic landscapes around them emphasizes family instead of community, individuals rather than groups of people, single farmsteads rather than neighborhoods. The paradox was that as people made their houses bastions against the world's stresses, the yards around them simultaneously became more efficient workplaces where men and women forged new links with the marketplace and the larger landscape of community.

Chapter 8

Community

On March 30, 1846, Julius Robbins left his home in the Wisdom section of Deerfield to help David R. Wait drive twenty-six cattle to the Brighton market. Making about twenty miles per day, the two men traveled overland along a well-established route, stopping overnight in Athol, Westminster, Bolton, and Waltham. They reached Brighton on Saturday, April 4. In all they traveled about a hundred miles in five days, a steady pace with a drove of fat cattle. Although Wait headed home the following morning after selling his cattle, Robbins stayed on to take in the sights in Brighton and Boston. He left his hotel on the 7th, boarded the train in Waltham at 7:30 a.m., reached Fitchburg by 9:00 in time to catch the stage for Greenfield, and arrived home by 7:00 that evening. Robbins entered the details of the drive in his diary. Then, three years later, on April 10, 1849, he wrote, that he "went to the depo with our steers, 4 of them." In that one terse phrase Robbins recorded a cultural revolution: the age of the great cattle drives was over for Franklin County and a vast new landscape was within a day's train ride.[1]

Like many farmers in the region, Robbins was interested in the railroad. He attended political rallies and railroad conventions in Greenfield, watched the first cars come into town in 1846, and understood that a railroad would alter his world in profound ways. His train ride between Waltham and Fitchburg was apparently his first, and he had probably never traveled so fast. Yet Robbins referred to this new experience, like most other things he wrote in his diary, in a few succinct words. Many implications of the railroad were fuzzy in 1846 and only a bit more focused in 1849 when he brought his cattle to the depo. Newspaper editors and poets might rhapsodize about technological progress and manifest destiny, but Robbins's diary was filled with the homely details of everyday chores and experiences.[2]

These experiences were centered on his family and community. His trips to lyceums, church meetings, lectures, political gatherings, and the county agricultural fair marked him as a man who was interested in progress, who was attuned to current affairs, and who welcomed some of the changes wrought by capitalism. Yet Robbins was a rather ordinary man who maintained many of the working habits historians have associated with a pre-industrial economy. He continued the practice of changing work with his neighbors; he attended such communal activities as house raisings, dances, and turkey shoots; and he gathered much of his family's food supplies on his farm. He behaved, in short, like a man who blended the traditions of the pre-industrial world with a competitive capitalistic one and who did not agonize about contradictions between them.

Robbins was born in 1815 to Nathan and Nancy Bangs Robbins. He spent his entire life near his birthplace. He was living at home with his parents in 1840 when he began his diary at the age of twenty-five. In 1846 he built a new house across the road from the family homestead and he, his brother George, and his father ran the family farm in a cooperative manner; each New Year's Day Robbins recorded the market prices of stock and produce, listed the family's stock, and noted the amount of hay and grains they had raised the preceding year. This family reckoning was not undifferentiated. Robbins was careful to list who owned what; but individual ownership was a subset of the family's stock, and the family farm was a conceptual unit even though it had separate owners. In most years the family followed a mixed strategy of agriculture, raising grains like rye, wheat, corn, and oats, field crops of potatoes and peas, orchard products such as apples, and livestock including beef cattle, hogs, and sheep. The women produced butter and cheese and managed the poultry. Much of this output was for household consumption, but they also produced for the market to pay for purchased goods. Their cash crops included fattened beef, logs and cordwood from their wood lot, and produce for the Greenfield and New England market. The items they bought were as essential as flour, and as desirable but unnecessary as carpet and wallpaper for the bedroom. They read newspapers, kept track of what the market was doing, and valued the conveniences and opportunities capitalism and commerce brought them. Often they bought locally, but they knew their prices and were prepared to go long distances to get what they wanted.[3]

This mixing of tradition and change, of family, community, and market, was embodied in the construction and form of Robbins's house and in its location in the neighborhood of Wisdom. The timbers for the frame came from the family wood lot up on the hill and the flooring was cut at the Stebbins mill in Deerfield's south meadows. To secure enough common boards at a good price, Robbins looked first in Shelburne, the town adjacent to the family's farm, but he ended up buying the lumber from Banaker and Hill in Warwick, a half-day's journey by wagon. The sash and doors were made in Erving at a factory that specialized in millwork. Finally, he located facing stones for the house's foundations in Colrain. This pattern of purchasing building mat-

Figure 8:1. Julius Robbins House, Deerfield, Massachusetts, 1846.
(Photograph by the author.)

erials in a regional rather than local market was evidence of how far market processes had penetrated into the experiences of ordinary men and women, but Robbins built a house that merged traditional features with the innovations that were reshaping the area's landscape.[4]

Robbins's house was similar to the structure Stephen Alexander built in Northfield (Fig. 8:1). It had a room on either side of the front entry and a flight of stairs that ran up in a straight line to the second floor, but unlike the Alexander house, Robbins's kitchen was in the ell that extended from the gable end of the house to the south. Viewed from the front, the house looked like a traditional New England one-and-a-half-story structure, but the front door faced the drive rather than the road. Here again was the segmentation, the withdrawal from direct public access that builders such as George Stearns had used in Northfield and that businessmen like Henry Clapp included in Greenfield workers' housing in the 1840s and 1850s. (See Figs. 7:48 and 7:49.) Beyond the house and at right angles to it was Robbins's English three-bay barn, a form that harked back to the beginnings of New England settlement. Traditions persisted in Robbins's rural world, then, in the shape of his house and barn, and in his social relations, but change was palpable too. In the construction of an ell, the siting of the house, the purchase of a cookstove, and in the gathering of materials from five separate towns, Robbins resonated to the activities of a modern economy even as his home remained one unit among many in a web of kin, neighbors, and community associations.

The example of Julius Robbins has aspects that are unique to him, but the same types of family ties, interests, and ambitions that drove him also stirred others. Kin and community were the first social loci of infants, and many children in Franklin County learned the lay of the land as a series of relationships — ties that both bound and supported them in their communities and across town lines. As they grew to adulthood, youths inevitably confronted the expectations of their families and their desires to live their own lives. Some, like Robbins, welcomed the emotional and financial support that stable ties provided, others found family and community confining; many dutifully fulfilled family responsibilities when called upon. George Fuller studied to be an artist until his family's fortunes compelled him to leave a promising career; he returned to Deerfield in the 1850s to manage the family farm. Two decades later, in a desperate struggle to save his family's land, he would return to his art, earning lasting fame and fortune as a painter. Oliver Chapin was born in Leyden in 1811. He attended Northfield Academy for two terms and at twenty-one started working for his father for eleven dollars per month. One winter he taught school. He eventually took over his father's farm and bought out the other heirs after his father's death. Samuel Dudley of Leverett received a common-school education and worked for other farmers as a laborer when he turned seventeen. When he was twenty he bought a small farm and did some lumbering. He later moved to nearby Shutesbury to follow the same business. Lorenzo Munn of Gill was born in 1815 and helped his father Seth run the family farm and operate a ferry that ran across the Connecticut River. He shared ownership of the farm after his father's death. Each of these men responded a bit differently to the choices presented them. Each went through a kind of rite of passage between youth and adulthood during which they experimented with careers, moved to different parts of the county, or simply waited for their time to come.[5]

The expansion of career options was a continuing process. "Much as it is to be regretted," Henry Colman observed in 1841, "few farmers find their sons willing to follow the profession of their fathers." He went on to point out that alternative employments with the prospect of more rapid financial gains encouraged children to leave the family farm, and he criticized the practice of dividing estates equally among several heirs because it created pressure to sell the farm out of the family. Colman's observations only pointed out what was already clear to many thoughtful people who were interested in the welfare of the region's farmers and the preservation of traditional values. Farming was becoming one alternative among many for making a living. As the decades passed, as the landscape became settled and ordered, it was apparent that not all children could or wanted to follow in their parents' footsteps and continue farming. For most families a shortage of good farmland forced children to consider cooperative arrangements like the one Robbins and his brother accepted, migration, non-farm occupations, wage labor, or a protracted wait for the control of the family patrimony. As they assessed their goals and opportunities, more and more children, both men and women, sought alternatives and revised their expectations about living in rural New England.[6]

The expansion of career choices for the region's men and women was the result of complex factors: improvements to the region's transportation networks, the creation of capital markets to sustain industrialization, and shifting expectations about material life and family security. The impact of these factors on the economic and social history of the region proceeded unevenly, but in general terms geographic and occupational mobility increased, the signs of regional culture slowly faded, and population shifts occurred as uplanders migrated to lowland manufacturing villages, coastal cities, and the West. Frequent movement of families was common in the colonial period, and it continued in the nineteenth century as people sought new opportunities to better themselves, but Franklin County's genealogical records suggest it was increasingly common to see children moving much further distances than they had earlier. Vermont, upstate New York, North Carolina, Michigan, Illinois, and cities such as Boston and New York were among their destinations. These places were either far removed or, in the case of cities, were morally suspect for a great many rural folk. Still, the attractions of these places were seductive — plenty of rich land at cheap prices in the rural areas, better business opportunities, a chance to start fresh, or the stimulation of urban living.[7]

Transportation quickened communication with these other communities and steadily diminished the insularity of rural life. All of the region's families witnessed cultural change from the growth of markets and improvements to transportation. In the eighteenth century, the county's trade was oriented primarily in two directions — eastern Massachusetts via overland routes and Connecticut and New York via the Connecticut River. Both routes had geographic complications. The falls at Enfield, Connecticut, were passable to small boats by means of vigorous poling, but the falls at South Hadley, Massachusetts, required a portage until they were eventually bypassed. By the 1790s, overland transportation to eastern Massachusetts ports, especially Boston, was not prohibitively expensive for certain types of products, and a substantial business in teaming developed by the early nineteenth century. While the habits of everyday living often followed a dreary routine that some rural youth sought to escape, families were not entirely isolated from contact with a broader world. Both eastern *and* southern market centers were familiar to many in the region by the 1780s. After that period, lands to the north in Vermont and Canada, and to the west in upstate New York and beyond would also become familiar. Kinship ties, marketing strategies, and commercial exchange cemented the aggregate of contacts that linked the area with the Atlantic world.[8]

As settlement in Franklin County proceeded, transportation improvements to the river took several forms. In 1792, the Massachusetts legislature incorporated the Proprietors of the Locks and Canals on the Connecticut River, a private stock company established to circumvent navigational impediments at Turners and South Hadley Falls. Work first began at South Hadley following the decision to build a canal and lock system around the falls, but construction was slowed by a shortage of capital and qualified hydraulic engineers. A transfusion of Dutch capital and design changes that led to the building of an inclined plane enabled the work to go forward. The falls at South Hadley were bypassed in 1794 and a moderately successful canal at Turners Falls was opened about the same time. Both developments increased exchanges on the north/south axis within the limitations of technology.[9]

In 1809, a new bridge across the Connecticut River at Hartford closed the route north to all but barge traffic. Initially, the size of barges depended upon the capacity of boat crews to pole the craft upstream over the falls of Enfield. George Sheldon later recalled that there were two kinds of boats. The cheapest type was built of pine in the upper sections of the river and was taken down to Hartford on a one-way trip. At Hartford, the boats were sold for their lumber and the crew returned northward. The process was repeated next spring with boats built during the winter. More permanent boats were built of oak with a cabin and carried a crew of five. "These boats were about seventy-five feet long, fourteen or fifteen wide at the mast, twelve or thirteen at the bow, eight or ten at the stern, with a capacity of from thirty-five to forty tons. They were rigged with a mast about twenty-five feet high, which stood about twenty-five feet from the bow with shifting shroud and forstays, a topmast to be run up at pleasure, square mainsail thirty by eighteen feet and a topsail twenty-four by twelve." The boats had no keel and were built of two-inch-thick white oak planks spiked to oak ribs. The bottom was flat from the mast back but it tapered slightly from the mast area to the bow. Freight was stacked in the center of the boat, leaving the sides free for poling or rowing. Oars were used only for downstream traffic. When the wind was not from the right direction, which was much of the time, upstream travel required poling, a procedure by which the bowman set a fifteen-to-twenty-foot-long ash pole into the bottom of the river, placed the opposite end on his shoulder, and walked aft the full length of the boat. Another man followed while the first man returned forward. Working vigorously a strong crew could pole the craft north at a speed of about 1.5 miles an hour. In areas with swift current the poling was assisted by teams of oxen who pulled the boat by a long rope from the shore. It was hard monotonous work and boat crews had a tough reputation, but they made possible sizable shipments of freight to and from Franklin County.[10]

River transportation improved markedly in the 1820s due to the self-interested boosterism of two rival commercial centers. In 1822, New Haven businessmen, eager to arrogate the valley's trade through their community, succeeded in chartering a canal corporation to improve commercial ties with north-central Connecticut and western Massachusetts. Although Hartford and Middletown merchants dominated the river trade by virtue of strategic location, the Connecticut River turns to the southeast below Middletown, and away from a major port. On paper a canal that extended north from New Haven through Farmington and then on to Northampton would be a more direct link with New York City. Despite the engineering obstacles and the impractical character of this scheme, Hartford businessmen reacted vigorously to this threat by chartering a company to bypass the last major obstacle on the lower Connecticut River, the falls at Enfield. Their plan was to build locks around the falls and to operate steamboats on the river. The competition of the two schemes set off a contest to find backers, raise capital, and win public support.[11]

The Hartford-based Connecticut River Company won the race to get into business. They were so anxious to be first that they constructed a steamboat that would fit the proposed locks and took the Enfield Falls at full speed. The first attempt to get by the Falls failed but the second succeeded and the vessel headed north up the river on a triumphant voyage that generated considerable attention. Church bells were rung, village cannon were fired, and crowds assembled to witness this great event. The scene caused a sensation as the vessel steamed past farms and villages, and as newspapers and pundits solemnly intoned the passing of an era and the coming of a new one. The celebrating was slightly premature. It was nearly three years before the locks were completed at Enfield, and steamboat traffic on the upper river never reached the expectations of the first enthusiasts. The Connecticut River Valley Steamboat Company was organized in 1831 to tow flat boats upriver, but the venture was overbuilt for the volume of business and freight rates proved to be too high. Ironically, larger companies failed while smaller, more flexible operations did reasonably well in the bid to manage the river traffic.[12]

Despite the initial success and momentum of the river forces, the canal interests pressed their program forward. Their progress was slow. The river interests were merely applying new technology to an existing water route. The canal group had to create an entire waterway from scratch. Furthermore, once the river interests had demonstrated their scheme's practicality, financial support for the canal declined. The ditch was pushed on to Northampton with difficulty and the first canal boat arrived in 1835, but canal operations were plagued with a series of problems, and red ink predominated. Between 1838 and 1839 canal receipts were poor. Only after New Haven voted to subsidize the canal's operations in 1841, could the company continue. It was too late; the railroad arrived in Northampton in 1845, and the canal closed. The competition of a faster and more reliable form of transportation was too much to overcome. The goal of making New Haven the entrepot to the upper Connecticut Valley was not practical (Fig. 8:2).[13]

The failure of the canal was related to a number of factors including poor management, insufficient water, high maintenance costs, and technological obsolescence, but the chief reason was that there was not enough trade from the valley to justify two similar systems of transportation. Farmers benefited from better transportation, but the seasonal cycles of agriculture insured that highly capitalized transportation systems would encounter cash-flow problems. Elihu Hoyt, one of the county's state senators in 1829, understood the difficulties of securing sufficient capital to pay for transportation improvements in a rural landscape. Although Hoyt favored the river interests, he was already hearing from railroad promoters who wanted state subsidies to build lines out to the Connecticut Valley and beyond. In a letter to his son on February 3, 1829, he observed that "the time I think has not yet come to make railroads to any great extent in this Country. the population is not sufficiently numerous & we have no great commodity to transport across our mountainous country that cannot now be easily transported to market by water." Better than many of his contemporaries Hoyt understood that expensive transportation projects needed a critical mass of population to insure a volume of business that would pay for them. He also knew that the water route south was only one of the commercial directions people in the region looked to. A considerable portion of the area's trade went overland to Boston. Only after the 1840s, did Franklin County and other areas in the region have enough industry to warrant construction of a transporation system that could operate in all seasons.[14]

While the river traffic was an important stimulus to the local economy, people depended upon a reliable network of roads to bring goods to market and to facilitate community life. As towns that were new in the 1770s matured and developed, local residents worked steadily on improving that network. Cattle went to the slaughterhouses and meatpackers in Brighton over the county's roads. Teamsters transported pork, cheese, butter, and poultry eastward and brought back store goods. Fourteen hundred pounds was considered a good load. The growth in teaming accelerated after investors promoted the construction of turnpikes in the 1790s and early 1800s to hasten long-distance road travel. Similarly, bridges over some of the larger rivers

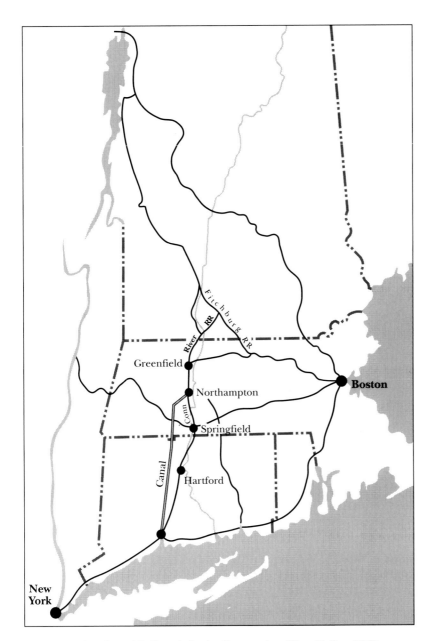

Figure 8:2. Canals and Railroads in the Connecticut River Valley, 1850.
(Drawn by the author.)

dramatically shortened some trips and helped encourage trade. In November of 1792, a large crowd watched the opening of the new 620-foot-long, four-arch bridge over the Connecticut River between Greenfield and Montague. The bridge simultaneously improved highway transportation with the East and served as a symbol of the area's progress. After the War of 1812, stage

coaches ran both north-south and east-west from Greenfield on regular schedules. The trip by stage took two days from Greenfield to Boston over reasonably good roads, many of them turnpikes. By the 1820s the volume of traffic
over Massachusetts roads was great enough to encourage state legislators to
consider building a canal from Boston to the Connecticut Valley. Even on
the local scene, roads were touted as important economic assets. When Crom-
well Bullock's house in Erving was sold to cover his debts in 1807, the advertisement qualified the meagerness of "a smallish house thereon, and fifteen
acres under improvement," by noting that the property was only a half-mile
from the turnpike from Greenfield to Boston. Clearly, local folks understood
the importance of good roads to the area's economy (Fig. 8:3).[15]

The Massachusetts legislature chartered turnpikes because some investors had found them profitable and because local road taxes were often insufficient to pay for improvements town taxpayers either could not or would
not spend money on. Obadiah Dickinson summed up the problems in a petition for a turnpike from Northfield to Sunderland. He pointed out that part
of the route lay on unincorporated land and that an expensive bridge was
necessary to cross the Miller's River. He added that the existing road and
bridge were in poor repair and concluded by arguing that "the road must be
made through lands but thinly inhabited, and the inhabitants very unable
to purchase, make and keep in repair said road." Few other turnpike petitions
printed in the county newspaper were so expansive, but the goals of such petitions were frequently the same. Petitioners hoped that local taxpayers would
not have to pay for expensive roads out of their own pocket, that the public
would benefit by harnessing the capital of local and outside investors, and that
investors presumably would make money.[16]

Farm families considered better roads as the most tangible example of
easier mobility, but better transportation was not merely technological change
in the form of roads, steamboats, and canals. It was also the result of political
competition centered on the issue of economic influence—down the valley
to the South, overland to the East, and from midwestern states. There were
winners and losers in this competition. The political issue was whether and
how the region's volume of trade would be controlled, and if so, then by
whom, and for whose benefit. Forward-looking people often came down on
opposite sides of the issue with equal certainty and conviction because they
perceived their interests differently. Nowhere was the issue more divisive
politically than the debate over the coming of the railroad. Roads and rivers
were adequate for agricultural trade, but with the emergence of industry,
transportation needs changed quantitatively and qualitatively. Factory work
was by the clock, not by nature's rhythms, and the manufacturing process
required a fairly even flow of raw materials and finished goods throughout the

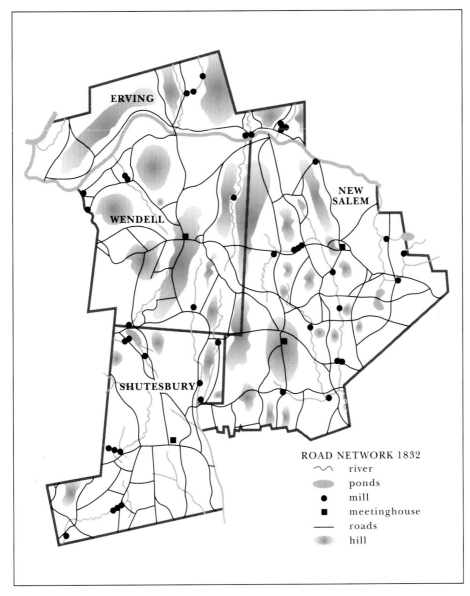

Figure 8:3. Road Network, Erving, Wendel, Shutesbury, and New Salem, Massachusetts, 1832. (Drawn by the author, based on Arthur W. Hoyt's 1832 map of Franklin County.)

entire year. As the number of factories increased and as they became larger in the 1840s, the pressures to secure better transportation intensified. One result was agitation for the railroad.[17]

Entrepreneurs were not the only ones interested in railroads, and the clamor over them in Franklin County and the Connecticut Valley came even before industry had developed in some areas. As railroad technology improved and became reliable in the mid to late 1830s, local investors and wealthy capitalists proved anxious to expand New England's railroad network. Each town had advocates who foresaw advantages in having a railroad right-of-way. More to the point, they saw disadvantages in not having one, in letting some other town get the advantage. Northampton was a classic case of how the fear of losing economic position prompted community leaders to agitate for a railroad. With an east-west line from Boston to Massachusetts's western border scheduled to pass well to the south through Springfield and another line proposed to the north for Greenfield, Northampton businessmen were spurred to action. As early as 1836, Northampton citizens were interested in a railroad line, but the panic of 1837 dried up capital and delayed plans. As the depression's effects eased in the early 1840s, planning went forward, but a proposal to build a line through Greenfield instilled a sense of urgency. Construction of a line north from Springfield began in 1843. Late in 1845, the railroad reached Northampton and there were proposals to extend it north to Greenfield. Thus there were now two proposals to build railroads through Franklin County—one linking the region to the South and one with the East. The time had come for people in the region to decide if they really wanted a railroad.[18]

The pro-railroad arguments were forcefully addressed at a convention held in Greenfield on October 25, 1845. The address was directed to stockholders of the Vermont and Massachusetts railroad company in an attempt to lure their support over to the proposal for a southern route to Northampton, but it also expressed the general sentiments of those who felt the railroad was in their best interests. "With a railroad communication direct to Greenfield, and thence to New York, the Erie Canal, and the great Lakes, will not the natural course of much of the merchandise be over your road to Greenfield, and thence down the Connecticut River Railroad to seek its shortest and cheapest course to the south and west?" While the address was clearly self-serving, it appealed to one of the principal interests of the Boston capitalists who financed much of the railroad building in New England. They had long explored schemes by which trade with the West could be brought directly from the Erie Canal to Boston, bypassing rival New York and insuring the continued vigor of Boston as a commercial port. The reasoning behind the argument was also appealing because the executives of the Vermont and Massachusetts railroad, led by Fitchburg industrialist Alvah Crocker, had not intended to link up the railroad with Greenfield, planning instead to run their railroad beside the Miller's River in eastern Franklin County and thence north and west to Brattleboro, Vermont. Greenfield might be linked with a spurline but it was not to be on the main route west.[19]

Railroad linkage with Boston was highly desirable and Greenfield interests held out hope of persuading Crocker's company to switch the Vermont and Massachusetts route to Greenfield. Meanwhile, boosters from Northampton attended meetings in Franklin County to champion the cause of the Connecticut River Railroad and the route south. After it became clear that Greenfield was not going to be on the main route from Boston to Troy, Franklin County entrepreneurs joined their forces with the supporters of the Connecticut River Railroad, apparently believing that a southern route was better than none at all. Meanwhile, the Massachusetts Legislature had already issued a charter for the line between Northampton and Greenfield in January 1845. The subscription book had been opened in April, and some local people began buying shares in the railroad extension. Not everyone greeted the prospect of a railroad with approbation. A number of local farmers in the Greenfield area objected to the line, pointing to the competition the railroad would bring by carrying western produce to the East—produce that would drive down prices eastern farmers received. Their objections were not shared by everyone; some prosperous farmers along the route actually bought shares of stock, but at one hundred dollars a share and with their wealth invested in fixed capital costs, relatively few farmers could afford to buy much stock in the railroad.[20]

Most of the railroad's stock was bought by capitalists outside of the area, many of them from Boston. Ten percent of the stockholders owned 50 percent of the company's issue. Even so, there were a number of local and regional investors, for 25 percent of the railroad's stock was owned by people living in towns along the right-of-way. In Franklin County, the towns of Deerfield and Greenfield showed particular interest in the road, subscribing more for the Northampton to Greenfield section than did Northampton investors. Leading the list of the local investors was Henry W. Clapp, Greenfield's wealthiest businessman, who had convinced local people that the north-south route was a practical alternative to an east-west route to Boston and that it would offer the opportunity for a future link with the Bay. Allied with Clapp was a group of substantial lawyers and the local industries, including Russell Cutlery, Lamson and Goodnow in Shelburne Falls, the woolen mills in Greenfield's Factory Hollow and the Griswold mills in Colrain. Farmers in Whately and Deerfield also bought shares. Wealthy farmers like Asa, Rowland, and Henry Stebbins owned twenty shares between the three of them; Ralph and George Williams owned five; and Horatio Hawks, Zebadiah Graves, and Christopher A. Stebbins also had shares. Some prosperous lowland farms supported the railroad, while other New Englanders eyed the railroads suspiciously. Perhaps these farmer investors sensed a need to diversify under the pressure of change. Perhaps they could afford to.[21]

For farmers the railroad proved to be a mixed blessing. While the improvement in transportation opened wider markets and brought cheaper consumer goods, the railroad also disrupted long-standing patterns. The fall/spring price difference for fat cattle virtually disappeared, further decreasing the profits that stall feeders had once enjoyed. While the railroad decreased transportation expenses by cutting the costs of drovers and ended the stock's weight loss that formerly occurred during the drive to market, the earlier system's inefficiencies had once been part of the reason for profit margins. If the railroad brought more order to the market system, it also increased competition. During the 1850s, more and more farmers in the lowland towns turned to alternatives to beef raising. Some got out of farming entirely . . . or tried to.[22]

Once begun, the expansion of the railroad network within the county continued. When Alvah Crocker of the Vermont and Massachusetts Railroad realized that a competing line had beaten his company to the northern route through Vermont, he reassessed his decision not to build on a route through Greenfield, North Adams, and on to Troy. Greenfield people and others in the eastern and western parts of the county were pleased. The line he proposed would offer better transportation opportunities for uplanders, not just those who lived in the Connecticut Valley lowlands. In 1848, Crocker petitioned the legislature for permission to revise the route of an east-west railroad from its northern course through Vermont to a more southerly route through Franklin County. He buttressed his request by claims that the route was more direct and that it would open up some of the last sites of good waterpower left in the state. One memorandum to the legislature optimistically claimed that "the valley of the Deerfield affords sites for factories [at] intervals of half a mile" and that "Shelburne Falls alone furnishes waterpower sufficient for ten or twelve manufacturing establishments of the largest class." Perhaps even more convincing was the potential power of the Connecticut River where it crashed over the rocks at Turners Falls. Although the Turners Falls site was not developed until after the Civil War, it must have seemed an attractive possibility for investment to men like Crocker. Convinced, the legislature agreed to incorporate the Troy and Greenfield Railroad in 1849. By 1851, work crews began laying track west of Greenfield amid real uncertainty as to whether the road could be financed.[23]

Complicating the prospects for successful completion of the line was the problem of how to get a railroad over or through Hoosac Mountain. The solution turned out to be a four-mile-long tunnel (then the world's longest) through unyielding granite. This project alone would absorb millions of dollars and it quickly became apparent that local capital could not finance the project. The legislature rebuffed the early requests for loans but approved an outlay of 2 million dollars in 1854 to push the project forward. Not until 1873 — nineteen years, 195 lives, and millions of dollars in state funds later — was the tunnel completed. In the interim, tracks were built westward up the Deerfield

River Valley, through Shelburne and Charlemont to the mouth of the tunnel. By 1858, the county map showed railroads running roughly north-south and east-west at about the middle of the county's geographic boundaries. These railroad lines intersected in Greenfield, reinforcing that town's long domination of the region's transportation routes.[24]

The consequences of the railroad were soon apparent. Greenfield gained the most from the new construction and in the 1850s went through an unprecedented period of growth. Its population had grown steadily in the 1830s and 1840s, but previous increases hardly compared with what happened in the 1850s. Between 1840 and 1860, the town's population grew from 1800 to 3200, and much of that increase occurred after 1846. Greenfield's growth as a transportation center was exceptional, but other towns also underwent considerable change after the trains came. Manufacturing blossomed in the Cheapside district of Deerfield, just south of the Deerfield-Greenfield line. At the opposite end of the town, the village of South Deerfield expanded from a modest crossroads to a real village center complete with a pocketbook factory. Meanwhile, the old street near the center of town remained agricultural, dominated by the prosperous farmers who were descendants of the town's old families.[25]

Farther to the west, the railroad contributed significantly to the growth of a small industrial village at Shelburne Falls. It was hardly coincidental that Lamson and Goodnow, the county's largest cutlery manufacturer, began construction of a new factory as rails were pushed westward from Greenfield. The railroad permitted the company to expand and with it the community on both sides of the river. The industrial commercial nexus, not the old agricultural community in the center of town, would be the new social sculptor of these upland villages. Like the original village of Deerfield, Shelburne's center did not take part in the new industrial growth. The positions of older geopolitical village centers that served an agricultural system throughout New England were often eclipsed under the pressures of commercial development and new forms of transportation. But the key word is *eclipsed*; like Julius Robbins's neighborhood in Wisdom the older farm communities did not simply disappear because of industrial growth. They continued to bide their time in the shadows outside more brightly illuminated landscapes.[26]

Among the changes to the county's landscape, none was more important than the new culture of work as men and women adjusted cultural discourse to include an industrial order alongside older agrarian traditions. Craftspeople continued to practice their trades, following established traditions of custom or "bespoke" work. Blacksmiths, carpenters, millwrights, joiners, weavers, hatters, coopers, and others had worked for generations to fill local needs for goods and services. In the eighteenth century most of these craftspeople worked within the network of family ties and community needs, but a few had reputations that extended beyond town borders. Some were people like Samuel Partridge of Hatfield whose skills as a joiner were sought for elaborate doorways in Deerfield, Hatfield, and Stockbridge houses. Others, such as Joseph Barnard, a Deerfield merchant who contracted with his uncle to produce canvas for the maritime trade in Salem, tied local production to larger markets. While men like Barnard and Partridge were clear exceptions, their activities were not unique. Craftspeople did move around and merchants used long-distance connections as part of their business practices. Some of the best craftspeople relied on their skills to make a living. Others combined a trade with some farming. A few married into the valley elite, but most were people of middling income who were able to make do with a variety of trades and who seldom reached the very top of the socioeconomic scale.[27]

Between 1790 and 1820, some craftspeople began to expand production beyond local markets. The case of the stoneware potteries in Whately is illustrative of the process. Most folks in Whately made their living farming, but as early as 1778, Jonathan Pierce, who had come from Wethersfield, Connecticut, was using local clays to make cheap redware pottery. By 1797, Stephen Orcutt was working in the same area making redware that was sold locally. In 1816, Orcutt bought land from Luther Wait and began a partnership with Luke and Obadiah Wait. The new pottery shop had water rights to Luther Wait's dam, and water was carried several rods in wooden troughs to a waterwheel that the partners used to power a pug mill that kneaded the clay to a workable consistency, an unusually sophisticated feature at the time. Even more unusual was the fact that the firm was potting stoneware, a higher-quality product than ordinary local earthenwares. Stoneware could not be made with local clays, and Orcutt must have imported the proper clay from Long Island or perhaps New Jersey. Obadiah Wait sold out his share in the works several months after the group had purchased the water rights. In 1817, Orcutt sold out to Luke Wait who ran the shop by himself for six more months before selling the business. Simultaneously, Daniel Goodale and Roderick Harwood, "potters," appear to have operated a shop beginning in 1817, but like Orcutt and Wait they dissolved their association a few years later. By 1821, Daniel Goodale was living in Hartford, where he made stoneware products that were nearly identical to those that Orcutt and Wait had made.[28]

Another potter, who began making redware in 1803, made Whately a center for ceramics production. In partnership with Justice White, Thomas Crafts began making redware teapots in 1822, copying a style introduced to the area by Sanford S. Perry, who started business in 1821 but who moved on to Troy, New York, by 1824. Crafts and White teapots were derived from

English designs. The inexpensive redware body was covered with a combination of manganese and galena (a sulphurite of lead) that was available locally and that, when mixed in the correct proportions and applied to the teapot, produced an opaque black metallic luster. In 1822, Crafts and White won a "gratuitous premium" at the Hampshire, Franklin, and Hampden Agricultural Society Annual Cattle Show and Fair held in Northampton. In an advertisement in the *Franklin Herald* the firm of Crafts and White announced "that they are carrying on the Manufactory of Tea Pots, on an extensive scale, at Whately. They flatter themselves that they can manufacture as good pots as are made anywhere in the United States." White left the partnership in 1823, but Crafts continued making teapots until 1832. In its heyday the operation employed six laborers and grossed four thousand dollars a year, apparently exporting teapots to Philadelphia and New York (Figs. 8:4 and 8:5).[29]

The Crafts family was to dominate the pottery business in Whately. After

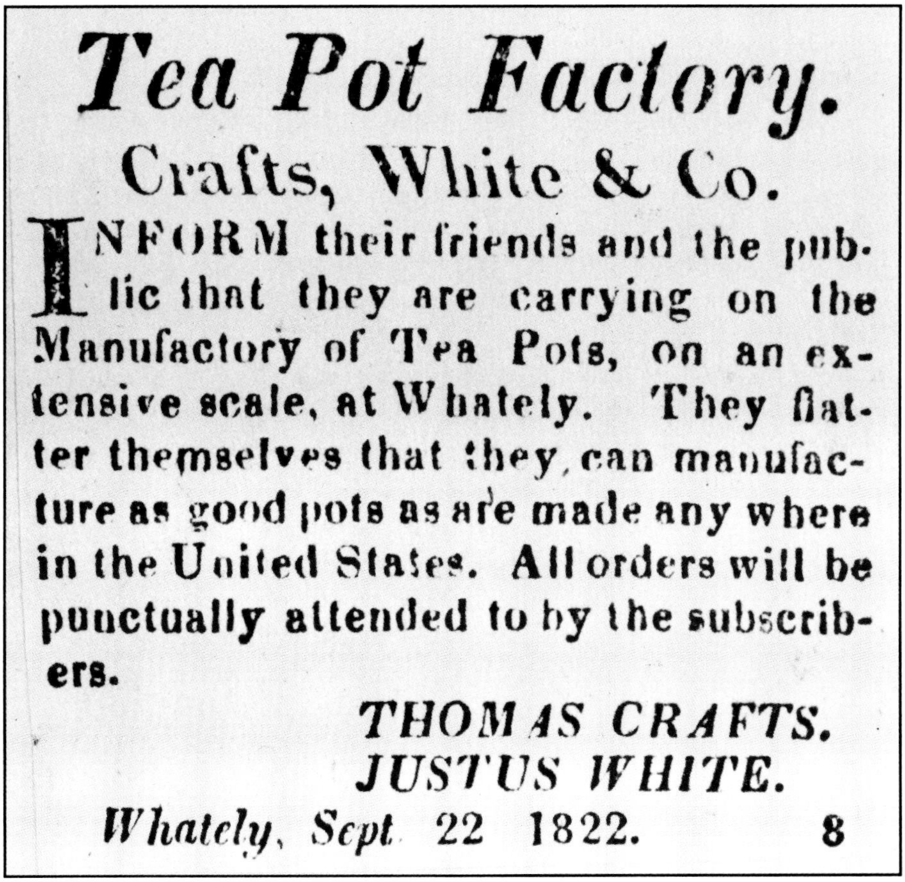

Tea Pot Factory.
Crafts, White & Co.

INFORM their friends and the public that they are carrying on the Manufactory of Tea Pots, on an extensive scale, at Whately. They flatter themselves that they can manufacture as good pots as are made any where in the United States. All orders will be punctually attended to by the subscribers.

THOMAS CRAFTS.
JUSTUS WHITE.
Whately, Sept 22 1822. 8

Figure 8:4. Advertisement for Teapots, *Greenfield Gazette*, September 29, 1822. (Courtesy, Henry N. Flynt Library.)

discontinuing teapot production in 1832, Crafts started making stoneware under the name Thomas Crafts and Company in 1833. He made a varied line of inexpensive commercial products: pots, jugs, butterpots, churns, jars, pitchers, chamberpots, inkstands, flower pots, mugs, beer bottles, blacking bottles, ice jars, and kegs. The clay came from New Jersey and was shipped up the river in quantity aboard flatboats to Whately. There, it was unloaded and drawn by team to the pottery three miles away. His son James recalled years later that if two or three boats came in at once his father needed as many as twelve to fifteen teams to haul the clay to the factory. By 1837, the company employed five workers and manufactured about $3,000 worth of stoneware per year. In 1842, Thomas Crafts's son, James, took over the company and changed the name of the firm to James M. Crafts and Company. During these poor economic years, business declined. In 1845 the company had only four employees and did only $1675 worth of business. Sometime in the middle of the 1840s James's brother, Thomas S. Crafts, became a partner in the firm and a few years later left for California. Other members of the Crafts family, however, continued making pottery into the 1850s.[30]

Between 1783 and 1861, twenty-one potters worked in Whately, and their influence went far beyond the town's borders. Starting with the production of simple redware forms similar to those made by other New England potters, Whately craftspeople branched off into the production of stoneware and specialized in producing a distinctive earthenware teapot that was exported to distant markets. Craftspeople who were trained in Whately influenced pottery traditions in Hartford, Connecticut; Portland, Maine; Keene, New Hampshire; and Troy, New York. Their operations were not related to the factory system, but neither were they typical of local potters producing for a local market. None of the potteries was highly capitalized, yet in at least one case a pottery made use of water power. It is unclear why pottery became such an important business in Whately. Individual enterprise, imagination, a good deposit of clay for redware production, a ready supply of fuel for firing the pots, and proximity to the Connecticut River were contributing factors, but the town *was* remote from both large markets and from the proper raw materials for stoneware production. Whately pottery was made in the craft tradition, but the scale of work was not typical of those who worked in small shops as individual craftspeople. The potteries that succeeded exploited the expanding market for ceramics, competing successfully with foreign imports. Their scale of production and market networks indicated that there were alternatives to farming, that goods could be produced successfully in small factories, and that society in the region was becoming complex enough to encourage specialization.[31]

Even upland communities entertained visions of manufacturing enter-

Figure 8:5. Teapot, Crafts and White, Whately, Massachusetts, ca. 1822–30. (Courtesy, Pocumtuck Valley Memorial Association.)

prises. The Franklin Glass Works began as an idea of Dr. Ebenezer Hall, one of the most ambitious and colorful men in the history of Warwick. Warwick was a rather isolated community located in the rolling uplands next to Northfield. It was a town of modest farmers when Hall was hired in 1805 to teach in one of the community's schools. A man of personal charm, Hall impressed everyone. William Cobb approvingly noted in his diary the day he visited Hall's school that he was "extraordinarily entertained with the good management and conduct of the school." Cobb was not the only one to be impressed. Hall managed to persuade Olive Rich, the daughter of one of the town's wealthiest men, to marry him, and from 1808 to 1811 he was elected to the prominent office of town clerk.[32]

Among Hall's intellectual pursuits was a fascination with science. Sometime before 1812, he became interested in the production of glass, and his curiosity and ambition led him briefly to Williamstown, Massachusetts, to a glasshouse built by a local farmer named Sherman. Although Sherman had never used this glasshouse, Hall secured permission to experiment with glass making, and upon returning to Warwick was able to persuade area residents to finance the creation of a glass factory. The schoolteacher, physician, politician, and patent medicine inventor carried the town along on his visionary scheme. A large number of local families invested in the idea; some even mortgaged their farms to raise money. Most seemed to believe, along with Hall, that manufacturing glass would lead them to prosperity. In the fall of 1811, a local farmer, Jonathan Blake, surveyed the ground for a glasshouse. In January, Hall contracted with a local mason, David Bishop, to construct the glasshouse, and James Symes, a glassmaker, arrived in Warwick to assist with its design, construction, and management. A month later Hall, his father-in-law, and several of the town's more prominent men formed a corporation known as The Franklin Glass Factory Company, the first glasshouse to be built in western Massachusetts.[33]

By September, months of construction were showing signs of progress. As glassmaker, Symes moved his family into a commodious house built for him. A tenement for the glassblowers who would work in the factory was put up across the road. As the factory neared completion in the winter of 1812–13, Hall set off with his wife and sister for Hopkinton, New York, to find glassblowers. William Cobb, president of the company, noted in his diary on March 22, 1813, that "Dr. Hall returned from Westward, where he had been engaged for 24 days to engage glassblowers having engaged 5 to come in a short time, paying them a bounty of 500 dollars each." The expenditure of $2500 to entice glassblowers to move to the new factory elicited immediate criticism from Warwick's hardworking farmer/stockholders. Many of them did not make $500 for a year's worth of labor and in their view the bounty was excessive if not unnecessary. Hall evidently explained that skilled glassblowers were hard to find and that glass companies made it a common practice to recruit skilled men by enticing them away from other firms with bounties.[34]

By late April of 1813, several glassblowers had moved to Warwick. Hall departed for Philadelphia in search of the clay necessary for making the glass melting pots. During the second week in July the factory was complete enough to begin making glass. On July 9, the workers began to heat the first furnace. On the 28th, "the furnace melting cap gave away before the glass was melted sufficiently to blow and the furnaces and ten pots were lost." Despite this setback, the furnace was rebuilt, a fire was started, and on September 5, 1813, William Cobb wrote, "The Franklin Glass Company began to blow glass on Sunday—the furnace stands well." A week later the company advertised that it was in complete operation and that it was producing window glass. Although the company had successfully produced glass, expenses mounted rapidly and the fledgling concern was forced to assess stockholders an additional $25 per share. Those who failed to pay would forfeit their shares at a public auction. After a warning notice on October 19, a list of shares to be sold was included in the October 31st paper. Things worsened rather quickly. Ebenezer Hall returned to town on November 27 from a visit to a glass factory in Woodstock, New York, where he had spent some time studying glassmaking. His expenses amounted to $500. Perhaps in disgust with the way things were going, James Symes, the company's glassmaker, left town a few weeks later to take up a new position with the Crown Glass Works in Sand Lake, New York. Abel Minard, one of the company's glassblowers, was appointed to take his place. Neither Hall's recipes for glass or Symes's departure improved the firm's cash problems. Another assessment on the shareholders was ordered and thirty-three shares had to be put up for auction. The only bright spot in the gloomy prospects was that William Cobb succeeded in raising $1305 by selling forty-four shares to a Boston merchant, Ebenezer Nickerson.[35]

The company struggled through 1814 without further mishap, until October 23, when Abel Minard died. He had served as glassmaker since James Symes departed and his fellow workers respected him. After his death, they erected a tombstone in his memory, specifically noting that it was "Erected by his Brother Workmen." Once again William Cobb went to Boston and tried to raise more money. He was not successful. Discouraged, he resigned the office of president and treasurer, and confided in his diary that he did so "calculating to pursue some other employment more conducive to my health and comforts." Although orders for glass did come in, they were not sufficient. The company was failing. Resignation notwithstanding, Cobb tried again to interest Ebenezer Nickerson in the project. Nickerson toured the works on February 3 and observed the workmen blowing glass, but Cobb did not record in his diary that Nickerson was prepared to invest in more shares, dashing hopes that outside money would help save either the factory or local stock owners. Then, on February 8, 1815, a local resident, Samuel Fay, called in the debts the company owed him, touching off a panic of suits from worried creditors, many of them local. Bankruptcy was avoided only after Stephen Ball stepped in and hired the glass factory for six months. Ball was a local man and his show of confidence allowed the company to reorganize, sell new stock, and pay off its debts.[36]

Debts continued to mount, creditors constantly appealed for payment, and the War of 1812 finally ended, unleashing a flood of European goods to compete with American manufacturers. In November of 1815, the furnace failed and the factory closed. Cobb settled with the workmen. On February 14, 1816, the factory was auctioned for $2,350, after last minute moves to salvage the company failed. The purchaser, Mark Moore, almost immediately resold the property to Ebenezer Nickerson and a consortium of Warwick men. These men in turn tried to restart the factory. The economic situation in Warwick meanwhile was becoming increasingly difficult. Each failure further depressed the town's financial health, making collection of debt more difficult, and insuring depreciation of local property. The final desperate move to restart glass production was dashed on June 26, 1816, when the cap of the glass furnace failed. Warwick's attempt to tie its fortunes to industry were at an end. During the next several years, the proprietors of the bankrupt firm tried to settle the company's debts. The factory was razed in 1820 and the land sold. The enterprising but ill-starred Dr. Hall headed for Keene, New Hampshire, to superintend a glassworks there. That factory also soon closed.[37]

Warwick's glass factory failed for a number of reasons. The town was geographically remote from raw materials, none of the original directors of the firm had extensive business experience particularly with a technologically complex industry, skilled labor was difficult to find and keep, neither the directors of the company nor those townspeople who invested in the project realized the tremendous capital resources required, and the investment of outside capital proved to be too little, too late. Finally, the company foundered on bad luck—furnaces that cracked at the wrong moments, the resumption of foreign competition at a time when the firm was most vulnerable, and the collapse of public confidence when a few months' faith might have made a difference. The failure of the glassworks obscures the fact that the citizenry of Warwick had very nearly succeeded in pulling off what more practical people would never have thought of. During the five years the company existed, it had raised thousands of dollars in capital, largely from local sources, built a factory complex of workers' housing, warehouses, barns, and a glasshouse in a remote upland town, and successfully manufactured glass. The investors in the glasshouse for the most part were local people, not eastern capitalists. Their vision to start a sophisticated industry, however unrealistic, came from people who were eager to develop their resources and opportunities, and who were willing to risk a great deal on the dream that their lives could be bettered by investing hard-earned savings in a factory instead of the farm.

In contrast to Warwick's experiment with glass, industrial development in the rest of the county followed a somewhat more typical if less colorful pattern. Factory Hollow in Greenfield was one site where the proper combination of topographic features and a good supply of water attracted development (Fig. 8:6). By 1790, a sawmill, a gristmill, and a fulling mill were using the water there. About 1812, local businessmen built a woolen mill, beginning the history of mechanized textile manufacture in the area. The venture was successful enough to attract the attention of two of Greenfield's most prosperous merchants, Lyman Kendall and Nathaniel Russell, and the two men purchased the mill in 1825. Although they had no experience with manufacturing, both men had contacts. Kendall was related by marriage to the Dwight family of Springfield, and Russell, his partner, was connected to old families

Figure 8:6. Factory Hollow, Greenfield, Massachusetts, 1852.
(Courtesy, Greenfield Historical Society.)

in Deerfield. The Dwights had supplied venture capital to help Kendall open his store in Greenfield, and they probably helped again by providing funds to help purchase the mill and finance its expansion. By 1826, the new owners had added a second mill and a dye house, and increased the number of employees to eighty by 1827. In that year Kendall moved to Cleveland to look for greater rewards than Greenfield provided, leaving Russell in charge of the store and factory. Unfortunately for Russell, the factory burned down on November 19, 1828, after an oil lamp overturned and started a fire. In 1830 Russell rebuilt with granite; the new mill was forty-five by a hundred feet, and was four stories tall with a gambrel roof and clerestory windows on the top floor. A bell tower was located near the midpoint of the long side. The new factory was powered by a forty-five-foot wheel that ran three pickers, eleven carding machines, five spinning jennies with a total of 320 spindles, forty looms, two fulling mills, and some cotton machinery. The equipment alone cost forty thousand dollars (Fig. 8:8). Financial backing for the operation seems to have come from Boston capitalists. The new factory produced high-quality cotton broadcloth, satinet, and doeskin (a soft fabric popular as coating material). Despite the infusion of capital, the textile industry was not particularly successful in Franklin County. Profits declined after 1837. In 1840, a Boston businessman, Theodore Leonard, reorganized the operation's finances, but the mill was never a particularly prosperous operation.[38]

The most profitable industries used materials that had to be imported, processed, and exported. By 1860, two of the nation's largest and most innovative cutlery factories were located in Franklin County. Together the two firms accounted for almost half of the cutlery manufactured in the United States. The trade in steel blades began indirectly. In 1819, a group of local businessmen sent John Russell, whose father was a Greenfield jeweler and silversmith, to Savannah, Georgia, to speculate in cotton. During the next thirteen years he did well, earning a modest personal fortune. In 1832, during a family visit to Greenfield, he happened upon *The Practical Tourist*, an account of the travels of Zachariah Allen, a prominent American textile manufacturer. As the story was later told, Russell was particularly struck by a section of the book in which Allen described the cutlery industry in Sheffield, a center for British tool and knife manufacturing. In 1833, he and his brother Francis formed a company to make chisels. They bought an old tannery, installed a steam engine, hired local labor, and started up production. From the beginning, the chisels established a reputation for excellence, winning a premium at the 1834 American Institute Fair. By 1835, the company employed ten men and expanded operations by making butcher and carving knives.[39]

The steam engine proved inadequate for Russell's needs, and he searched for a site with water power, finally settling on a former textile mill near the Greenfield-Deerfield line. Russell refitted the mill for forging and grinding, but just as they began production the forge shop burned to the ground. Two months later, in May, a spring flood smashed the remaining buildings and carried equipment and machinery all the way to the Deerfield meadows. Despite these twin disasters, Russell collected four thousand dollars from an insurance policy and rebuilt. He also benefited from a timely investment by Greenfield entrepreneur, Henry W. Clapp. In 1835, at the age of thirty-seven, Clapp retired to Greenfield after a career manufacturing jewelry in the New York City firm of Palmer and Clapp, where he made a considerable fortune. Clapp put up ten thousand dollars to help the company get started again. His conditions were simply that Russell not sell the firm without his consent, and that Clapp receive a third of the profits during the next seven years.[40]

The firm was reorganized as the John Russell Manufacturing Company with John Russell, Francis Russell, and Henry Clapp as partners. It included a forging room with twelve trip-hammers, a separate building with seventy grindstones, and one hundred emery wheels. Another shop was reserved for tempering the blades and affixing handles. The company was back in operation in 1837 with seventy employees, and profits began flowing in. Efforts by Sheffield cutlers to put Russell out of business were forestalled by the panic of 1837, which had little impact on Russell's business, but provided some protection in the form of a tariff that Congress levied in an attempt to raise revenue. Faced with the tariff and other business uncertainties, the Sheffield cutlers waited too long to undersell the new competition. Russell's cutlery soon established a reputation and the firm's success was assured. (See Fig. 8:7.) In the long run the company may have benefited from its near failure. The flood forced the owners to build a new factory, incorporating the experience they had gained. Not only did the company survive the panic of 1837

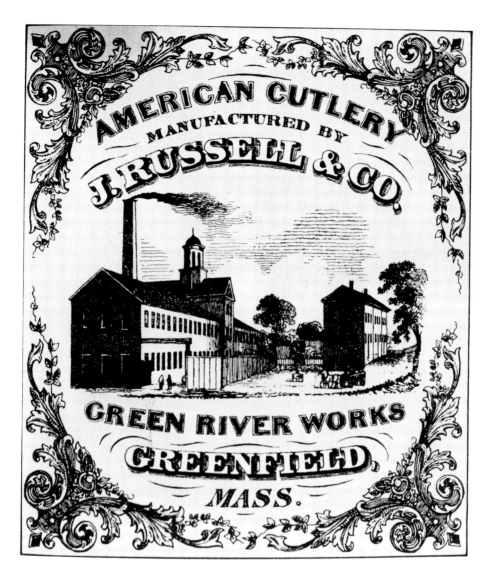

Figure 8:7. J. Russell and Co., Deerfield, Massachusetts, ca. 1850.
(Courtesy, Pocumtuck Valley Memorial Association.)

in fine shape, but it also expanded as the depression's effects wore off in the mid 1840s. As the figures in Table 8:1 show, sales were excellent. Dividends during the fifteen-year period averaged 35 percent of capital. For a region accustomed to the slow accumulation of wealth from farming, the company's spectacular profits illustrated the potential for success via industrialization.[41]

The Russell Company was not the first cutlery firm in the valley, and it soon had a competitor in Shelburne, Massachusetts. Among the small industries that started in the area around Shelburne Falls was a firm owned

Table 8:1
Growth of the John Russell Company, 1845-1860

Date	Capital	Employees	Value of Products (Annually)
1845	$ 20,000	80	$ 60,000
1850	$ 40,000	200	$125,000
1855	$ 75,000	300	$250,000
1860	$175,000	300	$280,000

by Silas Lamson that specialized in the manufacture of bent-scythe snaiths. Silas's sons, Nathaniel and Ebenezer, expanded operations in 1836, turning out more than twenty thousand snaiths yearly. In 1842 they ventured into making cutlery, and two years later joined with Abel and Ebenezer Goodnow to form the Lamson and Goodnow Manufacturing Company. The snaith factory was moved to Windsor, Vermont, in 1848, and the factory at Shelburne Falls began manufacturing cutlery exclusively. Like the Russell firm, Lamson and Goodnow used modern manufacturing techniques and were highly successful, introducing a number of innovations to the industry. In 1845 the firm was modestly capitalized. Five years later capital stood at $75,000. In 1851, the firm built a dam across the Deerfield River and erected a factory on the Buckland side of the river. Within ten years the firm had become the largest cutlery factory in the country, employing 340 workers, and holding capital assets valued at $500,000. And as the company grew, the hamlet of Shelburne Falls expanded and became a commercial/industrial village.[42]

The success of the cutlery industries in Franklin County defies any simple explanations about industrialization. The area's chief economic assets — low taxes, relatively abundant water power, and plenty of timber — might explain the origins of snaith making, box factories, and turning mills, but they do not easily account for the process by which highly capitalized factories were built in remote farming regions. Unlike textile mills that needed large amounts of unskilled or semi-skilled labor and that might make use of the area's agricultural products like wool, the cutlery factories employed highly skilled, expensive labor and imported most of the materials needed. The companies that did best in the region were those whose leaders had solid business experience and outside contacts. The Russell Company succeeded in part because it began producing cutlery so early that it established a reputation before competitors existed. Its directors were able businessmen who successfully incorporated technological innovations to compete with British firms. In retrospect, Russell's move to found a cutlery factory was highly audacious.

Neither he nor his brothers knew much about manufacturing cutlery, nor was there any assurance that the venture would succeed in competing with the reputation of Sheffield wares. What Russell did have was business experience, honed by more than a decade of familiarity with the volatile cotton market, and a family tradition of working with metals.[43]

Russell also had other conditions in his favor. Without a skilled labor force that used traditional technology, he could embrace manufacturing innovations with little opposition from workers. This freedom to experiment enabled him to compete effectively with established European cutlery firms. From the beginning he used steam power. He also introduced the use of powered trip-hammers to cutlery manufacture, speeding up the production of cutlery blanks, and making it possible to forge the knife blank, tang, and bolster from one piece of steel. By 1851, Russell had begun pressing knife blanks with dies, a process that had been developed by his competitors, Lamson and Goodnow, a few years earlier. Such innovations enabled both manufacturers to increase productivity from 150 to 3,000 pieces per worker per day, a major factor in both firms' ability to compete successfully with Sheffield cutleries.[44]

The introduction of industry and the expansion of business opportunity had complex results. Industrialization created a new kind of landscape. Steam-powered factories such as the Greenfield Tool Company's works had tall smokestacks that signaled their locations with clouds of coal smoke (Fig. 8:8). When the John Russell Cutlery built its new factory in Cheapside, it fostered the creation of a new neighborhood around it, a cluster of boardinghouses, small cottages, and modest homes for factory workers. A view of the scene, painted in 1864, documents a landscape that differed considerably from towns with dispersed settlement or nucleated villages like Sunderland, Deerfield, and

Figure 8:8. View of Greenfield Tool Company, Greenfield, Massachusetts, 1852. (Courtesy, Greenfield Historical Society.)

Figure 8:9. William Sommers, View of Cheapside, 1864.
(Courtesy, Pocumtuck Valley Memorial Association.)

Northfield (Fig. 8:9). The mechanics of Cheapside lived in homes that were small and clustered tightly together near the factory. Behind the houses were gardens, privies, laundry on lines, and fences. Developers, not the residents, dominated the architectural decisions. Many of the houses were built exactly alike, distinguished by the alterations their occupants or owners were able to make on the landscape adjacent to the house. All of them reflected a desire for housing and a plot of land. Most of them belonged to immigrants with cultural and ethnic backgrounds different from the dominant Yankee culture in the region.[45]

As the county's population density increased, the sense of its being a single geopolitical community was replaced by an emphasis on neighborhoods or groups. By the mid 1850s these neighborhoods often corresponded to specific points on the landscape: the local district school, a community burying ground, a factory village, and, sometimes, a church. Where families educated their children, buried their dead, and worshipped came to signal *place*, some sense of spatial responsibility, and even social loyalty. This neighborhood sense of community was central to the process of adapting to larger, more complex and specialized communities. No single institution within the life of a community could continue to serve as a symbolic unifying center for most people in town. Towns were too big, congregations could not all fit into one building, and there were multiple centers of religious gravity. The old mythic world of peaceable kingdoms was in retreat following the Great Awakening, and throughout the mid eighteenth century and the Revolutionary era new intellectual, political and spiritual attachments vied for the hearts and minds of the region's inhabitants.[46]

These changes were reflected on the region's landscape. By the 1790s the sacred canopy of the New England church which had served to knit the congregations and communities of the Connecticut Valley together was unraveled, to be replaced by a more competitive form of sectarianism. As if to underscore the centrifugal forces that were pulling apart the world of orthodox Congregationalism, the Deerfield congregation appointed the Reverend Samuel Willard Pastor of their church in 1807. Willard was Harvard trained and his Unitarian views on the divinity of Christ quickly led to trouble with other valley churches. Local ministers who examined Willard's credentials politely expressed esteem and affection for the candidate but refused to ordain him on the grounds that his theology was unacceptable. Deerfield's church members would not back down and imported more sympathetic ministers from eastern parts of the state who went forward with Willard's ordination. His appointment was one more sign of how impotent the valley's once-powerful clergy had become in the face of determined local opposition. Although Willard held his Deerfield flock together despite his theological views, his successors were not so fortunate. In 1838, a group of orthodox parishioners separated to form a trinitarian church, splintering the religious unity that had long marked village life and burdening church members with the support of two ministers and buildings.[47]

Deerfield's experience was not unique nor was religious dissent limited to the rise of Arminians or Baptists, or divisions between Old Lights and New Light theology following the Great Awakening. During the early decades of the nineteenth century, other communities witnessed splits in congregations experiencing the tug of religious revivalism. Itinerant preachers, immigration of new ethnic groups, and the tide of evangelicalism would reshape the religious landscape of the county. These new sects did not seek to replace those that had long dominated, but they insisted upon equal opportunity to win the region's unconverted. The Congregational way would be challenged successively by Baptists, Unitarians, Episcopalians, Methodists, Catholics, and Lutherans. While the county's original churches sometimes looked upon these contenders with alarm, there was little that they could do to compel obedience to the original congregation.

The fracturing of religious life into sects resulted in the construction of many new meetinghouses. Some of these new buildings stood adjacent to or

Figure 8:10. Congregational Meeting House, Ashfield, Massachusetts, 1812.
(Photograph by the Historic American Building Survey, National Park Service.)

Figure 8:11. St. John's Episcopal Church, Ashfield, Massachusetts, 1825.
(Photograph by the Historic American Building Survey, National Park Service.)

nearby once dominant churches. Down the street from Ashfield's 1812 Congregational Meetinghouse with its soaring steeple, the congregation of St. John's Episcopal Church laid the cornerstone of their new sanctuary in 1825. Although its size and ornamentation were little challenge to the magnificence of the earlier church, the two buildings marked the social and religious discourse of a community in which alternate religious truths had achieved legitimacy and could coexist on the same street (Figs. 8:10 and 8:11). There was nothing in the architecture of the two structures that indicated to casual outside observers the particular doctrinal positions of either congregation. Regardless of its iconoclastic theological antecedents, the Congregational meetinghouse in Ashfield looked more like a church than the plain style meetinghouses that once dominated the religious architecture of the valley.

In some towns congregations replaced and repositioned their churches to respond to the new architectural styles and cultural changes sweeping through New England. In Deerfield, the fourth meetinghouse was demolished in 1824, after the town's congregation built a new brick building. The new structure was a close copy of a church built several years earlier as the Second Congregational Church of Greenfield, reflecting the sense of rivalry with the county seat that the older town still seemed to feel. More importantly, the new Deerfield church was built to one side of the town common, partially on land that the church had to buy from the Hoyt family. The new site opened up the common and made it more park-like, but in a literal sense the community had moved religion out of the center of its public life (Fig. 8:12). The new meetinghouse remained a prominent fixture in community life, yet the displacement of the building symbolized a trend that was taking place in other communities. There was no longer an errand into the wilderness, no single city on the hill to serve as a beacon for the rest of civilization. Communal unity would require a metaphor other than a single church.[48]

What was left on the common in Deerfield was a brick schoolhouse. While this structure burned not long after John Warner Barber recorded his view of the town, the position of the school in the 1810s–1830s was appropriate. Throughout the towns of Franklin County and the rest of New England, school committees busily carved up the landscape into school districts, built schoolhouses, and hired schoolteachers. There were earlier schoolhouses of course, but the district school system dramatically expanded both the scale and the basis of local education. A look at the county's 1858 map reveals that district schools were scattered throughout the entire county. Their location was not random, for they were associated with identifiable places or neighborhoods. The Wapping schoolhouse (1839) built in the Wapping section of Deerfield is one surviving example of a district school. It was a single room, heated by a stove, with a shed addition where the privies were located and wood was stored (Fig. 8:13).

As such structures went, the Wapping schoolhouse was better appointed than most, with some attention given to exterior appearance and interior comfort. Like other schoolhouses it was built to equip children with the educational skills to live in an increasingly competitive and specialized society. In a sense district schools were a tacit admission that the older, less-structured approach to education through family, church, and schools was no longer disciplined enough, that children would have to go for varying lengths of time

Figure 8:12. View of Deerfield. From John Warner Barber, *Historical Collections*, 1839. (Courtesy, Pocumtuck Valley Memorial Association.)

to a specialized building to learn what they needed to know, and that this form of instruction would supplement what they received at home. While the buildings were usually built on marginal or insignificant pieces of land that reformers such as Horace Mann, Massachusetts's most famous educational reformer, criticized as unhealthy, their location was chosen largely to prevent long walks for schoolchildren, to keep them under the watchful gaze of parents and neighbors, and to preserve a measure of parental and local control. The timing of the creation of district schools varied somewhat within each community, but in general it coincided with efforts to rebuild the region's barns, to improve the efficiency of domestic space by building ells, and to increase productivity in the workforce through more disciplined work habits. As state and town authorities in the first half of the nineteenth century moved away from regulating citizens' religious lives, they shifted their attention to the schools as a way of inculcating social and cultural norms. Increasingly, then, schools became a symbol of community, a common space in towns where such land was rare.[49]

Not many communities in Franklin County had as generous a common as Deerfield's. Most towns simply had small sections of open land that served as a common near the intersection of several roads. Except for the nucleated villages surrounded by common fields in the lowlands, most of the landscape around the area's town commons was built up slowly. (See Fig. 7:44.) Greenfield's common was originally located near its eighteenth-century church but, as the town grew, population was concentrated in the village along the street

Community   237

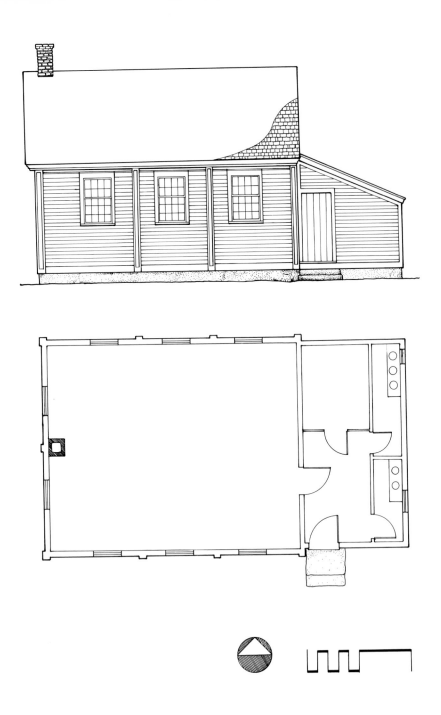

Figure 8:13. Wapping Schoolhouse, 1839, Deerfield, Massachusetts. (Redrawn by the author from originals by the Historic American Building Survey, National Park Service: original drawing by Harry Gulesian.)

near the south end of the town. At the village's principal intersection, one portion of the street was widened to form a small triangle of open land. This small plot served the function of public space while the original common two miles to the north was virtually ignored. Although the county's towns never had large commons, the public spaces that were set aside in villages became more controlled over time. Many towns put up fences around their commons to limit the access of vehicles and livestock. Some towns or groups of residents improved their commons by consciously landscaping the common with trees and walks. This concern for appearance helped to define community pride and marked the location of centers of power and public business. Central villages around these common spaces became core neighborhoods within the larger town to which other neighborhoods looked for goods and services.

The dominance of these core neighborhoods was reinforced by the presence of public and commercial buildings. By the 1790s most of these neighborhoods had at least one building that could hold public gatherings. Most of the time a village center would have a tavern, some of which had ballrooms or assembly rooms that were used for public gatherings, a church, or possibly a public hall. If these spaces were unavailable, there was always the district school or a large private home. As the county seat, Greenfield had several public spaces for large gatherings by the 1820s, several of which were built in brick, a material associated with urban centers. Surrounding the town common was the Second Congregational Church, which accommodated large public events such as the agricultural society's annual meeting. On the opposite corner was the Mansion House, the county's biggest hotel, with several function rooms, and down Deerfield Street was the County Courthouse built in 1817 (Fig. 8:14). Greenfield also had the county's first town hall built to provide space for public functions and the town offices, increasing the distance between it and most other rural towns of the county less able to capitalize on geographic position (Fig. 8:15). Some towns, such as Montague, built competing structures, but most communities could not afford to erect such buildings (Fig. 8:16). Greenfield's central location and its public amenities insured that it would remain the dominant political and social center in the county because there were few other spaces where large gatherings could occur. Other communities and neighborhoods would revolve around this central nucleus which in turn orbited in the shadows of larger metropolitan regions.

The emergence of neighborhoods as distinct places within larger towns was demonstrated in another way—where families chose to bury their dead. In the eighteenth century most towns in the region had a single burying ground where they placed their deceased. Sometimes the burying ground was associated with the community's meetinghouse, but not always. Early towns like Deerfield created a burying ground out of ministerial lands. After 1800, there

Figure 8:14. Mansion House, Greenfield, Massachusetts, 1852.
(Courtesy, Greenfield Historical Society.)

Figure 8:15. Town Hall, Greenfield, Massachusetts, 1852.
(Courtesy, Greenfield Historical Society.)

Figure 8:16. Town Hall, Montague, Massachusetts, 1858. (Photograph by the author.)

were no more ministerial lands left and in towns like Deerfield the old burying ground was nearly full. In some cases a new burying ground was laid out, in other cases a church developed its own graveyard for church members and their families, and in others, neighborhoods set aside a piece of land designated for burials. By the 1850s these small graveyards were scattered about the landscape of many towns in the region. The headstones usually reveal the names of local families who were laid to rest among friends and neighbors and who held fast to the notion of communal values by creating new ways to delineate community.[50]

In 1823, at the annual address to the Hampshire, Franklin, and Hampden Agricultural Society, Isaac Bates ebulliently proclaimed: "The country must be filled with activity and industry, not of the plough and spade merely;

but of the spindle and loom; the forge and hammer and all the busy machinery of the manufacturing process. It is this and this only that can make you rich." Had they been among the audience privileged to hear this address, many people would have embraced Bates's call for industrialization. Certainly they behaved as if they did, for throughout Franklin County and New England men and women busily searched for a way to participate in commerce and manufacturing. In the braiding of palm leaf for hats, the production and export of pottery in Whately, the attempt to establish a glass factory in Warwick, the creation of a cutlery industry, the improvements to transportation, and in myriad other ways, individuals reshaped older agrarian landscapes and communities.[51]

Reformers and intellectuals like Bates at first called for and believed in a balance between agriculture and industry, with each working to improve the circumstances of the other. The problem was that this balance was tough to achieve. Farmers moved to the contrapuntal rhythms of natural processes as much as social or economic ones. Manufacturing and commerce evolved initially within the sphere of an agricultural system, but the logic of factory work was human and artificial. Judged against the pace of a commercial system, the long-term strategies of farming were perceived by many as rather dull. Although Julius Robbins and other rural youth persisted on the family farm, many young people were driven away by the desire to seize new chances. Loyalty to family and kin would persist, but many young people detached themselves from deference to age, place, work roles, and the geographic community. New opportunities not declining ones made many youth impatient with traditions their elders sometimes held dear. Believing that a short-sighted drive for quick success threatened the moral fiber of American families, men like Henry Colman hoped to check the flight from the region's farms by trying to reify agricultural labor with dignity, claiming, "This confidence of progress, this hope of ultimate success, certain to persevering and judicious labor, is the great encouragement which is to sustain us."[52] So long as farming was the principal occupation shared by most families in the county, such words must have comforted. In 1833, when Colman spoke these sentiments, however, economic specialization was proceeding rapidly and the words must have sounded a bit hollow.

If the tensions between agricultural and industrial systems still seemed balanced in the 1830s, the scales were tipping by the 1850s as the direction of commercial growth became clearer. Farming, once the dominant strategy for living, seemed eclipsed in the northeast by a world of commerce, factories, and wage labor. To some, the temper of the times seemed bad. During his address at the first annual meeting of the Franklin County Agricultural Society, Joseph Buckingham lamented the current state: "That so many young men are tempted to quit the farm and the workshop and enter countinghouses and stores in cities, inspired with the hope of realizing a wealthy independence, in the shortest possible time, is much to be regretted, and the results too often presents a melancholy picture."[53] What Buckingham and many other commentators forgot in the midst of their jeremiads about the decline of youth, was that what constituted progress depended on one's perspective. People in Franklin County were developing a pluralistic system of values in which personal relationships forged in factories, neighborhoods, schools, churches, political parties, and far-flung networks of exchange would come to define communities of action and belief. Few men or women could regularly muster sufficient solidarity of interests to assert issues of majority will or class consciousness as long as most individuals held memberships in these different communities with competing goals.[54] Like the region's physical landscape, the topography of community was constantly adjusting to new life cycles of growth and decay.

Chapter 9

Conclusion

As a young man, Charles Hoyt socialized with the children of prominent Deerfield families and lived a sheltered and self-indulgent life. His father, Elihu Hoyt, was a state legislator; his mother, Hannah Taylor, was the daughter of a minister. He grew up in an ambitious and achievement-oriented family, surrounded by kin who mirrored his parents' desire to seize the main chance and shape the world. His father had high hopes for his eldest son, but parental expectations are sometimes heavy burdens and Charles early showed impatience and vagueness of purpose. Because his father was away from home serving in the Massachusetts legislature during extended periods in the winter, Charles was expected to shoulder considerable responsibility for the farming operations. He was not much interested in farming and, like many other youths in the town, paid more attention to social diversions than school. During a legislative session in Boston in 1822 his father testily wrote to his wife, "I understand you wish me to decide whether Charles is to go to school at the academy or not. I confess that I did not expect that he would be able to take care of the farming affairs, attend the dancing school, & go to the academy. I had hoped you know that the dancing school might have been dispensed with for this winter, in which case it was my intention to send Charley to the academy." He grudgingly acquiesced to Charles's wishes, permitting his son to attend dancing school and limiting his attendance at Deerfield Academy to half a quarter, but his exasperation was apparent. He grumbled about the expense pointedly noting, "I trust Charley will consider that all these advantages must be considered a finish to his education, & I hope he may profit accordingly." He was wrong; Charles Hoyt's education was far from over.[1]

By 1826, it was quite clear that Charles Hoyt was too restless to settle down as a farmer. The problem was to settle on something else. Using family connections, his father found him a job as a schoolteacher in Athol, but Charles soon found he detested schoolteaching. He reported mournfully to his sister Julia on January 18 that he had "completed the eighth week but the remaining four weeks seem to be longer to look forward [to] than to look backward upon the eight." His teaching days over, he asked his father for help in finding a business position in Boston. Although he had doubts about his son's qualifications for a job in one of Boston's mercantile establishments, Elihu Hoyt went to some trouble to look for openings. On January 31, 1826, he wrote to Charles from Boston with glum news: "I have not failed to look out for a position for you but without success so far, the best terms I can hear of in Boston are to board a young man, give him barely enough to clothe him, & generally nothing more than board him, & after all you cannot tell into whose hands you may fall but in all cases they will require good qualifications in bookkeeping, writing and arithmetick, my own views are that a place in a country store would be far preferable, the risk is less in business & in many respects, I think, much preferable." His father may have had in mind a position in a country store like the one operated by Orlando Ware, and later his son Edwin, a few hundred feet from the family's front door (Fig. 9:1). To Charles, life in a country store with its predictably slow pace and close supervision by his family or someone else's was something to escape. Ignoring his father's well-intentioned advice, he turned in another direction.[2]

On his own initiative this time, Charles Hoyt headed west. In the late spring of 1826, he secured a job aboard the packet boat "Albany" that traveled

Figure 9:1. Edwin Ware Store, Deerfield, Massachusetts, ca. 1858–68. (Drawn by the author from a photograph in the collections of the Pocumtuck Valley Memorial Association.)

from Schenectady to Utica via the Erie Canal. The work had little real potential, but it was exciting for a time and provided him with the adventure that he had missed at home. He wrote enthusiastically to his brother Henry that there was "no end to the travel on the canal . . . it would suit you to come and see it there are all kinds of people and things to be seen all life and bustle." He added that, despite what some people in Deerfield said, he was not homesick and that, if circumstances permitted, he planned to stay away. Despite his adolescent bravado, the adventure on the packet boat ended by the time the canal iced up for the winter, and he returned home. A year and a half later he set out on his own for New York City to try to find a position in business. He hoped to use the connections of Deerfield neighbor Theodore Nims who had settled in New York, but he found the job search discouraging and plaintively confessed to his brother Henry, "It is a hard world to get a living in and we must all of us see trials that in boyhood days we think little of." The ebullience he expressed during his canal adventure was gone and a more mature tone permeated his letters home. Sanctimoniously he cautioned his brother, "now I am left to shift for myself I begin to see the cares we must all go through in this world of trials to obtain a situation in society that cannot be impeached, remember what I now say to you." He added that he had decided to leave his present employment because he believed he could do better elsewhere.[3]

Alarmed, Elihu Hoyt wrote to his son with advice. Charles's unstable career search was a considerable worry to him and his concern was apparently intensified by the belief that he would once again have to bail his adult son out of a bad career choice. In his letter he stressed that the state of family finances precluded any significant help from the home front. Charles would have to manage on his own. After expressing his opinions on the importance of hard work and perseverance, he wrote: "I hope by this time that you have settled down again in a steady business, even if it is not so very profitable, for I know of nothing that can be done here to any advantage. it never was harder or duller times, nothing presents itself unless indeed we go to raising corn & potatoes, & this is unprofitable business at this day. beef is selling at about its cost last fall & I know not how the people are to meet their expenses, this spring, I know I cannot meet mine."[4] Like it or not, he could see little future for his restless son in Deerfield.

A month after he received his father's letter, Charles became seriously ill. He had been working as a clerk in a New York store, but now the disease confined him to bed and he lost his job. For nearly a month he was close to death and his recovery was protracted. Theodore Nims looked after Charles as best he could, writing about the patient's condition to the family, but Nims had his own affairs to attend to and could only do so much. By May, Charles was out of danger but was too weak to write. His job was gone; his debts for medicines, lodging, and food were mounting. At Charles's request, Nims wrote to Elihu Hoyt to ask for help, observing that he was "sorry to say that fortune has been rather unkind since he has been a resident of this city; but his sickness, was the unkindest cut of all." His father managed to pay the bills, and once again Charles returned home.[5]

His dreams of quickly becoming a businessman shattered, Charles turned to a new direction—medicine. By February, he was in Pittsfield studying medicine at the Berkshire Medical Institute where his uncle, Stephen West Williams, had lectured. More trouble intervened. His name was implicated in a grave-robbing incident in Montague in which the recently buried body of a teenage girl was dug up and taken. Stealing cadavers for dissecting classes at medical schools was officially frowned upon and socially proscribed, but medical schools occasionally resorted to the practice because it was so difficult to acquire suitable specimens for study. Montague citizens were outraged, but quick work by his father, who had a political career to look after, evidently kept Charles's name out of the newspapers. In any case, Charles's associations with the incident were only implied because he attended the school; officially he was cleared of any wrongdoing. Coincidentally or not, he decided to change medical schools and turned to his father for the tuition. Elihu Hoyt wrote in reply that he could not afford any additional expenses, but two weeks later he relented and wrote to Charles to say that he should not worry about the expenses too much and suggested that he investigate the medical schools at Hanover, New Hampshire, and Woodstock, Vermont. While he favored the school in Hanover, Charles chose the one in Woodstock.[6]

In 1833, Elihu Hoyt died, probably from complications related to his long struggle with chronic asthma. Two years later, in 1835, Charles Hoyt moved to Jacksonville, Florida, with a friend, Elijah Williams, apparently to help Williams with a scheme to raise capital for a railroad. Unaccustomed to the Florida climate and local diseases, he and Williams died a few months after their arrival. Charles was thirty-one. To the end he was still looking for a post in an occupation that he considered worthy and profitable. His brother, Henry, was content to remain on the family farm in the land of "steady habits," where he led a quiet and rather uneventful life. A moderately successful farmer, it seemed Henry Hoyt lacked the aggressive political drive that characterized his father or the craving for adventure that had taken his brother in so many directions.[7]

The transformation of the New England rural landscape was the result as much of a cognitive as of an economic process, in which old strategies for living were merged with new ones. For those who thought about what was happening, it was often confusing and disturbing. Although the seeds of a profit-oriented commercial world were carried over the Atlantic by the earliest settlers, the scale of the early nineteenth-century market economy in both urban centers and rural hinterlands was unprecedented. As the number of consumer goods and commercial opportunities expanded, rural folk developed various strategies to accommodate and participate in changing economic modes. The result was the simultaneous existence of two rather different systems of cultural organization, complementary but not fully interchangeable. By 1860 the larger of these two systems was agrarian. Theoretically, farm life provided families with considerable opportunity to act as independent economic units, capable of meeting many needs from the resources at hand. In practice few families actually had sufficient land, tools, and draft power to act independently. Local inequalities were reconciled by local exchanges within kin or neighborhood networks. These exchanges usually followed a kind of common-sense notion of efficiency in which farmers traded on the level that yielded the maximum return, economically, socially and/or psychically, for the most reasonable effort. Foodstuffs and labor were the core of these face-to-face exchanges and were based on household needs. Other purchases, however, might or might not occur on a local level. Many rural people used market centers for purchases of consumer goods because they often found they could obtain greater selection and better prices. They based their exchanges on a system of reciprocity in which social and psychological rewards were as important as economic ones.

This preponderance of local trade and an emphasis on reciprocity did not mean that farmers or rural folk were uninterested in or unaware of either profits or personal gain. Certainly Charles Hoyt's flight from the constraints of the family farm and his search for economic opportunity was one story among many of a youth searching for personal advancement via the marketplace. What distinguished the agrarian system he was trying to leave from industrial capitalism was that nature rather than humanity was the controlling force in many costs. Farm accounts and household production strategies thus emphasized control of debts. The concern with debts was not because the preindustrial world was isolated from markets. What drove many farmers to keep track of their debts was their lack of control over the fixed costs imposed by nature and market prices for agricultural products. Only by controlling debts could many farmers hope to manage household accounts. Many farm strategies, therefore, hinged on the ability of families to match consumption to production whether or not it was commercial or subsistence in nature. Typically the result was a mixture of household and market production strategies. The challenge was to maintain a balance as farm families' growing expectations as consumers made the control of debts infinitely more difficult.

Many farm families searched for ways of increasing production to attain their expectations. The widespread use of outwork systems such as palm leaf hat braiding became one way farm families could increase production and income — so were efforts to redesign houses and barns for expanded or more efficient production, to reorganize the landscape by investing labor in clearing and fencing, and to discipline the workforce by public educational efforts in district schools or agricultural fairs. These attempts to produce more efficiently were ways of maintaining family security.

Environmental and cultural conditions limited family choices. Uplanders had quantities of good grazing land, and lowlanders owned good tillage. These circumstances predetermined the range of choices farmers could make even within the traditions of general mixed agriculture. Upland farms often supported modest amounts of tillage for family use, but few hill farmers were in a position to undertake extensive commercial grain production. Instead they developed commercial practices that made the most of the relative abundance of pasturage and woodland while maintaining substantial production of foodstuffs for home use. By contrast lowlanders with abundant tillage raised surpluses of grains that could be exported or used to fatten cattle. By the 1840s, these factors account for the patterns of per capita production in which some commodities were raised equally among the county's towns and other items were confined to particular sections of the region.

Production for commercial markets introduced another set of variables into the family decision process. Market prices fluctuated, and the effects of these fluctuations penetrated rural areas in rather direct ways. Family food needs remained relatively constant depending on the size of the household and its age distribution, but market demand changed from week to week and year to year. In order to make choices about production for market, farmers had to receive a flow of information about prices and to stay sufficiently flexible to take advantage of changes in market opportunities. During the 1820s, newspapers began to publish weekly quotations of market prices; before that, information was passed by word of mouth. What farmers did with this information depended upon the limitations inherent in farming and their own holdings. These limitations were often considerable. Changing farm strategies often meant finding a marketable product that could be raised on the family's fields, that fit in the barn or shed, or that could be managed by the labor at hand. Moreover, any new strategy had to function within landscape systems that usually had been determined by earlier generations, systems that were often difficult to change. Raising broom corn or buying tools to increase efficiency were not viable choices if the growing season was too short or farms too small to justify using labor-saving machinery. The key to successful farm strategies for the region was not technological innovation, improved transportation, or better agricultural practices, although all of these things were important influences in the commercialization of farm production. But more often successful farm management was based on the ability to develop marketable commodities that could be raised within pre-existing conditions of the region's landscape. The alternative was to produce only for family use and thus to lose ground in the struggle to control debt and live within accepted standards of social respectability.

Rural youths like Charles Hoyt wanted the social respectability connoted by dancing schools and business careers, but in their impatience with farming's slow gains they frequently overestimated the opportunities that existed elsewhere or the time it would take to achieve their goals. The dilemma they faced was that agriculture represented a slow, hard path to financial success and social position. At a lyceum lecture reported in the Greenfield paper in September 1830, C. J. Ingersoll declared

> It is the general complaint that FARMS in New England are unprofitable; and that farmers tell us they are growing poor, — their sons fly to the west, south or north to seek THEIR fortunes, casting back an eye of contempt on the poverty of the New England hills, and keeping at a low point the population of these good old states. Goods formerly made in families, are now furnished so cheap by manufacturers, that they must be purchased, and the females permitted to live in comparable idleness.

Ingersoll rejected the oft-repeated suggestion that people "retrench" and learn to live within their means, arguing that it was much easier to talk about giving up unnecessary expenses than it was to actually do it. The alternative that he proposed, one that was fairly common to reformers of the time, was to put women back to work on productive activities that would add to the family profits. Since women were spending so much on silks, he reasoned, they might just as well take up silk culture at home, add to the family stock, and lessen the nation's dependence on foreign imports.[8]

By itself, Ingersoll's lecture was little more than a footnote in history, but his comments reflected some of the trends underway in early nineteenth-century New England and elsewhere. While Ingersoll and many others repeated the conventional wisdom that farms were unprofitable, what they really meant was that farms were not profitable enough at a time when expectations about the quality of life were changing rapidly. Sons and daughters did leave to seek their fortunes elsewhere, impatient with a system built on hard work and, frequently, self-denial. As business opportunities expanded, urbanization accelerated, and the nonagricultural sector grew, there were more choices for aspiring children like Charles Hoyt. The departure of the region's youth was deeply troubling to many families. Parents pointed out the financial risks of going west, away from the supportive web of family and friends. "Among those who emigrate to the western wilds, from the populous towns in New England," said Epaphras Hoyt at an agricultural society meeting, "how few do we find satisfied with their lonely condition? They hear of the fertile soil of the west . . . , and they must grasp the seductive boon." He pointed out that what new settlers encountered was "the toil attending the clearing and bringing under cultivation a new farm; where roads are to be cut out through forests and morrasses; bridges, mills, dwelling houses and barns erected."[9]

Conservative talk about the nobility of agriculture did little to dam the flow of youth to business. During the 1810s and 1820s, commercial activities were viewed as alternatives to farming rather than antagonists. Farm families in rural Warwick risked family security and their property on a visionary scheme to establish a glass factory. On a smaller but more successful scale, potters in Whately developed a series of potting ventures that went beyond the level of a single craft operation on a part-time basis. By the 1830s, a few entrepreneurs with access to outside capital were building factories for the production of textiles and cutlery, using the region's waterpower sites. As commerce and manufacturing grew, investors sponsored transportation improvements, hoping to develop profitable opportunities for both farming and manufacturing. Better transportation helped manufacturers move raw materials and finished products to and from market centers, but many farmers found that agricultural competition increased as canals and railroads linked them with other rural areas. Over time these changes helped shift the political and ideological debate from the concept of the complementary nature of agriculture and industry to a relationship with adversarial overtones. Yet Ingersoll was wrong; as census takers learned in 1860, the rise of manufacturing and migration to the West did not leave the New England hills destitute.

On the eve of the Civil War census takers made their rounds in Franklin County to gather information on the region's farms. The landscape they documented did not always justify reformer's jeremiads that New England farms were in decline, but the signs of profound changes were evident. Unlike the provincial tax valuation of 1771 when the age of settlement was a predictor of material well-being for the county's towns, the key factor by 1860 was geography. Upland communities were no longer rough-hewn outposts in which families struggled to clear land and build a farm. Hill towns had evolved and matured in their own distinctive ways. In the valleys below, lowland communities continued the trend of specializing for market production, taking advantage of fertile soils, longer growing seasons, and the location of transportation systems to increase the value of agricultural lands. Inequalities

Table 9:1

Land, and Livestock, Selected Towns, Franklin County Massachusetts, 1860

	Mean Acres Improved	Mean Acres Unimproved	Mean ($) Value of Farm	Mean No. of Horses
Western Uplands				
Ashfield	87	40	1998	1.3
Charlemont	72	53	2330	1.5
Conway	121	16	2640	1.3
Shelburne	111	26	4031	1.6
Lowlands				
Northfield	55	33	2982	1.5
Greenfield	95	29	4381	1.7
Montague	85	53	3264	1.3
Deerfield	58	16	3625	1.3
Sunderland	44	19	2932	1.5
Whately	80	14	3363	1.4
Eastern Uplands				
New Salem	66	50	1801	1
Shutesbury	62	66	1388	1

persisted among families, neighborhoods, and towns, and some of these in-equalities were visible in the material standards of the three major sections of the county—the western uplands, the eastern uplands, and the lowlands. These patterns provide a context for the changing fortunes of New England farmers and help to explain why youths like Charles Hoyt pursued careers in business.[10]

The census returns of 1860 recorded the value of farms in each town, the acres of improved and unimproved land, the number and value of various types of livestock, the quantity of many kinds of agricultural commodities, and the value of home manufactures. By analyzing the same towns recorded in the 1771 tax valuation list, we can see the drift of some patterns over time and assess the similarities and differences between the two sections of hill towns and the lowlands (Tables 9:1 and 9:2). In general farmers in the low-lands owned farms of greater value than those in the uplands. Mean farm values in the lowlands were near or above $3000, and in several towns were substantially above that figure. Two of the towns in the western uplands, Shelburne and Conway, were also close to or above that figure, while more

Mean No. of Cows	Mean No. of Oxen	Mean No. of Other Cattle	Mean No. of Sheep	Mean No. of Swine	Mean ($) Value of Livestock
3.3	1.2	4.4	16.7	1.6	404
3.3	1	4.4	13	1.2	402
3.3	1.5	5.6	6.8	1.5	528
4	2	7.5	16	2	671
1.6	.9	4.5	7.7	2.4	372
3.9	1.7	6.1	3.1	2.4	555
2.9	1.7	4.1	3.2	2.2	371
2.7	1.1	3.2	2.8	2.6	373
2.7	.3	2.4	1	3.2	303
3	1.1	3.7	1	2.8	350
2.6	1.5	2.3	2.2	1.4	248
2	2.2	2.2	2	1.4	252

remote communities such as Ashfield and Charlemont ranked somewhat lower. Shelburne's mean value was the second highest of the twelve towns in the sample, Greenfield being in first place with a mean value of $4381. Both of these towns contained substantial industries and relatively small numbers of farms; evidently the growth of industry worked to reduce the number of marginal farmers with small holdings and elevated the means for these two towns. By contrast, the farmers in the eastern hill towns maintained lower ratios of improved to unimproved lands and lived on holdings that were significantly lower in mean value than their counterparts to the west. The poorer soils and rugged topography of Shutesbury created conditions in which farms were less than half the mean value of lowland towns and less than all of the western hill towns surveyed. Based on this evidence alone it is clear that we must be very cautious about assigning normative patterns to hill and lowland towns or of accepting at face value the assertions that New England towns were in decline. Under reasonably favorable conditions such as those enjoyed by farmers west of the lowlands, farming could be profitable for many families. It also appears that industrialization and business expansion benefited

Table 9:2

Crops and Products, Selected Towns, Franklin County, Massachusetts, 1860

	Mean Bushels Wheat	Mean Bushels Rye	Mean Bushels Corn	Mean Bushels Oats	Mean Bushels Potatoes	Mean Tons Hay	Mean Lbs. Tobacco
Western Uplands							
Ashfield	8.7	.8	39	10.8	78.3	26.9	26.1
Charlemont	3.8	8.6	69.1	34	64.2	19.6	
Conway	8.4	5	73.3	26.3	40.8	24.6	244.8
Shelburne	26.6	6.8	95.8	20.3	84	34.1	.45
Lowlands							
Northfield	9.4	25.7	112	74.6	60.5	17	328
Greenfield	7	28.3	130	52.6	78.5	31.1	360.8
Montague	8.3	55.9	106.4	41.3	76.4	19.8	359.3
Deerfield	11.9	32.2	59.1	63.53	55.7	18.7	874
Sunderland	3.1	30.4	102	37.8	41.1	12.3	675
Whately	5.5	25.9	89	34.2	65.5	18.1	2627.6
Eastern Uplands							
New Salem	4.1	6.2	34	15.5	67.5	12.8	
Shutesbury	1.3	6.5	28	16.7	123.5	11.3	

the better-situated and wealthier farmers in towns like Greenfield and Shelburne by expanding local markets for produce and by increasing real estate values.

These local and metropolitan markets clearly affected agricultural strategies in several ways as farm families reacted rationally to local conditions. Some trends that we have already explored continued. Horses were widely distributed among all the region's towns, mirroring the widespread demand for transportation and mobility. Swine were more numerous in the lowlands, where farm population densities were higher and where there were larger quantities of grains for feeding hogs. Other types of livestock followed different patterns. Farmers in the western uplands raised more livestock than those in the rest of the county and became associated with pastoral forms of husbandry. They raised the largest mean numbers of sheep and cattle and produced the greatest quantities of butter and cheese. Eastern farmers also kept livestock, but the mean numbers were smaller, reflecting that section's more marginal farming conditions and the tendency to farm for household and local use rather than sale.

Mean Lbs. Butter	Mean Lbs. Cheese	Mean Value of Orchard Products	Mean Lbs. Maple Sugar	Mean Lbs. Wool	Mean Value of Animals Slaughtered ($)	Mean Value of Home Manufacturers ($)
361.9	133.3	12.80	358.6	56.6	49	11.30
295.7	140.4	17.60	136.5	49.5	51.20	5.41
436.2	121.7	15.70	275	24.5	75.35	6.91
564.8	133.5	25.59	236.6	55.7	91.11	.93
194.7	35.31	14.15	12	17.5	84.57	3.53
505.4	26.6	32.60	37.8	9.86	314.5	.23
335.4	.62	24.82	88.8	11.45	69.41	
333.4	32.1	17.07	33.5	7.7	75.35	6.92
324.9	30.2	22.82	125	4	85.12	6.19
379	70.9	21.06	11.6	2.4	73.49	4.25
171.9	113.9	7.48	4.61	8.16	39.94	10.5
180.6	55.2	7.29	17.01	5.7	46.52	1.04

In the production of tillage crops lowland farmers with better soils on level gradients held obvious advantages. Despite these advantages, hill farmers in the western uplands often raised equally large or greater crops of wheat and potatoes, and they were not very far behind in the production of corn. Lowlanders raised substantially higher amounts of rye and oats. In the eastern uplands farm families raised meagre amounts of grain crops, consistent with the pattern of livestock. One of the reasons the lowlanders did not show greater production of grains than the hill towns is that much of their tillage was devoted to market crops, especially tobacco. No upland community was comparable to lowland towns in the production of the frost-sensitive crop, although a few farmers in Conway did grow significant amounts. Tobacco production expanded further south in the county. Whately outstripped all others in mean production, followed by Deerfield and Sunderland. Quantities diminished up the valley but were still significant in view of the fact that many farmers continued broom-corn production, a commodity the standardized census forms did not account for. The size of this market production, coupled with substantial quantities of livestock and grain and the proximity to transportation routes to the South and East, made lowland farms relatively valuable and profitable, but the value of these farms was still based on a mixed strategy of production rather than on a single cash crop.

Despite the advent of an industrial economy, this mixed strategy encouraged many families to maintain certain agricultural traditions to pay debts and earn store credit. Although the quantities seem to have declined, lowlanders continued stall-feeding beef even in the face of western competition. The mean values of animals slaughtered was higher in most lowland towns than in the uplands, in spite of the fact that mean ownership of cattle was higher in the western uplands than in the lowlands. Evidently lowland stall-feeders continued buying cattle from the hill farmers. Maple sugar production, however, was skewed toward the western hill farmers, who processed impressive amounts of sap into sugar, presumably for household purposes and the market. Household manufacturing also continued in nearly all of the county's towns. The mean value of home manufactures was significantly lower in Shelburne and Greenfield. Evidently the factories in or near those towns reduced the appeal of outwork and home manufacturing when wage labor positions were available.

As we tease out patterns from the agricultural census, what emerges is a complex picture. While broad categories such as "western uplands, lowlands, and eastern uplands" demonstrate relationships, the census figures compare only farms rather than the entire population of the sample towns. After 1830, the population of most upland towns declined; outmigration occurred because young people found it more difficult to buy a farm as real estate values rose and because there were other more appealing jobs elsewhere. Marginal farm land was abandoned, but good farms survived. In the region's oldest towns, landowners did not close off all opportunity for youths. Deerfield had the largest number of farmers (258) for a single town in the 1860 census, yet the mean value of its farms was the third highest in the sample at $3625. Northfield had 191 farm families by 1860 with a mean farm value of $2982. While the means do not account for the very real differences between those at the top or the bottom of the farm hierarchy, it is clear that the expansion of farm households was made possible by the intensification of land use as well as the growth in the number of farms. Although the lowlands were used more intensively than the more pastoral uplands, farmers in both areas contributed to the creation of material prosperity. Only in the poorer lands of the uplands, especially to the east of the valley lowlands, was the picture gloomy. There, people moved away, turned to other more profitable occupations, or lived modestly as impersonal market forces and human ambition pushed and pulled people into making choices within limited resources (Fig. 9:2).

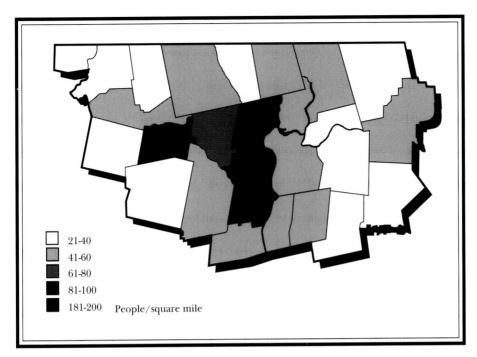

Figure 9:2. Population Density, Franklin County, Massachusetts, 1840.
(Drawn by the author.)

These changes to the landscape and the spread of mass-produced consumer goods reflected and fueled a quiet but measured shift in material expectations that affected almost everyone in antebellum America. The consequences of these changes were hard to grasp and even harder to evaluate. Critics decried what they saw as a preoccupation with material wealth, the folly of fashion, or the substitution of transient "elegancies" for things of more enduring worth, such as virtue and moral character. One statement in the Greenfield newpaper put it thus:

Hand to the Plough
Wife to the Cow
Boy to the Mow
Maid to the Sow
Will pay the rent now.
But — Man with his Tally-ho
Wife's squalling Piano
Girls with her Satin oh!
Boy with his Latin oh!
Is splash, dash, and must end in ruin oh!

Others made the same points less poetically, "Are there no items of family expense which you might expunge, and yet neither suffer, nor considerably feel the want of them? . . . be content with food and plain attire and the bare necessaries and essential comforts of life." Such advice was widely circulated, but in the same newspapers were advertisements for a great variety of consumer goods to tempt anyone who was tired of "bare necessaries and essential comforts." Farm families especially were the targets of such well-meaning advice. Everyday life on the farm involved hard work for relatively slow returns. The distinctions between lifestyles on rural farms and more urbanized market centers were apparent to observers. As early as 1802 an item in the *Greenfield Gazette* summarized the distinctions as follows:

> If the farmer's income be less abundant than that of a merchant, it is much more certain: if greater bodily fatigue attaches to his employment, he has much less anxiety of mind; if he has not an equal access to the elegancies of life, he is better assured of its real necessaries and comforts. Every farmer that is not in debt and has in himself the fee of his land, is a prince within his own domain; and provided his farm produces competent support, there is in his power as much independence as can fall to the lot of man.[11]

The problem with this advice is that few people behaved as if they really believed in it. It was fine to champion the goals of independence, the work ethic, and the contentment brought by living within one's resources, but the pressures to do otherwise were enormous. What in fact was a "competent support" in a world of rapidly developing industrial potential? At what point did an "elegancy" start to become a necessity? In a society with the expressly stated politics of equality of opportunity why should farmers believe they were better off with independence than "equal access to the elegancies of life"? What good was it to be a "prince within his own domain" if that domain was narrow and confined? Participation in the commercial world hitched farm strategies to hopes and desires for a more comfortable and abundant life (Fig. 9:3). The drive for profits was seldom analyzed philosophically. Money, credit, and profits conferred the opportunity to acquire land, hired labor to share work, better livestock, a clock for the parlor, an improved corn sheller, a cookstove to warm house and food, education for the children, travel, a good book, and countless other possibilities. Why should farmers' lives produce less abundantly? Was not the desire to share in material comforts cause for anxiety of mind?

The desire to share in material abundance was further stimulated by the imperatives of social discourse. Objects conveyed status and gentility, and few families were immune to or consciously rejected the competition. The interest in clothing, social ritual, and appearance prompted Elihu Hoyt to write to his wife in 1825:

You tell us of a wonderful display of elegance & taste at Mr. Wells wedding. It is pleasing to meet our friends at such entertainments but I fear no good generally comes out of them. They are the cause of much expense, & will probably be inducements for others to follow suit, by which means we shall some of us find ourselves unable to foot our bills. I hope, however, that this practice will not increase among us so far as to draw in those who will find themselves for fassions sake to make themselves such unnecessary expenses & to perplex & embarass themselves thereby.[12]

Hoyt knew well the pressures to conform to social norms, partly because his political career depended upon his standing with constituents and partly because his son's experiences reminded him about the costs of conformity. Charles Hoyt's attendance at dancing school, and his freedom to pursue a wide variety of careers—most of which ended up costing his parents money—was made possible by prosperity and by youthful enthusiasm about the shortest path to success. Wells's elegant wedding established new metaphors for social classification and served as a precedent for others. Setting the standard was less of an issue than making sure the family did not fall too far behind. Soon enough the "unnecessary expenses" inherent in such social gatherings would become expected and mandatory. The transformation of the landscape, the coming of industrial capitalism, then, was part of a process in which Americans increasingly defined their personal and family well-being in material terms.[13]

What the houses, barns, and material life of the county recall to consciousness is that the transformation of American culture was played out in three-dimensional as well as human terms. By the 1830s work was increasingly located in the back spaces of houses, in sheds, and kitchen ells, linked to but separated from the more formal and private quarters of public and family spaces. Domestic architecture was becoming specialized, efficient, and in the word from the period, "convenient." Similarly, the barns built out back or to one side of these houses were reshaped for more efficient production. The traditional English barn was increasingly replaced by a New England type with the runway between the gable ends. Such barns more efficiently accommodated larger herds which in turn generated the manure that fertilized the fields that grew the improved hay and grains that fed the herd. It was the landscape, the buildings on it, and the ways in which men and women organized and used their resources that made possible a rise in productivity. Rather than fancy newfangled agricultural implements, these landscape modifications and changed work habits were the real tools by which New Englanders effected economic growth and a general (but still stratified and unequal) improvement in the standard of living.

Both men and women contributed in different ways to the economy and to improved material standards. Men might shoulder heavy household and outdoor farm work, but women's chores were no less onerous. In addition to child care and housekeeping, women's activities in the dairy making butter and cheese, in gardens, and in outwork production such as palm leaf hats contributed significantly to the purchasing power of families intent upon acquiring such amenities as new crockery, clocks, silver spoons, books, furniture, paint, carpeting, wallpaper, lighting devices, clothing, education, musical instruments, kitchen sinks, cookstoves, curtains, and countless other items that were part of the trappings and pleasures of genteel living. Men might satirize women's frivolous consumer habits, they might lampoon pianos as a symbol of wasteful idleness, but their wives and daughters contributed significantly to the income that made such purchases possible and women thereby gained measurable influence over family spending priorities and the direction of cultural change. Epaphras Hoyt once wrote his brother Elihu about getting calico for the children, but his *wife* told him what to get and how much to pay for it. Similarly, when Elihu Hoyt wrote home with news of market prices, he suggested his wife send *her* chickens to market because the prices were good. These economic contributions added to the family stock, gave women more control over family expenses, and increased the quantity of material comforts in middle-class homes.[14]

The expansion of the market and the ordering of the landscape sharpened inequalities and class lines even as most families benefited in differing degrees from a rise in their standard of material comfort. The intimacy of community relationships that characterized the frontier stages of the region diminished. It was no longer possible to know everyone in the town, and exchanges became based more on contract and less on custom. Outside of family and kin, men and women structured relationships more abstractly and formally—with the neighborhood, the school district, a church, and various associational groups. There simply were more choices and more decisions to make.

Such choices were not always easy. Evaluating future prospects, children like Charles Hoyt had to weigh the rewards of farming against those of other occupations, of waiting for their inheritance, or of going off from home to seek their fortunes. Many of the region's youth moved before settling down and forming families. Some moved away for a time and then returned; others left never to come home. In their search for the main chance they encountered greater choices than their parents and grandparents, and, frequently, greater risks. In the process of improving their farms and communities, men and women not only competed for economic and political power, they learned to count success by their ability to exercise some control over their own lives.

As long as they conceived of control and human improvement in materialistic terms, they could accept stronger links with a market economy and give up some elements of customary relationships. Acceptance was made possible because men and women insisted upon maintaining basic values—respect for God, family, human affection, mutuality, and face-to-face relationships—while participating in the commodification of other traditional forms of discourse. Those at the top shared enough material opportunities to diffuse the violent consequences of class conflict, for even poor people usually owned enough to have something to lose in confrontations.[15]

This sharing of opportunity for material advancement, however modest, dampened political dissention and reduced to some extent the frustrations of the less well-to-do. So did the efforts of ministers and reformers who sought ways of helping men and women attain personal and civic virtue by living frugal and moral lives. It was an uphill struggle. Referring to the need for more economical, less pretentious houses, Isaac Bates sarcastically noted that the general response was "But who would live in a little hutch of a place! . . . and away goes all of man's philosophy on the subject."[16] The concern with appearances, with the outward and visible trappings of success, with the need to keep up with changing notions of comfort and convenience was a potent force that drove many people to seek new ways of making money. Reformers might agonize about men turning from true virtue to materialistic excess, but in the minds of most people in the county, success was not measured by abstract numbers in ledger books, nor by who controlled the means of production. Rather, it was increasingly gauged by the kind of lifestyle and personal reputation that one was able to build. Thoreau and other reformers aside, who indeed "would live in a little hutch of a place"?

The present landscape of Franklin County, then, still speaks to us of a process of change that was acted out on the late eighteenth-century landscape after the Revolution. Too often as we reflect on the values of our own era, we amplify a nostalgic longing for a world of closer communities, of face-to-face relationships, and of simpler times that we want to believe once existed. We forget that the things our forebears struggled to find and to build and that we so often value today—greater convenience, higher material standards of living, and increased personal freedom—were judged to be worthy goals even when they erased previous ones. Their struggle, and ours, to make a better world, is powerfully written on our landscape. If we would seek a more useable past, we must understand that landscape is a potent historical legacy and that living together requires continual effort to recognize and cherish things of enduring worth.

Plants in Williams Herbarium

It is rare to have a period catalog of plants for a specific region in antebellum America. Stephen West Williams, a Deerfield physician, prepared an herbarium of native plants in 1819. The list below gives the English names for plants he recorded. Such lists are particularly useful for specialists interested in the historic landscape and in reproducing planting types.

Adder's Tongue
Agrimony
Alder Black
American Camomile
American Senna
Annual Fleal Bane
Arrow Head
Asparagus
Aster
Avens

Balsam Fir
Balsamine
Bear Berry Bell Flower
    Clasping
Bethlehem Star-Yellow
Birds Nest
Bittersweet .
Black Alder
Black Nightshade
Black Spriger
Bladder Wort
Blessed Thistle
Blue Bottle
Blunt Leaved Silk Weed

Bone Set
Borage
Broad Leaved Panic Grass
Broom Grass
Buckwheat
Bull Bush
Burdock
Burr Reed
Bushy Gerardia
Butterfly Weed
Button Bush

Caducous Polygala
Canada St. Johns Wort
Canada Thistle
Cancer Root
Cardinal Lobelia
Carpet Weed
Castor Oil Plant
Catmint
Cat Tail Grass
Cedar, White
Chaffy Sedge
Chenopodium
Cherry, Winter
Chick Leaved Wintergreen

Chickweed
China Aster
Chiques Berry
Cinquefoil
Climbing Staff
Clove Tree
Clustered Solomons Seal
Cockle Corn
Coltsfoot
Comfrey
Common Blue Vervain
Common Hemlock
Common Life
    Everlasting
Common Mallow
Common St. Johns Wort
Common Yarrow
Cornel, White Berried
Cotton Grass
Cow Wheat
Cranberry
Crow Foot
Crow Foot Water
Cuckold
Cucumber Root
Cud Weed Culver

Devil's Bit
Dodder
Dogs Bane
Dog's Tongue
Dragon Root
Ducks Meat
Dwarf Dandelion
Dwarf Tree Primrose

Elastic Gum Risen Tree
Enchanter's Nightshade
Eupatorium
Eupatorium Semle

Falve Grapes
Fennel Flower
Farmatory
Farm, Male (5 varieties)
Field Trefoil
Fig Wort
Fimbriated Orchis
Flat Club Moss
Flower de Luce
Four Leaved Loose Strife
Four O'Clock
Fragrant Water Lily

Garden Artichoke
Garden Saffron
Gay Feather
Gerardia, Yellow, Purple, Bushy
Germander, Wild
Gill Grow by the Ground
Golden Rod
Greenbriar
Ground Nut

Hard Hack
Hawk Weed
Hawkweed, Kalm's
Hedysarum (5 varieties)
Hemlock Tree
Hemlock, Water

Hemp
Henbane
Herb Robert
Hone Wort
Hooded Willow Herb
Horned Spur
Horntail, Field
Horsemint
Horse Weed
Hybiscus
Hynop

Jacob's Ladder
Jagged Silphium
Jersey Tea
Jerusalem Artichoke
Jerusalem Oak

Indian Hemp
Indian Tobacco
Indian Turnip
Indigo, Wild

Ladies Traces
Lageta
Larkspur
Laurel, Narrow Ear
Life Everlasting
Lime Grass
Lime Tree
Lobelia Cardinal
Lobelia, Pale
Locust Tree
Loonstrife (3 varieties)
Love Apple
Lycopodium

Mad Dog Weed
Maiden Hair
Male Fern
Mallow, Common
Maple
Maple, Swarf or Canada
Marigold

Mayflower, Common
Meadow Grass Common
Meadow Rue
Meadow Sweet
Mercury, Three Seeded
Mignonette
Miklot Clover
Millet
Monkey Flower
Mother's Wort
Mountain Mint
Mouse Ear Chickweed

Narrow Leaved Dock
Neottia
Nettle
Nettle, Water
New England Spice
Noble Liverwort

Orchard Grass
Orchis (4 varieties)
Ox-eyed Daisy

Panic Grass (3 varieties)
Panicled Andromeda
Partridge Berry
Pea, Sweet
Pen Vine
Penny Royal
Pepper Mint
Petty Morrel
Pickerel Weed
Pink
Pink Clove
Pinweed
Piperidge Tree
Plantain, Water
Pleurisy Root, Whiteweed
Pointed Clivers
Polygonum, Spotted
Poppy, White
Pot Amaranth

Primrose Tree
Prince's Feather

Rattle Box
Red Raspberry
Red Rose
Red Top
Red Willow
Richweek
Round Leaved Sida
Rue
Rush, Slender

Saffron Falre
Saffron, Garden
Sage, Garden
Sand Wort
Sanicle
Sarsaparilla, Wild
Satin Plant
Savins
Savory, Summer
Scratch Grass
Scullcap Hynop Leaved
Scullcap, Side Flowering
Scurvy Grass
Sea Burdock
Sea Weed
Sedge, Chaffy
Sedge, Round Spiked
Seed Box

Self Heal
Sheep's Sorrel
Side Saddle Flower
Silkweed, Water
Skoke
Smooth Speedwell
Snake Head
Snakewort
Soapwort
Soapwort Gentian
Soft Bulrush
Solomon's Seal, Clustered
Sorrel Wood Upright
Spear Grass, Common
Spikenard
Spleen Wort
Sun Flower
Sundew, Round Leaved
Swamp rose
Sweet Fern
Swine Lettuce

Tall Anenome
Tansy
Thatch
Thistle Spear
Thorn Apple
Thorough Wort
Thousand Root
Thyme, Virginia
Timothy Grass

Toad Flax
Touch-me-not
Traveller's Joy
Trichortima
Trumpet Weed
Tuberous Cymbidium

Vegetable Oyster
Vervain, Common Blue
Virgin's Bower
Virginia Orpim
Virginia Rhexia

Water Agrimony
Water Crowfool
Water Horehound
White Topped Aster
White Weed
Wild Basil
Wild Cress
Willow, Conebearing
Willow Herb
Winter Cherry
Wintergreen (4 varieties)
Wood Anenome
Woodbine
Wormcress (3 varieties)

Yarrow Common
Yellow Diervilla
Yellow Violet

Glossary

Architrave. A trim piece, usually with moldings, surrounding openings such as doors and windows.

Baseboard. A board nailed to the bottom of interior walls to provide a tight seal beween walls and floors.

Bay. A unit of a structure delineated by portions of the framing or dimensional units.

Bead. A rounded molding made with a plane on the edge of a board or timber.

Bent. A section of framing defining one side of a bay; a term usually applied to the framing elements of barns.

Brace. A diagonal piece of timber used to stiffen a braced-frame structure.

Collar. A framing member used to tie rafters together to keep them from spreading.

Common rafter. One in a series of equally or almost equally sized rafters, the framing member used to support the roof sheathing.

Cornice. A molding of wood, plaster or other material, usually at the base of a roof, or top of an interior wall.

Ell. An addition built at right angles to the principal or front facade of a structure; New Englanders commonly refer to any addition that stretches to the rear of a house as an ell regardless of whether it is at right angles to the structure or not.

Gambel roof. A roof with two slopes in which the upper slope is flatter than the lower one; usually used to gain additional space under the roof or to create a more monumental scale.

Girt. A horizontal framing timber used to support ceilings or floors.

Graining. Applied paint that simulates another surface or material, usually wood but sometimes stone.

Hetchelled (heckled or hackled). A process of drawing fibrous plants through a comblike object (a *hetchel*) made of sharp iron prongs driven through a board. The term is usually applied to flax but was also used to describe the practice of separating seed from broom brush.

Hipped roof. A roof that slopes on all four sides of a rectangular or square building.

Joist. A timber, hewn or sawn, used to support the floors of a structure.

Lath. Strips of split (riven) or sawn wood, nailed to studs and used to support plaster.

Lean-to. A period term for an addition or integral part of a structure that fit within the main roof of a building; normally lean-tos resulted in a distinctively asymmetrical roof slope when viewed from the gable end of a building. Popular terminology today tends to call these structures "saltbox" buildings.

Mortise and tenon. A framing joint in which a tongue (the tenon) cut into one timber fits into a slot (the mortise) cut into another and is held in place with a wooden pin.

Passage. A period term analogous to the modern term "hall" or "corridor"; ordinarily an unheated space containing stairs, connecting rooms, or allowing access to the outside.

Piers. 1) Masonry supports located at intervals to support a frame above the ground; 2) the structural unit between two windows.

Pile. 1) A term referring to the depth of a building as defined by structural bays; single-pile structures are one room deep and double-pile structures are two rooms deep; 2) a chimney mass.

Plate. A horizontal timber, supported by posts, that supports the roof framing.

Pocket doors. A door or pair of doors that roll into recesses in a wall opening rather than swinging on hinges.

Post. A vertical load-bearing timber used in frame buildings, fences, signs, and for other landscape purposes.

Principal rafters. In braced-frame buildings, principal rafters were heavy rafters used in opposing pairs; usually they supported purlins which in turn stiffened lighter common rafters at their mid-points.

Purlin. A horizontal timber, parallel to the ridge of a roof, that supports common rafters at their approximate mid-points.

Quoins. In masonry structures these are cut blocks of stone that project slightly from the corners of buildings and help stiffen the wall; in wooden structures quoins serve as a form of decoration.

Rail. A horizontal section of timber framed into two posts that provides a solid surface for nailing on vertical siding.

Ridgepole. A horizontal framing member at the apex of a roof frame into which the rafters are nailed or joined.

Sash. The framed sections of wood used to hold glass panes in place.

Shouldered post. A post that swells toward the top where a girt and plate are joined, sometimes referred to in popular literature as "gunstock" posts because of their vague resemblance to inverted gunstocks.

Sill. 1) A horizontal framing member set on top of a foundation upon which the rest of a structure sits; 2) the bottom horizontal member of a window frame.

Stud. A vertical timber, lighter than posts, that was nailed or framed into the sill and girt or plate; in braced-frame structures studs were used as secure nailing surfaces for siding and lath rather than as load-bearing supports.

Wing. An addition to or secondary unit of a structure, generally with smaller proportions, that runs in the same direction as the ridge of the main roof.

Notes

Preface

1. Fernand Braudel, *Capitalism and Material Life, 1400–1800*, trans. Miriam Kochan (New York, 1973), xii.

Chapter 1
Introduction

1. Henry Colman, *Fourth Report of the Agriculture of Massachusetts, Counties of Franklin and Middlesex* (Boston, 1841), 164; for more information on Henry Colman see Donald B. Marti, "The Reverend Henry Colman's Agricultural Ministry," *Agricultural History* 51 (July 1977), 524–39.
2. Marti, "The Reverend Henry Colman," 528–29.
3. The literature on the transformation of the northern economy is vast and growing rapidly. For a useful summary see Allan Kulikoff, "The Transition to Capitalism in Rural America," *William and Mary Quarterly*, 3d. Ser., 46 (January 1989), 120–44. Also see Steven Hahn and Jonathan Prude, eds., *The Countryside in the Age of Capitalist Transformation: Essays on the Social History of Rural America* (Chapel Hill, 1985); Gary M. Walton and James F. Shepherd, *The Economic Rise of Early America* (Cambridge, 1979); Stuart Bruchey, *The Roots of American Economic Growth, 1607–1861* (New York, 1965); John J. McCusker and Russell R. Menard, *The Economy of British America, 1607–1789* (Chapel Hill, 1985), 17–90. The theoretical underpinnings of this book depend upon the work of Michel Foucault, especially *The Archaeology of Knowledge*, trans. A. M. Sheridan Smith (New York, 1972); Herbert L. Dreyfus and Paul Rabinow, *Michel Foucault: Beyond Structuralism and Hermeneutics*, 2d. ed. (Chicago, 1983), 44–103; Rhys Isaac, "Ethnographic Method in History: An Action Approach," *Historical Methods* 13 (1980), 43–61; Henry Glassie, "Meaningful Things and Appropriate Myths: The Artifact's Place in American Studies," in *Material Life in America, 1600–1860*, Robert St. George, ed. (Boston, 1988), 30–49; Ian Hodder, *Reading the Past: Current Approaches to Interpretation in Archaeology* (New York, 1986), 18–33, 118–70.

4. Fernand Braudel, *Capitalism and Material Life*, ix–xii; James Deetz, *In Small Things Forgotten: The Archaeology of Early American Life* (Garden City, N.Y., 1977); Jules David Prown, "Mind in Matter: An Introduction to Material Culture Theory and Method," *Winterthur Portfolio* 17 (1982), 1–19; Fred B. Kniffen, "Folk Housing: Key to Diffusion," *Annals of the Association of American Geographers* 55 (1965), 551; Wilbur Zelinsky, *The Cultural Geography of the United States* (Englewood Cliffs, N.J., 1973), 13; Peirce Lewis, "Axioms for Reading the Landscape: Some Guides to the American Scene," in *Material Culture Studies in America*, Thomas J. Schlereth, ed. (Nashville, Tenn., 1982), 174–82.

5. McCusker and Menard, *The Economy of British America*, 17–34, 211–35.

6. James A. Henretta, "Families and Farms: *Mentalité* in Pre-Industrial America," *William and Mary Quarterly*, 3d. Ser., 35 (January 1978), 3–32; Michael D. Merrill, "Cash is Good to Eat: Self-Sufficiency and Exchange in the Rural Economy of the United States," *Radical History Review* 3 (1977), 42–71; Christopher Clark, "Household Economy, Market Exchange and the Rise of Capitalism in the Connecticut Valley, 1800–1860," *Journal of Social History* 13 (1979), 169–89.

7. Robert St. George, "'Set Thine House in Order': The Domestication of the Yeomanry in Seventeenth-Century New England," in *New England Begins: The Seventeenth Century*, Jonathan L. Fairbanks and Robert F. Trent, eds., 3 vols. (Boston, 1982), 2:159–88; Stephen Innes, *Labor in a New Land: Economy and Society in Seventeenth-Century Springfield* (Princeton, N.J., 1983); E. P. Thompson, "The Moral Economy of the English Crowd in the Eighteenth Century," *Past and Present* 50 (February 1971), 76–136; E. P. Thompson, "Time, Work-Discipline, and Industrial Capitalism," *Past and Present* 38 (1967), 56–97; Winifred B. Rothenberg, "The Emergence of Farm Labor Markets and the Transformation of the Rural Economy: Massachusetts, 1750–1855," *Journal of Economic History* 48 (September 1988), 537–66.

8. Winifred B. Rothenberg, "The Emergence of Farm Labor Markets," 550–59; Jeremy Atack and Fred Bateman, *To Their Own Soil: Agriculture in the Antebellum North* (Ames, Iowa 1987).

9. Bernard Herman has argued many of the same points in *Architecture and Rural Life in Central Delaware, 1700–1900* (Knoxville, 1987), 10–11; Also see James Deetz, *In Small Things Forgotten*; Roland Barthes, *Elements of Semiology*, trans. Annette Lavers and Colin Smith (New York, 1967), 35–57; Hodder, *Reading the Past*, 118–46; Glassie, "Meaningful Things and Appropriate Myths"; St. George, *Material Life in America* 3–10.

10. Herman, *Architecture and Rural Life in Central Delaware*, 109–243; Joan Jensen, *Loosening the Bonds: Mid-Atlantic Farm Women, 1750–1850* (New Haven, 1986); Jack Larkin, *The Shaping of Everyday Life, 1790–1840* (New York, 1988); Thomas Hubka, *Big House, Little House, Back House, Barn: The Connected Farm Buildings of New England* (Hanover, N.H., 1984); Sally McMurray, *Families and Farmhouses in Nineteenth-Century America: Vernacular Design and Social Change* (New York, 1988).

11. Nancy Cott, *The Bonds of Womanhood: "Women's Sphere" in New England, 1780–1835* (New Haven, 1972); McMurry, *Families and Farmhouses*, 87–134.

12. Richard D. Brown, "The Emergence of Urban Society in Rural Massachusetts, 1760-1820," *Journal of American History* 61 (June 1974), 29-51; Margaret Richards Pabst, *Agricultural Trends in the Connecticut Valley Region of Massachusetts, 1800-1900*, Smith College Studies in History, 26:nos. 1-4 (Northampton, Mass., 1941); Thomas Dublin, "Women and Outwork in a Nineteenth-Century New England Town," in *The Countryside in the Age of Capitalist Transformation*, 51-69; Gerald F. Reid, "Local Merchants and the Regional Economy of the Connecticut River Valley," *Historical Journal of Massachusetts* 18 (Winter 1989), 1-16; Richard D. Brown, "The Agricultural-Industrial Transition in New England," *New England Quarterly* 61 (1988), 160-68.

Chapter 2
The Past

1. Obituary of Eunice Allen, *The Franklin Herald*, July 18, 1818; George Sheldon, *History of Deerfield, Massachusetts* (Deerfield, 1895), 1:545-50, 2: Gen. 12.
2. John Fraser Hart, *The Look of the Land* (Englewood Cliffs, N.J., 1975), 1-2; John R. Stilgoe, *Common Landscape of America, 1580-1845* (New Haven, Conn., 1982).
3. Neil Jorgensen, *A Guide to New England's Landscape* (Chester 1977); Betty Flanders Thomson, *The Changing Face of New England* (Boston, 1977), 141-56; Hans Kurath, *Handbook of the Linguistic Geography of New England* (Providence, 1959), see especially the map on pp. 241 and 242.
4. For a deeper perspective on the contact period see Peter A. Thomas, "In The Maelstrom of Change: The Indian Trade and Cultural Process in the Middle Connecticut River Valley, 1635-1665." Ph.D. diss., University of Massachusetts, 1979; William Cronon, *Changes in the Land: Indians, Colonists, and the Ecology of New England* (New York, 1983); Douglas R. McManis, *Colonial New England: A Historical Geography* (New York, 1975), 42-85.
5. Thomson, *Changing Face*, 1-18; George W. Bain and Howard A. Meyerhoff, *The Flow of Time in the Connecticut Valley* (Springfield, 1963), 1-15.
6. Bain and Meyerhoff, 19-35; Thomson, *Changing Face*, 19-32.
7. Thomson, 2-3; Bain and Meyerhoff, *Flow of Time*, 4-51; Jorgensen, *A Guide to New England's Landscape*, 48-59.
8. *Soil Survey: Franklin County, Massachusetts*, United States Department of Agriculture, Soil Conservation Society in Cooperation with Massachusetts Agricultural Experiment Station (Washington, D.C., 1967), 1-7; Jorgensen, *A Guide to New England's Landscape*, 48-59.
9. *Soil Survey*, 1-7; Henry Colman, *Fourth Report of the Agriculture of Massachusetts*, 3-5. See for example *Greenfield Gazette*, January 19, 1797; Thomson, *Changing Face*, 157-74.
10. *Soil Survey*, see the soil map at the back of the survey and pp. 2-5. For a summary of the region's population figures, see *Abstract of the Census of Massachusetts, 1865, with Remarks on the Same, and Supplementary Tables* (Boston, 1867).

11. *Soil Survey*, 55–197.

12. Ibid., 197–202; Lester Earl Klimm, *The Relation Between Certain Population Changes and the Physical Environment in Hampden, Hampshire, and Franklin Counties, Massachusetts, 1790–1925* (Philadelphia, 1933); Robert Paynter, *Models of Spatial Inequality: Settlement Patterns in Historical Archaeology* (New York, 1982), 45–111, 151.

13. The year of 1816 was a difficult one for farmers throughout the county and many records during the year were broken. For a fuller discussion see Randolph Roth, *The Democratic Dilemma: Religion, Reform, and the Social Order in the Connecticut River Valley of Vermont, 1791–1850* (New York, 1987), 81–82. Also see Christopher Clark, "Household, Market and Capital: The Process of Economic Change in the Connecticut Valley of Massachusetts, 1800–1860," Ph.D. diss., Harvard University, 1982.

14. Rodolphus Dickinson, *Elements of Geography, or An Extensive Abridgement Thereof; Exhibiting a View of the Natural and Artificial Features of the Various Divisions of the Earth; and Embracing Those Branches of Statistics Most Intimately Connected with Geographical Science* (Boston, 1813), 128–30.

15. *Soil Survey*, 197–202; David Ludlum, *The Country Journal New England Weather Book* (Boston, 1976), 62–85, 138–43.

16. For a useful discussion of this see James A. Henretta, *The Evolution of American Society, 1700–1815: An Interdisciplinary Analysis* (Lexington, Mass., 1973), 31–39; for additional work on the concept of time see E. P. Thompson, "Time, Work Discipline, and Industrial Capitalism," 56–97; Susan Geib, "'Changing Works': Agriculture and Society in Brookfield, Massachusetts, 1785–1820," Ph.D. diss., Boston University, 1981; Mark Kramer, *Three Farms: Making Milk, Meat and Money from the American Soil* (Boston, 1980), 3–107.

17. Howard Russell, *A Long Deep Furrow: Three Centuries of Farming in New England* (Hanover, N.H., 1976), 21; John R. Stilgoe, *Common Landscape of America*, 46–58; *Soil Survey*, 202.

18. Jorgensen, *A Guide to New England's Landscape*, 140–220; Sylvester Judd, *The History of Hadley* (1905; rpt. Somersworth, N.H., 1976), 96–103, 426–27; Elbert L. Little, Jr., *Atlas of United States Trees, I.: Conifers and Important Hardwoods*, USDA, Misc. Publ. No. 1146 (Washington, D.C., 1971).

19. Judd, *The History of Hadley*, 426–27; Timothy Dwight, *Travels in New England and New York*, 1821–22; (rpt. Cambridge, Mass., 1969), 1:21–30; George Sheldon, *History of Deerfield*, 1:101. A dedicated local physician gathered specimens of plants and trees in the Deerfield/Franklin County area: see Stephen West Williams, "Botanical Description and Medical, Culinary and Other Uses of the Plants in the First Volume of My American Herbarium," 1817, PVMA.

20. Stilgoe, *Common Landscape*, 3–7.

21. Judd, *History of Hadley*, 1–21; Stephen Innes, *Labor in a New Land*; Sheldon, *History of Deerfield*, 1:81–178; J. A. Temple and George Sheldon, *A History of Northfield, Massachusetts* (Albany, 1875); John Montague Smith, *A History of Sunderland, Massachusetts* (Greenfield, 1899).

22. Michael D. Coe, "The Line of Forts: Archaeology of the Mid-Eighteenth Century on the Massachusetts Frontier," in *New England Historical Archaeology*, Peter Benes, ed., Annual Proceedings, Dublin Seminar for New England Folklife (Boston, 1977), 44–55; also see Gregory H. Nobles, *Divisions Throughout the Whole: Politics and Society in Hampshire County, Massachusetts, 1740–1775* (New York, 1983), 107–31. See Table 3.1 in Paynter, *Models of Spatial Inequality*, 54.

23. Paynter, 45–112; Louis H. Everts, *History of the Connecticut Valley in Massachusetts with Illustrations and Biographical Sketches* (Philadelphia, 1879), 2:577–793.

24. Hart, *Look of the Land*, 45–52; McManis, *Colonial New England*, 41–85; David G. Allen, *In English Ways: The Movement of Societies and the Transferral of English Law and Custom to Massachusetts Bay in the Seventeenth Century* (Chapel Hill, 1981); Sheldon, *History of Deerfield*, 2:487–511; Kevin M. Sweeney, "The Children of the Covenant; the Formation and Transformation of a Second Generation New England Community," paper, Henry N. Flynt Library, Deerfield, Mass., 1971.

25. Richard I. Melvoin, *New England Outpost: War and Society in Colonial Deerfield* (New York, 1988).

26. Richard I. Melvoin, "Communalism in Frontier Deerfield," in *Early Settlement in the Connecticut Valley*, John W. Ifkovic and Martin Kaufman, eds. (Deerfield, Mass., 1984), 36–61; Sheldon, *History of Deerfield*, 2:768–72; "Records of the Proprietors of the Common Fields" PVMA.

27. Allen, *In English Ways*, 223–42. Allen modifies the long-standing tradition of a single type of town pattern by pointing out how different the experiences of the earliest settlers were. The point is that the alternatives for town planning in such an insecure part of New England were limited; Joseph S. Wood "Village and Community in Early Colonial New England," *Journal of Historical Geography*, 8 (1982), 333–46; Sheldon, *History of Deerfield*, 1:768–72. Sheldon was fairly explicit about the nuisance factor of the Common Field Fence. By the mid 1800s, the existence of the fence was cause for social contention rather than communal harmony. Sheldon, for one, wrote about the system purely in economic terms rather than social ones. As soon as economic self-interest changed for enough people, the fence was removed.

28. Temple and Sheldon, *History of Northfield*, 94–164; Lucy Cutler Kellogg, *History of Bernardston, Franklin County, Massachusetts, 1736–1900* (Greenfield, Mass., 1902), 1–48.

29. See for example McManis, *Colonial New England*, 41–85; James L. Garvan, "The Range Township in Eighteenth-Century New Hampshire," in *New England Prospects: Maps, Place Names, and the Historical Landscape*, Peter Benes, ed., Annual Proceedings, 1980, The Dublin Seminar for New England Folklife (Boston, 1981), 47–68. Many upland towns in Franklin County were laid out much like the towns Garvan discusses in N.H; Joseph Sutherland Wood, "The New England Village as an American Vernacular Form," *Perspectives in Vernacular Architecture, vol. 2*, Camille Wells, ed. (Columbia, 1986), 54–63; Joseph S. Wood, "Elaboration of a Settlement System: The New England Village in the Federal Period,"

Journal of Historical Geography 10 (1984), 331–56; Richard D. Bushman, *From Puritan to Yankee: Character and the Social Order in Connecticut, 1690–1765* (Cambridge, Mass., 1967), 74–82.

30. Deane Lee, ed., *Conway, 1767–1967* (Amherst, Mass., 1967), 3–18. The list of original proprietors of Conway contains 41 names. All but a few were names of Deerfield residents. It was the men of the nucleated town of Deerfield who decided how Conway was to be divided, not some outside speculator; Garvan, "The Range Township," 62–63; Roy H. Akagi, *The Town Proprietors of the New England Colonies: A Study of Their Development, Organization, Activities and Controversies, 1620–1770* (1924; rpt., Gloucester, Mass., 1963), 294–96. Bushman, *From Puritan to Yankee*, 74–82.

31. Mary Beth Pudup, "South Deerfield; A Place between Towns Becomes a Town between Places," paper, Henry N. Flynt Library, Deerfield, Mass., 1977, 4–7; Probate Inventory, Nathan Frary, Registry of Probate, Hampshire County Courthouse, Northampton, Mass. Probate Inventory, Elijah Arms, Registry of Probate, Franklin County Courthouse, Greenfield, Mass. Elijah Arms' real estate consisted of a farm with 158 acres, a pasture lot of 18 acres, another lot of 99 acres, a farm in the Mill River section of Deerfield with 364 acres, a pasture with 24 acres, and a farm in Conway of 160 acres. Arms's estate placed him near, but not at the top of the estates probated in Deerfield. The point here is that his holdings were unusual for the amount of land and farms that he owned. Within each farm, however, land was held in contiguous lots, and that pattern was fairly common until holdings were subdivided and sold later on in the nineteenth century.

32. Peirce F. Lewis, "Axioms for Reading the Landscape: Some Guides to the American Scene," in *Material Culture Studies in America*, Thomas J. Schlereth, ed. (Nashville, 1982), 175–91.

33. Dwight, *Travels in New England and New York*, 1:218.

34. Dwight, *Travels in New England and New York*, 2:212.

35. *Massachusetts Tax Valuation List of 1771*, Betty Hobbs Pruitt, ed. (Boston, 1984), 442–65.

36. Bettye Hobbs Pruitt, "Self-Sufficiency and the Agricultural Economy of Eighteenth-Century Massachusetts," *William and Mary Quarterly* 41 (July 1984), 340–45.

37. *Greenfield Gazette*, January 1, 1795, January 5, 1797, October 8, 1795, October 13, 1796; Maxwell advertised his land for sale in 100 to 150 acre lots. Prices for Deerfield's North Meadows appear in probate records, and family papers.

38. This appears to be borne out in a wide variety of records. See Bettye Hobbs Pruitt "Agriculture and Society in the Towns of Massachusetts, 1771: A Statistical Analysis," Ph.D. diss., Boston University, 1981. The percentage of land listed as unimprovable varied considerably. See for example Massachusetts, General Court, Committees, Valuations, "A List of the Polls and the Estates, Real and Personal, of the Several Proprietors and Inhabitants of the Town . . . 1792," Microfilm, Henry N. Flynt Library, Deerfield, Mass.; U.S. Secretary of the Treasury, Surveyor of the Revenue, Massachusetts and Maine Direct Tax

Census, 1798, Microfilms of Hampshire County Direct Tax Census in Henry N. Flynt Library, Deerfield, Mass.

39. Rodolphus Dickinson, "A Geographical, Statistical, and Historical View of the Town of Deerfield in the County of Franklin, and State of Massachusetts" (Deerfield, Mass., 1815), 11–12. Northfield had more good pasturage than Deerfield. See Rodolphus Dickinson, "A Description of Northfield and Lexington: Intended as an Exhibition of the Plan of a Contemplated Gazetteer of Massachusetts Proper" (Deerfield, Mass., 1818), 5–6.

40. U.S. Secretary of the Treasury, Direct Tax Census, 1798; see the Sections on Colrain, Deerfield, Shelburne, Whately, and Sunderland, for example; Pruitt, "Agriculture and Society in the Towns of Massachusetts, 1771; Richard L. Bushman, "Family Security in the Transition from Farm to City, 1750–1850," *Journal of Family History* 6 (1981), 238–56; Kenneth Lockridge, "Land, Population and the Evolution of New England Society, 1630–1790; and an Afterthought," in *Colonial America: Essays in Politics and Social Development*, Stanley N. Katz, ed. (Boston, 1971), 467–91.

41. *Massachusetts Tax Valuation List of 1771*, 450–51.

42. Stephen West Williams to Elihu Hoyt, February 1, 1829, Hoyt Family Papers, PVMA.

43. Nobles, *Divisions Throughout the Whole*, 117–21; Nobles calculated that more than half of Alvord's business was with these newly settled towns.

Chapter 3
Change

1. Chronology of Wilson's Stay in Canada, Wilson Papers, Pocumtuck Valley Memorial Association (hereafter PVMA); George Grinnell to John Wilson, January 18, 1864, Wilson Papers, PVMA.

2. Elihu Hoyt to Julia Hoyt, February 20, 1832, Hoyt Papers, PVMA; Robert A. Gross, "Culture and Cultivation: Agriculture and Society in Thoreau's Concord," *The Journal of American History* 69:1 (June 1982), 42–61.

3. For a good biography of John Wilson, see: Laurie Mitchel, "An Enterprising Soul: John Wilson of Deerfield" paper, Henry N. Flynt Library, Deerfield, Mass., 1979; George Sheldon, *A History of Deerfield* 2:826: John Wilson to James Woolwich, April 22, 1812, Wilson Papers, PVMA.

4. See Barbara Robinson, "The History of the John Wilson Printing Office," paper, Henry N. Flynt Library, Deerfield, Mass., 1978: John Wilson, Memorandum Book, April 30, 1816, Wilson Papers, PVMA.

5. Robinson, "The History of the John Wilson Printing Office," 13–23; Wilson, Memorandum Book, December 15, 1819; April 28, 1820; March 29, 1821; PVMA.

6. Wilson's contract with the town may be found in Overseers of the Poor, misc. folder, Deerfield Town Papers, PVMA.

7. See Petition for a Patent for a Plough, February 12, 1839, Wilson Papers, PVMA;

Mitchel, "An Enterprising Soul," 10–12; Wilson, Memorandum Book, June 18, 1819; May 20, 1823; March 8, 1828; Paul Jenkins, *The Conservative Rebel: A Social History of Greenfield* (Greenfield, Mass., 1982), 50, 63, 78, 186; Sheldon, *History of Deerfield*, 2:389; Henry Colman, *Fourth Report on the Agriculture of Massachusetts*, 176–77.

8. Wilson, Memorandum Book; Henry K. Hoyt to Elihu Hoyt, January 19, 1832, Hoyt Papers, PVMA.

9. Mitchel. "An Enterprising Soul," 20–23; William H. Sumner, *A History of East Boston* (Boston, 1858), 500, 572.

10. Sumner, *A History of East Boston*, 572, 500.

11. Deposition of John Wilson, December 19, 1849, Wilson Papers, PVMA; *Greenfield Gazette* and *Franklin Herald*, April 14, 1835.

12. Mitchel, "An Enterprising Soul," 23–24.

13. John Wilson's copy of Colman's report on agriculture is preserved in the PVMA Library. The book was signed by Henry Colman and dedicated to him as a friend; John Wilson, Memorandum Book, April 27, 1851, June 7, 1852, PVMA; probate docket of John Wilson, Registry of Probate, Franklin County Courthouse, Greenfield, Mass.

14. Northfield's valuation lists are on microfilm in the Northfield Town Library, Northfield, Mass.

15. Lucy Simler, "Tenancy in Colonial Pennsylvania: The Case of Chester County," *William and Mary Quarterly*, 3d ser., 43 (October 1986), 542–69.

16. Others have also examined the trend to limit family size in order to retain the value of family farms. For a discussion of this issue, see Maris A. Vinovskis, *Fertility in Massachusetts from the Revolution to the Civil War* (New York, 1981), 80–88.

17. For evidence of hiring Irish workers see Elijah Fuller, Diary, Fuller Family Papers, PVMA.

18. For further discussion of the practice see Susan Geib, "'Changing Works'"; Christopher F. Clark, "Household, Market and Capital"; Robert Gross, "Culture and Cultivation: Agriculture and Society in Thoreau's Concord," 52–55; Jonathan Hoyt, Diary, June 6, 1800, Hoyt Family Papers, PVMA. Other examples of Hoyt working are detailed in the diary; see Jonathan Hoyt, Diary, April 8, 1800; May 6, 1800; January 2, 1805; May 1, 1805; Winifred Rothenberg, "The Emergence of Farm Labor Markets and the Transformation of the Rural Economy: Massachusetts, 1750-1855."

19. For a discussion of seasonality in Deerfield see Daphne L. Dervan, "Wholesome, Toothsome, and Diverse: Seasonality in the Foodways of Deerfield, Massachusetts," research report, Henry N. Flynt Library, Deerfield, Mass., 1982; Mark Kramer, *Three Farms*, 3–107; Carl O. Sauer, "Homestead and Community on the Middle Border" in *Changing Rural Landscapes*, Ervin H. and Margaret M. Zube, eds. (Amherst, Mass., 1977), 5–15. Sauer noted for Missouri that the farm economy " . . . from its beginnings was based on marketing products, but it also maintained a high measure of self-sufficiency" (p. 11). Similar observations could

be made about the early nineteenth-century economy of rural Massachusetts; Clark, "Household, Market and Capital: The Process of Economic Change," 42–115.

20. Information on agricultural equipment was gleaned from consulting probate inventories located in the Franklin County Courthouse. Copies of these inventories are located on microfilm in the Henry N. Flynt Library, Deerfield, Mass. The Memorial Hall Museum maintains an excellent collection of agricultural equipment that was locally owned.

21. Peter H. Cousins, *Hog, Plow and Sith: Cultural Aspects of Early Agricultural Technology* (Dearborn, Mich., 1973), 7–9.

22. Calvin Stearns, Day Book, December 1817, January 1818. Also see: Peter Cousins, "'That Shall He Also Reap': The Mechanization of Harvesting," Henry Ford and Greenfield Village *Herald* 2 (1982), 6–18.

23. Elisha Wells to Elihu Hoyt, July 18, 1833, Hoyt Family Papers, PVMA.

24. Robert Paynter, *Models of Spatial Inequality*, 45–111, 251.

25. John G. Palfrey, *Statistics of the Condition and Products of Certain Branches of Industry in Massachusetts, for the Year Ending April 1, 1845* (Boston, 1846), 189–212; Francis DeWitt, *Statistical Information Relating to Certain Branches of Industry in Massachusetts for the year Ending June 1, 1855* (Boston, 1856), 172–209.

26. Ibid.

27. Mark Mastromarino, "'The Best Hopes of Agriculture': The History of the Agricultural Fair in Massachusetts," honors thesis, Boston College, 1983, 112–46.

28. *Greenfield Gazette and Courier*, September 30, 1850; Julius Robbins, Diary, September 25, 1850, PVMA; *Transactions of the Franklin County Agricultural Society for the Year 1853* (Greenfield, Mass., 1853); Mastromarino, "'The Best Hopes of Agriculture,'" 130–38; Wayne C. Neely, *The Agricultural Fair* (New York, 1935).

29. *Franklin Democrat*, October 8, 1855; *Greenfield Gazette and Courier*, September 30, 1850; October 3, 1853.

30. Carole Shammas, "How Self-Sufficient Was Early America?," *Journal of Interdisciplinary History* 13 (Autumn 1982), 247–72; Henry Colman, *Fourth Report*, 183, 159.

31. Henretta, "Families and Farms: Mentalité in Pre-Industrial America," 3–32; Richard L. Bushman, "Family Security in the Transition from Farm to City, 1750–1850; Joyce O. Appleby, *Capitalism and the New Social Order: The Republican Vision of the 1790s* (New York, 1984); Hannah Hoyt to Elihu Hoyt, February 7, 1807, Hoyt Papers, PVMA.

Chapter 4

Lowlands

1. A shorter version of this chapter appeared as "Farm Dynamics and Regional Exchange: The Connecticut Valley Beef Trade, 1670–1850," *Agricultural History* 61 (August 1987), 1–17. I am grateful to that journal for permission to reprint por-

tions of that paper. John Adams, *Diary and Autobiography of John Adams*, L. H. Butterfield, ed. (Cambridge, Mass., 1962), 2:17; George Sheldon, *A History of Deerfield, Massachusetts*, 2: Gen. 244.

2. Stephen Innes, *Labor in a New Land*, 8–9; George Sheldon, "Tis Sixty Years
   Since: The Passing of the Stall Fed Ox and the Farm Boy," in *History and Pro-
   ceedings of the Pocumtuck Valley Memorial Association, 1890–1898*, 3 (1901), 472–90;
   Rodolphus Dickinson, "A Geographical, Statistical, and Historical View," 9–11.

3. John and Seth Sheldon, Account Book, 1791–1858, PVMA. This account book
   lists purchase prices and sale prices of stall-fed oxen; Sheldon, "Tis Sixty Years
   Since," 475–77; Colman, *Fourth Report*, 51–80.

4. Jonathan Hoyt, Diary, May 14, 1805, July 8, 1805, Hoyt Papers, PVMA; Solomon C. Wells, Diary, April 23, 1833, PVMA.

5. Colman, *Fourth Report*, 5–8; Sheldon, "Tis Sixty Years Since," 473–75; Jonathan
   Hoyt, Diary, January 21, 1800, Hoyt Papers, PVMA.

6. Adams, *Diary*, 2:17; Bettye Hobbs Pruitt, "Self-Sufficiency and the Agricultural
   Economy of Eighteenth Century Massachusetts," 333–64.

7. Elihu Hoyt's letters are a particularly valuable source of information; see Henry
   K. Hoyt to Elihu Hoyt, March 11, 1831, Hoyt Papers, PVMA.

8. Ibid.; John and Seth Sheldon, Account Book, 1791–1858, PVMA; Joseph Barnard, Daybook, 1738–1785, PVMA; Sheldon, "Tis Sixty Years Since," 474–75.

9. Sheldon, "Tis Sixty Years Since," 475–77.

10. Ibid., 476–78; Colman, *Fourth Report*, 51–80.

11. Sheldon, "Tis Sixty Years Since," 478, 477–80.

12. Ibid., 479–84.

13. Ibid., 482.

14. For weight estimates, see James W. Thompson, *A History of Livestock Raising in
    the United States, 1607–1860* (Washington, D.C., 1942), 32–34; Sylvester Judd, *His-
    tory of Hadley*, 368; Howard Russell, *A Long Deep Furrow*, 158–61; Joseph Barnard,
    Daybook; Colman, *Fourth Report*, 51–80, Rodolphus Dickinson, "A Geographical,
    Statistical, and Historical View," 9–12. Using Dickinson's estimate of 400 cattle
    weighing 440,000 lbs. in 1815, the live weight of animals probably averaged
    about 1100 lbs. by that date. Also see John and Seth Sheldon, Account Book,
    and Sheldon, "Tis Sixty Years Since" 478–80.

15. See for example: Charles Hitchcock to Elihu Hoyt, February 10, 1806; Charles
    Hitchcock to Elihu Hoyt, February 4, 1809; Charles Hitchcock to Elihu Hoyt,
    February 3, 1806; Elihu Hoyt to Hannah Hoyt, June 7, 1819; Elihu Hoyt to
    Hannah Hoyt, December 10, 1820; Elihu Hoyt to Hannah Hoyt, January 9,
    1821, Hoyt Papers, PVMA.

16. Sheldon, "'Tis Sixty Years Since,'" 480–84; John and Seth Sheldon, Account
    Book; Jonathan Hoyt, Diary, April 15, 1800; Elihu Hoyt to Hannah Hoyt, Feb-
    ruary 27, 1805; Elias Joyner to Elihu Hoyt, August 10, 1801; Stephen W. Williams
    to Elihu Hoyt, February 10, 1827; Elihu Hoyt to Henry Hoyt, January 10, 1832,
    Hoyt Papers, PVMA. By the late 1820s the Greenfield newspaper was publish-

ing the prices of the Brighton market. See *Greenfield Gazette and Franklin Herald*, October 13, 1829.

17. John and Seth Sheldon, Account Book; Sheldon, "'Tis Sixty Years Since,'" 485–87.

18. *Greenfield Gazette*, September 8, 1796; Robert Paynter, *Models of Spatial Inequality*, 34–111; Clark, "Household, Market and Capital," 125–92; David C. Smith and Anne E. Bridges, "The Brighton Market: Feeding Nineteenth-Century Boston," *Agricultural History* 56 (January 1982), 3–19; Gerald F. Reid, "Local Merchants and the Regional Economy of the Connecticut River Valley," *Historical Journal of Massachusetts* 18 (Winter 1989), 1–16.

19. *Greenfield Gazette*, July 25, 1808, August 1, 1808, March 6, 1808, April 4, 1809.

20. Ibid., January 18, 1808.

21. Ibid., April 4, 1809, July 10, 1810; Elihu Hoyt to Hannah Hoyt, March 1, 1809, Hoyt Papers, PVMA.

22. Dickinson, "A Geographical, Statistical and Historical View," 10–11.

23. Elihu Hoyt, to Hannah Hoyt, February 18, 1814; Elihu Hoyt to Hannah Hoyt, June 7, 1819, Hoyt Papers, PVMA.

24. Winifred B. Rothenberg, "The Emergence of a Capital Market in Rural Massachusetts," 789–91.

25. Colman, *Fourth Report*, 64–80; Isaac Bates, "An Address to the Hampshire, Franklin, and Hampden Agricultural Society, Northampton, Mass., Oct. 23, 1823" (Northampton, 1823), PVMA; Elihu Hoyt to Hannah Hoyt, January 9, 1821, Hoyt Papers, PVMA.

26. Colman, *Fourth Report*, 80. Similar observations on the importance of manures may be found in Joyce O. Appleby, "The Changing Prospect of the Family Farm in the Early National Period," Regional Economic History Research Conference *Working Papers* 4 (1981), 1–25.

27. Sheldon, "'Tis Sixty Years Since,'" 473; Henry Colman, "An Address Before the Hampshire, Franklin and Hampden Agricultural Society, October 23, 1833" (Greenfield, 1833), PVMA, 15. Colman claimed: "The most splendid bouquet, which ever poured out its delicious perfumes on the unsullied bosom of youthful innocence and beauty, is the luxuriant offspring of the manure heap." Not everyone agreed with him, but he put it beautifully.

28. Charles Jones, "The Broom Corn Industry in the Counties of Franklin and Hampshire and in the Town of Deerfield in Particular," *History and Proceedings of the Pocumtuck Valley Memorial Association* 4 (1899-1909), 105, 106.

29. Ibid.

30. George Sheldon, Broom Corn, Deerfield Town Papers, PVMA.

31. Jones, "The Broom Corn Industry," 107; Colman, *Fourth Report*, 30–32.

32. Sheldon, Broom Corn.

33. Jones, "The Broom Corn Industry," 107-108.

34. Ibid., 109; Gregory Nobles, "Commerce and Continuity: A Case Study of the Rural Broommaking Business in Antebellum Massachusetts," *Journal of the Early Republic* 4 (Fall 1984), 287-308.

35. Jones, "The Broom Corn Industry," 108–109; Sheldon, Broom Corn.

36. Sheldon, Broom Corn; Jones, "The Broom Corn Industry," 109, 110; Nobles, "Rural Manufacture and Urban Markets," 10–21.

37. Jones, "The Broom Corn Industry," 109.

38. Nobles, "Commerce and Continuity," 289–305. Nobles points out correctly that broom making was not factory production either but something in between; Colman noted that over time this pattern changed. Price fluctuations and competition encouraged many farmers to get out of the manufacturing business and simply raise broom corn as a cash crop. See Colman, *Fourth Report*, 30–32.

39. Jones, "The Broom Corn Industry," 109–10.

40. Ibid., 110–11; E. W. to Elihu Hoyt, July 18, 1833, July 31, 1833, Hoyt Papers, PVMA. E. W. probably stands for Elisha Wells. On at least one occasion, when the merchants in New York would not give him the price he wanted, Wells took his brooms to Philadelphia.

41. Jones, "The Broom Corn Industry," 109–10; Nobles, "Commerce and Continuity," 287–308.

42. John Bigelow, *Statistical Tables: Exhibiting the Condition and Products of Certain Branches of Industry in Massachusetts for the Year Ending April 1, 1837* (Boston, 1838), 94–105; John G. Palfrey, *Statistics for 1845*, 189–212; Francis DeWitt, *Statistical Information for 1855*, 172–209.

43. Jones, "The Broom Corn Industry," 109–11.

44. Elijah Fuller, Diary, Fuller Family Papers, PVMA.

45. Ibid., May 13, 1851.

46. Ibid., May 13, 1851, August 4, 5, 1851, September 17, 1951, October 8, 10, 1851.

47. Ibid.

Chapter 5
Uplands

1. Kevin M. Sweeney, "River Gods in the Making: The Williamses of Western Massachusetts," in *The Bay and the River*, Peter Benes, ed., Annual Proceedings, 1981, Dublin Seminar for New England Folklife (Boston, 1982), 101–17; Kevin M. Sweeney, "River Gods and Related Minor Dieties: The Williams Family and the Connecticut River Valley, 1637–1790," Ph.D. diss., Yale University, 1986.

2. John Williams, Memoirs of John Williams, handwritten transcription by Alberta C. Woodruff, Williams Papers, PVMA, 1–2.

3. Ibid., 5.

4. Ibid. The memoir was apparently citing a diary at this point. The date was given as June 29, 1789, 6.

5. Ibid., April 1791, October 16, 1791.

6. John Williams, Journal, Wastebook, Memorandum Book, Northampton Historical Society, Northampton, Massachusetts. This memorandum book was

given to the historical society by a descendant. It confirms many of the details provided by the Williams memoir in the PVMA collections.

7. Philip Greven, *Four Generations: Population, Land and Family in Colonial Andover, Massachusetts* (Ithaca, N.Y., 1970); Robert A. Gross, *The Minutemen and Their World* (New York, 1976); Kenneth L. Lockridge, "Land, Population, and the Evolution of New England Society, 1630-1790; and an Afterthought," in *Colonial America: Essays in Politics and Social Development*, 461-91.

8. Lockridge, "Land, Population, and the Evolution of New England Society," 470-90; Gross, *The Minutemen*, 79-89; *Abstract of the Census of Massachusetts, 1865, with Remarks on the Same, and Supplementary Tables* (Boston, 1967), Lester Earl Klimm, *The Relation Between Certain Population Changes*.

9. Klimm, *The Relation Between Certain Population Changes*; Paynter, *Models of Spatial Inequality*, 251.

10. Isaac C. Bates, "An Address to the Hampshire, Franklin, and Hampden Agricultural Society," 30-31.

11. Louis H. Everts, *History of the Connecticut Valley in Massachusetts*, 645.

12. Ibid., 648.

13. Ibid., 654.

14. Isaac Bates criticized the practice of partable inheritance, charging that giving the farm to a favorite son and charging him to pay off the other children created an intolerable debt burden. See Bates, "An Address to the Hampshire, Franklin, and Hampden Agricultural Society," 18-19.

15. Charles Hitchcock to Elihu Hoyt, February 4, 1809, Hoyt Papers, PVMA. Hitchcock wrote, "I wish you to write me your opinion whether it will be best to buy or be early with what we have got. . . . if the weather is so constantly cold for sometime longer our upland farmers will consume a very great part of their hay. as you know the universal answer to cattle buyers is 'I have hay enough I can keep them as well as not' but I will not say their answer will be the reverse next April."

16. *Franklin Herald*, February 12, 1802.

17. Clark, "Household, Market, and Capital," 3-36.

18. *Greenfield Gazette*, September 12, 1808.

19. Ibid., September 8, 1796; June 13, 1803. Notice of proprietors' shares for auction appeared annually through the first decade of the nineteenth century.

20. Gerald F. Reid, "Local Merchants and the Regional Economy of the Connecticut River Valley," *Historical Journal of Massachusetts* 18 (Winter 1989), 8-10; Rodolphus Dickinson, "A Geographical, Statistical, and Historical View," 10; Julius Robbins, Diary, March 26, 1840, PVMA.

21. John G. Palfrey, *Statistics for 1845*, 189-212.

22. John Bigelow, *Statistical Tables for 1837*, 94-105; Howard S. Russell, *A Long Deep Furrow*, 290-91, 351-53; Percy W. Bidwell and John I. Falconer, *History of Agriculture in the Northern United States, 1620-1860* (Washington, D.C., 1925), 217-21, 259-60.

23. *Franklin Herald*, September 13, 1814; John Wilson, Memorandum Book, September 1824, June 1, 1825, Wilson Papers, PVMA.

24. Bidwell and Falconer, *History of Agriculture*, 220–21; Colman, *Fourth Report*, 92–99.

25. Colman, *Fourth Report*, 105, 109; Bigelow, *Statistical Tables for 1837*, 94–105; Palfrey, *Statistics for 1845*, 189–212; Francis DeWitt, 172–209.

26. Palfrey, *Statistics for 1845*, 189–212; DeWitt, *Statistical Information for 1855*, 172–209.

27. For a more detailed view of the outwork system, see Thomas Dublin, "Women and Outwork in a Nineteenth-Century New England Town," 51–70.

28. Elihu Hoyt to Hannah Hoyt, January 18, 1820, Hoyt Papers, PVMA; Sally McMurry, *Families and Farmhouses in Nineteenth-Century America*, 56–86.

29. For a later perspective see Hal Barron, *Those Who Stayed Behind: Rural Society in Nineteenth-Century New England* (Cambridge, Mass., 1984), 51–111.

Chapter 6
Farmsteads

1. Dwight, *Travels in New England and New York*, 2:231.

2. Massachusetts, General Court, Committees, Valuations, Aggregates of the Polls and of the Valuation of the Real and Personal Property in the Towns of Massachusetts, 1791, microfilm, Henry N. Flynt Library, Deerfield, Mass.

3. This is an interpretive issue that not every one would agree with. I am in agreement here with the definition provided in Gary M. Walton and James F. Shepherd, *The Economic Rise of Early America*, 8. For a radically different interpretation, see Michael Merrill, "Cash is Good to Eat: Self-Sufficiency and Exchange in the Rural Economy of the United States," 42–71; also see Robert B. St. George, "'Set Thine House in Order,'" 2:159–88; Thomas Hubka, *Big House, Little House*, 52–85.

4. This information is based on observations of more than 50 houses in Franklin County. Also see John Stilgoe, *Common Landscape of America, 1580–1845*, 16, 149–70; Julius Robbins, Diary, March 23, 1840, PVMA; Rudy J. Favretti and Joy Putman Favretti, *Landscape and Gardens for Historic Buildings: A Handbook for Reproducing and Creating Authentic Landscape Settings* (Nashville, 1978), 11–45.

5. Calvin Stearns, Daybook, October 26–November 2, 1816, May 3, 1817, June 1820, Northfield Historical Society. The acorns on the Doak fence are the only references I have located to a finial on a picket fence in Franklin County. Evidently they were rare.

6. Stilgoe, *Common Landscape*, 188–92; Sheldon, *History of Deerfield*, 768–71.

7. See, for example, Jonathan Hoyt, Diary, April 8, 1800, Hoyt Family Papers, PVMA; Judd, *The History of Hadley*, 431–32; J. H. Temple and George Sheldon, *A History of Northfield, Massachusetts*, 102.

8. The uses of fencing to control production have been effectively investigated by Steve Hahn, *The Roots of Southern Populism: Yeoman Farmers and the Transformation of the Georgia Upcountry, 1850–1890* (New York, 1983), 59–63; also see Bernard

L. Herman, "Fences," in *After Ratification: Material Life in Delaware, 1789–1820* J. Ritchie Garrison, Bernard L. Herman, and Barbara M. Ward, eds. (Newark, Del. 1989), 7–20.

9. Jonathan Hoyt, Diary, Sept, 17, 1810, PVMA; David Hoyt, Account and Memorandum Book, June 13, 1802, PVMA.

10. Gregory Gross, "Good Fences Make Good Neighbors: A Study of Deerfield Fencing, 1670–1900," paper, 1983, Henry N. Flynt Library, Deerfield, Mass.; Stilgoe, *Common Landscape*, 188. One of the clearest descriptions of fencemaking I know of is in Roy Underhill, *The Woodwright's Companion* (Chapel Hill, N.C., 1983), 77–84.

11. Jonathan Hoyt, Diary, March 22, 1810, November 5, 1804; Winifred Rothenberg, "The Emergence of Farm Labor Markets," 537–65; *Soil Survey; Franklin County, Massachusetts*, United States Department of Agriculture, Soil Conservation Society in Cooperation with the Massachusetts Agricultural Experiment Station (Washington, D.C., 1967), 202.

12. Dudley Woodbridge, Journal of a Trip from Cambridge to Deerfield, original, Massachusetts Historical Society, photocopy, PVMA; Nigel Harvey, *A History of Farm Buildings in England and Wales* (Newton Abbot, Eng., 1970); 48–110; Henry Glassie, *Pattern in the Material Folk Culture of the Eastern United States* (Philadelphia, 1968), 55–62, 89–92, 146–50, 153–61; Robert St. George, "The Stanley-Lake Barn in Topsfield, Massachusetts: Some Comments on Agricultural Buildings in Early New England," *Perspectives in Vernacular Architecture*, vol. 1, Camille Wells, ed. (Annapolis, 1982), 7–11; Henry Glassie, "The Variation of Concepts within Tradition: Barn Building in Otsego County, New York," *Geoscience and Man* 5 (June 1974), 177–235.

13. U.S. Secretary of the Treasury, Direct Tax Census, 1798, microfilm, Henry N. Flynt Library, Deerfield, Mass.

14. *Greenfield Gazette*, August 16, 1802, January 3, 1803, February 30, 1804, February 5, 1811; Hubka, *Big House, Little House*, 32–9.

15. MS, List of Houses, Out Houses &c. own'd by D. Hoit, Feby 8th 1799, PVMA; Massachusetts General Court, Aggregates of the Polls, 1791; U.S. Secretary of the Treasury, Direct Tax Census, 1798.

16. See especially the illustration on p. 215 in John Faragher, *Sugar Creek: Life on the Illinois Prairie* (New Haven, Conn., 1987).

17. Hubka, *Big House, Little House*, 55–61.

18. Justin Hitchcock to Elihu Hoyt, June 4, 1804, PVMA; Sheldon, *History of Deerfield*, 1:454; 2:381–84; *Greenfield Gazette and Courier*, May 22, 1848.

19. I am indebted to Richard Candee for pointing out that early machine-headed cut nails were available in New England by the 1790s.

20. This information was gathered from a barn survey conducted in the 1970s by Frank White and John Mott for the Department of Research, Old Sturbridge Village, Sturbridge, Massachusetts.

21. See Benjamin A. Clark, Map of the Town of Deerfield. This wall map depicts the houses of several of Deerfield's wealthier inhabitants around the edges of the

map. Zebina Stebbins's house is the only example of a structure in which house and barn were probably built simultaneously. The map is on view in the reading room of the Henry N. Flynt Library, Deerfield, Mass. Mary Mix Foley, *The American House* (New York, 1980), 138; Talbot Hamlin, *Greek Revival Architecture in America: Being an Account of Important Trends in American Life Prior to the War Between the States* (London, 1944), 159–86. On 167, Hamlin notes that the Greek Revival flourished in new or rapidly growing towns, and singled out the Connecticut Valley (168–73) as an area interested in the Greek style. Thomas Hubka, "The Connected Farm Buildings of Northern New England," *Historical New Hampshire* 37 (Fall 1977), 86–115; Wilbur Zelinsky, "The New England Connecting Barn," *The Geographical Review* 47 (October 1958), 540–53; John Warner Barber, *Historical Collections: Being a General Collection of Interesting Facts, Traditions, Biographical Sketches, Anecdotes, Etc. Relating to the History and Antiquities of Every Town in Massachusetts, with General Descriptions* (Worcester, Mass., 1839), 254, 271; Hubka, *Big House, Little House*, 5–30.

22. Elihu Hoyt to Henry Colman, 1831; Jonathan Hoyt, Diary, November 22–27, 1810, PVMA.

23. Stearns, Daybook, June 12–27, 1835, Northfield Historical Society, Northfield, Mass.

24. List of Houses, Out Houses &c own'd by D. Hoit, PVMA; Sumpter T. Priddy, "The Sheldon Hawks House," paper, 1974, Henry N. Flynt Library, Deerfield, Mass.; Brooke S. Blades, "Cultural Behavior and Material Culture in Eighteenth-Century Deerfield, Massachusetts: Excavations of the Dr. Thomas Williams House," report, 1977, Henry N. Flynt Library, Deerfield, Mass.; Calvin Stearns, Daybook. The evidence in Stearns's accounts may be misleading since non-carpenters might have moved buildings, but the diaries and account books consulted for this study also do not support the concept that farm families frequently moved structures; Hubka, *Big House, Little House*, 161–78.

25. William Stoddard Williams, "plan of sowing the following seeds in my garden," Williams Family Papers, PVMA; also see Mary Plant Spivy, "Gardens in Nineteenth-Century Deerfield: A Rabbit's Eye View of the Street," (paper, Henry N. Flynt Library, Deerfield, Mass., 1975); Dwight, *Travels*, 1:29, 30; See, for example, *Greenfield Gazette*, May 1, 1793; *Franklin Herald*, April 1, 1817.

26. John Wilson, Memorandum Book, Wilson Papers, PVMA; David Hoyt, Account and Memorandum Book, Hoyt Papers, PVMA; J. B. Russell, *Genuine Garden Seeds*, 1828, Broadside Collection, American Antiquarian Society, Worcester, Mass.; although most real estate advertisements in the Greenfield newspapers did not specifically list orchards, the advertisements that did list them stated that the orchards produced cider. See Dwight, *Travels*, 1:27, 28; Hoyt's observations were published in Daniel Adams, ed., *The Medical and Agricultural Register for the Year 1806* (Boston, 1806), 95; William Cobb's observations were also published in Adams, *Medical and Agricultural Register*, 127; John G. Palfrey, *Statistics for 1845*; Francis DeWitt, *Statistical Information for 1855*.

27. Jennie Maria Sheldon, *The Life of a New England Boy, A True Sketch* (Boston, 1896); Colman, *Fourth Report*, 174.

Chapter 7
Dwellings

1. George Washington, *The Diaries of George Washington*, John C. Fitzpatrick, ed. (Boston, 1925), 2, 30; Dell Upton, *Holy Things and Profane: Anglican Parish Churches in Colonial Virginia* (Cambridge, Mass., 1986), 199–232. Bernard L. Herman has observed similar patterns in the tidewater regions of Delaware. See "Ordinary Mansions," in *After Ratification: Material Life in Delaware, 1789–1820*, 49–63.

2. Other than the Sheldon house, we cannot be certain that the hastily drawn buildings on this single page actually depicted Deerfield dwellings, but it is probable that they did. See Dudley Woodbridge, "Travel Journal, October 1–October 10, 1728," in Massachusetts Historical Society *Proceedings* 18 (1789–1880), 337–40.

3. Richard I. Melvoin, *New England Outpost*.

4. Thomas Anburey, *Travels through the Interior Parts of America*, William Harding Cater, ed., 2 vols. (Boston 1923), 2:28, Robert Blair St. George, "Artifacts of Regional Consciousness in the Connecticut River Valley, 1700–1780," in *The Great River: Art & Society of the Connecticut Valley, 1635–1820*, William N. Hosley, Jr., and Gerald W. R. Ward, eds. (Hartford, Conn., 1985), 29–40; Kevin M. Sweeney, "Mansion People: Kinship, Class, and Architecture in Western Massachusetts in the Mid-Eighteenth Century," *Winterthur Portfolio* 19 (1984), 231–55; Also see Sweeney, "River Gods and Related Minor Dieties."

5. William N. Hosley, "Architecture," in *The Great River: Art & Society of the Connecticut Valley, 1635–1820*, 63–133; The Reverend William Bentley, *The Diary of William Bentley, D. D.* (Salem, Mass., 1905), 1:92.

6. Similar houses have been identified by Myron Stachiw, John Worrell, and other members of the research staff at Old Sturbridge Village: Myron Stachiw and Nora Pat Small, "Tradition and Transformation: Rural Architectural Change in Nineteenth Century Central Massachusetts," in *Perspectives in Vernacular Architecture*, vol. 3, Thomas Carter and Bernard L. Herman, eds. (Columbus, 1989), 135–48.

7. Henry Glassie, *Folk Housing in Middle Virginia* (Knoxville, Tenn., 1977); James Deetz, *In Small Things Forgotten*, 28–43; Lee Soltow, "Egalitarian America and Its Inegalitarian Housing in the Federal Period," *Social Science History* 9 (Spring 1985), 199–213.

8. Brooke S. Blades, "Cultural Behavior and Material Culture in Eighteenth-Century Deerfield, Massachusetts"; Thomas Hubka, *Big House Little House*, 44–50, 122–28. Hubka has written extensively on the formation of these ell spaces in Maine, and the patterns he describes are similar to those for Franklin County.

9. The evidence for the Stearnses' work is contained in the account and daybooks

of Calvin Stearns, owned by the Northfield Historical Society, Northfield, Massachusetts; also see: J. Ritchie Garrison, "Calvin Stearns, Carpentry, and Domestic Architecture in Northfield, Massachusetts, 1799–1850," forthcoming, *Perspectives in Vernacular Architecture*, vol. 4, Thomas Carter and Bernard Herman, eds. (Columbus, Missouri, 1991).

10. Calvin Stearns, Daybook, May–December 1816, Northfield Historical Society.

11. Ibid., July–December 1832.

12. References to the Samuel Stearns House are scattered through Calvin Stearns's Daybook between 1820 and 1824.

13. Sally McMurry, *Families and Farmhouses in Nineteenth-Century America*, 56–134.

14. Garrison, "Calvin Stearns, Carpentry, and Domestic Architecture in Northfield."

15. Personal communication, Agnes Hammond, July 18, 1987.

16. Personal communication, Dr. John Worrell, Director of Research, Old Sturbridge Village, Sturbridge Massachusetts, August, 5, 1989; John E. Worrell, "Scars Upon the Earth: Physical Evidence of Dramatic Social Change at the Stratton Tavern" in *Proceedings of the Conference on Northeastern Archaeology*, James A. Moore, ed., Amherst, University of Massachusetts, Department of Anthropology, *Research Reports*, 19 (January 1980); Ruth Schwartz Cowan, *More Work for Mother: The Ironies of Household Technology from the Open Hearth to the Microwave* (New York, 1983).

17. Calvin Stearns, Daybook, June 1, 1835; Cowan, *More Work for Mother*.

18. J. Ritchie Garrison, "'All These Conveniences Combined': The Evolution of Cookstoves in Nineteenth-Century America," paper presented at a conference on Nineteenth-Century Domestic Technology, West Chester State College, November 18, 1989.

19. Measurements of the George Stearns house were made in the summer of 1987; Probate Inventory, George Stearns, Registry of Probate, Franklin County Courthouse; Dell Upton, "Pattern Books and Professionalism: Aspects of the Transformation of Domestic Architecture in America, 1800–1860," *Winterthur Portfolio* 19 (Summer/Autumn 1984), 104–50.

20. Clifford E. Clark, Jr., "Domestic Architecture as an Index to Social History: The Romantic Revival and the Cult of Domesticity in America, 1840–1870," *Journal of Interdisciplinary History* 7 (1976), 33–56.

21. U.S. Secretary of the Treasury, Direct Tax Census, 1798; Michael Steinitz, "Rethinking Geographical Approaches to the Common House: The Evidence from Eighteenth-Century Massachusetts," in *Perspectives in Vernacular Architecture*, vol. 3, Thomas Carter and Bernard L. Herman, eds.

22. For comparative evidence see Herman, "Ordinary Mansions," 51–54; Dell Upton, "Vernacular Domestic Architecture in Eighteenth-Century Virginia," *Winterthur Portfolio* 17, no. 2/3 (Summer/Autumn 1982), 95–120.

23. U.S. Secretary of the Treasury, Direct Tax Census, 1798; Hubka, *Big House Little House*, 32–50.

24. "Land Use and Community in Deerfield, an Historic Archaeological Survey,"

National Endowment for the Humanities Grant, RO-21199, on file in Office of Academic Programs, Historic Deerfield, Inc.

25. Sweeney, "Mansion People," 21–23; Paul Jenkins, *The Conservative Rebel*, 49–61; William N. Hosley, "Asher Benjamin: Builder's Guides and the Country Builder, A Survey," paper, Henry N. Flynt Library, Deerfield, Mass., 1976; *History and Tradition of Shelburne, Massachusetts* (Springfield, Mass., 1958), 177, 178; Dwight, *Travels*, 2:247–48.

26. Dwight, *Travels*, 2:48; John Warner Barber, *Historical Collections*, 256–59; Hosley, "Asher Benjamin"; Abbott L. Cummings, "An Investigation of the Sources, Stylistic Evolution, and Influence of Asher Benjamin's Builder's Guides," Ph.D. diss., University of Ohio, 1950; Jenkins, *The Conservative Rebel*, 63; Jack Quinan, "Asher Benjamin and American Architecture," *Journal of the Society of Architectural Historians* 38 (October 1979), 244–56.

27. Jenkins, *The Conservative Rebel*, 51, 62–63; Hosley, "Asher Benjamin," 1–33. An important exception is Jack Larkin, *The Reshaping of Everyday Life, 1790–1840* (New York, 1988), 105–48. Alice Hanson Jones, *Wealth of a Nation to Be: The American Colonies on the Eve of the Revolution* (New York, 1980); Gloria Main, "The Standard of Living in Southern New England, 1640–1773," *William and Mary Quarterly*, 3d. Ser., 45 (January 1988), 124–34; Lois Green Carr and Lorena S. Walsh, "The Standard of Living in the Colonial Chesapeake," *William and Mary Quarterly*, 3d. Ser., 45 (January 1988), 135–59.

28. Main, "The Standard of Living" and Carr and Walsh, "The Standard of Living"; also see: Garrison, "'All These Conveniences Combined."

29. Claude Levi-Strauss, *Myth and Meaning* (New York, 1979), 5–24, 34–43.

Chapter 8
Community

1. Julius Robbins, Diary, March 30–April 7, 1846, PVMA.
2. Ibid.; John Kasson, *Civilizing the Machine: Technology and Republican Values in America, 1776–1900* (New York, 1976).
3. Robbins, Diary, March 23, 1844, April 1–18, September 25, 1845, January 1–18, 1846; George Sheldon, History of Deerfield 2: Gen., 270.
4. Robbins, Diary, November 4–6, 11–18, December 16–18, 21, 1846.
5. Suzanne L. Flynt, *George Fuller: At Home, 1822–1884* (Deerfield, Mass., 1984), 4–16; Louis H. Everts, *History of the Connecticut Valley in Massachusetts*, 754, 763; Joseph Kett, *Rites of Passage: Adolescence in America, 1790 to the Present* (New York, 1977).
6. Henry Colman, *Fourth Report of the Agriculture of Massachusetts*, 173; Kett, *Rites of Passage*; Thomas Dublin, ed., *Farm to Factory, Women's Letters, 1830–1860* (New York, 1981).
7. Francis X. Blouin, Jr., "The Boston Region 1810–1850: A Study of Urbanization

on a Regional Scale," Ph.D., diss., University of Minnesota, 1978; Richard D. Brown, "The Emergence of Urban Society in Rural Massachusetts, 1760-1820," 29–51; Jonathan Prude, *The Coming of Industrial Order; Town and Factory Life in Rural Massachusetts, 1810-1860* (Cambridge, 1983), 3–33, 67–132; Katherine Curtis Donahue, "Time is Money: Households and the Reorganization of Production in Northern New England, 1790 to 1900," Ph.D., diss., Boston University, 1981; John Adams and Alice B. Kazakoff, "Migration and the Family in Colonial New England: The View from Genealogies," *Journal of Family History* 9 (Spring 1984), 24–43; Maris Vinovskis, *Fertility in Massachusetts*, 117–44.

8. George Rogers Taylor, *The Transportation Revolution, 1815–1860* (New York, 1951); Thelma M. Kistler, "The Rise of the Railroads in the Connecticut River Valley," *Smith College Studies in History* 23 (1937–38), 11–16.

9. Kistler, "Rise of the Railroads," 15–16; Timothy Dwight, *Travels in New England and New York*, 1:234–36; Sheldon, *History of Deerfield*, 2:906–14.

10. Sheldon, *History of Deerfield*, 2:908–909.

11. Kistler, "Rise of the Railroads," 16–18.

12. Ibid., 16–18, 23; Betsey Hoyt Wilson, Diary, December 1, 1826, PVMA.

13. Kistler, "Rise of the Railroads," 24–28.

14. See *Franklin Herald and Public Advertiser*, October 28, 1822; Kistler, "Rise of the Railroads," 47–66; Elihu Hoyt to Henry K. Hoyt, Hoyt Papers, PVMA.

15. *Greenfield Gazette*, November 29, 1803; Paul Jenkins, *The Conservative Rebel*; Kistler, "Rise of the Railroads," 17. Kistler and others may have understated the amount of teaming. Estimates made in the mid 1820s of freight wagons moving overland through Bolton, Massachusetts, to Boston reported that on the average, ten wagons a day carrying one ton each traveled every day of the year (including Sundays the report lamented). The report went on to add that the wagons "come from or go to that region of country, on or near the route from hence to Greenfield." While the report was probably optimistic and not all of the freight would have originated in Greenfield or Franklin County, it does give some indication of the magnitude of teaming. On the basis of the Bolton estimate, it is possible that nearly 15,000 tons of freight were funneling through Bolton heading for the Boston market, much of this tonnage originating in Western Massachusetts. See *Report of the Commissioners of the State of Massachusetts, on the Routes of Canals from Boston Harbour to Connecticut and Hudson Rivers* (Boston, 1826), appendix 38, 59–60; *Greenfield Gazette*, February 9, 1807.

16. *Greenfield Gazette*, April 6, 1801.

17. Kistler, "Rise of the Railroads," 39–44; E. P. Thompson, "Time, Work-Discipline, and Industrial Capitalism, 56–97.

18. Kistler, "Rise of Railroads, 54–66; *Hampshire Gazette*, December 12, 1843; Jenkins, *Conservative Rebel*, 95–97.

19. "Address to the Stockholders of the Vermont and Massachusetts Railroad Company adopted by the Convention Held at Greenfield, October 25, 1845," (Greenfield, 1845), 11, PVMA; *Hampshire Gazette*, January 9, 1844; Kistler, "Rise of Railroads," 61–63; Jenkins, *Conservative Rebel*, 96–98.

20. Jenkins, *Conservative Rebel*, 96; Kistler, "Rise of Railroads," 89–91.

21. Kistler, "Rise of Railroads, 114–18.

22. Ibid., 120.

23. Julius Robbins, Diary, November 23, 1846, April 10, 1849; Jenkins, *Conservative Rebel*, 96–101; Kistler, "Rise of the Railroads," 52–62; "Address to the Stockholders of the Vermont and Massachusetts Railroad Company," 11–16.

24. Jenkins, *Conservative Rebel*, 100–101.

25. Ibid., 101–102; Everts, *History of the Connecticut Valley in Massachusetts*, 600–18.

26. Robert Paynter, *Models of Spatial Inequality*, 45–111; Robert Paynter, "Surplus Flows Between Frontiers and Homelands," in *The Archaeology of Frontiers and Boundaries*, Stanton W. Green and Stephen M. Perlman, eds. (New York, 1985), 181–89.

27. Amelia F. Miller, *The Connecticut Valley Doorway: An Eighteenth-Century Flowering* (Boston, 1983); Susan Gunn, "Tramp As Writ or Weaving in Deerfield Prior to 1800," paper, Henry N. Flynt Library, Deerfield, Mass., 1974, 3, A-8; Sheldon, *History of Deerfield*, 2:68. This was increasingly true after 1820. In a letter to the editor, one writer claimed: "It is not to be disguised that the mechanics generally speaking do not in their whole lifetime raise themselves above a comfortable subsistence, and many, very many not above actual want." See *Greenfield Gazette and Franklin Herald*, January 29, 1828.

28. James M. Crafts, *History of Whately, Massachusetts, 1661–1899* (Orange, Mass., 1899), 290; Ena Cane, *Whately, Massachusetts 1771–1971* (Northampton, Mass., 1972); Leslie Keno, "The Pottery of Whately, Massachusetts," paper, Henry N. Flynt Library, Deerfield, Mass., 1978, 6–13.

29. Leslie Keno, "The Pottery of Whately, Massachusetts," 13–19; Registry of Deeds, Franklin County Courthouse, Greenfield, Mass., 55:219; Laura Woodside Watkins, *Early New England Potters and Their Wares* (Cambridge, Mass., 1950), 102–103; *Franklin Herald*, September 22, 29, 1822.

30. John Bigelow, *Statistical Tables for 1837*, 104–105; John G. Palfrey, *Statistics 1845*, 360; Watkins, *Early New England Potters*, 102–103; Keno, "The Pottery of Whately, Massachusetts," 15–19.

31. Keno, "The Pottery of Whately, Massachusetts," 1–29.

32. William Cobb, Diary, December 31, 1805, Warwick Public Library, Warwick, Mass.; Jonathan Blake, *History of the Town of Warwick, Massachusetts* (Boston, 1873), 94; Peter H. Templeton, "Making It With Sand: Glass Manufacture in 19th Century Western Massachusetts," paper, Henry N. Flynt Library, Deerfield, Mass., 1979.

33. Templeton, "Making It With Sand," 6–7; Julia D. Snow, "The Franklin Glass Factory—Warwick's Venture," *The Magazine Antiques* 12 (August 1927), 133–39; Cobb, Diary, November 11, 1811; Jonathan Blake, Diary, September 25, 1811, Warwick Public Library, Warwick, Mass.; Commonwealth of Massachusetts, *Private and Special Statues of the Commonwealth of Massachusetts, February 1806 to February 1814*, vol. VV (Boston, 1823), ch. 96, p. 377.

34. Cobb, Diary, March 22, 1813, April 3, 1813, April 10, 1813.

35. Cobb, Diary, April 5, 1813, July 28, 1813, September 5, 1813, November 27, 1813,

December 8, 19, 1813, December 29, 1813; *Franklin Herald*, September 11, 1813, October 19, 31, 1813.

36. Templeton, "Making It With Sand," 13. Minard's gravestone still stands in Warwick; Cobb, Diary, January 31, 1815, February 3, 1815, February 8, 10, 1815.

37. Cobb, Diary, March 7, 1815, May 23, 1815, November 18, 1815, December 16, 1815, February 14, 21, June 26, 1816; *Franklin Herald*, May 28, 1816; Templeton, "Making It With Sand," 22–23; Blake, Diary, November 13, December 14, 23–15, 1816, January 17, 1817.

38. Jenkins, *Conservative Rebel*, 63–64, 73–76.

39. Martha Van Hoesen Taber, "A History of the Cutlery Industry in the Connecticut Valley," *Smith College Studies in History 41* (1955), 4; Robert L. Merriam and Deerfield Academy American Studies Group, *The History of the John Russell Cutlery Company, 1833–1936* (Greenfield, Mass., 1976); Jenkins, *Conservative Rebel*, 76–84.

40. Taber, "A History of the Cutlery Industry," 18; Jenkins, *Conservative Rebel*, 76–77.

41. Bigelow, *Statistical Tables for 1837*, 98–99; Taber, "A History of the Cutlery Industry," 20.

42. Taber, "A History of the Cutlery Industry," 24; H. E. Walling, Map of Franklin County (Philadelphia, 1858).

43. Jenkins, *Conservative Rebel*, 76–79.

44. Taber, "A History of the Cutlery Industry," 37.

45. The painting is owned by the Pocumtuck Valley Memorial Association. For more information on Cheapside, see Jenkins, *Conservative Rebel*, 102; Stacey Flaherty, "Cheapside's Story," paper, Henry N. Flynt Library, Deerfield, Mass., 1978, 9–16.

46. Michael Zuckerman, *Peaceable Kingdoms: New England Towns in the Eighteenth Century* (New York, 1970).

47. The literature on the effects of the Great Awakening is extensive. See, for example, Gregory H. Nobles, *Divisions Throughout the Whole*; Richard Bushman, *From Puritan to Yankee*; Patricia J. Tracy, *Jonathan Edwards, Pastor: Religion and Society in Eighteenth-Century Northampton* (New York, 1980); William G. McLoughlin, *New England Dissent, 1630–1833: The Baptists and the Separation of Church and State* (Cambridge, Mass., 1971); C. C. Goen, *Revivalism and Separatism in New England, 1740–1800: Strict Congregationalists and Separate Baptists in the Great Awakening* (New Haven, Conn., 1962); Sheldon, *History of Deerfield*, 2:784–801.

48. Stephen Marini, "Evangelical Itinerancy in Rural New England: New Gloucester, Maine, 1757–1807," in The Dublin Seminar for New England Folk Life, Annual Proceedings, 1984, *Itinerancy in New England and New York*, Peter and Jane Benes, eds. (Boston, 1986), 49–64; Randolph Roth, *The Democratic Dilemma*, 41–79. Information on the two Ashfield churches was taken from the Historic American Building Survey, Library of Congress; Sheldon, *History of Deerfield*, 2:800–4.

49. Maris Vinovskis, *Fertility in Massachusetts*, 66–72; Maris Vinovskis, "Trends in Massachusetts Education, 1826–1860," *History of Education Quarterly* 12 (1972), 501–29.

50. Benjamin A. Clark, "Map of the Town of Deerfield."

51. Isaac C. Bates, "An Address," 29.

52. Henry Colman, "An Address," 17.

53. Joseph T. Buckingham, "Address Delivered Before the Franklin County Agricultural Society at Greenfield, September 25, 1850," (Greenfield, Mass., 1850), 24.

54. Thomas Bender, *Community and Social Change in America* (Baltimore, 1982), 121–42; Walter Nugent, "Toqueville, Marx, and American Class Structure," *Social Science History* 12 (Winter 1988), 327–47.

Chapter 9
Conclusion

1. George Sheldon, *A History of Deerfield*, 2:Gen., 216; Elihu Hoyt to Hannah Hoyt, January 10, 1822; Elihu Hoyt to Hannah Hoyt, January 16, 1822; Elihu Hoyt to Hannah Hoyt, February 1, 1822, Hoyt Papers, PVMA.

2. Charles Hoyt to Julia Hoyt, January 18, 1826; Elihu Hoyt to Charles Hoyt, January 31, 1826, Hoyt Papers, PVMA.

3. Charles Hoyt to Henry K. Hoyt, June 12, 1827; Elihu Hoyt continued to search for a business job for his son during this period. See Elihu Hoyt to Hannah Hoyt, 1828, Hoyt Papers, PVMA. Charles Hoyt to Henry K. Hoyt, January 9, 1829; Elihu Hoyt responded to the change by writing "I have not heard anything further from Charles, what does he mean by changing his business. I cannot learn what he is doing," Elihu Hoyt to Hannah Hoyt, February 13, 1829, Hoyt Papers, PVMA.

4. Elihu Hoyt to Charles Hoyt, March 19, 1829, Hoyt Papers, PVMA.

5. Theodore Nims to Elihu Hoyt, April 24, 1829; Theodore Nims to Elihu Hoyt, May 11, 1829, Hoyt Papers, PVMA.

6. Elihu Hoyt to Charles Hoyt, February 27, 1831; Hoyt noted that no medical students ought to engage in stealing cadavers " . . . in a project of this kind while public opinion remains such as it is." He further suggested that dissecting specimens could be obtained in cities without exciting public outcry; Elihu Hoyt to Charles Hoyt, January 12, 1832; Elihu Hoyt to Charles Hoyt, January 26, 1832; Elihu Hoyt to Charles Hoyt, February 3, 1832, Hoyt Papers, PVMA; Paul Starr, *The Social Transformation of American Medicine* (New York, 1982); Barnes Riznik, *Medicine in New England, 1790–1840* (Sturbridge, Mass., 1965); Joseph Carvalho III, "Rural Medical Practice in Early Nineteenth-Century Rural New England," *Historical Journal of Western Massachusetts 4* (Spring 1975), 144.

7. Sheldon, *History of Deerfield*, 2:Gen. 216; Amelia F. Miller, "The History of the Ebenezer Hinsdale Williams House," report, Henry N. Flynt Library, Deerfield, Mass.

8. *Greenfield Gazette and Franklin Herald*, September 7, 1830.

9. Epaphras Hoyt, "Address delivered at Northampton before the agricultural society, October 25, 1821," Hoyt Papers, PVMA.

10. United States Bureau of Census, Agricultural Census of 1860, microfilm, Henry N. Flynt Library, Deerfield, Mass.

11. *Franklin Herald*, September 17, 1816, January 7, 1817; *Greenfield Gazette*, July 26, 1802; Carole Shammas, "How Self-Sufficient Was Early America?," 247–72.

12. Elihu Hoyt to Hannah Hoyt, February 1, 1825, Hoyt Papers, PVMA.

13. For the most complete discussion of this trend to date, see Neil McKendrick, John Brewer, and J. H. Plumb, *The Birth of a Consumer Society: The Commercialization of Eighteenth Century England* (Bloomington, Ind., 1982); also see Carole Shammas, "Consumer Behavior in Colonial America," *Social Science History* 6 (Winter 1982), 67–86.

14. Elihu Hoyt to Hannah Hoyt, January 25, 1805; Epaphras Hoyt to Elihu Hoyt, January 25, 1805, February 11, 1806, February 1, 1825, Hoyt Papers, PVMA.

15. Thomas Bender, *Community and Social Change in America*, 121–42; Walter Nugent, "Tocqueville, Marx, and American Class Structure," 327–47, esp. 340-43.

16. Isaac C. Bates, "An Address," 19.

Bibliography

Manuscript Sources

American Antiquarian Society, Worcester, Mass.
Russell, J. B. Genuine Garden Seeds, 1828. Broadside Collection.

Henry N. Flynt Library, Deerfield, Mass.
Clark, Benjamin A. Map of the Town of Deerfield. Philadelphia 1855, privately owned.
Craftsman's File. Education Dept., Historic Deerfield, Inc.
Massachusetts General Court, Committees, Valuations. "A list of the Pols and Estates, Real and Personal, of the Several Proprietors and Inhabitants of the Town, 1811." Microfilm.
Massachusetts General Court, Committees, Valuations. "A list of the Pols and Estates, Real and Personal, of the Several Proprietors and Inhabitants of the Town, 1791." Microfilm.
Pierce, George. Daybook, September 13, 1852–March 27, 1855.
Pierce and Johnson's Ledger 1834–35.
Pierce, Samuel. Account Book, 1821–26.

Jones Library, Amherst, Mass.
Anonymous. Account Book. List of Shipments on the Connecticut River, 1752–54.

Northfield Historical Society, Northfield, Mass.
Map of Bennet Meadows, Northfield, Mass., ca. 1710–20.
Calvin Stearns. Account and Day Books, 1799–1857.

Northampton Historical Society, Northampton, Mass.
Williams, John. Journal, Waste Book, and Memorandum Book, 1805–25.

Pocumtuck Valley Memorial Association Library, Deerfield, Mass. [PVMA]
Barnard, Joseph. Daybook, 1738–85.
Boutelle, Charles O. Plan of Deerfield and the North Meadows, 1837.
Childs, James. Journal, in Childs and Rice Account Book, 1841–43.
Fragment of Proprietor's Map of Deerfield and the North Meadows, ca. 1671.

The Franklin Herald, 1812–22.

Fuller, Elijah. Diary. Fuller Papers, 1859–64.

Greenfield Gazette, 1792–1811.

Greenfield Gazette and Courier, 1841–60.

Greenfield Gazette and Franklin Herald, 1827–37.

Hawks, Zur. Diary, 1819–20.

Hoyt, Arthur W. Map of Franklin County, 1832.

Hoyt, Charles. Papers, 1831–32.

Hoyt, David. Account and Memorandum Book, 1789–1803.

————. Diary, 1768–1803.

Hoyt, Epaphras. "Address Delivered at Northampton before the Agricultural Society, October 25, 1821."

Hoyt, Elihu. Papers, 1801–33.

Hoyt, Jonathan. Diary, 1800–10.

Hoyt, Julia. Papers, 1809–33.

Hoyt, Hannah. Papers, 1804–32.

Hoyt, Henry. Papers, 1825–32.

Nims, Edward. Diary, 1830–31.

Overseers of the Poor. Misc. folder, Deerfield Town Papers.

Records of the proprietors of the Common Fields, Deerfield, Massachusetts, 1733–1866.

Robbins, Julius. Diary, 1840–82.

Sheldon, George. Broom Corn. Deerfield Town Papers, N.d.

Sheldon, John and Seth. Account Book, 1791–1858.

Wells, Solomon C. Diary, 1832–51.

Williams, John. Memoirs. Transcription by Alberta C. Woodruff, N.d.

Williams, Stephen West. "Botanical Description and Medical, Culinary and Other Uses of the Plants in the First Volume of my American Herbarium," 1817.

Wilson Papers, 1812–39.

Wilson, Mary Hoyt. Diary, 1826–28.

Wilson, John. Memoradum Book. Wilson Papers, 1850–60.

Warwick Public Library, Warwick, Mass.

Blake, Jonathan. Diary.

Cobb, William. Diary.

Registry of Probate

Franklin County Courthouse, Greenfield, Mass., 1811–60.

Hampshire County Courthouse, Northampton, Mass., 1770–1811.

Published Sources

Adams, Daniel, ed. *The Medical and Agricultural Register for the Year 1806*. Boston: Manning and Loring, 1806.

Adams, John. *Diary and Autobiography of John Adams*. L. H. Butterfield ed. 4 vols. Cambridge: Belknap Press of Harvard University Press, 1962.

Adams, John, and Kazakoff, Alice B. "Migration and the Family in Colonial New England: The View from Genealogies." *Journal of Family History* 9 (Spring 1984), 24–43.

"Address to the Stockholders of the Vermont and Massachusetts Railroad Company adopted by the Convention Held at Greenfield, October 25, 1845." Greenfield: Miriam and Mirick, 1845.

Akagi, Roy H. *The Town Proprietors of the New England Colonies: A Study of Their Development, Organization, Activities and Controversies, 1620–1770*. 1924. Rpt., Gloucester: P. Smith, 1963.

Allen, David Grayson. *In English Ways: The Movement of Societies and the Transferral of English Law, Local Law, and Custom to Massachusetts Bay in the Seventeenth Century*. Chapel Hill: University of North Carolina Press, 1981.

Anburey, Thomas. *Travels Through the Interior Parts of America*, William Harding Cater, ed. 2 vols. Boston: Houghton Mifflin, 1923.

Appleby, Joyce O. *Capitalism and the New Social Order: The Republican Vision of the 1790s*. New York: New York University Press, 1984.

————. "The Changing Prospect of the Family Farm in the Early National Period." Regional Economic History Research Conference, *Working Papers* 4 (1981), 1–25.

Atack, Jeremy, and Bateman, Fred. *To Their Own Soil: Agriculture in the Antebellum North*. Ames: Iowa State University Press, 1987.

Bain, George W., and Meyerhoff, Howard A. *The Flow of Time in the Connecticut Valley*. Springfield: Connecticut Valley Historical Museum, 1963.

Barber, John Warner. *Historical Collections: Being a General Collection of Interesting Facts, Traditions, Biographical Sketches, Anecdotes, Etc. Relating to the History and Antiquities of Every Town in Massachusetts, with General Descriptions*. Worcester, Mass.: Door, Howland & Co., 1839.

Barron, Hal. *Those Who Stayed Behind: Rural Society in Nineteenth-Century New England*. Cambridge: Cambridge University Press, 1984.

Barthes, Roland. *Elements of Semiology*. (French original, 1965.) Trans. Annette Lavers and Colin Smith. New York: Hill and Wang, 1968.

Bates, Isaac. "An Address to the Hampshire, Franklin, and Hampden Agricultural Society, Northampton, Mass., Oct. 23, 1823." Northampton, Mass.: Thomas W. Shepard, 1823.

Bender, Thomas. *Community and Social Change in America*. 1978. Rpt., Baltimore: Johns Hopkins University Press, 1982.

Bentley, William. *The Diary of William Bentley, D.D.* 4 vol. Salem, Mass.: Essex Institute, 1905–14.

Bidwell, Percy W. "The Agricultural Revolution in New England." *American Historical Review* 26 (1921), 683–702.

———. "Rural Economy in New England at the Beginning of the 19th Century." Connecticut Academy of Arts and Sciences, *Transactions* 20 (1916), 241–399.

Bidwell, Percy W., and Falconer, John I. *History of Agriculture in the Northern United States, 1620–1860.* Washington, D.C.: Carnegie Institution, 1925.

Bigelow, John. *Statistical Tables: Exhibiting the Condition and Products of Certain Branches of Industry in Massachusetts for the Year Ending April 1, 1837.* Boston: Dutton and Wentworth, State Printers, 1838.

Blake, Jonathan. *History of the Town of Warwick, Massachusetts.* Boston: Noyes, Holmes, 1873.

Braudel, Fernand. *Capitalism and Material Life, 1400–1800.* 1967. Rpt., New York: Harper Colophon Books, 1973.

Brown, Richard D. "The Agricultural-Industrial Transition in New England." *New England Quarterly* 61 (June 1988), 160–68.

———. "The Emergence of Urban Society in Rural Massachusetts, 1760–1820." *Journal of American History* 61 (June 1974), 29–51.

Bruchey, Stuart. *The Roots of American Economic Growth, 1607–1861: An Essay in Social Causation.* 1965. Rpt., New York: Harper Torchbooks, 1968.

Buckingham, Joseph T. "Address Delivered before the Franklin County Agricultural Society at Greenfield, September 25, 1850." Greenfield, Mass.: Charles A. Mirick, 1850.

Bushman, Richard L. "Family Security in the Transition from Farm to City, 1750–1850." *Journal of Family History* 6 (1981), 238–56.

———. *From Puritan to Yankee: Character and the Social Order in Connecticut, 1690–1756.* Cambridge: Harvard University Press, 1967.

Cane, Ena. *Whately, Massachusetts, 1771–1971.* Northampton: Gazette Printing, 1971.

Carr, Lois Green and Walsh, Lorena S. "The Standard of Living in the Colonial Chesapeake." *William and Mary Quarterly*, 3d. ser., 45 (January 1988), 135–59.

Carvalho, Joseph III. "Rural Medical Practice in Early Nineteenth-Century Rural New England." *Historical Journal of Western Massachusetts* 4 (Spring 1975), 1–15.

Clark, Christopher. "Household Economy, Market Exchange and the Rise of Capitalism in the Connecticut Valley, 1800–1860." *Journal of Social History* 13 (Winter 1979), 169–89.

Clark, Clifford, Jr. "Domestic Architecture as an Index to Social History: The Romantic Revival and the Cult of Domesticity in America, 1840–1870." *Journal of Interdisciplinary History* 7 (1976), 33–56.

Coe, Michael D. "The Line of Forts: Archaeology of the Mid-Eighteenth Century on the Massachusetts Frontier." In *New England Historical Archaeology*, Peter Benes, ed. Annual Proceedings, Dublin Seminar for New England Folklife. Boston, 1977.

Colman, Henry. "An Address Before the Hampshire, Franklin, and Hampden Agricultural Society, October 23, 1833." Greenfield: Phelps and Ingersoll, 1833.

———. *Fourth Report of the Agriculture of Massachusetts: Counties of Franklin and Middlesex.* Boston: Dutton and Wentworth, State Printers, 1841.

Cott, Nancy. *The Bonds of Womanhood: "Women's Sphere" in New England, 1780–1835.* New Haven: Yale University Press, 1977.

Cousins, Peter H. *Hog, Plow, and Sith: Cultural Aspects of Early Agricultural Technology.* Dearborn, Mich.: Greenfield Village and Henry Ford Museum, 1973.

———. "'That Shall He also Reap': The Mechanization of Harvesting," *Henry Ford and Greenfield Village Herald* 2 (1982), 6–18.

Cowan, Ruth Schwartz. *More Work for Mother: The Ironies of Household Technology from the Open Hearth to the Microwave.* New York: Basic Books, 1983.

Crafts, James M. *History of Whately, Massachusetts, 1661–1899.* Orange, Mass.: D. L. Crandall, 1899.

Cronon, William. *Changes in the Land: Indians, Colonists, and the Ecology of New England.* New York: Hill and Wang, 1983.

Danhof, Clarence. *Change in Agriculture: The Northern United States.* Cambridge: Harvard University Press. 1969.

Deetz, James. *In Small Things Forgotten: The Archaeology of Early American Life.* New York: Anchor Press/Doubleday, 1977.

Demos, John. *A Little Commonwealth: Family Life in Plymouth Colony.* New York: Oxford University Press, 1970.

DeWitt, Francis. *Statistical Information Relating to Certain Branches of Industry in Massachusetts for the Year Ending June 1, 1855.* Boston: William White, Printer to the State, 1856.

Dickinson, Rodolphus. "A Description of Northfield and Lexington: Intended as an Exhibition of the Plan of a Contemplated Gazeteer of Massachusetts Proper." Deerfield, Mass.: C. J. Newcomb, 1818.

———. *Elements of Geography, or An Extensive abridgement Thereof; Exhibiting a View of the Natural and Artificial Features of the Various Divisions of the Earth; And Embracing Those Branches of Statistics Most Intimately Connected with Geographical Science.* Boston: Bradford and Read, 1813.

———. "A Geographical, Statistical, and Historical View of the Town of Deerfield in the County of Franklin, and State of Massachusetts." Deerfield, Mass.: C. J. Newcomb, 1817.

Dreyfus, Hubert L., and Rabinow, Paul. *Michel Foucault: Beyond Structuralism and Hermeneutics.* 2d. ed. Chicago: University of Chicago Press, 1983.

Dublin, Thomas. *Farm to Factory: Women's Letters, 1830–1860.* New York: Columbia University Press, 1981.

———. "Women and Outwork in a Nineteenth-Century New England Town: Fitzwilliam, New Hampshire, 1830–1850." In *The Countryside in the Age of Capitalist Transformation: Essays on the Social History of Rural America,* Steven Hahn and Jonathan Prude, eds. Chapel Hill: University of North Carolina Press, 1985.

Dwight, Timothy. *Travels in New England and New York.* 4 vols. 1821–22. Rpt., Cambridge: Harvard University Press, 1969.

Everts, Louis H. *History of the Connecticut Valley in Massachusetts with Illustrations and Biographical Sketches.* 3 vols. Philadelphia: L. H. Everts, Press of J. B. Lippincott, 1879.

Faragher, John Mack. *Sugar Creek: Life on the Illinois Prairie*. New Haven: Yale University Press, 1986.

Favretti, Rudy J., and Favretti, Joy Putman. *Landscape and Gardens for Historic Buildings: A Handbook for Reproducing and Creating Authentic Landscape Settings*. Nashville: American Association for State and Local History, 1978.

Flaherty, David H. *Privacy in Colonial New England*. Charlottesville: University Press of Virginia, 1972.

Flynt, Suzanne. *George Fuller: At Home, 1822–1884*. Deerfield: Pocumtuck Valley Memorial Association, 1984.

Foley, Mary Mix. *The American House*. New York: Harper and Row, 1980.

Foucault, Michel. *The Archaeology of Knowledge*. Trans. by A. M. Sheridan Smith. New York: Harper Colophon, 1972.

Garrison, J. Ritchie. "Calvin Stearns, Carpentry, and Domestic Architecture in Northfield, Massachusetts, 1799–1850." In *Perspectives in Vernacular Architecture*, vol. 4, Thomas Carter and Bernard L. Herman, eds. Columbus: University of Missouri Press, 1991.

———. "Farm Dynamics and Regional Exchange: The Connecticut Valley Beef Trade, 1670–1850." *Agricultural History* 61 (August 1987), 1–17.

Garvin, James L. "The Range Township in Eighteenth-Century New Hampshire." In *New England Prospect: Maps, Place Names, and the Historical Landscape*, Peter Benes, ed. Annual Proceedings, The Dublin Seminar for New England Folklife, 1980. Boston: N.d.

Giedion, Sigfried. *Mechanization Takes Command: A Contribution to Anonymous History*. New York: Oxford University Press, 1948.

Glassie, Henry. *Folk Housing in Middle Virginia*. Knoxville: University of Tennessee Press, 1977.

———. "Meaningful Things and Appropriate Myths: The Artifact's Place in American Studies." In *Material Life in America, 1600–1860*. Robert St. George, ed. Boston: Northeastern University Press, 1988. Pp. 63–92.

———. *Pattern in the Material Folk Culture of the Eastern United States*. Philadelphia: University of Pennsylvania Press, 1968.

———. "The Variation of Concepts within Tradition: Barn Building in Otsego County, New York." *Geoscience and Man* 5 (June 1974), 177–255.

Goen, C. C. *Revivalism and Separatism in New England, 1740–1800: Strict Congregationalists and Separate Baptists in the Great Awakening*. New Haven: Yale University Press, 1962.

Grant, Charles S. *Democracy in the Connecticut Frontier Town of Kent*. New York: Columbia University Press, 1961.

Greven, Philip I., Jr. *Four Generations: Population, Land, and Family in Colonial Andover, Massachusetts*. Ithaca: Cornell University Press, 1970.

Gross, Robert A. "Culture and Cultivation: Agriculture and Society in Thoreau's Concord." *The Journal of American History* 69, no. 1 (June 1982), 42–61.

———. *The Minutemen and Their World*. New York: Hill and Wang, 1976.

Hahn, Steven. *The Roots of Southern Populism: Yeoman Farmers and the Transformation of the Georgia Upcountry, 1850–1890*. New York: Oxford University Press, 1983.

Hahn, Steven, and Prude, Jonathan, eds. *The Countryside in the Age of Capitalist Transformation: Essays on the Social History of Rural America.* Chapel Hill: University of North Carolina Press, 1985.

Halsted, Byron D. *Barns, Sheds, and Outbuildings.* 1881. Rpt., Brattleboro, Vt: Stephen Greene Press, 1977.

Hamlin, Talbot. *Greek Revival Architecture in America: Being an Account of Important Trends in American Life Prior to the War Between the States.* London: Oxford University Press, 1944.

Hart, John Fraser. *The Look of the Land.* Englewood Cliffs, N.J.: Prentice-Hall, 1975.

Harvey, Nigel. *A History of Farm Buildings in England and Wales.* Newton Abbot, Eng.: David and Charles, 1970.

Henretta, James. *The Evolution of American Society, 1700–1815: An Interdisciplinary Analysis.* Lexington, Mass.: D. C. Heath, 1973.

———. "Families and Farms: *Mentalité* in Pre-industrial America." *William and Mary Quarterly,* 3d. ser., 35 (January 1978), 3–32.

Herman, Bernard L. *Architecture and Rural Life in Central Delaware, 1700–1900.* Knoxville: University of Tennessee Press, 1987.

———. "Fences." In *After Ratification: Material Life in Delaware, 1789–1820,* J. Ritchie Garrison, Bernard L. Herman, and Barbara McLean Ward, eds. Newark: Museum Studies Program, University of Delaware, 1988. Pp. 7–20.

———. "Ordinary Mansions." In *After Ratification: Material Life in Delaware, 1789–1820,* J. Ritchie Garrison, Bernard L. Herman, and Barbara McLean Ward, eds. Newark: Museum Studies Program, University of Delaware. 1988. Pp. 49–63.

History and Tradition of Shelburne, Massachusetts. Shelburne: Shelburne, Mass., 1958.

Hodder, Ian. *Reading the Past: Current Approaches to Interpretation in Archaeology.* New York: Cambridge University Press, 1986.

Hosley, William N. "Architecture." In *The Great River: Art & Society of the Connecticut Valley, 1635–1820,* William N. Hosley and Gerald W. R. Ward, eds. Hartford, Conn.: Wadsworth Atheneum, 1985. Pp. 63–133.

Hubka, Thomas C. *Big House Little House, Back House, Barn: The Connected Farm Buildings of New England.* Hanover, N.H.: University Press of New England, 1984.

———. "The Connected Farm Buildings of Northern New England." *Historical New Hampshire* 37 (Fall 1977), 86–115.

———. "Maine's Connected Farm Buildings." *Maine Historical Society Quarterly* 18 (Winter 1978), 139–70; 19 (Spring 1979), 217–45.

Innes, Stephen. *Labor in a New Land: Economy and Society in Seventeenth-Century Springfield.* Princeton: Princeton University Press, 1983.

Isaac, Rhys. "Ethnographic Method in History: An Action Approach." *Historical Methods* 13 (1980), 43–61.

Jedrey, Christopher M. *The World of John Cleveland: Family and Community in Eighteenth-Century New England.* New York: W. W. Norton, 1979.

Jenkins, Paul. *The Conservative Rebel: A Social History of Greenfield, Massachusetts.* Greenfield, Mass: Town of Greenfield, 1982.

Jensen, Joan. *Loosening the Bonds: Mid-Atlantic Farm Women 1750–1850.* New Haven: Yale University Press, 1986.

Jones, Alice Hanson. *Wealth of a Nation To Be: The American Colonies on the Eve of the Revolution.* New York: Columbia University Press, 1980.

Jones, Charles. "The Broom Corn Industry in the Counties of Franklin and Hampshire, and in the Town of Deerfield in Particular." *History and Proceedings of the Pocumtuck Valley Memorial Association* 4 (1879–1904), 105–10.

Jorgenson, Neil. *A Guide to New England's Landscape.* Chester, Conn.: Globe Pequot Press, 1977.

Judd, Sylvester. *The History of Hadley.* 1905. Rpt., Somersworth: New Hampshire Publishing, 1976.

Kasson, John. *Civilizing the Machine: Technology and Republican Values in America, 1776–1900.* New York: Penguin, 1976.

Kellogg, Lucy Cutler. *History of Bernardston, Franklin County, Massachusetts, 1736–1900.* Greenfield, Mass.: E. A. Hall, 1902.

Kett, Joseph. *Rites of Passage: Adolescence in America, 1790 to the Present.* New York: Basic Books, 1977.

Kistler, Thelma M. "The Rise of the Railroads in the Connecticut River Valley." *Smith College Studies in History* 23 (October 1937–July 1938), 1–289.

Klimm, Lester Earl. *The Relation Between Certain Population Changes and the Physical Environment in Hampden, Hampshire, and Franklin Counties, Massachusetts, 1790–1925.* Philadelphia: University of Pennsylvania Press, 1933.

Kniffen, Fred B. "Folk Housing: Key to Diffusion." *Annals of the Association of American Geographers* 55 (December 1965), 549–77.

Kramer, Mark. *Three Farms: Making Milk, Meat and Money from the American Soil.* Boston: Little, Brown, 1980.

Kulikoff, Allan. "The Transition to Capitalism in Rural America." *William and Mary Quarterly,* 3d. ser., 46 (January 1989), 120–44.

Kurath, Hans. *Handbook of the Linguistic Geography of New England.* Providence, R.I.: Brown University, 1959.

Larkin, Jack. *The Shaping of Everyday Life, 1790–1840.* New York: Harper and Row, 1988.

Lee, Deane, ed. *Conway, 1767–1967.* Conway, Mass.: Town of Conway, 1967.

Lemon, James T. *The Best Poor Man's Country: A Geographical Study of Early Southeastern Pennsylvania.* Baltimore: Johns Hopkins University Press, 1972.

Levi-Strauss, Claude. *Myth and Meaning.* New York: Schocken, 1979.

Lewis, Peirce F. "Axioms for Reading the Landscape: Some Guides to the American Scene." In *Material Culture Studies in America,* Thomas J. Schlereth, ed. Nashville: American Association for State and Local History, 1982. Pp. 174–82.

Little, Edward L. *Conifers and Important Hardwoods.* Washington, D.C.: United States Department of Agriculture, Miscellaneous Pub. No. 1146, 1971.

Lockridge, Kenneth A. "Land, Population, and the Evolution of New England Society, 1630–1790; and an Afterthought." In *Colonial America: Essays in Politics and Social Development,* Stanley Katz, ed. Boston: Little, Brown, 1971. Pp. 461–91.

————. *A New England Town, The First Hundred Years, Dedham, Massachusetts, 1636–1736*. New York: Norton, 1970.

Lockwood, John H., et al. *Western Massachusetts: A History*. New York: Lewis Historical Publishing, 1926.

Ludlum, David. *The Country Journal New England Weather Book*. Boston: Houghton Mifflin, 1976.

Main, Gloria. "The Standard of Living in Southern New England, 1640–1773." *William and Mary Quarterly*, 3d. ser., 45 (January 1988), 124–34.

Main, Jackson Turner. *The Social Structure of Revolutionary America*. Princeton: Princeton University Press, 1965.

Marini, Stephen. "Evangelical Itineracy in Rural New England: New Gloucester, Maine, 1757–1807." In *Itinerancy in New England and New York*, Peter and Jane Benes, eds. Annual Proceedings, The Dublin Seminar for New England Folk Life, 1984. Boston: Boston University, 1986. Pp. 49–64.

Marti, Donald B. "The Reverend Henry Colman's Agricultural Ministry." *Agricultural History* 51 (July 1977), 524–39.

Martin, Margaret E. "Merchants and Trade of the Connecticut River Valley, 1750–1820." *Smith College Studies in History* 24 (October 1938–July 1939), 1–284.

Massachusetts, Commonwealth of. *Private and Special Statues of the Commonwealth of Massachusetts, February 1806 to February 1814 VV*. Boston: Wells and Lilly, 1823.

McCusker, John J., and Menard, Russell. *The Economy of British America, 1607–1789*. Chapel Hill: University of North Carolina Press, 1985.

McHenry, Stewart G. "Eighteenth-Century Field Patterns as Vernacular Art." *Old Time New England* 69 (July–December 1978), 1–21.

McKendrick, Neil; Brewer, John; and Plumb, J. H. *The Birth of a Consumer Society: The Commercialization of Eighteenth-Century England*. Bloomington: Indiana University Press, 1982.

McLoughlin, William G. *New England Dissent, 1630–1833: The Baptists and the Separation of Church and State*. Cambridge: Harvard University Press, 1971.

McManis, Douglas R. *Colonial New England: A Historical Geography*. New York: Oxford University Press, 1975.

McMurry, Sally. *Families and Farmhouses in Nineteenth-Century America: Vernacular Design and Social Change*. New York: Oxford University Press, 1988.

Melvoin, Richard I. "Communalism in Frontier Deerfield." In *Early Settlement in the Connecticut Valley*, John Ifkovic and Martin Kaufman, eds. Deerfield: Historic Deerfield, and Institute of Massachusetts Studies, 1984. Pp. 36–61.

————. *New England Outpost: War and Society in Colonial Deerfield*. New York: Norton, 1988.

Merriam, Robert, and the Deerfield Academy American Studies Groups. *The History of the John Russell Cutlery Company, 1833–1936*. Greenfield, Mass.: Bete Press, 1976.

Merrill, Michael. "Cash is Good to Eat: Self-Sufficiency and Exchange in the Rural Economy of the United States." *Radical History Review* 3 (1977), 42–71.

Miller, Amelia F. *The Connecticut Valley Doorway: An Eighteenth-Century Flowering*. Boston: Published by Boston University for the Dublin Seminar for New England Folklife, 1983.

———. "Connecticut Valley Doorways: An Eighteenth-Century Flowering." In *The Bay and the River: 1600–1900*, Peter Benes, ed. The Annual Proceedings, The Dublin Seminar for New England Folklife, 1981. Boston: Boston University, 1982. Pp. 60–72.

Nobles, Gregory. "Commerce and Continuity: A Case Study of the Rural Broommaking Business in Antebellum Massachusetts." *Journal of the Early Republic* (Fall 1984), 287–308.

———. *Divisions Throughout the Whole: Politics and Society in Hampshire County, Massachusetts, 1740–1775*. New York: Cambridge University Press, 1983.

North, Douglas C. *The Economic Growth of the United States, 1790–1860*. New York: Norton, 1961.

Nugent, Walter. "Toqueville, Marx, and American Class Structure." *Social Science History* 12 (Winter 1988), 327–47.

Pabst, Margaret Richards. "Agricultural Trends in the Connecticut Valley Region of Massachusetts, 1800–1900." *Smith College Studies in History* (October 2, 1940–July 1941), 1–138.

Palfrey, John G. *Statistics of the Condition and Products of Certain Branches of Industry in Massachusetts, for the Year Ending April 1, 1845*. Boston: Dutton and Wentworth, State Printers, 1846.

Paynter, Robert. *Models of Spatial Inequality: Settlement Patterns in Historical Archaeology*. New York: Academic Press, 1982.

———. "Surplus Flows between Frontiers and Homelands." In *The Archaeology of Frontiers and Boundaries*, Stanton W. Green and Stephen M. Perlman, eds. New York: Academic Press, 1985. Pp. 181–89.

Prown, Jules David. "Mind in Matter: An Introduction to Material Culture Theory and Method." *Winterthur Portfolio* 17 (1982), 1–19.

Prude, Johnathan. *The Coming of Industrial Order: Town and Factory Life in Rural Massachusetts, 1816–1860*. Cambridge: Cambridge University Press, 1923.

Pruitt, Bettye Hobbs. "Self-Sufficiency and the Agricultural Economy of Eighteenth-Century Massachusetts." *William and Mary Quarterly*, 3d ser., 41 (July 1984), 333–64.

Quinan, Jack. "Asher Benjamin and American Architecture." *Journal of the Society of Architectural Historians* 38 (October 1979), 244–56.

Reid, Gerald F. "Local Merchants and the Regional Economy of the Connecticut River Valley." *Historical Journal of Massachusetts* 18 (Winter 1989), 1–16.

Report of Commissioners of the State of Massachusetts, on the Routes of Canals from Boston Harbour to Connecticut and Hudson Rivers. Boston: True and Greene, State Printers, 1826.

Riznik, Barnes. "Medicine in New England, 1790–1840." Booklet. Sturbridge, Mass.: Old Sturbridge Village, 1965.

Roth, Randolph. *The Democratic Dilemma: Religion, Reform, and the Social Order in the Connecticut River Valley of Vermont, 1791–1850*. New York: Oxford University Press, 1987.

Rothenberg, Winifred B. "The Emergence of Farm Labor Markets and the Transformation of the Rural Economy: Massachusetts, 1750–1855." *Journal of Economic History* 48 (September 1988), 537–66.

———. "Farm Account Books: Problems and Possibilities." *Agricultural History* 58 (April 1984), 106–12.

———. "The Market and Massachusetts Farmers." *Journal of Economic History* 41 (June 1981), 300–12.

———. "A Price Index for Rural Massachusetts, 1750–1855." *Journal of Economic History* 39 (December 1979), 975–1001.

Russell, Howard S. *A Long Deep Furrow: Three Centuries of Farming in New England.* Hanover, Mass.: University Press of New England, 1976.

Salisbury, Stephen. "Economic History: Then as Now: 'The Economic History of the United States' in Light of Recent Scholarship." *Agricultural History* 53 (October 1979), 796–814.

Saur, Carl. "Homestead and Community on the Middle Border." In *Changing Rural Landscapes,* Ervin H. and Margaret J. Zube, eds. Amherst: University of Massachusetts Press, 1977. Pp. 5–15.

Schlebecker, John T. *Whereby We Thrive: A History of American Farming, 1607–1972.* Ames: The Iowa State University Press, 1975.

Shammas, Carole. "Consumer Behavior in Colonial America." *Social Science History* 6 (Winter 1982), 67–86.

———. "How Self-Sufficient Was Early America?" *Journal of Interdisciplinary History* 13 (Autumn 1982), 247–72.

Sheldon, George. *A History of Deerfield, Massachusetts.* Deerfield: Pocumtuck Valley Memorial Association, 1895–96.

Sheldon, George. "'Tis Sixty Years Since': The Passing of The Stall Fed Ox and the Farm Boy." *History and Proceedings of the Pocumtuck Valley Memorial Association, 1890–1898* 3 (1901), 472–90.

Sheldon, Jennie Maria. *The Life of a New England Boy: A True Sketch.* Boston: N.P., 1896.

Shover, John. *First Majority—Last Minority: The Transformation of Rural Life in America.* DeKalb: University of Iowa Press, 1976.

Simler, Lucy. "Tenancy in Colonial Pennsylvania: The Case of Chester County." *William and Mary Quarterly*, 3rd ser., 43 (October 1986), 542–69.

Smith, David C., and Bridges, Anne E. "The Brighton Market: Feeding Nineteenth-Century Boston." *Agricultural History* 56 (January 1982), 3–19.

Smith, John Montague. *A History of Sunderland, Massachusetts.* Greenfield, Mass.: E. A. Hall, 1899.

Snow, Julia D. "The Franklin Glass Factory—Warwick's Venture." *The Magazine Antiques* 12 (August 1927), 133–39.

Soltow, Lee. "Egalitarian America and Its Inegalitarian Housing in the Federal Period." *Social Science History* 9 (Spring 1985), 199–213.

St. George, Robert B. "Artifacts of Regional Consciousness in the Connecticut River Valley, 1770–1780." In *The Great River: Art & Society of the Connecticut Valley, 1635–1820,* William N. Hosley and Gerald W. R. Ward, eds. Hartford. Conn.: Wadsworth Atheneum, 1985. Pp. 29–40.

———. *Material Life in America, 1600–1860*. Boston: Northeastern University Press, 1988.

———. "'Set Thine House in Order': The Domestication of the Yeomanry in Seventeenth-Century New England." In *New England Begins*, Jonathan L. Fairbanks and Robert F. Trent, eds. 3 vols. Boston: Museum of Fine Arts, 1982. 2:159–88.

———. "The Stanley-Lake Barn in Topsfield, Massachusetts: Some Comments on Agricultural Buildings in Early New England." In *Perspectives in Vernacular Architecture*, Camille Wells, ed. Annapolis: The Vernacular Architecture Forum, 1982. Pp. 7–23.

Stachiw, Myron and Small, Nora Pat. "Tradition and Transformation: Rural Architectural Change in Nineteenth Century Central Massachusetts." In *Perspectives in Vernacular Architecture*, vol. 3., Thomas Carter and Bernard L. Herman eds. Columbus: University of Missouri Press, 1989. Pp. 135–48.

Starr, Paul. *The Social Transformation of American Medicine*. New York: Basic Books, 1982.

Steinitz, Michael. "Rethinking Geographical Approaches to the Common House: The Evidence from Eighteenth Century Massachusetts." In *Perspectives in Vernacular Architecture*, vol. 3, Thomas Carter and Bernard L. Herman eds. Columbus: University of Missouri Press, 1989. Pp. 16–26.

Stilgoe, John R. *Common Landscape of America, 1580 to 1845*. New Haven: Yale University Press, 1982.

Suits, D. B. "The Determinants of Consumer Expenditure: A Review of Present Trends." In *Impacts of Monetary Policy*. Englewood Cliffs, N.J.: Prentice-Hall, 1963. Pp. 1–57.

Sumner, William H. *A History of East Boston*. Boston: J. E. Tilton, 1858.

Swedlund, Alan C. and Boyce, A. J. "Making Structure in Historical Populations: Estimation by Analysis of Surnames." *Human Biology* 55 (May 1983), 151–262.

Swedlund, Alan C.; Meindle, Richard S.; Nydon, Judith; and Gradie, Margaret I. "Family Patterns in Longevity and Longevity Patterns of the Family." *Human Biology* 55 (February 1983), 115–29.

Sweeney, Kevin. "Mansion People: Kinship, Class, and Architecture in Western Massachusetts in the Mid-Eighteenth Century." *Winterthur Portfolio* 19 (Winter 1984), 231–55.

———. "River Gods in the Making: The Williamses of Western Massachusetts." In *The Bay and the River*, Peter Benes, ed. Annual Proceedings, The Dublin Seminar for New England Folklife, 1981. Boston, 1982. Pp. 101–17.

Swierenga, Robert P. "Agriculture and Rural Life; The New Rural History." In *Ordinary People and Everyday Life: Perspectives on the New Social History*, James B. Gardiner and George Rollie Adams, eds. Nashville: American Association for State and Local History, 1983.

Taber, Martha Van Hoesen. "A History of the Cutlery Industry in the Connecticut Valley." *Smith College Studies in History* 41 (1955), 1–138.

Taylor, George R. *The Transportation Revolution, 1815–1860*. 1951. Rpt., White Plains, N.Y.: M. E. Sharpe, N.d.

Temkin-Greener, Helena and Swedlund, Alan. "Fertility Transition in the Connecticut Valley, 1740–1850." *Population Studies* 32 (1978), 27–41.

Temple, J. H., and Sheldon, George. *A History of Northfield, Massachusetts.* Albany: Joel Munsell, 1875.

Thompson, E. P. "The Moral Economy of the English Crowd in the Eighteenth Century." *Past and Present* 50 (February 1971), 76–136.

———. "Time, Work-Discipline, and Industrial Capitalism." *Past and Present* 38 (1967), 56–97.

Thompson, James W. *A History of Livestock Raising in the United States, 1607–1860.* Washington, D.C.: U.S. Department of Agriculture, Agricultural History Series, no. 5, 1942.

Thomson, Betty Flanders. *The Changing Face of New England.* Boston: Houghton Mifflin Company, 1977.

Tracy, Patricia J. *Jonathan Edwards, Pastor: Religion and Society in Eighteenth-Century Northampton.* New York: Hill and Wang, 1980.

Underhill, Roy. *The Woodwright's Companion.* Chapel Hill: University of North Carolina Press, 1983.

Upton, Dell. *Holy Things and Profane: Anglican Parish Churches in Colonial Virginia.* The Architectural History Foundation. Cambridge: MIT Press, 1986.

———. "Pattern Books and Professionalism: Aspects of the Transformation of Domestic Architecture in America, 1800–1860." *Winterthur Portfolio,* 19 (Summer/Autumn 1984), 104–50.

———. "Vernacular Domestic Architecture in Eighteenth-Century Virginia." *Winterthur Portfolio* 17, no. 2–3 (Summer/Autumn 1982), 95–120.

U.S.D.A. Soil Conservation Service in Cooperation with the Massachusetts Agricultural Experiment Station. Soil Survey: Franklin County, Massachusetts. Washington, D.C.: U.S. Government Printing Office, 1967.

Vinovskis, Maris A. *Fertility in Massachusetts from the Revolution to the Civil War.* New York: Academic Press, 1981.

———. "Trends in Massachusetts Education, 1826–1860." *History of Education Quarterly* 12 (1972), 501–29.

Walton, Gary M., and Shepherd, James F. *The Economic Rise of Early America.* Cambridge: Cambridge University Press, 1979.

Warner, Oliver D. *Abstract of the Census of Massachusetts, 1865: With Remarks on the Same and Supplementary Tables.* Boston: Wright and Potter, State Printers, 1867.

Washington, George. *The Diaries of George Washington,* John C. Fitzpatrick, ed. Boston: Houghton Mifflin Company, 1925.

Watkins, Laura Woodwide. *Early New England Potters and Their Wares.* Cambridge: Harvard University Press, 1950.

Wilson, Harold F. *The Hill Country of Northern New England: Its Social and Economic History, 1790–1930.* New York: Columbia University Press, 1936.

Wines, Richard S. "The Nineteenth-Century Agricultural Transition in an Eastern Long Island Community." *Agricultural History* 55 (January 1981), 50–63.

Wood, Joseph S. "Elaboration of a Settlement System: The New England Village in the Federal Period." *Journal of Historical Geography* 10 (1984), 331–56.

———. "The New England Village as an American Vernacular Form." In *Perspectives in Vernacular Architecture*, vol. 2, Camille Wells, ed. Columbia: University of Missouri Press, 1986. Pp. 54–63.

Woodbridge, Dudley. "Travel Journal, October 1–October 10, 1728." In *Massachusetts Historical Society Proceedings* 18 (1879–1880), 337–40.

Worrell, John. "Scars Upon the Earth: Physical Evidence of Dramatic Social Change at the Stratton Tavern." *Research Reports* 19 (January 1980), Proceedings of the Conference on Northeastern Archaeology, James A. Moore, ed. Amherst: Department of Anthropology, University of Massachusetts. Pp. 133–45.

Zelinsky, Wilbur. *The Cultural Geography of the United States.* Englewood Cliffs, N.J.: Prentice-Hall, 1973.

———. "The New England Connecting Barn." *The Geographic Review* 47 (October 1958), 540–53.

Zemsky, Robert. *Merchants, Farmers and River Gods.* Boston: Gambit, Inc., 1971.

Zuckerman, Michael. *Peaceable Kingdoms: New England Towns in the Eighteenth Century.* New York: Alfred Knopf, 1970.

Unpublished Sources

Blades, Brooke S. "A Summary of Archeological Excavations Conducted at the Frary House, Deerfield, Massachusetts." Report, 1978. Henry N. Flynt Library. Deerfield, Mass.

———. "Cultural Behavior and Material Culture in Eighteenth-Century Deerfield, Massachusetts: Excavations at the Dr. Thomas Williams House." Report, 1977. Henry N. Flynt Library, Deerfield, Mass.

Blouin, Jr., Francis X. "The Boston Region 1810–1850: A Study of Urbanization on a Regional Scale." Ph.D. diss., University of Minnesota, 1978.

Bowen, Joanne V. "Account Books and the Study of Subsistence on the New England Farm: Comments on Methods and Results." Paper given at a colloquium on Early American Account Books: Needs and Opportunities for Study, Deerfield, Mass., March 24, 1984.

Clark, Christopher. "Household, Market and Capital: The Process of Economic Change in the Connecticut Valley of Massachusetts, 1800–1860." Ph.D., diss., Harvard University, 1982.

Cummings, Abbott Lowell. "An Investigation of the Sources, Stylistic Evolution, and Influence of Asher Benjamin's Builder's Guides." Ph.D. diss., University of Ohio, 1950.

Dervan, Daphne. "Wholesome, Toothsome and Diverse: Seasonality in the Foodways of Deerfield, Massachusetts." Report, 1982. Henry N. Flynt Library, Deerfield, Mass.

Donahue, Katharine Curtis. "Time is Money: Households and the Reorganization of Production in Northern New England, 1790–1900." Ph.D., diss., Boston University, 1981.

Flaherty, Stacy. "Cheapside's Story." Paper, 1978. Henry N. Flynt Library, Deerfield, Mass.

Folbre, Nancy R. "The Politics of Reproduction: Hampshire County, Massachusetts, 1680–1800." Paper read at a colloquium on Recent Research in Western Massachusetts, Historic Deerfield, Deerfield, Mass., 1978.

Garrison, J. Ritchie. "'All These Conveniences Combined': The Evolution of Cookstoves in Nineteenth-Century America," paper presented at a conference on Nineteenth-Century Domestic Technology, West Chester State College, November 18, 1989.

Geib, Susan. "'Changing Works': Agriculture and Society in Brookfield, Massachusetts, 1785–1820." Ph.D. diss., Boston University, 1981.

Gross, Gregory. "Good Fences Make Good Neighbors: A Study of Deerfield Fencing, 1670–1908." Paper, 1983. Henry N. Flynt Library, Deerfield, Mass.

Gunn, Susan. "Tramp as Writ or Weaving in Deerfield Prior to 1800." Paper, 1974. Henry N. Flynt Library, Deerfield, Mass.

Hirtle, Peter. "Agrarian Economy in Flux: The Agriculture History of Deerfield, 1670–1760." Paper, 1973. Henry N. Flynt Library, Deerfield, Mass.

Hosley, William N. "Asher Benjamin: Builders Guides and the Country Builder, A Survey." Paper, 1976. Henry N. Flynt Library, Deerfield, Mass.

Keno, Leslie. "The Pottery of Whately, Massachusetts." Paper, 1978. Henry N. Flynt Library, Deerfield, Mass.

Lehman, Rebecca. "The Spoon Speaks Out: Eating Utensils in Deerfield Inventories, 1674–1800." Paper, 1974. Henry N. Flynt Library, Deerfield, Mass.

Mastromarino, Mark. "'The Best Hopes of Agriculture': The History of the Agricultural Fair in Massachusetts." Honors thesis, Boston College, 1983.

Mitchell, Laurie. "An Enterprising Soul: John Wilson of Deerfield." Paper, 1979. Henry N. Flynt Library, Deerfield, Mass.

Priddy, Sumpter T. III. "The Sheldon Hawks House." Paper, 1974. Henry N. Flynt Library, Deerfield, Mass.

Pruitt, Bettye Hobbs. "Agriculture and Society in the Towns of Massachusetts, 1771: A Statistical Analysis." Ph.D. diss., Boston University, 1981.

Pudup, Mary Beth. "South Deerfield: A Place between Towns Becomes a Town between Places." Paper, 1977. Henry N. Flynt Library, Deerfield, Mass.

Reader, William A. "Yankees, Immigrants, and Social Climbers: A Study of Social Mobility in Greenfield, Massachusetts, 1850–1970." Ph.D. diss., University of Massachusetts, 1973.

Robinson, Barbara. "The History of the John Wilson Printing Office." Report, 1978. Henry N. Flynt Library, Deerfield, Mass.

Schumacher, Max G. "The Northern Farmer and the Markets During the Late Colonial Period." Ph.D. diss., University of California, 1965.

Spivy, Mary Plant. "Gardens in Nineteenth-Century Deerfield: A Rabbit's Eye View of the Street." Paper, 1975. Henry N. Flynt Library, Deerfield, Mass.

Stevens, Mary Lynn. "No Complaints: Agriculture in Deerfield 1760–1810." Paper, 1976. Henry N. Flynt Library, Deerfield, Mass.

Sweeney, Kevin M. "The Children of the Covenant; the Formation and Transformation of a Second Generation New England Community." Paper, 1971. Henry N. Flynt Library, Deerfield, Mass.

———. "River Gods and Related Minor Deities: The Williams Family and the Connecticut River Valley, 1637–1790." Ph.D. diss., Yale University, 1986.

Templeton, Peter H. "Making It with Sand: Glass Manufacture in Nineteenth-Century Western Massachusetts." Paper, 1979. Henry N. Flynt Library, Deerfield, Mass.

Thomas, Peter A. "In the Maelstrom of Change: The Indian Trade and Cultural Process in the Middle Connecticut River Valley, 1635–1665." Ph.D. diss., University of Massachusetts, 1979.

Index

Landscape and Material Life in Franklin County, Massachusetts, 1770–1860 was composed in Baskerville by Lithocraft, Inc. ITC New Baskerville display type was set on the Macintosh at The University of Tennessee Press. Printed on 70–pound Warren's Patina by Braun-Brumfield, Inc. Designed by Dariel Mayer.